# The Anthropocene: Politik—Economics—Society—Science

Volume 19



**Series editor**

Hans Günter Brauch, Mosbach, Germany

More information about this series at http://www.springer.com/series/15232
http://www.afes-press-books.de/html/APESS.htm
http://www.afes-press-books.de/html/APESS_19.htm

Dumisani Ngwenya

# Healing the Wounds of Gukurahundi in Zimbabwe

## A Participatory Action Research Project

Springer

DUT DURBAN UNIVERSITY OF TECHNOLOGY

Dumisani Ngwenya
Grace To Heal
Bulawayo
Zimbabwe

More on this book is at: http://afes-press-books.de/html/APESS_19.htm

ISSN 2367-4024 ISSN 2367-4032 (electronic)
The Anthropocene: Politik—Economics—Society—Science
ISBN 978-3-319-66817-8 ISBN 978-3-319-66818-5 (eBook)
https://doi.org/10.1007/978-3-319-66818-5

Library of Congress Control Number: 2017951986



Cover photo: The photo on the book cover of the Victoria Falls was taken by © Hans Günter Brauch on 10 September 2015 who has granted permission to use it here.
The photo on page iii shows a man holding the log that was used by the 5th brigade to beat him during the Gukurahundi atrocities in 1983. Use of such logs on defenceless villagers was a common occurrence.


Copy-editing: PD Dr. Hans Günter Brauch, AFES-PRESS e.V., Mosbach, Germany
Style and English Language Editor: Claire Mortimore

Printed on acid-free paper

This Springer imprint is published by Springer Nature
The registered company is Springer International Publishing AG
The registered company address is: Gewerbestrasse 11, 6330 Cham, Switzerland

*This book is dedicated to the people of Matebeleland who have continued to walk proud and tall in the face of adversity.*
*We are hard pressed on every side, yet not crushed; we are perplexed, but not in despair; persecuted, but not forsaken; struck down, but not destroyed*
*(2 Corinthians 4:8–9).*

Map of Zimbabwe. *Source* University of Texas at Austin, University Libraries, Perry-Castañeda Library Map Collection, at: http://www.lib.utexas.edu/maps/zimbabwe.html (2 May 2017). This map is in the public domain

# Foreword

For most of my academic life, I followed the traditional path in supervising postgraduate theses and in carrying out my own research. That is, I focussed almost entirely on exploring a problem and added, at the very end, a list of recommendations for the relevant authorities to consider. I suspect I always knew that the authorities were extremely unlikely to read what I or my students had written and were even less likely to change anything as a result. I also realised that policy change is an extremely slow process. But I hoped that these contributions to knowledge would eventually contribute to shifting policy and planning in desirable ways and thus bring about change.

As I have got older, I have become much less patient with such an approach. Happily, I became acquainted with an alternative approach—action research—where researchers not only explore a problem but plan, implement and evaluate an intervention designed to tackle the problem. The most obvious benefit of action research is that some peace is built immediately. It is also possible that the micro-level outcomes sought from action research might spread more widely.

Dumisani Ngwenya's action research with a small group of survivors of *Gukurahundi* is a classic example of this kind of research. It was highly participatory, with the group members deciding what to do and how and when to do it. It took place slowly, over a 30-month period. And it had modest outcomes—'a measure of healing' in the words of one participant—which hopefully will become more solid over time and also spread to the families and friends of the group members.

I learned a great deal in the course of this project and feel privileged to have been a small part of it.

Geoff Harris
International Centre of Nonviolence,
Durban University of Technology

Photograph of cottages in the vicinity of the elementary school of Ngoma close to the Hwange National Park in Matabeleland North in Zimbabwe. *Source* The photograph was taken by © Hans Günter Brauch on 9 September 2015, who has granted permission to use it here

Photograph of children of the elementary school of Ngoma close to the Hwange National Park in Matabeleland North in Zimbabwe. *Source* The photograph was taken by © Hans Günter Brauch on 9 September 2015, who has granted permission to use it here

# Acknowledgements

My sincere gratitude extends to my supervisor, Prof. Geoff Harris, who not only 'teaches peace', but always strives to practice what he teaches. I cherish the many hours we spent, face to face and via email, discussing this work. You have become more than a supervisor; you are a mentor, colleague and friend. Thank you for all those 'You might find this useful' emails! To the women and men who agreed to embark on this learning journey with me, thank you for teaching me so much and for sticking it out over such a long period of time. To Reshma, thank you for the 'crash course' in coding and analysis; you are a good teacher. To my parents for your foresight; without your guidance, my path would not have ended up here.

To my wife Nokuthaba and my children Mayibongwe and Nobukhosi, who have endured many years of an absent husband and father; thank you for lending me to this project. You can have me back now.

Many thanks to the editor of this series Hans Günter Brauch for holding my hand through this journey, for looking out for my interests and your wise counsel. You do a good job.

Last but not least, to the many nameless people behind this project, the anonymous reviewers, the senior editor Johanna Schwarz in Heidelberg (Germany), the project managers and typesetters in Chennai, Tamil Nadu (India) and the many other people in many countries involved with this book with Springer Nature publishers. Thank you all for your work.

Bulawayo, Zimbabwe
March 2017

Dumisani Ngwenya

Memorial to women burnt alive by the 5th brigade. *Source* Photograph of the author

Memorialisation of mass grave in progress. *Source* Photograph of the author

# Contents

# List of Figures

# List of Tables

# Abbreviations

| | |
|---|---|
| AAD | Adversity Activated Development |
| APs | Assembly Points |
| AU | African Union |
| CCJP | Catholic Commission for Justice and Peace |
| CIO | Central Intelligence Organisation |
| DDR | Disarmament Demobilisation and Reintegration |
| INGOs | International Nongovernmental Organisations |
| POSA | Public Order and Security Act |
| POTRAZ | Post and Telecommunication Regulatory Authority of Zimbabwe |
| PTSD | Post Traumatic Stress Disorder |
| SADC | Southern Africa Development Community |
| TOL | Tree of Life |
| ZANLA | Zimbabwe African National Liberation Army |
| ZANU | Zimbabwe African National Union |
| ZAPU | Zimbabwe African People's Union |
| ZIPRA | Zimbabwe People's Revolutionary Army |
| ZNA | Zimbabwe National Army |
| ZVT | ZIPRA Veterans Trust |

Map of Zimbabwe. *Source* University of Texas at Austin, University Libraries, Perry-Castañeda Library Map Collection, at: http://www.lib.utexas.edu/maps/zimbabwe.html (2 May 2017). This map is in the public domain

# Chapter 1
# Healing the Wounds of *Gukurahundi*

*We have to heal ourselves, we have to continue, we have to live.*
Participant

## 1.1 Introduction

Although the concept of peacebuilding is conceived differently by politicians and peace practitioners (Ghali 1992; Lambourne 2004; Clancy/Hamber 2008), it has become widely acceptable in political circles that post-armed conflict reconstruction or transitional mechanisms must also include peacebuilding as an integral element of recovery. In the 1980s, Zimbabwe experienced the most serious state-perpetrated violence against a section of its citizens[1] (see Sect. 2.2). Conventional wisdom dictates that the nation should have undertaken some form of healing process to address the causes and consequences of the violence, which was perceived to be ethnically motivated. However, this did not happen, the December 1987 Unity Agreement between the two political parties only served to stop the violence and to grant immunity to the antagonists. The elite pact between the political parties involved only served to entrench impunity and suppression and left a section of the nation hurting, fearful, bitter and resentful. Up to the present, no form of truth recovery and reconciliation on the issue of *Gukurahundi* has been carried out. Calls for official healing processes for the survivors of the 1980s' atrocities have gone unheeded.

This thesis seeks to answer the question of whether it is possible for those affected by the atrocities to heal themselves in the absence of an official apology or

[1]Between 1983 and 1986 the government of Zimbabwe carried out an operation ostensibly to counter dissidents. However, the especially trained army unit was involved in gross human rights violations which left an estimated 20 000 civilians dead. It was known as *Gukurahundi*, a Shona word meaning the rains that wash away the dirt before the planting season. See Chap. 2 for a fuller discussion on this.



D. Ngwenya, *Healing the Wounds of Gukurahundi in Zimbabwe*,
The Anthropocene: Politik—Economics—Society—Science 19,
https://doi.org/10.1007/978-3-319-66818-5_1

healing programme. It also explores possible ways and approaches that individuals and communities might employ in an effort to find relief from the decades of hurts and pain.

I start this chapter with an acknowledgement of my lack of experience in participatory action research (PAR). This, coupled by the intricate nature of the topic under consideration, the self-healing of communities affected by political violence in the absence of official healing programmes or apology, made the present research project highly challenging. However, my desire to undertake this research was driven by a desire to see the communities in Matebeleland liberated from the painful memories they have endured for almost three decades and to develop an effective approach that could be used with the wider society in the pursuit of relief for the affected communities. My actions and beliefs about this project were guided by Freire's (1970) philosophy of conscientisation. While it might be possible that the participants found it difficult to articulate and engage in the technical aspects of the healing of trauma as discussed in Chaps. 3 and 4, my approach here was not a theoretical or academic discussion of the topic, but an attempt to discover a methodology that could result in the healing of the affected individuals and their communities. The intention was to facilitate a process where participants could engage in an informative, reflective and critical dialogue about their experiences, through dialogue and participating in several consciousness-raising activities (McIntyre 2007). Concerning this process of self-discovery and naming one's world, Freire (1970, p. 72) counsels that the 'development of subjectivities, is not an "armchair revolution". The discovery cannot be purely intellectual, but must also involve action, nor can it be limited to mere activism, but must include serious reflection; only then will it be praxis.' Praxis must be conceptualised as reflection upon and action in the world in order to transform it. Thus, I was not seeking an elitist but practical knowledge that would result in the liberation of the participants as they embarked on this journey of self-discovery. The participants would know if the approach contributed to their healing or not and I was certain that they would be able to describe in their own terms and ways what has happened to them and how. While they might not have the jargon, they would have had the experience.

## 1.2 Motivation for Research

While it has been almost three decades since *Gukurahundi* came to an end, its repercussions on the survivors and the Matebeleland communities in general are still being keenly felt (see Sect. 2.3). Our experience at Grace to Heal (see Sect. 1.7) is that these issues are still very much alive at a very deep and personal level. A case in point is one man from Tsholotsho who kept the log that was used to beat him in

1983 and has vowed to keep it until justice was done. Unfortunately, because of old age, he might die before this happens. This kind of response seems to be the norm rather than the exception in Matebeleland.

This means that there are many people who, to use Father Michael Lapsley's statement,[2] 'are caught in a moment of history' and have not been afforded the opportunity to deal with the painful memories and the traumas of the past. My work at Grace to Heal entailed frequent interaction with communities, families and individuals who were affected by *Gukurahundi*. By virtue of being part of the Ndebele community, I also carry vicariously the wounds of my people and might need healing in one form or the other.

Chapter 12 part six of the new constitution, which came into effect in 2013 in Zimbabwe, has a provision for a National Peace and Reconciliation Commission to address issues of national healing, unity and cohesion. The reality on the ground indicates that *Gukurahundi* is unlikely to be dealt with seriously under the present circumstances. In fact, it is not possible for this to happen right now (see Sect. 4.1). The question that begs an answer is, how long should these people have to wait before they are allowed to deal with their needs for healing and restoration?

From a peacebuilding perspective, we know that, after violent conflicts or wars, there is a need for nation building at both the socio-political and economic levels (Ndlovu-Gatsheni 2003; Staub et al. 2005, see also Sects. 3.1 and 4.1). This, as we have already noted, has not happened yet in post-conflict Matebeleland.

While I am aware of studies done around the issues of *Gukurahundi,* I am not aware of any study that has used action research to explore self-healing techniques or mechanisms that victim communities and individuals can use as a grassroots, self-generated approach to community healing. The doctoral research of Stauffer (2009) and Motsi (2010) focused on the role of narratives in shaping the discourse around *Gukurahundi* and the role of pastoral care in transforming trauma caused by *Gukurahundi* respectively and used quite different research designs to my study.

This topic has therefore been chosen so that the researcher, together with the co-researchers who are direct victims of *Gukurahundi*, might learn how self-healing can be systematically practised and what sort of resiliencies people have developed to cope with their traumas and bad memories. Most people I have met in the course of my work with Grace to Heal do not display any overt and typical symptoms of trauma or PTSD and seem to live 'near normal' lives. Yet from time to time, flashes of anger, resentment and hatred for the Shona manifest themselves. The aim was that, if this project was successful, it would be of benefit not only to the participants but to the wider communities as well and would contribute significantly to Grace to Heal's good practice ethos. This research tried to address a problem that is urgent,

[2]Father Lapsley, an anti-Apartheid campaigner, became victim of a parcel bomb by the Apartheid government of South Africa, and has developed a programme called the 'Healing of Memories', which helps victims of violence to deal with their painful memories.

practical and pertinent to the communities in Matebeleland in particular, and for Zimbabwe as a nation in general.

## 1.3 Research Question and Objectives

In light of this history of violence and suffering and the absence of any concrete government programme to address the issues of trauma, forgiveness and reconciliation, the research aim was to engage in a participatory action research project with victims of *Gukurahundi* aimed at the healing of memories.

The overall research question was: What is the nature and extent of trauma-related challenges for victims of *Gukurahundi* and what can be done to facilitate their amelioration in the absence of an official apology or healing programmes?

The research objectives were:

(i) To review the recent literature on
   (a) the nature, extent and consequences of trauma following community violence.
   (b) healing processes, with particular reference to healing groups of victims in the absence of official apology or reconciliation programme.
(ii) Together with a group of victims of *Gukurahundi,* to identify contexts, barriers, and issues that may be significant in the healing process for people traumatised by political violence, with specific reference to the *Gukurahundi* violence.
(iii) To develop a sustainable and replicable model which can facilitate self-healing for victims of *Gukurahundi.*
(iv) Together with these victims, to assess the potential of such and the possibility of its widespread usage.
(v) In the course of the research, to consciously reflect on the strengths and limitations of participatory action research in such settings.

The research sought to explore whether it is possible for individuals affected by the violence of *Gukurahundi* to find ways and means of healing themselves in the absence of an official apology and/or healing and reconciliation programme. Indeed, it sought to determine how useful these self-healing initiatives might be, given the accepted conditions that make for effective healing (Barsalou 2005, see also Sect. 4.4).

Objective (i) was achieved through the review of literature, describing and analysing the healing of bad memories caused by violence. In addition, literature that describes participatory action research and the experiences of the practitioners of this approach was consulted to give me an in-depth understanding of this method, its strengths and its limitations.

Objectives (ii), (iii) and (v) were achieved by the setting up of the action research group of 10 individuals who are survivors of *Gukurahundi*. (I have chosen to refer to the participants as 'survivors' rather than 'victims' out of respect for the many affected communities, families and individuals who are courageously and silently living their lives resiliently and have not succumbed to the intents of their victimisers). The participants were selected purposively from the communities in which Grace to Heal works. This approach was chosen due to the sensitive nature of the subject and the hostility towards any discussions of *Gukurahundi* by the authorities. Because this is a 'taboo' subject, people are not usually comfortable discussing this topic in public and view such engagements by outsiders with great suspicion. Besides, an indiscriminate random selection of participants might have attracted unwarranted attention from the state security agents, thus exposing participants to unnecessary harm or interference with the project. The issue of doing no harm to research participants and their communities is one of the important considerations in research ethics (see Sect. 6.7). I had originally planned that participants would come from Tsholotsho; some 115 km from Bulawayo where I am based, but this changed at implementation (see Sect. 6.2.1).

## 1.4 Scope of the Study and Delimitations

This study was carried out with a small group of particular people in a particular environment over a period of time and may not reflect the findings of the communities of Matebeleland as a whole.

## 1.5 Theoretical Framework

This research was done within the broad context of peacebuilding, as opposed to clinical psychology or psychiatry, because the focus of the project was on social transformation. Within the peacebuilding ambit, restorative justice and conflict transformation theories in particular, are theories that are more relevant for this study.

*Restorative justice* has been described as 'a process whereby all the parties with a stake in a particular offence come together to resolve collectively how to deal with the aftermath of the offence and its implications for the future' (Dignan 2005, p. 3). For communities coming out of war or genocide, the focus of restorative justice on nonviolence offers a potentially sustainable platform for a community to build its future upon. There is no denying, however, that retributive justice may have some role to play within the peacebuilding framework (Huyse 2003, pp. 97–102), or that restorative justice also has its limitations. As Braithwaite (2003) has pointed out, restorative justice cannot deal with the issues of structural injustices that advantage some communities and disadvantage others. However, he still insists that restorative justice offers 'better value' than retributive or criminal justice. This restoration is targeted not only at victims, but at perpetrators and the community at large during a situation of political transition from undemocratic rule to the beginnings of democracy and upholding of human rights (Villa-Vicencio 2000).

According to the South African Truth and Reconciliation Commission's Report, (vol. 1 chap. 5, paragraph 80f: 126),

> Restorative Justice seeks to redefine crime: it shifts the primary focus of crime from the breaking of laws or offences against a faceless state to a perception of crime as violations against human beings…It encourages victims, offenders and the community to be directly involved in resolving conflicts.

Restorative Justice brings in certain dimensions to the understanding of justice that are not always present in criminal justice. In a political context, it can involve former antagonists working together to address the violence of the past as a basis for building a stable future together. Included here is the restoration of moral worth and equal dignity for all persons, at the same time working to create a society where the various sectors in it have some measure of equality (Villa-Vicencio 2000). A list of eight goals which a community or nation coming out from a situation of atrocity should aim for has been suggested by Cobban (2007, pp. 22–23) and seem to fit in well within the tenets of restorative justice:

1. Overcome communal and official denial of the atrocity; gain public acknowledgement.
2. Obtain the facts in an account as full as possible in order to meet victims' need to know, to build a record for history, and to ensure minimal accountability of perpetrators.
3. Forge basis for a domestic democratic order that respects and enforces human rights.
4. Promote reconciliation across social divisions; reconstruct the moral and social systems devastated by violence.
5. Promote psychological healing for individuals, groups, victims, bystanders and offenders.
6. Restore dignity to victims.
7. Punish, exclude, shame, and diminish offenders for their offences.
8. Accomplish these goals in ways that render them compatible rather than antagonistic with the other goals.

In restorative justice, justice is realised in a context of human relations and not just through legal or criminal justice court systems. That is to say, it recognises the fact that wrong is done to people and, in seeking redress, it seeks to not only satisfy the legal requirements of the law but also to right the relationship with the individual and society, which has been ruptured by the act of violence. This means that issues of truth, acknowledgment, healing, forgiveness and reconciliation need to be addressed diligently and deliberately. As mentioned above, restorative justice is consummated through the process of restoration and rehabilitation of the perpetrators and not just through alienation and punishment. For justice to be said to have been fully attained, restitution and reparations must take place beyond the legal theory and codes of law (Biggar 2003).

While the restorative justice theoretical framework is the most ideal, it nevertheless is not appropriate for this research, because it requires the involvement of the victim, the perpetrator and community if it is to be effective. It needs to be noted that this study took place in the absence of such cooperation from those responsible for the harm done (see Chap. 2). The other point to note is that, apart from the few at the top, it would be extremely difficult to identify those that committed the atrocities, as the 5th Brigade was disbanded soon after the 1987 Unity Accord. Nevertheless, survivors deserve some respite from the hurts most of them have been carrying for over 30 years.

I therefore decided to use the *conflict transformation* theory, which emphasises the addressing of conflicts in the context of relationships. It has been described as a process of 'engaging with and transforming the relationships, interests, discourses and, if necessary, the very constitution of society that supports the continuation of violent conflict' (Miall 2006, p. 4). A crucial aspect has to do with the use of forgiveness and reconciliation as the means of bridging issues of trust and dealing with hurts, trauma hatred and desire for vengeance in the process of individual or community healing after violent conflicts. If these are not dealt with, they jeopardise progress towards sustainable peace for communities and individuals. Forgiveness and reconciliation have been dealt with considerably in the literature review below (Sect. 2.1). It should be noted that reconciliation requires two parties and as such it is not the focus of this study. Rather, the focus is on studying the resiliencies and agency, the inner fortification of the hurting communities and individuals so they can somehow address these hurts, independent of any action by the perpetrators.

## 1.6 Research Design

This research used participatory action research as its research design because this project aimed to offer participants an opportunity not only to reflect on their problems but to attempt to transform them too.

> Participatory action research is the term used by Fals-Borda to emphasise both the participative and action elements of research which is 'openly ideological' and thereby aims to transform socio-political inequities. This approach to social research integrates scientific investigation with education and political action. It is an interdisciplinary methodology enabling people to take control of their lives by combining formal and informal knowledge, and using that new knowledge to change their realities.... PAR produces knowledge which is valid and relevant because of its popular knowledge and science and the participation of the people experiencing the problems studied (Dickinson 1997, p. 2)

PAR utilises the exploratory and descriptive and uses 'thick' descriptions to convey the process and dynamics of the research (see Sect. 6.2). The qualitative research methodology was preferred in this project as it was action and process oriented and sought to understand the social context within the specific context in which the participants are located (Babbie/Mouton 2001). This collective trauma, self-healing process can be defined as a psychosocial approach. Thematic data analysis was used as the data analysis approach for the qualitative data collected. The analysis was largely inductive but was guided by a priori theoretical framework and the researcher's personal interests in the topic under study (see Sect. 6.5).

## 1.7 Proposed Data Collection Methods

Since my interest was to understand the subjective experiences of the participants and the processes and events flowing from our engagement within the participants' environment, a qualitative data collection approach was chosen. Originally, the data collection tools in the table below were to be used to collect the data for this research, although a different set of tools were used during the actual research (see Sect. 6.4). This partly stemmed from my inexperience with the research approach chosen (Table 1.1).

**Table 1.1** Proposed data collection tools. *Source* The author

| Tool | Activities | Purpose |
|---|---|---|
| Timeline | Participants draw/create a chronology of events before, during and after the traumatic incidents. | Produce facts of the incident(s)<br>Help clarify issues for individual and group.<br>Validate the participants' experiences<br>Provide a non-threatening way to relate the traumatic experiences. |
| Theatre | A simulation of a scene from *Gukurahundi.*<br>Brainstorm and discuss issues raised by drama. | Break the ice and stimulate participants to discuss their stories in an indirect way.<br>Remove pressure of focusing on self while still engaging with issues that are real |
| River of Life | Participants draw a river (a depiction of their lives) and place along it times of joy and sadness. | Help participants connect with their emotions.<br>Identify emotions rising from the traumatic experiences and how they are affecting their quality of life in the present. |
| Psychoeducation | Brief presentation of theories on the nature of trauma, traumatic experience and human responses to it. | Help participants gain technical appreciation of their responses to their traumatic experiences.<br>Provide framework in which to discuss their experiences.<br>De-pathologise their responses to the traumatic experiences, so that they see them as 'normal' reactions to situations like theirs. |

## 1.8 Placing Myself and My Work in the Context of This Study

I am a co-founder and executive director of Grace to Heal and my interest and active participation in the field of peacebuilding is quite recent, having only started 14 years ago. Apart from being involved in the day-to-day running of the organisation, I actively participate in the organisation's programmes, especially in the rural areas, which has afforded me the opportunity to interact directly with communities most affected by *Gukurahundi*. I view myself as a practitioner rather than an academic and my approach to this study reflects this.

I pioneered the programme described below and have spent a considerable amount of time listening to people narrate stories of state-sanctioned atrocities. In the context of this research, I was both an 'insider' and an 'outsider'. I was the former in the sense that, at one level, the participants were colleagues with whom I have worked and shared a bond, being from the same community which *Gukurahundi* sought to decimate; the latter because they shared extra experiences that set them apart from me that made the bonds between themselves stronger. They underwent guerrilla and military training, experienced both the liberation war and *Gukurahundi* as soldiers and are members of an organisation that identifies them as former ZIPRA combatants. In other words, they share affinities that set them apart from me, being part of a world which I was allowed to glimpse but could never fully appreciate or identify with.

Grace to Heal is a faith-based peacebuilding organisation, working mostly within the rural communities of Matebeleland North. At its inception in 2003, the organisation's sole mandate was to aid the victims of *Gukurahundi.* This included helping people to seek redress and assisting children of the deceased to acquire their parents' death certificates so they could apply for their own birth certificates[3] (see Sect. 2.4). We soon found out that we had no capacity for this and that, for most families, the most pressing issue had to do with their loved ones who were either lying in mass shallow graves or whose graves were unknown. People were unsettled as they felt that the spirits of the departed were unhappy and they attributed their misfortunes to the angry spirits (Eppel 2006). We teamed up with another organisation[4] that had experience in addressing this concern. The process involves bringing together families with loved ones in a particular grave to deliberate about what they want to do about it. This process is a long one as most

[3]It is difficult for families to get death certificates for people killed during *Gukurahundi,* since their deaths are not officially acknowledged. In Zimbabwe, by law a child needs to have their father present or at least their identity card in order to apply for a birth certificate and one cannot sit for the grade seven exams or proceed to secondary school without it. As a result, there are many people who are without identity documents who therefore have not been to school and cannot get any formal employment. Many have chosen to skip the border and find menial jobs in South Africa where they acquire South African documents fraudulently (see Kombanie 2011).

[4]The name of the organisation has been withheld for security reasons.

families have moved away from the communities where their family members were killed and, in most cases, we deal with the second generation who were young when this happened. Bringing the families together allows them to share and collaborate their stories. The families are then brought together with the community leaders and the witnesses who then share with them the events leading to the deaths and show them the grave.[5] Together with the community, the families make final decisions about what they want to do with the grave. People want the sites to be preserved and we assist them with building materials and with community labour whilst they construct the graves. Usually, people want them constructed in such a way that they can be exhumed if and when the opportunity arises, which means that the top is just covered with soil and left. Occasionally some families are satisfied with the preservation and so cover the top with concrete.

This event is treated as if it were a fresh burial with the community actively participating. It is a way of allowing the community to 'mourn' with the families and a way of integrating them back into society. People never had an opportunity to mourn and carry out the burial rites because the deceased were either buried hurriedly or by neighbours or occasionally by the soldiers, as people had fled their homesteads. After the 'burial' families usually perform their religious rites (Christian or African traditional religion) and often feel free to visit the site regularly according to their traditions. In the process of doing this, stories are recorded and data about the deceased are documented for future use. While no scientific study has been carried out about the effectiveness of this process, participants have often reported an improvement in their fortunes as they believe the spirits of the dead have been appeased and are no longer angry.

While this seems to work well for those with dead relatives, there are some victims of torture during *Gukurahundi* who are still alive. The organisation has dealt with such individuals on an ad hoc basis as and when they come forward. I became interested in carrying out this research because I was curious to find out how best to address this group's need for healing. Their suffering was different from those who had lost relatives in the sense that the physical pain had been inflicted on them. Hence, they carried both emotional and physical scars along with emotional and psychological wounds.

With time, community-based peacebuilding became a major focus of Grace to Heal's work as well and the twin interests and foci of my work—trauma healing and peacebuilding—form both the background and motivation for this study.

[5]To say these are graves is a misnomer because due to neglect these sites have been overgrown and one cannot tell where a grave might be. The land has become flat and animals and sometimes people walk over the graves unknowingly.

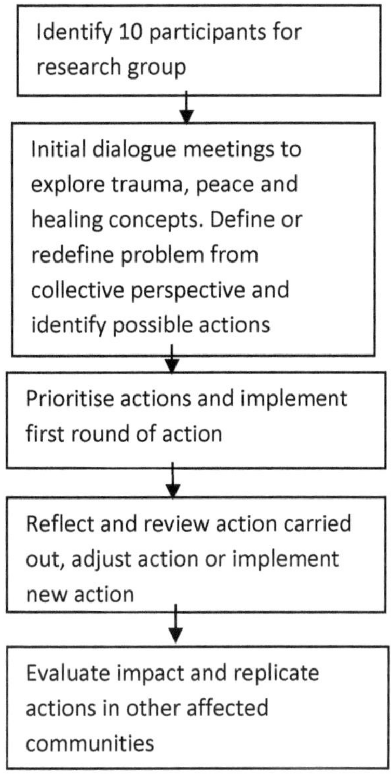


**Fig. 1.1** Research plan schematic presentation. *Source* The author

## 1.9 Research Plan

For conceptual clarity, the diagram below represents the steps taken in the execution of this research. However, being a PAR project, the actual implementation of the research was iterative and more complex than the diagram suggests (Fig. 1.1).

## 1.10 Structure of the Book

Chapter 2 looks at the background of the Ndebele-Shona tensions and how these have been used by politicians for their own selfish ends. It traces the intricate historical context that eventually led to the *Gukurahundi* era and discusses briefly the unfolding of the events as well as reviewing some of the atrocities visited upon the people and examining some of the damages this caused to the people of Matabeleland. It considers how this has affected relations between the two ethnic groups.[6]

[6]As Ndebele historians will point out, it is a misnomer to call the Ndebele an ethnic group as it is made up of seven distinct tribal groupings. The preferred view is that Ndebele is a nation made up of these groupings (see Ndlovu-Gatsheni 2008).

Chapter 3 discusses the psychological effects of armed violence on communities and individuals who experience it. It provides a detailed discussion of what trauma is and how it works. Papadopoulos' (2007) theory of Adversity Activated Development (AAD), which says that, besides increased resilience, individuals can grow from the traumatic situations experienced, is explored. The chapter questions the relevance of PTSD in non-Western settings and concludes that pathologising trauma does not always help when dealing with non-Western victims of trauma. It seeks to relate the issues of trauma, traumatic events and PTSD to the violence of the 1980s in Matabeleland and how they might be addressed. It further discusses the role of peacebuilding in post armed conflict and argues for a trauma-sensitive approach to peacebuilding. Lastly, the idea of collective emotions and collective trauma is explored.

Chapter 4 looks at what it means to heal after traumatic experiences. It examines the various components of the healing process and the theories that guide this work. It also looks at the conditions necessary for healing, which includes issues of forgiveness and reconciliation, which form the basis for most healing processes, and why this might be relevant for the situation in Matabeleland. It also delves into the optimum conditions for community recovery after violent conflicts and whether such conditions exist in Matabeleland at present. I argue that no such conditions exist currently and discuss how best to deal with this situation. Lastly, I discuss a few case studies of community-driven healing initiatives in other countries and how these have worked.

Chapter 5 reviews participatory action research as the research design used in this project, and presents a comparative analysis of some PAR cases that have been implemented in various places and under various circumstances.

Chapter 6 sets out the research design, research methodology and data collection methods used. It also explains the data analysis process. It offers a 'thick' description of the whole research process and narrates the challenges and successes of the project. I also reflect on my learning journey through this research project.

Chapter 7 evaluates how the PAR process itself measured up to PAR practice as reviewed in Chap. 5. It also evaluates the effectiveness of the collective actions undertaken by participants during the life of the project.

Chapter 8 discusses the analysis and findings of the study.

Chapter 9 carries on the discussion of chapter eight's findings but focuses on issues that were problematised by this research.

Chapter 10 offers a summary, conclusions and reflections on the research process.

## 1.11 Conclusion

This chapter has introduced the purpose and aims of the research. It has also discussed the research approach, the theoretical framework and the proposed data collection methods. It has offered the justification for the research and has placed me and my work within the context of the study.

Chapter 2 provides the history, background and consequences of *Gukurahundi*.

## References


Babbie, E and Mouton, J. 2001. *The practice of social research*. Cape Town: Oxford Press.

Barsalou, J. 2005. Trauma and transitional justice in divided societies. *United States Institute of Peace,* 135 (Special Report): 1–11. At: www.usip.org (12 June 2009).

Biggar, N. (ed.). 2003. *Burying the past: making peace doing justice after civil conflict.* Georgetown: Georgetown University Press.

Braithwaite, J. 2003. Restorative justice and a better future. In G. Johnstone (ed.), *A restorative justice reader: texts, sources, context.* Devon, Willan: Cullompton.

Clancy, M. A. C. and Hamber, B. 2008. Trauma, peacebuilding and development: an overview of key positions and critical questions. At: www.incore.ulst.ac.uk/research/projects/trauma/ (17 July 2010).

Cobban, H. 2007. *Amnesty after atrocity? Healing nations after genocide and war crimes.* Boulder, US: A Paradigm.

Dickson, G. 1997. Participatory action research and health promotion: the grandmothers' story. PhD Thesis, University of Saskatchewan.

Dignan, J. 2005. *Understanding victims and restorative justice*. Berkshire, England: Open University Press.

Eppel, S. 2006. 'Healing the dead': exhumation and burial as truth-telling and peace-building activities in rural Zimbabwe. In T. A. Borer (ed.), *Telling the truths: truth telling and peace building in post-conflict societies.* Notre Dame, Indiana: University of Notre Dame Press.

Freire, P. (1970) 1993. *Pedagogy of the oppressed.* New York: Continuum.

Ghali, B. B. 1992. An agenda for peace; Preventative diplomacy, peacemaking and peace-keeping. At: http://www.un.org/en/sc/repertoire/89-92/Chapter%208/GENERAL%20ISSUES/Item%2029_Agenda%20for%20peace_.pdf (08 March 2007).

Huyse, L. 2003. Justice. In D. Bloomfield, T. Barnes, and L. Huyse (eds.), *Reconciliation after violence: A hand book.* Stockholm: IDEA.

Lambourne, W. 2004. Post-conflict peacebuilding: meeting human needs for justice and reconciliation. *Peace, Conflict and Development*, 4: 1–24.

McIntyre, A. 2007. *Participatory action research*: Qualitative research methods series 52. L.A: SAGE.

Miall, H. 2006. Conflict transformation: a multi-dimensional task. At: http:www.berghof-handbook.net (10 February 2006).

Motsi, R. G. 2010. The trauma caused by the Matabeleland massacre of 1982–1986 in Tsholotsho and how the church can bring transformation using pastoral care. PhD Thesis. University of Pretoria.

Ndlovu-Gatsheni, S. J. 2003. The post-colonial state and Matebeleland: regional perceptions of civil-military relations, 1980–2002.

Papadopoulos, R. K. 2007. Refugees, trauma and adversity-activated development. *European Journal of Psychology and Counselling*, 9(3): 301–312.

Stauffer, C. S. 2009. Acting out the myths: the power of narrative discourse in shaping the Zimbabwe conflict of Matabeleland, 1980–1987. PhD Thesis, University of KwaZulu Natal.

Staub, E., Pearlman, L. A., Gubin, A. and Hagengimana, A. 2005. Healing, reconciliation, forgiving and the prevention of violence after genocide or mass killings: an intervention and its Experimental Evaluation in Rwanda. *Journal of Social and Clinical Psychology,* 24(3): 297–334.

Truth and Reconciliation Commission of South Africa. March 1999. TRC Report, Vol. 1, Cape Town.

Villa-Vicencio, C. 2000. Restorative justice: dealing with the past differently. In C. Villa-Vicencio and W. Verwoerd (eds.), *Looking back, reaching forward: reflections on the Truth and Reconciliation Commission of South Africa.* London: Zed.

# Chapter 2
# Background and History of Violence in Matebeleland

*When a group has entrenched itself in power, then it regards its rights and privileges to be sacrosanct.*

Mugabe (in Hill 2005, p. 1).

*Our votes must go together with our guns. After all, any vote we shall have shall have been the product of the gun. The gun which produces the vote should remain its security officer- its guarantor. The people's votes and the people's guns are always inseparable twins.*

Mugabe (in Meredith 2007, p. 16)

## 2.1 Preface

Zimbabwe, and particularly the Matebeleland region (the focus of this study), has a long history of violence which dates back to pre-colonial days (Alexander et al. 2000a). The history and memory of the past of the people of this region has been powerfully shaped by violence. These include the *mfecane* wars of the 1820s and 1830s; the 1893 and 1896 wars against the imperialists; the forced evictions and coercive agrarian interventions of the colonial state; black resistance and the white government repression of the 1960s; the violence of the war of liberation in the 1970s; and the 1980s' atrocities committed by the Zimbabwean armed forces (Ndlovu-Gatsheni 2003, p. 18).

Listening to victims of the 1980s' atrocities, one notices that most of them do not make a distinction between the war of liberation and the post-independence massacres. Their stories weave in and out of the two wars as if they were one and the same thing. For instance, an elderly lady interviewed in Tsholotsho concerning the killing of two of her children by the military, started talking about two Central Intelligent Organisation (CIO) agents who were killed in one part of Tsholotsho and how the people had rejoiced and composed a song at their death. It was later discovered from other sources that these had been killed during the war of



D. Ngwenya, *Healing the Wounds of Gukurahundi in Zimbabwe*,
The Anthropocene: Politik—Economics—Society—Science 19,
https://doi.org/10.1007/978-3-319-66818-5_2

independence by the freedom fighters and not by dissidents (GTH interviews 2009). This perhaps is an indication of how these communities have been immensely affected by all the episodes of violence that have affected them from time to time.

### *2.1.1 The Scale and Intensity of the Gukurahundi Massacres*

The intense and brutal violence of a genocide or ethnic-based war has a profound effect on those who survive it. According to Edkins (2003), those who themselves may not have been brutalised but witness it being done to others are also left as traumatised as if they were actually brutalised themselves. They feel a keen sense of shame because they feel as if they participated in the betrayal perpetrated by others. Staub et al. (2005) describe the impact as leaving the survivors' psychological needs frustrated; it also disrupts their identity, their understanding of their world and spirituality. The coexistence of these disruptions and the inability to control their emotional states create intense trauma symptoms among victims, which often leave them feeling vulnerable in what they perceive as a dangerous world (Staub/Pearlman 2001). This gives rise to feelings of insecurity, victimisation and a lack of trust; not to mention the desire for revenge and feelings of hatred, which further contribute to traumatisation (Zorbas 2004; Shriver 1999).

This study seeks to find out how such people, who are carrying emotional and psychological wounds, can be helped to move towards the healing of their memories, even in the absence of official healing processes.

## 2.2 Background to the Matebeleland Conflict

### *2.2.1 Violence Between the Ndebele and the Whites*

The Ndebele uprisings of 1893 and 1896 marked the beginning of the long history of violence between the blacks and white colonists. Although the colonists suffered heavy casualties during these wars, the Ndebele were eventually defeated and subjugated. They were systematically driven from their land and their cattle plundered.

In 1930, the Land Apportionment Act decreed that the people were to be moved from the land they occupied into the present Nkayi, Lupane and Tsholotsho areas. People were forcibly removed from their lands and literally dumped in the wild forests (Alexander et al. 2000a, pp. 45–66). This act was not meant just for

Matabeleland, but for the whole of the country. The increased disaffection of the black people eventually led to the struggle for independence, which saw black nationalists take up arms against their colonial masters.

The war of liberation, which lasted from about 1964 to 1979, was often brutal, with the civilian population bearing the brunt. The peasants were often accused of supporting the other side by both the Rhodesian (modern-day Zimbabwean) Forces and the Guerrillas. Those who stood accused of being 'sell outs' were usually summarily executed by the Guerrillas; while on the other hand, the Rhodesian army would also kill, torture, and detain those villagers suspected of providing support to the 'terrorists'. In Mashonaland, protective villages, referred to by the villagers as 'keeps', were used to try and prevent any contact between them and the freedom fighters (Kringer 1992, pp. 108–109). The Rhodesian government under the Rhodesian Front Party had very early on in its tenure, tightened security laws and introduced draconian amendments to the Law and Order (Maintenance) Act in 1962 (Meredith 2008). Ian Smith, the Prime Minister of Rhodesia, also declared a state of emergency in 1965 soon after the Unilateral Declaration of Independence from Britain. These laws provided for the detention without trial of anyone suspected of being in any way involved with the nationalist parties in their fight for independence. Under these laws, the security forces and other law-enforcing agents were immune from prosecution for any atrocities committed in their line of duty. These laws created a pervasive culture of impunity within the Rhodesian forces. Many nationalists and their followers were detained for numerous years without trial (Todd 2007).

Ironically, the State of Emergency and the Law and Order (Maintenance) Act remained unchanged post-independence until 1990, and were used by Mugabe against ZAPU in the 1980s (CCJP 2007, p. 44).

### 2.2.2 Violence Between the Ndebele and the Shona

> *They said, "Your forefathers ate our cattle—where are they?" We were attacked for being Ndebele. They actually said it.*
>
> Alexander et al. (2000a, p. 222)

The history of the relationship between the Shona and the Ndebele is shrouded in controversy and myth and has often been exploited for political advantage by both the colonialists and the two ethnic groups (Abrams 2006, pp. 24–25). This notion is also confirmed by Alexander et al. (2000a, p. 6).

We situate our analysis of post-colonial conflict firmly in political rivalry- in the Zanu (PF) government's desire to efface Zapu as a significant political counterweight, and in the insecurities of the first years of independence in which a legitimate and 'majoritarian' Zanu (PF) government sought to consolidate its power. Violence in post-colonial Zimbabwe was the product not of a disintegrating state nor ethnic antagonism—it was in no way the result of a 'retraditionalization' of politics. Rather, it was the consequence of the excesses of a strong state, itself a direct Rhodesian inheritance, and a particular interpretation of nationalism.

*The Pre-Colonial Era*

The roots of the Ndebele-Shona rivalry can possibly be traced back to the 1830s. According to Beach (1994), by 900 AD the Shona had emerged as a discernible language group. Shona states controlled the lucrative trade routes leading from the interior's gold mines to the Indian Ocean. However, by the 1700s their power and influence began to diminish because of Portuguese colonisation and the dwindling resources. With the scarcity of minerals, the Shona states turned upon each other in a bid to increase their wealth through land acquisition and cattle raiding. This resulted in the weakening of these states which opened the way for external groupings to enter the Shona territories, of which the Ndebele were but one.

Nguni-speaking groups from Southern Africa began moving up north in the 1820s and 1830s, settling briefly in the Shona territories of present day Zimbabwe. They soon moved on, leaving behind a power vacuum in these territories. In about 1838, the Ndebele, another Nguni speaking group led by Mzilikazi, moved in and established its kingdom. Mzilikazi's system of government required the Shona villages to pay a tribute to avoid being raided by his soldiers. The Ndebele language gradually grew to cover most of the south-western part of the country. Abrams (2006, p. 27) surmises that 'overall it was a relatively peaceful form of coexistence'.

This however is not the commonly held view of the history between the two ethnic groups. The mythical history of the *mfecane*, that propagates the existence of ethnic antagonism between the Shona and the Ndebele, has overshadowed this history and can be seen as a direct contributor to *Gukurahundi* in the 1980s.[1] This alternate history advanced by British, South African and Rhodesian historians and taken up by Shona historians too, appeared in the 1950s (Abrams 2006, p. 27). This is the history currently taught in Zimbabwean schools.

According to this view, beginning in the early 19th century, the Zulus of Southern Africa began moving up north. This movement caused a series of conflicts throughout the continent that became known as *mfecane*, a Zulu word meaning 'the crushing'. It is said that the *mfecane* was so violent that it led to massive depopulation of large parts of southern Africa, which opened the way for the white settlers to move onto what was now unoccupied land (Beach 1994). The migration of Mzilikazi and the Ndebele is placed within this period. While it is commonly believed that Mzilikazi was a general with close ties to Shaka Zulu's army, Beach maintains that there is little evidence to suggest that they had anything more than a

[1]Mythical in the sense that, although the event did take place, most of the facts have been manipulated to suit certain groups' agendas and plans.

superficial relationship (Beach 1994, p. 134). On arrival in Zimbabwe, the Ndebele overran the Shona tribes and established a despotic kingdom which thrived on raiding its subjects, killing, looting and selling them off as slaves. It is this version of history that has come to characterise the Ndebele as a warlike and ruthless nation which dominated and mistreated its Shona subjects. It is this very perception that came to dominate and motivate the violence and atrocities committed by the 5th Brigade between 1983 and 1987. It is interesting to note here that Beach (1980) in his book, *The Shona and Zimbabwe 900–1850*, records that the various Shona states practised the system of 'tribute' and the strong often raided the weak for their cattle and crops. In other words, it was a common practice of the day and was not exclusive to the Ndebele. I think there can be no doubt about the fact that raids were carried out by the Ndebele against the Shona; the bone of contention is whether this was a new practice introduced by the Ndebele.

### 2.2.3 The Struggle for Independence and the Growing of the Ndebele/Shona Polarisation

The period of colonial rule, by and large, did not perpetuate the legacy of the Ndebele/Shona antagonism. This period saw the black population united under a non-ethnic nationalist movement, working together to fight for their rights. Joshua Nkomo, a Ndebele, was the leader of this movement, which underwent several name changes due to its banning by the government of Rhodesia. However, in 1929/1930, there were clashes in Bulawayo between the Ndebele and Shona residents of that city. While Phimister/van Onselen (1979) argue that the outbreak of violence was caused by economic factors, Msindo (2006) insists that the 1929 violence had more to do with ethnicity than economics. This is not the platform to debate the merits and demerits of these two arguments. For the purpose of our discussion it is enough to show another period of Ndebele/Shona violence as we try to reflect on the root causes of the 1980s Matabeleland massacres.

In 1957, the Southern Rhodesia African National Congress (ANC) was formed in order to pressurise the government to abolish discriminatory laws and give voting rights to Africans. It was subsequently banned in 1959, when the government realised the threat it posed. Several of its leaders were arrested, but Nkomo managed to escape. Soon after, the National Democratic Party (NDP) was formed to replace the ANC, with a more revolutionary demand—majority rule. Nkomo became its leader (Meredith 2008, p. 28). It was also banned in 1962 and was replaced immediately by the Zimbabwe African People's Union (ZAPU). By now some of the nationalist leaders had become disenchanted with Nkomo's leadership and his strategy of seeking external influence to pressurise the British to accede to the nationalist demands. In 1963 they broke away, led by Ndabaningi Sithole, and formed the Zimbabwe African Nationalist Union (ZANU). Sithole was elected to lead it with Robert Mugabe chosen in absentia to be its secretary general.

While ZAPU's top leadership had a good mix of both Ndebele and Shona, it nevertheless eventually came to draw its support from Matabeleland and Midlands Province. Meanwhile, Enos Nkala, who had an abiding hatred for Nkomo, was just about the only Ndebele in the top leadership of ZANU (Meredith 2008, p. 32). Addressing a press conference after the formation of ZANU, Nkala is reported to have said: 'Now I am going to see to it that Joshua Nkomo is crushed' (Meredith 2008, p. 32). Ironically, another of Nkala's inflammatory speeches years later is blamed for the violence that flared up between ZIPRA and ZANLA combatants at Entumbane (see below Sect. 2.3.1). The struggle to assert themselves led to a rivalry between the two parties which resulted in a period of black on black violence in the years 1963–1964. Gang warfare, arson, petrol bombing, stoning and assaults became the order of day. This situation eventually assumed ideological and ethnic dimensions that were never transcended (Meredith 2008, p. 33). The Rhodesian government under Ian Smith took advantage of this situation by fanning the tribal fires, pitting one side against the other in order to divide the nationalists and keep them weakened. During this time, little attention was paid to the whites or to the nationalist cause for which they were meant to be fighting (Meredith 2008, p. 33).

By 1964, both parties were convinced that armed confrontation was necessary to achieve independence. A year later, in 1965, Ian Smith proclaimed the Unilateral Declaration of Independence for the state of Rhodesia (Abrams 2006, p. 32; Meredith 2008, p. 35). The race to establish military wings to fight against the Rhodesian regime served to increase the gap between the two nationalist parties. The fact that, initially they had to compete for recruits from the same pool of black people living outside Rhodesia, worsened the relations even further. ZAPU established the Zimbabwe African People's Revolutionary Army, while ZANU formed the Zimbabwe African National Liberation Army. The ZAPU/ZANU antagonism naturally spilled over to the respective armed forces and the war period was characterised as much by the clashes between ZIPRA and ZANLA as by the fight against the Smith regime (Abrams 2006, p. 32). ZIPRA despised ZANLA combatants whom they saw as ill-trained, unprofessional and not matching their own training. Whenever they met within Rhodesia, they faced each other as enemies (Alexander et al. 2000a, pp. 145–147).

Several attempts by other African leaders were made to unify the two factions of the two armies but with little success, as the level of trust was never high enough to bridge the gap. One such attempt to form a combined army ended in disaster. Combatants from ZIPRA and ZANLA were sent to Tanzania in an attempt to form a combined army—the Zimbabwe People's Army (ZIPA). In June 1976, in the training camps of Mgagao and Morogoro, fighting broke out over the use of the kitchens and ZANLA quickly armed themselves and fired on unarmed ZIPRA soldiers. Dozens were killed, although a number managed to escape. It was the same story in Mozambique: some ZIPRA soldiers sent to train as part of ZIPA, were tortured and forced to denounce ZAPU. Such acts only served to harden the existing antagonism between both ZANU and ZAPU and ZIPRA and ZANLA (Alexander et al. 2000a, p. 147).

A further contributor to the suspicion and mistrust between the two was the strategy adopted by ZIPRA to train and equip a regular army with modern weapons. This regular army was kept in reserve and was not sent into Rhodesia to fight. This prompted ZANU to believe that they were being withheld for an eventual war with itself. This contributed to an already overflowing conundrum of mistrust and antagonism between the two organisations (Meredith 2008, p. 38).

Although in 1979 the two parties managed to unite under the Patriotic Front banner, the union only lasted till the end of the Lancaster House Conference, which brought an end to minority rule. As soon as the conference was over, Mugabe announced that ZANU would stand for the elections alone. This announcement, made unilaterally when Mugabe had already left London and without prior notice to Nkomo, only served to stoke the fires of mistrust and antagonism further (Meredith 2008, p. 38).

In the elections of February 1980, Mugabe won 57 of the 100 seats, while Nkomo won 20, all in Matabeleland. The other 20 were reserved for whites and a further three were won by Muzorewa's United African National Council, {UANC} (Abrams 2006, p. 35). Mugabe offered Nkomo the largely ceremonial post of President but he turned it down saying he did not want to be caught up in 'an official prison' (Meredith 2008, p. 39). He was later given the Ministry of Home Affairs. The relationship between the two men never really improved. On Independence Day, Nkomo and his wife were relegated to an obscure seating position away from the public sight and reserved for junior ministers. Nkomo felt slighted and he reports that his wife could not hold back her tears at the humiliation (Meredith 2008, pp. 39–40). From the beginning, Mugabe had wanted a one-party state and now the only thing that stood between him and his ambition was Nkomo and his ZAPU party. Once again this did not bode well for the future.

## 2.3 The Matabeleland Violence 1980–1987

*Nkomo and his guerrillas are germs in the country's wounds and they will have to be cleaned up with iodine. The patient will have to scream a bit.*

Edgar Tekere (in Meredith 2008, p. 60)

### *2.3.1 The Genesis of the Post-Independence Conflict*

As in every post-conflict situation, the problems of Disarmament, Demobilisation and Reintegration posed a huge threat in the already polarised and high-tension environment of Zimbabwe. To facilitate this process, ZIPRA and ZANLA guerrillas were required to be confined to Assembly Points (APs) where they would either be demobilised or integrated into the new Zimbabwe National Army (ZNA). From the beginning, the process was fraught with suspicions, mistrust and irregularities. To start with, the exercise was to be supervised by the Rhodesian army, the very enemy ZIPRA and ZANLA had fought against. This left the guerrillas feeling insecure and suspicious; they were to be disarmed by an armed enemy which left them vulnerable to it. This was compounded by the fact that most guerrillas felt that they should have been consulted over the disarmament issue and that the Lancaster House agreement was a sell-out (Alexander et al. 2000a, pp. 182–183).

Because of the deep misgivings over the whole process, both ZIPRA and ZANLA had fighters who stayed away from the assembly points, fearing that this might be a trick to entrap them. Indeed, there were reports that a bus load of ZIPRA guerrillas was attacked by air on their way to an assembly point in Lupane. Large quantities of arms were also cached by both ZIPRA and ZANLA (Alexander et al. 2000a, pp. 182–183). This was to later provide Mugabe with a perfect excuse to, once and for all, get rid of his nemesis ZAPU and everything associated with it. Those men who stayed out of the APs began to roam the country side causing havoc and committing acts of banditry (Todd 2007, pp. 5–7). In the eastern part of the country, ZANU PF had deliberately left out some of its fighters to campaign for the forth-coming elections. Complaints of harassment and intimidation of civilians were made against all the parties, but ZANLA was singled out to be the worst culprit. Nkomo urged the governor, Lord Soames, to disqualify ZANU PF from the elections. In Matabeleland, the ZAPU regular army rounded up some 400 errant guerrillas and delivered them to Khami prison.

After the elections and his victory, Mugabe chose to ignore the acts of ZANLA and to highlight the activities of the errant ZIPRA guerrillas. The tone shifted from bandits and unruly elements to dissidents and the problem was represented increasingly in political terms. It was said they were disgruntled over ZAPU's electoral loss and were refusing to recognise Mugabe's government. Enos Nkala, the man who had once vowed to crush Nkomo, introduced a tribal element to the accusations. He said the dissidents were Ndebeles who were calling for a second war of liberation and that they should be shot down. He called Nkomo the 'self-appointed Ndebele King' who should be crushed (Alexander et al. 2000a, pp. 185–186). By calling Nkomo a Ndebele king, Nkala seems to have been accusing him of wanting to bring back the Ndebele domination of the Shona of the pre-colonial era and invoking the hatred and resentment for the Ndebeles. Whatever his reasons for the outburst, this allegory was not lost on the 5th brigade, which was to be soon unleashed in Matabeleland and some parts of Midlands Province (Meredith 2008, p. 60).

The process of integrating fighters from three armies proved to be an odious task and, by late 1980, several thousands of guerrillas were still stuck in the APs. In a bid to stop the rural banditry, provide better accommodation and to alleviate the problem of boredom among the ex-fighters, they were moved to new housing schemes in Chitungwiza near Harare and Entumbane in Bulawayo. This move brought the old foes into proximity and, in October 1980, brief gun fire was exchanged between ZIPRA and ZANLA in Chitungwiza. In November, Nkala came to address a rally in Bulawayo; at this rally, he once again stoked the fire of conflict with his reckless speech: 'As from today,' he said, 'ZAPU has become the enemy of ZANU-PF. The time has come for ZANU-PF to flex its muscles.' He urged the party supporters to form vigilante groups and challenge ZAPU on its home turf. If it meant 'a few blows' then they would 'deliver them'.

After the rally, party supporters clashed in the streets and this spilled over into the holding camps at Entumbane where ZIPRA and ZANLA lived adjacent to each other. The government subsequently moved a further 500 ZANLA guerrillas into Entumbane and several ZAPU officials were arrested (Alexander et al. 2000a, p. 186). These incidents led many guerrillas to believe that further conflict was still likely. Rumours of what had happened at Entumbane circulated to the APs and the newly integrated units of the ZNA, further increasing tension and distrust all round.

In the midst of these high tensions, Mugabe continued to goad Nkomo and ZAPU. In January 1981, in a cabinet reshuffle, Nkomo was demoted from the Home Affairs portfolio to Public Service and later to Minister without portfolio. Nkomo protested and warned of the possibility of unrest that such actions might arouse, but Mugabe did not heed his protestations. By this time the country was on a knife-edge and all it needed was the smallest of sparks to light the fires of violence (Meredith 2008, p. 61; Alexander et al. 2000a, p. 186).

A more serious fight broke out in February 1981, in a newly integrated Zimbabwe National Army (ZNA) unit stationed at Ntabazinduna and soon spread to other units around the country. The fight eventually made its way to the volatile Entumbane camps. When ZIPRA troops at Gwayi and Esigodini got wind of the fight at Entumbane, they headed for the city and were ironically only stopped by the Rhodesian army battalions that were still intact (White 2007; Alexander et al. 2000a; Meredith 2008). In the wake of these skirmishes, arms were cached by both sides, adding to those cached during the war and when moving into APs. Many guerrillas who had fled the fighting eventually returned but others left permanently. Others fled the country for Botswana or South Africa, some preferred to go back to their rural homes and some took to the bush and became dissidents.

By early 1982 the issues around DDR had been dealt with sufficiently for Mugabe to feel confident enough to make his final move on Nkomo and ZAPU. In February, he announced that arms caches had been found on ZAPU properties. This, he claimed, was clear proof that ZAPU had been planning a coup against his government (Todd 2007, p. 42; Alexander et al. 2000a, pp. 188–189; Meredith 2008, pp. 62–63). In addition, ZIPRA guerrillas were implicated in an attack on the prime minister's residence and shortly thereafter, six tourists were kidnapped and later killed by dissidents along the Victoria Falls road in Matabeleland North (Alexander et al. 2000a, p. 189). Nkomo and other ZAPU officials were expelled from government and many ZAPU officials including high profile ZIPRA figures like Dumiso Dabengwa and Lookout Masuku were arrested and tried. Although found not guilty, they were simply re-detained and only released in 1986. They were accused of orchestrating the dissidents' activities and, although the ZAPU leadership strenuously denied these charges and even condemned the dissidents, they were nevertheless deemed responsible by Mugabe and his coterie. Former dissidents themselves testify that they got very little if any support from any ZAPU structures (Alexander et al. 2000a, pp. 199–201).

The ZIPRA guerrillas, now integrated into ZNA, became victims of persecution in some of the units. Those accused of being 'dissident sympathisers' and 'disloyal elements' were purged, arrested or killed with such intensity that army officers apparently had to tour the ZNA units, assuring the soldiers that they would not be persecuted for their past affiliations (Alexander et al. 2000a, p. 189). Former ZIPRA combatants testified that many of their colleagues were killed, beaten up or victimised. They alleged that some of their numbers were taken away, never to be seen again. In other units they were disarmed and segregated. Many deserted the army and returned to their homes, but they continued to be hunted and harassed.

### *2.3.2 The Fifth Brigade* (Gukurahundi)

> *We want to wipe out ZAPU leadership. You've* (sic) *only seen the warning lights. We haven't yet reached full blast... the murderous organisation and its murderous leadership must be hit so hard that it doesn't feel obliged to do the things it has been doing.*
>
> Enos Nkala (in CCJP 1997, p. 60)

> *We have to deal with this problem, ruthlessly... Don't cry if your relatives get killed in the process.... Where men and women provide food for dissidents, when we get there, we eradicate them. We don't differentiate when we fight, because we can't tell who is a dissident and who is not...*
>
> Robert Mugabe—The London Times 1983

> *They said we were dissidents, but we had never seen a dissident. It was just a trick by the regime to kill the people*
>
> *Gukurahundi* survivor (in Blair 2002, p. 32)

In October of 1980, Mugabe had entered a secret deal with North Korea to train a new brigade to deal specifically with 'internal security'. However, this deal was only announced in 1982 when the North Korean instructors arrived in the country. This brigade, the 5th Brigade, was to be answerable to Mugabe directly and fell outside the command structures of the ZNA (Todd 2007, p. 37). It used different guns from the regular army and even its communication equipment was not compatible with that used by the other defence forces. This naturally raised suspicions within ZAPU, which saw the new unit as a private army meant to serve Mugabe's whims. The deployment of the regular forces and the Police Support Unit among others was more than sufficient and certainly a group of loosely connected, ill-equipped dissidents, numbering no more than 400 at their peak, did not warrant the creation of this new unit (Alexander et al. 2000a, p. 198). While the initial recruitment for the 5th Brigade included some ex-ZIPRA guerrillas, most were eventually purged, while others withdrew out of fear for their lives.

If there had been any doubt about the real intent for creating the 5th Brigade, this was soon dispelled at the pass out parade. The force was made up almost entirely of Shona speakers, almost all from the former ZANLA guerrillas. At the passing out parade the Fifth Brigade was officially called *Gukurahundi*, a Shona word meaning the rain that drives away chaff before the spring rains. To the people in Matabeleland and parts of Midlands it came to mean that the Ndebele were the dirt that needed to be washed away (CCJP 2007, p. 74; Meredith 2008, p. 66; Alexander et al. 2000a, pp. 191–192). Mugabe is reported to have said that 'the knowledge you have acquired will make you work with the people, plough and reconstruct' (CCJP 2007, p. 74). Perence Shiri, the brigade's commander, is said to have issued the following instructions: 'From today onwards I want you to start dealing with the dissidents. We have some of them here at this parade… Wherever you meet them, deal with them and I don't want a report' (CCJP 2007, p. 75).

From day one of its deployment, the brigade showed that it had taken these instructions from its commander and commander-in-chief seriously. From the moment it was deployed to the day it was withdrawn from Matabeleland, it caused an untold amount of suffering, death and chaos.

#### 2.3.2.1 The Acts of the Fifth Brigade

By January 25th reports of the work of the 5th Brigade started pouring in. The first were from Mbembesi, an area 50 km East of Bulawayo. Reports from here were brought to Nkomo that soldiers wearing red berets were carrying out mass beatings and killing civilians indiscriminately and that, within a matter of a few days, 95 people had been killed (Nkomo's Letter to Mugabe 7th June 1983). The brigade spread into the rest of the areas in Matabeleland North, into Tsholotsho, Lupane and Nkayi, and in a space of six weeks some 2000 civilians had been killed, many burnt alive inside huts. Thousands more were tortured. In Tsholotsho several areas had villages where people were burnt alive inside huts. In Mkhonyeni village, at least 27 women were placed in 4 huts and burnt, while in Silonkwe, not very far from Mkhonyeni, another 22 people died in a burning house (CCJP 2007, pp. 154–160). Usually, when the soldiers arrived at a village, people would be rounded up and interrogated about the whereabouts of dissidents. People would be beaten en masse with thick sticks. Sometimes they would be made to fight each other, climb on trees and bark like baboons, then throw themselves to the ground. Some of their perverse and grotesque torture methods included making relatives kill each other, forcing sons-in-law to have sex with their mothers-in-law and making husbands or sons watch while their wives or mothers were being raped. People were made to sing while being beaten and often, after the killings, people were made to dig shallow graves and bury the dead together in one grave. Then they would be made to sing and dance on top of the freshly buried, singing derogatory songs against Nkomo and ZAPU. At times, those to be killed were made to dig their own grave then lie on top of each other to be shot with a single bullet. Sometimes pregnant women were accused of carrying dissidents and would have their stomachs ripped open to reveal the 'dissident' they were carrying. One woman described how she was beaten on her stomach with the butt of a gun when she revealed she was pregnant. Rape was also common and the soldiers would tell their victims they were creating a generation of Shona babies in Matabeleland (Alexander et al. 2000b, p. 323; Blair 2002, p. 32).

The biggest single incident of mass killings was reported to have happened in Lupane where 62 men and women were shot by the banks of the Cewale River. Seven survived by pretending to be dead. All over Matabeleland North and South and some parts of Midlands Province, similar stories have been recorded. While the exact number of the dead can never be known with certainty, it has been estimated at 10,000–20,000 (Eppel 2006, p. 261). Although the researchers of the *Breaking the Silence* report, seem comfortable with a scientific estimate of about 6000 dead (CCJP 2007, pp. 8, 284–285), Meredith (2008, p. 75) puts the number at 10,000.

Stringent curfew regulations were introduced in these areas. No one was allowed in or out of these areas, and journalists were forbidden to go outside of Bulawayo. A dusk-to-dawn curfew was pronounced, stores were closed and granaries burnt where they were found (Ndlovu-Gatsheni 2003, p. 25), ostensibly to reduce food support for the dissidents. All drought-relief deliveries were stopped and all forms of transport were banned, including bicycles and scotch carts (Ndlovu-Gatsheni 2003, p. 78). At the time, there was a severe drought and people were reliant on drought relief for their survival. In addition to the beatings and killings, they were now being deliberately starved. This was especially so in 1984, when the government adopted the policy of using food as a weapon against the communities in Matabeleland (Ndlovu-Gatsheni 2003, p. 79).

While an argument can be made to the effect that the real motive for Mugabe to set the 5th Brigade upon the people of Matabeleland was to crush ZAPU and thus realise his dream of a one-party state, these actions suggest also a more sinister plot. From the onset, the 5th Brigade was never really meant to seriously fight against dissidents. Its focus was on Ndebele-speaking villagers.[2] While these atrocities took place within the context of 'fighting' dissidents, it is clear from the evidence gathered by the CCJP, that this unit had been trained to persecute and kill civilians in Matabeleland. Often, they arrived in a village armed with names of local ZAPU officials, who, if they were found, were promptly executed. Whenever former ZIPRA soldiers were found, they too were killed immediately, including those who were on official leave from the ZNA or had been officially demobilised. But the bulk of the people killed were ordinary civilians, including women and children. Across the whole of Matabeleland, the *modus operandi* was the same and there was a predictable pattern. The acts described above cannot have been the acts of undisciplined elements within the unit; the similarities of their actions all over Matabeleland suggest a different story. The bulk of their actions were aimed at civilians and only occasionally against dissidents. The dissidents themselves attested to this. In the words of one:

---

[2]For instance, GTH interviews with both victims and beneficiaries, reveal that those who were Shona, or could speak Shona, were often spared or escaped with minor beatings. On 24th November 2009, GTH interviewed one such woman, who survived being burnt along with other women at Mkhonyeni, because she became the translator for the 5th brigade (see also Alexander et al. 2000a, p. 223).

> The *Gukurahundi* wasn't a good fighting unit. It was trained to reduce the Matabeleland population, it was killing civilians. The *Gukurahundi* weren't soldiers, where do you see soldiers who sing when on patrol? They were looking for civilians not other soldiers, so we would come across them singing and we would take cover. Soon after you'd hear people crying in their homes… [W]e'd clash with them, but instead of following us, they'd call for the villagers. That's where you'd hear bazookas and AKs firing into homes (Alexander et al. 2000a, p. 200).

There are very few reported incidents of the 5th Brigade having killed or apprehended dissidents. There are also very few incidents reported of civilians caught in genuine crossfire between dissidents and government agencies. The Police Support Unit seems to have been the most efficient force in dealing with dissidents. Even commercial farmers interviewed by CCJP,[3] felt that the 5th brigade was more interested in 'politicking' than in going after dissidents, and whenever farmers reported the presence of dissidents to it, they hardly showed much interest (CCJP 2007, p. 82).

Testimonies from the villagers also indicate that the 5th Brigade itself often alluded to the fact that they had been ordered to kill the Ndebele people as some form of revenge for the ills of the past committed by the Ndebele ancestors on their ancestors. According to victim testimonies gathered by Alexander et al. (2000a, p. 222), the 5th Brigade told people that they had been told to 'wipe out all people in the area', 'to kill anything human'. They said they had been told that all Ndebeles were dissidents, thus making women and children targets too. However, in one area of Tsholotsho, it is reported that people were told that they were being punished for 'having parented those responsible for Entumbane and Connemara' (CCJP 2007, p. 82), a reference to the clashes between ZIPRA and ZANLA of 1980 and 1981. More common, however, were general accusations of having parented dissidents.

While other fighting units were reported to have harassed or killed civilians, especially the Central Intelligence Organisation (CIO), the damage they inflicted does not compare at all with that of the 5th Brigade, to which 80–85% of the atrocities committed—murders, rapes, torture, and property destruction—have been attributed (see CCJP 2007, pp. 266–274). There was too little contact between dissidents and the 5th Brigade to justify the stated official reason for its deployment as an 'elite force' to combat dissidents.

The evidence is very strong that the 5th Brigade was never really meant to fight dissidents but was created specifically to persecute and decimate the civilian population in Matabeleland, which was the support base of ZAPU, the arch enemy of ZANU PF. The actions of *Gukurahundi*, the harassment of ZAPU officials and the speech acts of the ZANU PF politicians convinced the people of Matabeleland that they were being persecuted and killed for being Ndebele. This served to create within the Ndebele population a persecution mentality and a deep mistrust of Shonas and ZANU PF. Coupled with this was a document purported to have been

[3]The Breaking the Silence report by CCJP and the Legal Resources Foundation provides extensive data of interviews with the victims, in some cases a village-by-village account of the events that transpired during the 1980s' disturbances.

crafted by the 'Shona elite' within ZANU in 1979, entitled 'The Grand Plan'. This document laid out several strategies to dominate and marginalise the Ndebele. While the authenticity of the document is debatable, what has been taking place in Matabeleland since 1980 mirrors the contents of this document precisely. In 2000, another document surfaced which was reviewing the progress made thus far in fulfilling 'The Grand Plan' (see Appendix A).

## 2.4 The Current Situation in Matabeleland

> *The belief that the fifth brigade's particular brand of violence was not an aberration but part of a plan orchestrated by ZANU-PF's leaders changed people's perceptions of the goals of the 1980's war fought not against dissidents but against the Ndebele and ZAPU.*
>
> Alexander/McGregor (1996, p. 6)

### *2.4.1 The Impact of* Gukurahundi

The perception by most Ndebeles that they were meant to have been annihilated by another tribe has left a general sense of anger, vulnerability and mistrust against Mugabe, ZANU PF and the Shonas in general. These sentiments are brought about by the realisation that, not only were they the targets of extermination, but that also everything that constituted their world, everything that made their life worth living —their work, their families and their children—was at the point of being wiped out too (Zorbas 2004, p. 30). As Zorbas points out, when a person has had such terrifying 'existential crisis', it makes the work of healing and reconciliation that much more difficult because the victim has to overcome major emotional, moral and mental challenges to get to a point where some kind of relationship with the perceived perpetrator is re-established. At this point, it is important to examine what effect these traumatic events had within the Ndebele communities.

#### 2.4.1.1 A Hardening of Ethnic Differences

The fact that the soldiers of the 5th Brigade predominantly spoke the Shona language, and that those who were Shona, or could speak the language, were often spared from death, served to worsen an already unhealthy relationship between the two ethnic groups. From that time on, anything done by the government of ZANU PF or Shonas in Matabeleland has been viewed with suspicion and interpreted as part of the continued effort to dominate the Ndebeles. When the 5th Brigade began building schools in Matabeleland, this was not seen as development assistance but a heralding of the introduction of Shona students into Matabeleland. We have already noted above how the rapes were seen as a way of creating a generation of ‘Shona babies’, another way of increasing the dominance of Shona over Ndebele.[4] By contrast, rapes committed by the ZNA soldiers or dissidents were seen simply as an abuse of power, unlike those of the 5th Brigade (Alexander et al. 2000a, p. 223). The ethnic differences were further hardened, by the 5th Brigade’s frequent reference to tribalistic justifications for their actions against the people of Matabeleland (see Sect. 2.4.2 below). Hence this ‘war’ came to be seen not as a fight against the dissidents but against the Ndebele and ZAPU:

> An attack on the Ndebele was an attack on Zapu and an attack on Zapu was an attack on the Ndebele; and an attack on Zapu as Ndebele made those who were not Ndebele come to see themselves as such. Such attacks struck at the root of people’s most cherished social and political identity (Alexander et al. 2000a, p. 223).

This conflict perhaps succeeded, more than any other in the history of the two groups, to concretise ethnic prejudice and foster a strong identification between ethnicity and political affiliation. If those ZAPU members who were Shona began to feel and see themselves as Ndebele because of these attacks, then the gap between Ndebele and Shona must have been even more pronounced. For a while it became dangerous to be Ndebele or ZAPU. Speeches from ZANU PF ministers and officials also contributed to the hardening of ethnic differences. Enos Nkala, the prominent Ndebele in ZANU PF, is constantly being quoted by people in Matabeleland as having said, ‘*Ngabe ubuNdebele buya gezwa ngabe sengabugeza*’ (‘If it were possible to wash away my being Ndebele I would have done it long ago’). Such comments served to further create perceptions and strong feelings of alienation and vulnerability among the people of Matabeleland. They had become the ‘enemy of the state’.

#### 2.4.1.2 Fear and Hatred

The intensity and extent of the acts of the 5th Brigade created a great sense of fear and hatred for Mugabe, ZANU PF and the military among the Ndebele. The politicisation of the military and the strong link between ethnicity and political affiliation, promoted a negative perception of the military. Since the violence of the 5th Brigade was state sanctioned, people perceived the military as a Shona-dominated institution and the Shona language as the official means of communication. Most of the people in Matabeleland, especially the elderly, are still terrified of the army. The possibility of the recurrence of the massacres is a distinct possibility to them. Even today sentiments remain like, ‘We can still be eliminated at any time’ and ‘*Amasotsha ngiyawesaba ngoba ayabulala*’ (‘I fear the soldiers because they kill’) (CCJP 2007, p. 96; Ndlovu-Gatsheni 2003, p. 30). This fear has even affected the voting patterns of most elderly people, who would rather vote for ZANU PF so that they can prevent the return of *Gukurahundi*. This again shows a strong association perceived by the people of the violence of the 1980s with ZANU PF. The younger generation is, by contrast, driven more by hatred than by

[4]See also Appendix A.

fear and, thus, will oppose anything ZANU PF. Hence, since the death of Joshua Nkomo in 1999 and the rise of the opposition, Matabeleland has become a strong base for the opposition (Ndlovu-Gatsheni 2003, p. 31). Mugabe as a person is not liked in Matabeleland. Mention of his name in the context of the suffering of the people in this region usually draws responses of open anger towards him. One victim's comment—'His behaviour makes us hate him. He has been killing us' (Blair 2002, p. 31)—is a fair representation of the feelings of most Ndebele people.

The hatred of the Shona in general is in reality, a more complex issue. Most Ndebeles have very cordial and friendly relations with Shona people at a personal level and there are intermarriages between the two groups. Yet, at another level, there is intense hatred for the Shona. This situation is best illustrated by what normally happens at soccer matches when Highlanders play against Dynamos. Highlanders are a team based in Bulawayo and the Ndebele like to see it as their last standing social institution. On the other hand, Dynamos is from Harare, and its support base is predominantly Shona. When the teams are playing in Bulawayo and Highlanders is losing or loses, the Highlanders' supporters usual chant anti- Shona songs. One of them is particularly poignant: '*Maye! Maye! Nanka amaShona engibulala!*' ('Oh! Oh! Here are the Shonas killing me!'). This song has been adapted from a folk song sung by their ancestors during the 1893/1896 Ndebele uprisings.

It is important to note that Highlanders is the only team that has had people from other ethnic groups play for it, almost from its formation in 1932. Currently the bulk of its players are Shona. While insults and often violence against the Shona is a common feature of these matches, one would not dare insult a Shona Highlanders player, as this would draw an immediate violent response from other supporters. This suggests that Dynamos, as a representative of a Shona institution, provokes and projects the pain of what a Shona-speaking army did in the 1980s. The pain of a Highlanders loss to a Shona team becomes the pain of the suffering at the hands of the Fifth Brigade. Dynamos and its Shona supporters become a proxy to which Ndebele give vent to their anger. It is perhaps not a Shona individual or Dynamos as a team that is a problem but what they represent—the collective Shona entity associated with the massacres of thousands of Matabele peoples.

#### 2.4.1.3 Economic Hardships

During the operations of *Gukurahundi* in Matabeleland, people lost homes and properties through arson and pillaging by the 5th Brigade and ZANU PF supporters. During those years, life came to a standstill for developmental programmes. Jobs were lost as people fled death and persecution and some were later denied their pensions for having broken their contracts without notice. Young and able-bodied men fled their rural homes for urban areas or across the borders. Others were killed. All this meant that a lot of families were left without breadwinners, which compromised their future. Children stopped attending school and some never went back after the violence. Many people could not get death certificates for their relatives and, as a result, children could not get birth certificates and families could not draw money from bank accounts in the names of the deceased, or collect the deceased's pensions. Those that suffered severe physical injuries were left unable to work in their fields and were forced to depend on the goodwill of family and neighbours for survival (CCJP 2007, pp. 142–143).

People from Matabeleland complain bitterly about economic marginalisation. They perceive that they are being deliberately discriminated against, when it comes to the sharing of the national cake. They see their region as lagging behind others in every aspect of developmental progress. People point out that there seems to be an unwritten law that people belonging to the Ndebele-speaking group must be disadvantaged on all fronts. For instance, the dominance of the Shona-speaking people in all spheres of life in Matabeleland is often cited as clear examples of marginalisation. Although the government has vehemently denied these claims, the existence of a document entitled 'The Grand Plan', authored in 1979 and a follow-up review of the same in 2000 (please refer to Appendix A) seem to give credence to this conspiracy theory. While it is difficult to verify the authorship and authenticity of these documents, it is equally difficult to deny that what has happened so far and continues to happen, is accurately reflected in these documents. As the review document reveals, the plan seems to be working well because every senior position in government offices, from the police to the state-owned entities, is headed by a Shona-speaking person, even in the most remote parts of Matabeleland. Reports of people being 'bussed in' from outside Matabeleland to take up employment and student places in tertiary institutions abound. As a matter of fact, my wife tried, without success, for three years in the 1990s, to enrol in one of the local teachers' colleges. In the end, she had to use the political influence of a relative to be accepted. Furthermore, delays in the implementation of projects like the Zambezi Matabeleland Water Project (meant to solve Bulawayo's perennial water shortages) and road construction are often cited as examples of marginalisation. However, this complaint is often dismissed as bitterness because of the 1980s (Ndlovu-Gatsheni 2003, p. 32).

#### 2.4.1.4 Psychological and Physiological Injuries

The unprecedented violence of the 1980s left people with emotional wounds and physical injuries. As one of them said, 'This wound is huge and deep…the liberation war was painful, but it had a purpose… The war that followed was much worse. It was fearful, unforgettable, and unacknowledged' (CCJP 2007, p. 96). Those that were beaten by the 5th Brigade and are still alive carry permanent disabilities, such as partial lameness, paralysis, deafness, recurring backaches and headaches, impotence, infertility and kidney damage (CCJP 2007, p. 143).

Emotional scars and bad memories of the violence of the 1980s are also some of the effects of *Gukurahundi*. According to the *Breaking the Silence* report, large numbers of the people in Tsholotsho showed signs of some degree of psychological trauma, leading to recurring depression, dizzy spells, anxiety, anger or permanent fear and distrust of government officials. Some children were left without one or both parents and with the trauma of having witnessed extreme violence done to those they loved. Some people do not know the whereabouts of their family members who were disappeared. These conditions affect those who are supposed to mourn their dead; their grief is not atoned for by a decent burial and the mourning process remains incomplete, what Timmerman (1987) calls 'impaired mourning'. Communities were left with the trauma of having seen their loved ones and neighbours humiliated, beaten and killed (CCJP 2007, p. 143).

### *2.4.2 The Unity Accord*

After sustained pressure by Mugabe and his state machinery, Nkomo finally gave in and entered talks with Mugabe. This eventually culminated in the signing of a peace accord between the two parties on 22 December 1987. The Unity Accord merged the two parties together into the new ZANU PF and this brought an end to the killings and some level of peace.

Unfortunately, the people of Matabeleland did not reap the peace dividend which the Unity Accord was meant to provide. Ndlovu-Gatsheni (2003, pp. 31–33) suggests five reasons why the Unity Accord fell dismally short of bringing healing to the victims and survivors of *Gukurahundi*, if indeed this was ever its original intent. To start with, it was not a product of a democratic process but was simply imposed on the people by the political elite. In fact, even today, not many know what is contained in the Unity Accord document. This was just one of the authoritarian nation building strategies of ZANU PF, which never carried any healing element for the ordinary people. Secondly, the Accord was not premised on any comprehensive post-conflict peacebuilding process, which is necessary for the reconstruction of relationships, reconciliation and nationhood. The Accord preoccupied itself mostly with power-sharing arrangements between the two parties. There was no social reconstruction programme that would have overseen the reintegration of the former dissidents into civil society, or any provision to address trauma caused by the massive violence against civilians. Thirdly, the Accord did not make any provision for compensation of any kind for the people of Matabeleland who were injured or who lost breadwinners and other family members. Fourthly, issues of justice were not addressed, war crimes were not investigated and no one was brought to book. Instead, in 1988, a blanket amnesty was granted to both dissidents and the 5th Brigade. Lastly, no programme of economic rebuilding was instituted for a region which had been severely disadvantaged developmentally by deliberate isolationist policies of the ZANU PF government and by the pillaging of the military and ZANU PF supporters (Ndlovu-Gatsheni 2003, p. 32). This simply means that most people in Matabeleland did not benefit from the Unity Accord. Their hurts, needs for justice and redress have gone largely unmet.

The people of Matabeleland have come to believe that they are discriminated against based on ethnic affiliation. They see this as a continuation of their persecution, but this time using a different form of violence—structural violence. The people, therefore, have nursed and are still nursing wounds and carry in them a great fear and suspicion, long after the 'peace accord' of 1987 (Alexander et al. 2000b, pp. 322–323).

## 2.5 Conclusion

This chapter has sought to trace the historical roots of the animosities between the Ndebele and the Shona and how these were manipulated and played out over the years, increasing the levels of polarisation between the two camps. It also discussed how these animosities contributed to the 1963 split of ZAPU, which was clearly along ethnic lines, further increasing the divisions, which resulted in a lot of mistrust between the political protagonists. All these events, plus the unfolding of events during the liberation war, the ceasefire negotiations and the incidents of the early 1980s, ultimately culminated in the atrocities of *Gukurahundi* between 1982 and 1987. The chapter also examined the after-effects of the atrocities and concludes that, far from getting better, the current environment has somewhat worsened the situation, especially since nothing has been done to address issues of justice, truth and healing, now almost three decades after the violence.

Chapter 3 begins to review the theories that guide this research. In particular, this chapter will discuss how the trauma caused by armed violence can be addressed in the context of peacebuilding, which is the theoretical framework upon which this research is grounded.

## References

Abrams, B. E. 2006. Strategy of domination: Zanu-PF's use of ethnic conflict as a means of maintaining political control in Zimbabwe, 1982–2006. MA, Tufts University. At: http://fletcher.tufts.edu (21 May 2009).

Alexander, J. and McGregor, J. 1996. Democracy, development and political conflict: rural institutions in Matabeleland North after independence. *International conference on the Historical Dimensions of Democracy and Human Rights in Zimbabwe*. Harare, September, 1996.

Alexander, J., McGregor, J. and Ranger, T. 2000a. *Violence and memory: one hundred years in the 'dark forests' of Matabeleland*. Oxford: James Curry.

Alexander J., McGregor, J. and Ranger, T. 2000b. Ethnicity and the politics of conflict: a case for Matabeleland. In E. W. Nafziger, F. Stewart, and R. Vayrynen (eds.), *War hunger and displacement: the origins of humanitarian emergencies: analysis*. Oxford: University Press, N.Y.

Beach, D. N. 1980. *The Shona and Zimbabwe 900–1850*. London: Heinemann Educational Books.

Beach, D. 1994. *The Shona and their neighbours*. Oxford: Blackwell.

Blair, D. 2002. *Degrees in violence: Robert Mugabe and the struggle for power*. London: Continuum.

CCJP. 2007. *Gukurahundi in Zimbabwe: a report on the disturbances in Matabeleland and the Midlands 1980–1988*. Johannesburg: Jacana Media.

Edkins, J. 2003. *Trauma and the memory of politics*. Cambridge: Cambridge University Press.

Kringer, N. J. 1992. *Zimbabwe's guerrilla war: peasant voices*. Cambridge: Cambridge University Press.

Meredith, M. 2008. *Mugabe: power, plunder and the struggle for Zimbabwe*. Jeppestown, South Africa: Jonathan Ball.

Msindo, E. 2006. Ethnicity, not class? The 1929 Bulawayo faction fights reconsidered. *Journal of Southern African Studies*, 1(3) September: 429–447.

Ndlovu-Gatsheni, S. J. 2003. The post-colonial state and Matebeleland: regional perceptions of civil-military relations, 1980-2002.

Nkomo, J. M. 1983. *Informative letter to Prime Minister Mugabe*. In *The Zimbabwe Independent*.

Phimister, I. and Van Onselen, C. 1979. The political economy of tribal animosity: a case study of the 1929 Bulawayo 'faction fight' (online). *Journal of Southern African Studies*, 3(2): 187–206. At: http://www.jstor.org/stable/2636770 (3 July 2014).

Shriver, D. 1999. The long road to reconciliation: some moral stepping stones. In R. Rothstein (ed.), *After the peace: resistance and reconciliation*. Boulder, Co: Lynne Rienner.

Staub, E. and Pearlman, L. 2001. Healing, reconciliation and forgiving after genocide and other collective violence. In R. Helmick and R. Peterson (eds.), *Forgiveness and reconciliation: religion, public policy and conflict transformation*. Radnor, Philadelphia: Templeton Foundation.

Staub, E., Pearlman, L. A., Gubin, A. and Hagengimana, A. 2005. Healing, reconciliation, forgiving and the prevention of violence after genocide or mass killings: an intervention and its Experimental Evaluation in Rwanda. *Journal of Social and Clinical Psychology*, 24(3): 297–334.

Timmerman, J. 1987. *Chile*. Alfred a knopf Inc.

Todd, J. G. 2007. *Through the darkness: a life in Zimbabwe*. Cape Town: Zebra.

White, L. 2007. 'Whoever saw a country with four armies?' the battle of Bulawayo revisited. *Journal of Southern African Studies*, 33(3) September: 619–631.

Zorbas, E. 2004. Reconciliation in post-genocide Rwanda. *African Journal of Legal Studies*, 1(1): 29–35.

# Chapter 3
# Armed Conflict, Trauma and Peacebuilding

*...the experience of trauma is one that remains 'unfinished' for many people who have been affected by trauma.*
Pumla Gobodo-Madikizela (2007, p. 42).

*War has a catastrophic effect on the health and wellbeing of nations. ...War destroys communities and families and often disrupts the development of social and economic fabric of nations.*
Murthy/Lakshminarayana (2006, p. 25)

## 3.1 Introduction

In this chapter, we examine the effects of armed conflicts at both individual and social levels. We will seek to define trauma and make a distinction between traumatising experiences and traumatic events. We will discuss issues surrounding Post-Traumatic Stress Disorder (PTSD), argue that it is not necessarily the correct term to describe the after-effects of violence and suggest that 'extreme trauma' is perhaps a better term to use, particularly in the Matabeleland context. Papadopoulos' (2007) theory of Adversity Activated Development (AAD) will also be explored, according to which the mere existence of a traumatising event does not mean that the person experiencing it will of necessity be traumatised by it. On the contrary, it might actually prompt such an individual to experience positive personal growth. The chapter will further explore the relevance of PTSD in non-western societies and discuss possible alternative theories that might be more suitable in these contexts. Since this whole dissertation is approached from a peacebuilding perspective, the relationship between trauma and peacebuilding will also be explored. Finally, the concepts of collective emotions and emotional climates in relation to peacebuilding and trauma are discussed.



D. Ngwenya, *Healing the Wounds of Gukurahundi in Zimbabwe*,
The Anthropocene: Politik—Economics—Society—Science 19,
https://doi.org/10.1007/978-3-319-66818-5_3

## 3.2 Psychological Effects of Armed Conflict

Armed conflicts, as well as natural disasters, have the potential to upset individual and community wellbeing. However, ethnic-based wars and political violence carry with them a particularly potent capacity to cause severe damage to the victims' psychological, emotional and spiritual wellbeing (Edkins 2003; Staub et al. 2005; Staub/Pearlman 2001; Zorbas 2004; Shriver 1999). The survivors'

> basic psychological needs are profoundly frustrated, their identity, their way of understanding the world, and their spirituality disrupted. These disruptions, along with those of interpersonal relationships, and the ability to regulate internal emotional states, co-exist with and give rise to intense trauma symptoms (Staub et al. 2005, p. 299).

Writing about state terrorism in Chile, which has strong similarities to the Matabeleland *Gukurahundi,* Agger/Jensen (1996) suggest that there are four categories of psychological warfare mechanisms that oppressive states tend to use in their efforts to oppress and dominate 'enemy groups'. These are:

- Direct repression, which includes violent arrests, arbitrary imprisonments, torture, disappearances and killings under false pretences. These actions are aimed at breaking an opponent down psychologically and even eliminating them physically.
- Indirect repression, in the form of using food and other basic necessities as political weapons; i.e. people are deprived of these basic human necessities on political or ethnic grounds.
- Social marginalisation which is a systemic process that deprives people of their social and political power.
- Individual marginalisation, whereby people, as a result of other forms of repressive strategies, experience a loss of skills and knowledge, cultural integrity and self-esteem. This tends to make individuals isolated and estranged from one another and results in pervasive fear throughout a community and is felt at all levels of human relationships (Agger/Jensen 1996, p. 68).

All these strategies are meant to disrupt communal and family support and coping mechanisms as a way of breaking down any political resistance that a unified community can present (see also Lemaire 2000, p. 73; Erickson 1995, p. 1) These disruptions to a person's wellbeing are seen as resulting in trauma and in some extreme cases in PTSD. However, as we shall see in Sect. 3.4, not all who experience such events will end up traumatised.

## 3.3 Trauma: A Discourse

The term trauma is usually used by different people (media practitioners, activists, politicians, medical practitioners and peace practitioners) to refer to various circumstances, ranging from, very stressful situations, to the effects or consequences of these situations (Saul 2000). There is normally no distinction between trauma as a noun, (i.e. the event) and trauma as an adjective (i.e. the experience of the event, as in a traumatic event). In everyday speech, the term is used to refer to both forms interchangeably. According to Papadopoulos (2000), when people use trauma as a noun they usually are referring to the painful and disturbing effects of an event on some individuals. Thus, it has come to be synonymous with terms like distressing, upsetting, stressful, etc. He points out that people tend to use trauma whenever they want to emphasise the enormity of human suffering to audiences, such as politicians and funding agencies. The Haiti earthquake tragedy of January 2010, serves as a recent example of this loose use of the term. The news media, aid organisations and politicians have been unanimous is pronouncing this quake, which left over 200 000 people dead and practically flattened the capital city, as being 'traumatic'. The IASC *Guidelines on Mental Health and Psychosocial Support in Emergency Settings* (2007) suggests that about 10–15% of the people could suffer from PTSD following a disaster.

Trauma, as Papadopoulos (2000, p. 92) sees it, is a product of social construction. In other words, it refers to the way one perceives and experiences a fact, rather than the phenomenon itself. That is to say, whether an event is traumatic or not, depends entirely on the individual's context and their interpretation of that event. The same event could be traumatic for one person and a heroic one for another. Concerning wars and political violence, people need to guard against the tendency to 'over-pathologise' human suffering and forget about the political and other dimensions (like religious beliefs for instance) that might give that suffering some meaning. Dillenburger et al. (2006, p. 98) concur with Papadopoulos when they point out that in Northern Ireland, violence was never experienced as a homogenous experience for the whole population. Rather, the experiences were unique and different for each person and resulted in different impacts on their lives and health. Even if their experiences are similar, events do not of necessity produce identical effects in different people (see also Bracken/Petty 1998, p. 54; Ehrenreich 2003, p. 20).

An analogy has been drawn by both Papadopoulos (2000) and Saul (2000) of a man who is, for example, arrested for 27 days for no apparent reason with a man like Nelson Mandela who spent 27 years in prison. The conclusion is that the person arrested for no reason, even if for 27 min, is likely to be traumatised by this; while Mandela's 27 years, in the context of his political beliefs, resulted in his becoming a hero, neither bitter nor severely affected psychologically by the event. In other words, the traumatic event in and of itself will not necessarily 'traumatise'; rather, it depends on how the individual and community perceive the event itself and what meaning, if any, they attach to it (Neller et al. 2005, p. 153). In our work with victims of *Gukurahundi* at Grace to Heal, we dealt with two men who were both arrested, detained and tortured by the 5th Brigade in their teens and at that time could not comprehend why they were being made to suffer. These men were still traumatised and struggling to make sense of their suffering 27 years later. Both got a certain amount of relief after undergoing trauma-processing sessions. On the other hand, those who were adults at the time, while still angry, bitter and wishing for revenge, did not seem to exhibit the same symptoms as these younger men.

This brings us back to the need to define what this term 'trauma' means. Having read many articles on trauma, I am struck by the fact that almost none give space to defining what trauma is; most plunging straight into discussing, the effects, consequences, treatment or other aspects of trauma. Given the complex and varied usage of the term 'trauma', it is necessary to explore the meanings of the word.

### 3.3.1 Defining Trauma

Trauma can be physical, psychiatric or psychological. Our interest here is the last, which has been defined variously in medical dictionaries as 'an experience that is emotionally painful, distressful, or shocking and which may result in lasting mental and physical effects' (internet reference 1). Another definition is that it is an 'emotional wound or shock that creates substantial, lasting damage to the psychological development of a person, often leading to neurosis; or an event or situation that causes great distress and disruption' (internet definition 2). Farwell/ Cole (2004, p. 25) describe it simply as a 'systematic shock that disrupts the balance of the affective, cognitive, and spiritual inner function'.

In other words, this is an injury that occurs in the emotions or mind which is so intense that the mind is overwhelmed and cannot process it in the normal way. Typical characteristics of a traumatising event include a sense of powerlessness, terror and helplessness (Neller et al. 2005, p. 151). It is important to note here that this is a normal response to an intense life-threatening event. When such an event occurs, the mind creates emotional memories of the distressing event, which are then stored in structures deep within the brain. So, trauma is distressing, upsetting, stressful and harrowing (Papadopoulos 2000, p. 92). Per Becker (2004, p. 6), the basic framework of trauma in situations of organised violence implies a notion of tearing, of rupture, of structural breakdown. It can only be defined and understood within a specific context which must be fully described. It is also a process that develops sequentially and contains both an individual, intra-psychic dimension and a collective, macro-social dimension that are interwoven.

Warren (2006, pp. 22–23) has classified trauma into two categories or types: Type 1 is individual trauma, which can be described as a blow to the psyche that breaks through one's defences so suddenly and with such brutal force that one cannot react effectively. Type 2 is collective trauma which is a blow to the basic tissues of social life that destroys the bonds that hold people together and impairs the prevailing sense of community. In peacebuilding, the prime concern is with the latter type. Type 1 is dealt with within the context of the community, unlike medical approaches which have tended to focus exclusively on the individual victim, without seeking to mitigate the unpeaceful relations involved.

According to Finch (2006), psychological trauma is experienced subjectively but, at the same time, it is a result of an objective and quantifiable action or incident. For instance, an act of torture can be exerted on two or more people, using a particular instrument or method for a certain amount of time and force. While everyone receives more or less similar action, how they experience it is unique and dependent upon one's perspective on life, and one's mental and emotional state, etc. A traumatic event will not necessarily produce similar reactions from the victims. Finch further compares trauma as a death experience. He says it is a death of the way things are. That is to say, an individual's worldview, perception of life, beliefs, values, etc. are usually radically altered by the experience and her/his image of a perfect world is shattered by the traumatic experience. However, he also points out that while this experience will inevitably take us to the limits of our physical (and we could add, psychological) existence, it nevertheless carries with it the potential to take us beyond ourselves, to the transcendent (Finch 2006, p. 29).

Papadopoulos' (2000) etymological study on the word trauma, has led him to a similar conclusion. According to this study, the Greek root of the word trauma comes from the word *teiro* and this has two meanings: 'to rub in' and to 'rub away' or 'off'. If the skin is rubbed vigorously with a rough object for some time, a mark or injury will result. On the other hand, something can be rubbed away or off as a way of cleaning it. Trauma could therefore be a wound resulting from an experience that has been 'rubbed in' leaving a mark; or it could leave a clean surface having been 'rubbed off' by the experience. He contends that trauma should therefore be seen as a neutral word and that any experience has the potential to have harmful or positive effects. Trauma could either scar a person for life or make that person a better person. This is a useful discussion to remember because invariably, in just about every situation of organised violence, there are people who seem to emerge stronger from evil situations. They have developed resiliencies either through the course of their lives or through the traumatic event. We shall discuss Papadopoulos' (2007) theory of Adversity Activated Development (AAD) below (Sect. 3.3.4).

### 3.3.2 The Effects of Trauma

It is therefore imperative that in our interactions with individuals and communities who have experienced traumatising events, we hold in tension the whole spectrum of the possible responses to the events. While some people may be devastated and their lives fall apart, others emerge stronger from the adversity, maybe with a renewed zeal for life, with greater commitment to new values. The discussion that follows shall be mainly guided by Papadopoulos' work on AAD.

### 3.3.3 Negative Outcome

When facing a threat, people have three options—*fight, flight* or *freeze*. In the *fight* response, the victim will attempt to retaliate (actual or fantasised), and expend their energy in this effort. This leads to feelings of anger, rage and frustration and might result in a determination to get even and result in anxiety or other types of disorder.

The *flight* response is motivated by the desire to escape from the trauma, and tends to create fear, guilt, and shame and lowered self-esteem, resulting in acute stress disorders. With the *freeze* response, one is unable to act in any way and feelings of terror and helplessness are experienced, as well as immobility. Often, it results in PTSD (Warren 2006, p. 4). Papadopoulos (2007) has further divided the negative effects of trauma into three categories, ranging from the everyday to pathological responses:

Firstly, there is what he calls ‘ordinary human suffering’ (OHS). This is the usual and natural way that humans respond to traumatic events in everyday life, i.e. when one’s expectations of a smooth life are not fulfilled. This response does not always result in a pathological condition. Suffering is part of human experience and there is no need to try to locate this within a medical/pathological framework. People who are well-integrated, with what he terms a ‘sufficiently intact psychological immune system’, are well able to deal with adversities, with the help of their family and social support systems.

Secondly, there is the ‘distressful psychological reaction’, a more severe form of OHS, where the person experiences a higher level of discomfort or suffering. This experience is still a common one and does not necessarily require specialist attention.

Thirdly, there is the ‘psychiatric disorder’, which manifests itself as PTSD (Papadopoulos 2007, pp. 305–306). This form goes on for longer and requires specialist professional help. Once someone has been dragged into what Finch (2006) calls the ‘black hole of trauma’, they become disoriented, and imprisoned by the living reality, powerless to change their situation and overwhelmed by the pain of the wounds and the new realities it brings with it. Erikson (1995, p. 1) sees it as a foreign object that ‘breaks in on you, smashing through whatever barrier your mind has set up as a line of defence’. Once this ‘alien intruder’ invades a person, it takes them over and becomes the controlling feature of what he calls one’s ‘interior landscape’. One is overwhelmed with the threat of being drained and left empty inside. Gobodo-Madikizela (2008, p. 173) describes it as an experience of loss of control, language, power and self. The person has no words to describe their pain and experience; what has been called ‘speechless terror’. ‘When people are traumatised, a “silent language” begins to occupy the space between words, rupturing speech and changing its rhythm.’ This ‘speechlessness’ further alienates individuals from their support systems; because they are unable to communicate their deep-felt pains:

> This ‘silent language’ in essence conveys the ‘lived memory’ of trauma and the struggle with its disruptive impact… without language and without a feeling of self-control there is no self. The connections between the self and the rest of humanity are severed as victims are reduced to objects by their tormentors and their personhood treated as worthless (Gobodo-Madikizela 2008, p. 173).

Furthermore, the trauma victim may be consumed by hatred and desire for revenge. This anger ‘justified as it might be, aimed at the perpetrator, tends also to affect all those around the victim and even the already injured self’ (Finch 2006,

p. 30). This is the negative and destructive human reaction to trauma. However, as Papadopoulos (2007) has pointed out, the fact that there are three possible negative effects to being exposed to trauma, alerts us to the fact that not all traumatic experiences will lead to PTSD. This, I believe, is particularly relevant to the Matabele communities. Although many of them express the desire for revenge and carry with them a hatred for the perpetrating ethnic group, they are not necessarily pathological or neurotic, and lead near normal everyday lives.

### 3.3.4 The Positive

Papadopoulos' (2007, p. 306) second category of how people react to adverse situations is what he calls 'Adversity-Activated Development' (AAD). This is a category of people who not only survive their traumatising events but who do so with a fair degree of 'intactness' and, in fact, are strengthened by their particular exposure. He therefore defines AAD as the 'positive developments that are a direct result of being exposed to adversity'. He argues that there is a significant number of individuals and groups who have found meaning in their sufferings and have been able to transform their negative experiences in a constructive way, gaining new strength and renewal. Again, the inimitable Nelson Mandela would be a very prominent example. Once the initial life-threatening adversity has been survived, this kind of people may begin to appreciate the chance for life in a whole new way, re-examining their values and priorities and beginning to live their lives in a more conscious and qualitative way. This giving of meaning to suffering can be transformative and might be the difference between neurosis and an integrated and wholesome life after adversity. This also could be the difference between harmonious living and the trans-generational transmission of hatred and a desire for vengeance among individuals, families and communities. As the Catholic con templative Richard Rohr has said: 'Pain not transformed is transmitted' (quoted in Nikondeha 2009, p. 2). The transmutation or transfiguration of adversity is a concept that needs further exploration.

Papadopoulos makes a strong distinction between AAD and other forms of positive growth responses to suffering, in particular post-traumatic growth (PTG). He indicates three reasons why the two are fundamentally different: Firstly, the basic point of departure for PTG is trauma. It assumes that all who experience PTG must have been traumatised. On the other hand, AAD uses adversity rather than trauma as its basis. This is consistent with his argument that not all who are exposed to suffering are necessarily traumatised. PTG sees growth as happening after the trauma and so PTG and PTSD are closely linked as they both focus on *post* trauma, hence assuming that all are traumatised. AAD recognises the fact that adversity may still continue after the initial experience, in perhaps another form other than the one already experienced. For instance, after suffering physical violence, victims may continue to experience other forms of suffering long after the violence or war has ceased.

Secondly, he points to the different terms these two concepts use: PTG uses 'growth' while AAD uses 'development'. He sees 'growth' as also carrying a negative connotation as in cancer growth, while 'development' is said to be more neutral, allowing for more variations of positive responses. AAD is characterised by

> Positive, 'growthful' developments which are a direct result of the experiences gained from being exposed to adversity/'trauma', as well as new elements—characteristics which did not exist prior to the adversity (Papadopoulos 2007, p. 307).

Thirdly, AAD happens because suffering exposes a person's limits. Suffering pushes people to the end of themselves, beyond their previous understandings and expectations and they feel they do not know how else to move forward with their lives. When these limits open up new horizons beyond the known to a new dimension of experiencing life and living, this experience can be said to be transformational. When this happens, a new perception of self, one's relationships and meaning and purpose of life emerge because of this transformational experience and

> …a new epistemology (a way of understanding how one knows) emerges which is the sum total of all new perceptions that lead to the acquisition of a new way of understanding, speaking, relating about oneself, others and life itself (Papadopoulos 2007, p. 308).

### *3.3.5 The Neutral*

Finally, Papadopoulos speaks of the third category of reactions to suffering/adversity as being neutral. He terms this response 'resilience' and argues that there is a difference between this and AAD, although existing literature makes no distinction between the two. Resilience is normally used to refer to the ability of an object to retain its characteristics after being subjected to some severe conditions. For instance, an object, say a child's toy, is said to be resilient if it can withstand adverse conditions. In the same manner, individuals, families or communities are said to be resilient if they can survive pressures without a change in their values, abilities and skills. This theory is supported by Ehrenreich (2003, p. 20) who points out that,

> Despite the fact that in some countries, virtually everybody in the entire country has been exposed to or witnessed multiple horrific events, people appear to be remarkably resilient. Despite ongoing symptoms of distress, more or less normal social functioning remains possible and for many, if not most, a tolerable quality of life is maintained.

Hence, 'the key characteristic of resilience is that, it retains qualities that existed before, whereas AAD introduces new characteristics that did not exist before' (Papadopoulos 2007, p. 308). Resilience is therefore neutral because nothing is altered by the pressure applied. According to Papadopoulos, the majority of individuals have no need for professional help after experiencing a traumatising event because a great deal of their healthy functioning remains intact and unaffected by the devastation.

These three categories of possible effects of trauma and the variations within them are very instructive indeed. They warn against the tendency of pathologising every experience of violence or traumatic situation that people and communities go through. My experience at GTH confirms these distinctions. Even though I might not have been aware of these reactions in the way that Papadopoulos has described them, I have noted that reactions of the victims of the violence of *Gukurahundi* are not uniform.

Notwithstanding Papadopoulos' very useful approach, there remains one more issue of discussion with regard to AAD and the 'resilient' responses. While Papadopoulos' theory might be correct, there is another possibility that needs to be considered: the question of coping and being resigned to one's fate. The question relates to how much of this positive outlook on life can be attributed to the fact that people have just accepted what has befallen them and resigned themselves to it. While I am attracted to his theory, it is difficult to determine accurately whether this sort of reaction is an AAD-inspired response, or the acceptance of a situation and a realisation that, nevertheless life must go on; a practical response to a very difficult reality.

## 3.4 The Relevance of Post Tramatic Stress Disorder in Non-Western Settings

> *To understand mass traumatisation in a way that focuses primarily on the symptoms of individuals and not on the impact of traumatic events on communities and cultures (both directly and as the sum of the experience of individuals comprising the social unit), falsifies the experience of the victims. It is an 'understanding' purchased at the price of incomprehension.*
>
> Ehrenreich (2003, p. 21)

> *To decouple individual from social suffering—to interpret symptoms narrowly in terms of disease and individual pathology—is to risk violating the experiences of sufferers and contributing to the very suffering mental health practitioners seek to remedy.*
>
> Uehara et al. (2002, p. 223)

The potency of contemporary political violence lies in its ability to control society by creating states of terror which permeate the entire social fabric and affect grassroots social relations, as well as subjective mental life (Summerfield 1996, p. 1). This is a deliberate ploy by armed groups to try and break all community support systems and thus isolate individuals who are left feeling vulnerable and exposed. It appears that the 'senseless' acts of torture, rape and other acts of violence against civilians are meant to serve this purpose rather than to extract information. We previously noted (Sect. 2.2) Agger/Jensen's (1996) four categories of mechanisms of psychological warfare: direct repression, indirect repression, social marginalisation and individual marginalisation. Each of these methods tends to eat away at human dignity, cultural dignity and self-esteem. As a result, there is a pervasive sense of fear felt at all levels of human relationships. In Argentina (1970s and 1980s), specific tactics were used by the military junta to break the social fabric and there was a deliberate act to target those areas that were sacred to the Argentinean society. Quite frequently, soldiers would invade homes and abduct victims at night. The home is the place where trust, relationship-building and safety are provided for and are first learnt. The military junta's attack on people in their homes was not just physical and psychological but extended to the social and cultural level as well (Robben 2000, pp. 70–74). Similar attacks on long-held familial, social and cultural norms were used by the 5th Brigade on the people of Matabeleland during the *Gukurahundi* era.

Hence, we note that, although individuals seem to be the prime targets of political violence, its execution is meant to have maximum effect upon the community. Its aim is to disrupt social 'safety nets', leaving individuals disconnected and feeling vulnerable, insecure and isolated from the community from which they derive their identity and being. To counter this process, one has to go beyond the individual and seek to heal the social fabric within which an individual's existence, identity and security lie. Summerfield (1996) points out that when violence constantly terrorises whole communities, the survivors of individual acts of extreme violence are more likely to regard their wounds as social rather than psychological. This is especially so in non-western societies where community is still very important, but is also true in western societies. The nature of war or political violence is such that it is experienced as a collective. The destruction of people's social world, which encompasses their identity, history and way of life, has the greatest impact upon those who witness it and 'is not a private injury carried by a private individual' (Summerfield 1996, p. 19). In other words, although the acts of brutality are carried out on individuals, it is because those individuals belong to a certain social grouping. Their persecution is linked to an identity which the perpetrators might wish to destroy, subjugate or marginalise. It is therefore important from a peacebuilding perspective not to employ healing methodologies that isolate the individual further from their community, but rather to seek to heal the individuals within the context of their community. This is because 'it is the community that offers a cushion for pain, the community that offers a context for the intimacy, the community that serves as the repository for binding tradition' (Summerfield 1996, p. 19).

A PTSD approach which focuses on individual, symptoms, pathology and therapeutic processes does not meet the need to address the community context of trauma (Wessells 2008; Summerfield 1996, 1999; Becker 2004). There can be no doubt that PTSD is a reality and does affect some people who experience traumatic events (Guess 2006; de Zulueta 2007). The problem is in universalising it at the expense of other, possibly more appropriate approaches to therapy for suffering brought about by wars and political violence. Simply importing the PTSD model wholesale into societies that do not necessarily share western value systems (particularly the emphasis on the individual, as opposed to community as the basis for the healing of painful memories), may be unproductive. While the medical/psychological nature of this approach might be seen in the West to be closer to the essence of being than the social and religious ones, it is these latter systems which tend to define the rest of the world. Family and community tend to take precedence over the individual as the centre of existence. Dependency and interdependency are cherished more than autonomy and individualism. Modern violent conflicts frequently aim at the harassment and destruction of entire communities, so brutal acts suffered by individuals are more likely to be felt as social rather than psychological (Summerfield 1996, p. 6).

Thus, the PTSD approach has been criticised by researchers and practitioners such as Summerfield (1996, 1999), Wessells (2008) and Becker (2004). Becker (2004, pp. 3–5) sees one of the weaknesses of PTSD being that it focuses on symptoms without reference to the cause of the symptoms. It is not possible, he believes, to carry out family (or community) diagnosis within the categories of PTSD. This paradigm focuses solely on the direct victim of a violent act, and does not recognise that the victim's family could suffer a degree of traumatisation because of what has been done to the victim. Interestingly, he points out that, while it can be said that the presence of PTSD means that trauma has happened, the absence of the same is no guarantee that trauma is absent. Other indicators of trauma, such as social behaviour and somatic and Psychosomatic symptoms, psychosomatic[1] do not feature in the definitions of PTSD. In addition, rigid time definitions in PTSD can result in a wrong diagnosis if the trauma symptoms are not observed within a certain time frame. While this could apply to natural disasters, it is not always the case with man-made disasters, where trauma symptoms have been known to appear ten, twenty or even fifty years after the event. He favours the term 'extreme traumatisation' which he defines as:

> An individual or collective process that occurs in reference and in dependency of a given social context: it is a process marked by its intensity, of extremely long duration in time, and the interdependency between the social and the psychological dimension. It exceeds the capacity of the individual and social structures to answer adequately to this process. Its aim is the destruction of the individual, his sense of belonging to the society, his social activities. Extreme trauma is characterised by a structure of power within the society that is based on the elimination of some members of this society by others of the same society. The process of extreme trauma in not limited in time and develops sequentially (in Losi 2000, p. 15).

This, of course, has implications for how we approach treatment in such contexts and is the subject of discussion in Chap. 3.

The use of 'post' in PTSD assumes that the traumatic event that occurred divides the time into two—a before and an after. It implies that the 'before' was wonderful and that everything 'post' the event is problematic, if not pathological (Papadopoulos 2000, p. 94). According to Papadopoulos (2000), trauma is not a

[1]These include high levels of alcohol abuse, family and social violence, suicides and increased levels of general illnesses (Mitchels 2003, p. 411).

result of a single event that happens at one specific time but is often a series of traumatic time sequences over a period of time. If people live in a chronic state of oppression, marginalisation and violence in one form or the other, constant stress may be the result. For instance, the people of Matabeleland have not only lived under a series of wars from the pre-colonial to the *Gukurahundi* of the 1980s and electoral violence since then, but continue to feel marginalised by what they perceive to be a deliberate policy which side-lines them from the mainstream economy and real political power (see Sect. 1.4).

Wessells (2008) assents that the trauma paradigm 'decontextualizes' human suffering by reducing it to individual terms, when many of the greatest sources of suffering are collective and are rooted in a socio-historic context of human rights violations (see also Saul 2000, pp. 103–105). He sees the 'universalisation' tendency in the field of trauma as a continual problem, resulting from the desire by psychologists to have psychology regarded as a science following universal laws. It becomes a natural step to export these methods and concepts developed in western countries to situations of violent conflict across different regions of the world, without regard to the huge differences in culture, situation, social, political, economic and historical systems that pertain in various parts of the world.

In Africa, civil wars tend to be low intensity and ongoing; as a result, it becomes difficult to talk about 'post trauma' as people more or less permanently live under chronic and accumulating stresses. Structural violence, poverty, weak governance and marginalisation also contribute to the distress of the affected communities, regularly more than direct forms of violence. Often civil society is so shattered by armed conflicts, as when people are internally displaced or become refugees, that people are left with no support systems or traditional coping mechanisms. The social fabric that is necessary for social cohesion is damaged, and mistrust, anger, hatred and a sheer lack of resources can make it impossible for people to support each other as neighbours. All these situations are likely to produce varying forms of distress other than PTSD (Wessells 2008, pp. 2–11). The traditional trauma approach does not take into account human rights abuses and does not consider the change of social conditions as a vital strategy for healing affected communities (Pintar 2000, p. 61). In view of the nature of conflicts in Africa, it becomes clear that the traditional trauma approach, with its emphasis on PTSD, is unlikely to work well in the continent.

There has been a recent shift from an emphasis on the PTSD paradigm towards a more holistic approach. For instance, the Inter-Agency Standing Committee's (IASC) *Guidance Note for Mental Health and Psychosocial Support in Emergency Settings 2007*, sees trauma as a small part of a larger ambit of mental health and psychosocial issues that impact on the wellbeing of victims following a man-made disaster. It seeks to normalise the reactions to traumatising events which have previously been classified as pathologies. While the trauma paradigm remains an issue, it is increasingly realised that there are other factors that are equally, if not more relevant—an important shift towards seeking a balance in approaches. The IASC further notes that local populations might experience collective cultural, spiritual and religious stresses because they are unable to exercise their healing and coping practices, which have been interrupted by a disaster. Humanitarian workers are urged to consider these practices as part of healing methods for people in conflict zones. In its *Guidance Note for Mental Health and Psychosocial support Haiti Earthquake Emergency Response-January 2010,* the IASC describes the symptoms normally apportioned to pathology as normal reactions to traumatising events. They also seek to discourage the use of the term 'trauma', rather 'suggesting' the use of terms like psychological and social or emotional problems, distress and stress, overwhelmed, etcetera (IASC 2010, p. 29). This departure from the long-held views about trauma is a welcome effort to balance it with the reality that pertains in non-western countries. It is also an effort, according to Ehrenreich, (2003, p. 18), to return to the original primary meaning of psychological traumatisation as 'the response of victims to violence committed against them'.

A potential danger with the trauma approach is that it puts people into a perpetual victim mentality. In a world where trauma is glorified and is often the means to get access to aid and other such benefits, one might not want to give up the victim status. This can easily lead to addiction and the creation of a cycle of dependency, perpetuating victimhood and victimisation (Papadopoulos 2000, p. 94; Lamott 2005, pp. 222–224). People will cling to the victim status simply because it pays to remain in that state for as long as possible. In most cases this aid, whether in the form of grants or asylum, depends on how well the 'victim' articulates his/her story in terms that fit PTSD categories, which in many cases might be meaningless to the person (Summerfield 1996, p. 11). Furthermore:

> The survivor is taught how to think about what he has experienced, completely independently of whether and to what extent this thinking coincides with his actual experiences; the authentic witness is very soon only in the way, he has to be pushed aside like an obstacle…. The survivor is robbed of his only possession: of his authentic experiences (in Lamott 2005, p. 222).

Such an approach to healing only serves to fulfil what Lamott (2005) calls the 'narcissistic' motives of the caregivers. In other words, the necessity and effectiveness of their work is justified by the apparent overwhelming numbers of people needing their specialised services (Summerfield 1996, pp. 11–14; Weine/Chae 2008, pp. 9–10). This raises the question of how effective the healing process can be in this case. Again, Summerfield (1996) has shown that the use of western trauma models, without regard to local approaches, can work against the good intentions of humanitarian workers. The terminologies, diagnostic and healing processes, which are often foreign to the victims, are bound to cause confusion and frustration and fail to assist victims recover from their pains, by focusing on the less important issues for them. 'The trauma field may be in danger of attending only to those cues which match their prior assumptions about the nature of victimhood, and the pre-eminence and universality of a psychological wound' (Summerfield 1996, p. 17).

## 3.5 Conceptualising Peacebuilding

> *Peacebuilding is a contested concept which gains meaning as it is practised.*
>
> John Heathershaw (2007, p. 219)

> *It is generally accepted that the central task of peacebuilding is to create positive peace, 'a stable social equilibrium in which the surfacing of new disputes does not escalate into violence and war.*
>
> Michelle Maiese (2003)

Before discussing the relationship between trauma and peacebuilding, we need to briefly look at the concept of peacebuilding. This concept has been defined variously by different authors and practitioners, including Boutros-Ghali (1995), Lambourne (2004), Clancy/Hamber (2008). Despite diverse definitions and perspectives on peacebuilding, it is generally agreed that peacebuilding is an integral part of any efforts aimed at addressing the root causes of conflict through the transformation of both the system and relationships. What makes peacebuilding such an elusive concept is that it takes different forms depending on the context and who is practising it (Clancy/Hamber 2008, p. 5).

There are basically two schools of thoughts when it comes to the practice and definition of peacebuilding. There are those who see it as solely a 'post-conflict' activity. These would include the UN and other organisations using track one diplomacy. Then there are those who see it as an activity that goes on before, during and after a violent conflict: these are usually those organisations which do track two diplomacy and tend to be more focused on local communities.

In his 1992 *Agenda for Peace*, Boutros Boutros-Ghali, then UN General Secretary, defined peacebuilding as a post conflict 'action to identify and support structures which will tend to strengthen and solidify peace in order to avoid a relapse into conflict' (Section vi. paragraph 55). Following a similar line of thought, The Conflict Management Toolkit (CMT) sees peacebuilding as a 'process that facilitates the establishment of durable peace and tries to prevent the recurrence of violence by addressing root causes and effects of conflict, reconciliation, institute building and political, as well as economic transformation' (internet definition 3). In other words, this school of thought considers peacebuilding in terms of sequencing. Maiese's (2003) definition makes this school of thought's perspective quite clear when she says peacebuilding is a 'long-term process that occurs after violence has slowed down or come to a halt' and 'takes place after peacemaking and peacekeeping'. This approach limits the potential of peacebuilding; by confining peacebuilding to a post-conflict context, opportunities for intervention at an earlier stage of the conflict are likely to be missed.

It is more helpful to view peacebuilding in terms of objectives and activities rather than just an issue of sequencing (Cockell 2003, p. 17), the tasks of which include, but are not limited, to the following:

- The creation of an environment conducive to self-sustaining and durable peace. This entails working with communities to encourage cooperation. The transformation of the social and economic systems forms an important part of this task.

- Reconciling the parties in conflict. Protracted violent conflicts usually have devastating effects on communities caught up in the violence and, as we saw in Sect. 2.2, their psychological and emotional wellbeing is greatly affected. In addition, relationships between the antagonistic groups are broken and enmity and desires for vengeance become prominent.
- Addressing the structural and social factors.
- Creating mechanisms that encourage cooperation and dialogue must be created so that communities learn how to manage their conflicts through peaceful means.

Fisher/Zimina (2009) see peacebuilding as:

> not primarily concerned with conflict behaviour but addresses underlying context and attitudes that give rise to violence, such as unequal access to employment, discrimination, unacknowledged and unforgiven responsibility for past crimes, prejudice, mistrust, fear, hostility between groups. It is a low-profile activity that can take place through all stages of the conflict, but is strongest either in later stages after a settlement and a reduction in violent behaviour or in earlier stages before any open violence has occurred (Fisher/Zimina 2009, p. 14).

The focus here is on peace-enhancing outcomes and there is a great concern for how things happen. In other words, it is as much about process as it is about the activity itself and its outcome (Fisher/Zimina 2009, p. 12). According to this view, peacebuilding can happen at any stage of the conflict but is most effective before the outbreak of overt violence or before its end. This allows for flexibility to seek opportunities for intervention anywhere along the trajectory of the conflict spiral. Peacebuilding from this perspective therefore 'encompasses measures in the context of emerging, current or post-conflict situations for the explicit purpose of preventing violent conflict and promoting lasting and sustainable peace' (DAC Manual 2005). We can illustrate this approach of the broadening of the peacebuilding concept from the traditional post-conflict to the inclusion of the period before overt conflict, by reference to Grävingholt et al. (2009) diagram (Fig. 3.1):

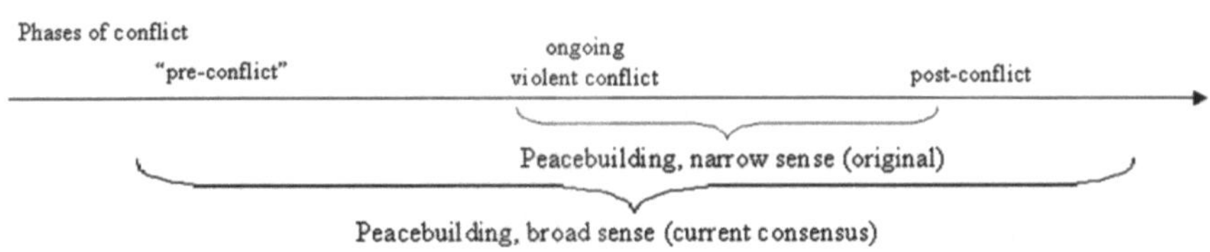


**Fig. 3.1** The broadening understanding of peacebuilding. *Source* Grävingholt et al. (2009, p. 5). The permission was granted by Cornelia Hornschild. Publication Office, German Development Institute. Bonn, Germany in April 2017

As can be observed from the diagram, the previous view of peacebuilding, which to some extent is still held by the UN and other INGOs has peacebuilding fixed narrowly from the ongoing conflict to a post-conflict situation (Maiese 2003). The broader understanding of peacebuilding, depicted by the bottom bracket, falls within the definition of peacebuilding by Galtung (1996) and Lederach (1997) among others. They view it as a set of processes occurring before, during and after a conflict: the lessening of structural violence and social asymmetries, the promotion of social justice and the transformation of those systems that encourage power and wealth imbalances (Wessells 2008, p. 19). Structures that promote injustice and inequality exist long before a conflict becomes overt; it therefore makes sense for those involved in communal peacebuilding activities to start dealing with these deep-rooted causes of conflicts. As Cockell has pointed out:

> Waiting for a conflict to produce a negotiation process or even a signed peace accord before engaging in the structural transformation of the roots of that conflict is to risk allowing opportunities for effective peacebuilding to pass by irretrievably (Cockell 2003, p. 18).

### *3.5.1 Transformative Versus Technical Peacebuilding*

Fisher/Zimina (2009) have made an important distinction between transformative and technical peacebuilding. The two broad definitions of peacebuilding discussed above, roughly correspond to technical and transformative approaches. 'Transformative' peacebuilding works to achieve deep-seated social and political change and is preoccupied with the transformation of the root causes of conflicts, structures and relationships. On the other hand, 'technical' peacebuilding is 'incremental activity, which aims to make a practical difference in a specific domain, without necessarily challenging the deeper context' (Fisher/Zimina 2009, p. 20). The major differences between the two are illustrated by their table below (Table 3.1).

The technical approach is important as a short-term measure but for deeper, more meaningful and lasting change, there is need to employ the transformative approach, which provides a long-term perspective to peacebuilding. This is the sort of approach that is needed to bring about a measure of healing to violence-torn societies. Local grassroots organisations are the ones that tend to adopt this approach more, as opposed to bigger and international organisations which tend to favour more conventional and diplomatic approaches, with a focus on the top levels of leadership, especially if they believe their interests would be better served by deference to the host state (Fisher/Zimina 2009, p. 27).

Peacebuilders need to ask which approach serves the communities best. It may very well be that both need to be carried out simultaneously, but the 'many' people approach as opposed to the 'key' people approach seems most likely to result in positive and lasting change in communities emerging from violent conflict. The key people approach holds the view that concentrating on a few key people and working

**Table 3.1** Technical and Transformative approaches to peacebuilding. *Source* Fisher/Zimina (2009)

| | | Technical approach | Transformative approach |
|---|---|---|---|
| Goals | Overall purpose | To end a specific situation or open conflict: 'negative' peace | In addition, to influence the underlying structure and culture as an integrated element in building something better: 'positive' peace |
| | Agenda | Set by funders and project holders, with some limited consultation with community | Set and continually reviewed with community, in consultation with funders and project holders |
| | Objectives | Achievement of project objectives | Promoting shared vision of/for community, of which programme work is part |
| | Priority | Content of programme | Solidarity; relationships as well as content |
| Strategy | Focus | A specific piece of work | Building elements of wider change into a specific piece of work |
| | Evaluation | Focus on efficiency, project successes | Efficiency plus bigger picture impact |
| | Learning | Downplaying failures | Taking failures as starting points; inclusion of self-reflection and action learning |
| | Issues | Solve present issue | Expand, change, transcend contested issues |
| | Theory of change | Implicit: change in immediate situation will ripple out | Explicit: developed in relation to analysis and systems thinking. |
| | Scope | One level, one sector | Multilevel, local-global, alliances across sectors |
| | Time horizon | Duration of project (plus extension) | Medium to long term |
| Values | Accountability | Primarily, in practice, to funders | Primarily to identified partners/ community |
| | Whose peace? | Power relations are unchallengeable: need to accommodate | Peace is for whole community, especially the weakest: option to work to change power relations if better future requires it |
| | Self image | A professional doing a good job | Agent of change, modelling struggle and transformation |
| | Context | Project and work-focused, done by project staff | Adds ongoing conflict analysis and future scenario planning, all undertaken with wider community |

(continued)

**Table 3.1** (continued)

| | | Technical approach | Transformative approach |
|---|---|---|---|
| Analysis | Actors | Good working relationship | In addition, works for change of perspective, goals, heart, will, inclusive sense of identity |
| | View of violence | Prevent and defuse it; ambivalent about its use | Race, gender and class dimensions are integral part of violence; transforming the energy into positive outcomes; active promotion of nonviolent approaches |
| | View of conflict | A problem in the way of achieving goals | Inevitable, an opportunity for development, and change; consider options to intensify |

to transform those individuals will result in social change quickly and effectively. It is doubtful, however, that focusing on individuals, albeit key ones, will have a far reaching social change. Individuals might be healed and their sense of trust and tolerance improved but such changes, unless coordinated and harnessed intentionally into action, are unlikely to result in social transformation. On the other hand, a programme that focuses on more people can achieve both individual and social transformation more effectively, particularly at local community level. Trauma-processing programmes carried out with the wider population will promote individual healing within the greater community, while programmes designed to help communities to advocate for change with regards to key conflict drivers can result in socio-political change (CDA 2009). There is a need to hold the tension between these two strategies if the Peace Writ Large[2] Peace Writ Large is to be realised. We now turn to the relationship between peacebuilding and trauma healing.

## 3.6 Trauma and Peacebuilding

*The entire affective world, constructed over the years with utmost difficulty, collapses with a kick in the father's genitals, smack on the mother's face, an obscene insult to the sister, or the sexual violation of a daughter. Suddenly an entire culture based on familial love, devotion, the capacity for mutual sacrifice collapses.*

Timerman (1981, p. 148)

[2]Peace Writ Large refers to an approach that seeks to make linkages between the individual, social and national levels in peacebuilding. Its outlook is macro rather than micro, it is concerned with the 'bigger picture'. (see Chigas/Woodrow 2009, also Fisher/Zimina 2009).

> *An end to the fighting will not bring an immediate return to normality. Basic trust and moral values take time to be restored. Even when a sense of security returns, the war may continue in people's minds.*
>
> de Jong et al. (2000, p. 2068)

Peacebuilders are concerned with trauma because it affects progress towards sustainable peace within families and communities. In situations of politically-motivated or ethnically-based violence, the individual's trauma is not dealt with outside the greater family or community dynamics.[3] It is for this reason that this thesis will not delve much into technical descriptions of psychological trauma and clinically-oriented healing methodologies. Rather than approach trauma as a medical concept, applying fundamentally to individuals, peacebuilders view trauma as a social and political process that refers to the entire community and which is understood within a political and cultural context (Becker 2004, p. 3).

Perhaps the most toxic effect of violent conflict is the divisions it causes between the 'aggressor' group and the 'victim' group.[4] Unfortunately, these conflicts are often based on ethnic or tribal lines and are intrastate, so that victims and offenders may be living side by side or within proximity of each other. In the wake of such conflicts, community cohesion and identity tend to form along narrower lines than those that encompass national citizenship. People will draw closer and close ranks as they seek security from those sharing the same experience with them. The experience of violence and atrocities and their remembrance within communities tend to aggravate feelings of hatred and fear which fuel on-going conflict (Lederach 2007, pp. 11–12).

In all this, the politics of memory plays a pivotal role in how a community deals with its violent past.[5] This particularly, refers to painful memories resulting from a community being deliberately targeted for persecution or 'cleansing'. In this case, the pain transcends the individual consciousness into that of society, thus making pain political. As Cole (2004, p. 87) has said: 'Not only is pain social, but it is also historically constituted and expressed, so that painful symptoms can in some cases be read as a kind of archive of historical memories.' There is a real probability that this may result in what has been described as 'trans-generational transmission' of the trauma or painful memories to the next generation (Ehrenreich 2003; Almqvist/Broberg 2003; Becker 2004; Wessells 2008; de Zulueta 2007). This school of thought argues that generations of traumatised people can pass on their trauma to the next generation through stories and attitudes towards the perpetrator group:

---

[3]Zelizer (2008) talks of two main types of peacebuilding activities: those that focus on structural sources of conflict and those which are concerned with improving relations between groups. These tend to be more community-based than the former which are elitist and policy-focused. (This is very similar to Fisher/Zimina's (2009) transformative and technical peacebuilding concept discussed in Sect. 3.5.1 above).

[4]In a conflict, typically, both sides will claim 'victim' status for themselves.

[5]Here again the aim is not to describe the pathological reactions of the brain to trauma nor so much the individual's memory as the collective memory.

> The language of violence is etched in the memory of many victims of violent conflict, and passed on to the next generation, and to the next, in the way that traumatic memory so often does, in ways subtle and not so subtle (Gobodo-Madikizela 2008, p. 174).

De Zulueta (2007, p. 228) sees what she terms the 'presence of the past in the microbiology' of the Israeli-born children of the Holocaust survivors whose lives seem to have adjusted well in their new country. That is, she sees in the current Israeli generation elements of hatred, fear and mistrust, which are as a result of their parents' Holocaust experiences. However, Sorabji (2006) cautions against the wholesale acceptance of this concept and argues that the younger generation are not simply passive recipients of their parents' anger, pain and hatred, but make conscious choices on what to do with the information surrounding them. Whether transmitted or inferred, unless the effects of past violence are not dealt with, it may well lead to a resumption of hostilities in the future. Coupled with perpetual marginalisation, asymmetrical power and economic sharing, memories of the painful past in the hands of unscrupulous power seekers can and will play a deadly role in inciting victimised communities. As Mitchels (2003, p. 407) reiterates: 'The effects of trauma can cause, exacerbate or perpetuate violence.' Writing about Kosovo, Lamott (2005, p. 227) says:

> Trauma was, as it were, conserved as the source of revenge and resistance against suppression … Clinging on to persecution not only serves memory but also represents a duty never to give up the struggle. It stirs up enmity and places trauma as a long-term potential mobilization strategy.

Rwanda provides a case in point, where decades of ethnically-related violence eventually lead to the 1994 genocide, which left close to a million Tutsis as well as some Hutus dead. As Newbury (2002) has amply illustrated, the facts and myths of the Rwandan history were cleverly used by Hutu extremist politicians to build up a frenzy of killings, probably unprecedented in modern history (see also Mamdani 2001). According to Weine/Chae (2008, p. 11), mass traumatisation can be both a consequence of prior failure of peacebuilding and a possible cause of future failure. Effective peacebuilding will take cognisance of this potential risk and seek to address this psychological aspect of the trauma of war, for, if left unattended, these powerful emotional and natural responses to traumatisation are likely to lead to revenge. In my experience working with victims of *Gukurahundi*, I concur somewhat with Barsalou's (2005, p. 4) comment—that chosen traumas can be transformed or glorified as they are retold to subsequent generations and develop the potential to be used to incite revenge and to restore the honour of the victimised group.

In the last few decades there has been a convergence between the fields of trauma healing and peacebuilding (Zelizer 2008; Weine/Chae 2008). According to Weine/Chae (2008, p. 11), trauma healing overlaps with peacebuilding in that it seeks to diminish fears and unhealthy representations of self and others at individual, family, community and societal levels. In this way, it contributes to consolidating peace. On the other hand, peacebuilding does not only focus on governments but also on human elements of peace, which include beliefs, relationships and communication. The governmental approach focuses on the reformation of institutions and policies, while the community approach focuses on improving relations between groups, its major activities hinging around civil society and seeking to improve trust and understanding between conflicting groups. It operates at the 'nexus of trauma and peacebuilding' (Zelizer 2008, p. 85). At the very least, peacebuilding should aim to ensure that activities do not further traumatise or cause psychological harm to people who are already suffering the effects of violence (see also the discussion on transformative and mechanical peacebuilding, Sect. 3.5.1).

While this move towards convergence is a positive development, the gap between the two still needs to be narrowed further. The trauma approach focuses on emergency and crisis, while peacebuilding is more preventative and involves trying to strengthen structures and supporting relationships in a move towards human equity, to prevent further violence. Both trauma healing and peacebuilding approaches see violence as springing from disparities and dissatisfaction over structural conditions. However, the trauma perspective tends to seek to restore the peace that once existed. On the other hand, some peacebuilding challenges structural violence in order to change the status quo. While trauma healing focuses solely on the victims, peacebuilding includes the perpetrators as well, wherever possible (Weine/Chae 2008, p. 12). The trauma theory is fundamentally a psychological one, while peacebuilding is primarily a social approach. The efforts to bring the two concepts together are in a way trying to move trauma healing into the social. For trauma theory to become more relevant, it should loosen its fundamental belief that trauma causes emotional and psychological pathologies (Weine/Chae 2008, p. 13). One such effort to conceptualise a new paradigm is Erikson's (1995) collective trauma theory.

## 3.7 Collective Emotions and Collective Trauma

> *It is the community that offers a cushion for pain, the community that offers a context for intimacy, the community that serves as the repository for binding traditions.*
>
> Kai Erikson (1995, p. 189)

> *The social, political and cultural context shapes a people's personal priorities and expectations, it shapes the meaning and the impact of violence on the individual...*
>
> Patrick Bracken (2000, p. 58)

The concepts of collective emotions and collective trauma offer some key insights into the understanding of how communities affected by violence process their collective pain. Communities which have experienced violence perpetrated against them carry a shared pain that identifies them as a victimised group. In other words, trauma has a social dimension and, as noted above, modern, political conflicts tend to destroy the social fabric of communities targeted by the violence. It was also noted how the individual's pain is understood within the context of a suffering community (Sect. 3.5). According to Erikson (1995, p. 1):

> Sometimes 'tissues' of a community can be damaged the same way as the tissues of mind and body… traumatic wounds inflicted on individuals can combine to create a mood, an ethos–a group culture, almost–that is different from (and more than) the sum total of the private wounds that make it up.

These traumatised communities, says Erikson, are different and distinct from assemblies of traumatised persons. This is particularly so if the community has been targeted for elimination or persecution based on its identity, whether it be ethnic, racial, religious or political. This induces common feelings of fear, hatred and insecurity, which have been termed collective or group-based emotions. The knowledge of these concepts, I believe, is crucial in community-based healing processes, as they assist in understanding why certain groups or communities feel the way they feel and behave the way they behave. This will of course inform methodologies and approaches as to how peacebuilders help a particular community deal with its wounds. This research also seeks to be informed by these understandings.

### 3.7.1 Collective Emotions and Group-Based Emotions

According to Bar-Tal et al. (2007, p. 442), collective emotions can be described generally as emotions which are shared by large numbers of individuals in a certain society. Group-based emotions, on the other hand, can be termed as 'emotions that are felt by individuals as a result of their membership in a certain group or society'. What this means is that individuals could experience emotions, not necessarily because of their personal life events, but as a reaction to collective or societal experiences in which only some of the group members have taken part (Bar-Tal et al. 2007, p. 442):

> The assumption here is that just as individuals may be known by a dominant emotion, societies also may develop a collective or communal emotional outlook. Unlike individual emotions, which are usually associated with a dispositional system or physiological mechanisms, these collective and group emotions are formed purely as a result of experiences that a community experiences in a particular social context (Bar-Tal et al. 2007, pp. 442–443).

These collective emotions are paramount in determining how individuals and societies react to conflicts and in the development of a context that maintains a certain long-term emotional state and emotional orientation. This emotional state is what has been referred to as the 'emotional climate' (Bar-Tal et al. 2007; Kanyangara et al. 2007; de Rivera/Paez 2007), which is the collective behaviour that a group displays when it is 'focused on the emotional relationships existing between members of the society' (Kanyangara et al. 2007, p. 388). What is important to note is that these collective feelings exist independently of an individual's personal feelings and mirror how individuals think most of the people are feeling in that particular community's present situation (de Rivera/Paez 2007, p. 234). Objective facts, institutional systems and political policies all contribute to the emotional climate but it is also influenced by how ordinary people behave. In other words, the emotional climate does not only depend on broader social dynamics but also on dynamics that take place at the individual level.

> An understanding of these dynamics is crucial in peacebuilding, particularly when dealing with communities or groups that have experienced violent conflicts. This understanding could help to determine the predictive power of climates.[6] That is to say we can use the predominant or prevailing emotional climate to predict group behaviour in certain circumstances. It can be expected that particular emotions will conjure specific perceptions of a situation and will determine how people react to it (de Rivera/Paez 2007, p. 242).

For instance, collective fear may be deeply entrenched into the psyche of community members and is associated with a culture of violence. This orientation affects the community's options in dealing with their conflicts or hurts because all expectations of the future are based solely on their past experiences. Fear therefore becomes a platform for violence, as the first reaction to any threat (perceived or real) is to fight. Another emotion that leads to negative behaviour is that of hatred. It is usually a reaction to perceived deliberate injustice and harm inflicted on a continuous basis. The perpetrators are viewed as being irredeemably evil and this arouses within the victims the desire to eliminate the hated group. This intense hatred leads to intractable conflicts, as the focus is not so much on the behaviour but the perceived fundamental character of the offending group. In such instances, reconciliation and forgiveness are difficult to achieve. Lack of security can also contribute to negative collective behaviours, as it brings with it feelings of frustration, fear and dissatisfaction which may result in extreme behaviours such as wars and violent conflicts, as well as genocide in some cases (Bar-Tal et al. 2007, pp. 449–450).

### *3.7.2 Collective Trauma*

In dealing with communities affected by armed conflict, like the people of Matabeleland, one needs to bear in mind the social dimension of hurts caused by the violence. A community will experience these collective negative emotions when it has undergone violation of its identity and existence as these are etched into its memory. The challenge is how to deal with such a 'collective wound' in a holistic manner, which can help bring about healing to the community at large. It is here that 'healing' approaches will determine whether efforts are beneficial to the

[6]It has been pointed out though that there currently isn't enough data to make definite pronouncement about how the emotional climate affects predictive power in collective behaviour (de Rivera/Paez 2007, p. 242).

affected communities. In as much as modern armed conflict is aimed at the destruction of a community's social fabric and coping mechanisms, it seems important for healing methodologies to focus on repairing the torn fabric by concentrating on approaches that promote community healing.

It is important at this juncture to make the two following points which follow from the material reviewed in this chapter and which influence the approach taken in this research: Firstly, there is no doubt that clinical psychology and the PTSD approaches to healing bring real value to the process of reconstruction of individuals and communities broken by the trauma of violence. What has been said above in no way demeans these approaches, but peacebuilders need not be restricted to these predominantly Western approaches when there are other approaches which are more contextual and better understood by the victim communities and therefore are more meaningful to them. However, during the research, the clinical therapy option was available if needed. That need never arose. Secondly, I am not a psychologist or counsellor by profession so it could be asked on what grounds I am basing my research and intervention. My response is that, as a grassroots peacebuilding practitioner and a member of the victim community, living in a country steeped in violence, I have seen and experienced the effects of violence upon communities and individuals that have gone through traumatising events. In fact, my work involves interacting with these individuals and their communities daily. My concern is from a peacebuilding perspective as noted in Sect. 2.6. Unhealed communities carry the added risk of either reigniting or further exacerbating violent conflicts.

## 3.8 Conclusion

In this chapter, we have discussed the effects of armed conflicts on individuals and seen how modern armed conflicts often seek to destroy the social fabric of a community, even though their acts of violence might be aimed at individual family or community members. We sought to define trauma, following Farwell/Cole (2002), as the systematic shock that disrupts the balance of the affective, cognitive and spiritual inner function. However, not all people exposed to 'traumatising' events are affected similarly. Traumatisation depends on the context and interpretation of the event. Trauma can be experienced at a collective level as a blow to the basic tissues; something that destroys the bonds that hold people together and impairs the prevailing sense of community.

The effects of trauma can be positive, neutral or negative. Activated Adversity Development (AAD) is the growth some people experience due to exposure to adverse circumstances, while resilience could be termed neutral insofar as people emerge intact from their experiences of suffering. PTSD, on the other hand, is the negative response to suffering. The fact that PTSD theories might not be the best approach to trauma healing in non-Western societies, was also discussed. This is because this approach tends to focus on individuals whereas, in many non-Western societies, community is emphasised more than the individual, and other value systems such as faith, world views and culture, need to be taken into consideration. The interplay between trauma theory and peacebuilding is crucial in the formulation of an effective and relevant response in post armed conflict societies.

Communities emerging from such violence can experience collective painful memories and peacebuilding activities must address this if they are to restore the torn social fabric, heal the social wounds and prevent further cycles of violence. We also discussed the concepts of collective emotions and emotional climate and saw how these are crucial in understanding the dynamics of how individuals and communities react to conflicts and the development of a particular predominant collective emotion in a particular society.

Chapter 4 will discuss the meaning of community trauma healing and explore how other communities have dealt with their traumas in the absence of state-sponsored healing programmes or apologies from the perpetrators who, in this case, happen to be the government of the day.

## References

Agger, I. and Jensen, S. B. 1996. *Trauma and healing under state terrorism.* London: Zed.

Almqvist, K. and Broberg, A. G. 2003. Young children traumatized by organized violence together with their mothers—the critical effects of damaged internal representation. *Attachment & Human development*, 5(4): 367–380.

Barsalou, J. 2005. Trauma and transitional justice in divided societies. *United States Institute of Peace,* 135 (Special Report): 1–11. At: www.usip.org (12 June 2009).

Bar-Tal, D., Halperin, E. and de Rivera J. 2007. Collective emotions in conflict situations: societal implications. *Journal of Social Issues*, 63(2): 441–460.

Becker, D. 2004. "Dealing with the consequences of organised violence in trauma work". In *Transforming ethnopolitical conflict* (pp. 403–420). VS Verlag für Sozialwissenschaften

Bracken, P. J. and Petty, C. 1998. *Rethinking the trauma of war.* London: Free Association Books.

Bracken P. 2000. Rethinking the trauma of war. In C. Becker (ed.), *Psychosocial and trauma response in war-torn societies: the case of Kosovo.* Psychosocial Notebook, Vol. 1, IOM.

Boutros-Ghali, B. 1992. An agenda for peace; Preventative diplomacy, peacemaking and peace-keeping. At: http://www.un.org/en/sc/repertoire/89-92/Chapter%208/GENERAL%20ISSUES/Item%2029_Agenda%20for%20peace_.pdf (08 March 2007).

Boutros-Ghali, B. 1995. *Supplement to an agenda for peace.* New York: United Nations.

CDA Collaborative learning projects, 2009. *R*eflecting on peace practice: participant training manual. At: http://cdacollaborative.org/wordpress/wp-content/uploads/2016/01/Reflecting-on-Peace-Practice-1-Participant-Training-Manual.pdf (22 April 2011).

Clancy, M. A. C. and Hamber, B. 2008. Trauma, peacebuilding and development: an overview of key positions and critical questions. At: www.incore.ulst.ac.uk/research/projects/trauma/ (17 July 2010).

Cockell, J. 2003. Conceptualising peacebuilding: human security and sustainable peace. In M. Pugh (ed.), *Regeneration of war-torn societies.* London: Macmillan.

Cole, J. 2004. Painful memories: ritual and the transformation of community trauma. *Culture, Medicine and Psychiatry*, 28(1): 87–105.

de Jong, K., Mulhern, M., Ford, N., van de Kam, S. and Kleber, R. 2000. The trauma of war in Sierra Leone. *The Lancet,* 355: 2067–2068.

de Rivera, J. and Paez, D. 2007. Emotional climate, human security, and cultures of peace. *Journal of Social Issues,* 63(2): 233–253.

Dillenburger, K., Akhonzada, R. and Fargas, M. 2006. Post-trauma: is evidence-based practice a fantasy? *International Journal of Behavioral and Consultation Therapy,* 2(1): 95–102.

Ehrenreich, J. H. 2003. Understanding PTSD: forgetting trauma'. *Journal of Social Issues*, 3(1): 15–28.

Edkins, J. 2003. *Trauma and the memory of politics*. Cambridge: Cambridge University Press.

Erikson, K. 1995. Notes on trauma and community. In C. Caruth (ed.), *Trauma: explorations in memory*. Baltimore: The John Hopkinson University Press.

Farwell, N. and Cole, J. B. 2002. Community as context of healing: psychosocial recovery of children affected by war and political violence. *International Journal of Mental Health,* 30(4): 19–41.

Fisher, S. and Zimina, L. 2009. Just wasting our time? Provocative thoughts for peacebuilders. *Berghof handbook.* At: http://citeseerx.ist.psu.edu/viewdoc/download?doi=10.1.1.550.1263&rep=rep1&type=pdf (03 October 2010).

Finch, R. J. 2006. Trauma and forgiveness: a spiritual inquiry. *Journal of Spirituality in Mental Health*, 9(2): 27–41. At: http://www.tandfonline.com/doi/abs/10.1300/J515v09n02_03 (14 September 2009).

Galtung, J. 1996. *Peace by peaceful means: peace and conflict, development and civilization*. UK: Sage.

Grävingholt, J., Ganzle, S., and Ziaja, S. 2009. The convergence of peacebuilding and state building: addressing a common purpose from different perspectives. Briefing Paper 4/2009. Bonn: German Development Institute / Deutsches Institut für Entwicklungspolitik (DIE).

Gobodo-Madikizela, P. 2003. *A human being died that night: a story of forgiveness*. Cape Town: David Philip.

Gobodo-Madikizela, P. 2008. Trauma, forgiveness and the witnessing dance: making public spaces intimate. *Journal of Analytical Psychology*, 53: 169–188.

Heathershaw, J. 2007. Peacebuilding as practise: discourses from post-conflict Tajikistan. *International Peacekeeping*, 4(2) April: 219–236.

Inter-Agency Standing Committee (IASC). 2007. *IASC Guidelines for on mental health and psychosocial support in emergency setting.* Geneva: IASC.

Inter-Agency Standing Committee (IASC). 2010. *Guidance note for mental health and psychosocial support: Haiti earthquake emergency response* (online). Geneva: IASC. At: https://www.apa.org/international/resources/info/haiti-guidelines.pdf (20 October 2010).

Kanyangara, P., Rimé, B., Philippot, P. and Yzerbyt, V. 2007. Collective rituals, emotional climate and intergroup perception: participation in 'Gacaca' tribunals and assimilation of the Rwandan genocide. *Journal of Social Issues*, 63(2): 387–403.

Lambourne, W. 2004. Post-conflict peacebuilding: meeting human needs for justice and reconciliation. *Peace, Conflict and Development*, 4: 1–24.

Lamott, F. 2005. Trauma as a political tool. *Critical Public Health,* 15(3): 219–228.

Lederach, J. P. 1997. *Building Peace: sustainable reconciliation in divided societies*. Washington, DC: USIP.

Lemaire, J. M. 2000. Disconcerting humanitarian interventions, and the resources of collective healing. In C. Becker (ed.), *Psychological and trauma response in war-torn societies: the case of Kosovo*. Psychological Notebook, Vol. 1, November, 2000, IOM.

Losi, N. 2000. Understanding the needs of the displaced: some elements on the Kosovo case. In C. Becker (ed.), *Psychosocial and trauma response in war-torn societies: the case of Kosovo.* Psychosocial Notebook, Vol. 1, IOM.

Maiese, M. 2003. What it means to building everlasting peace. *Beyond intractability*. At: http://www.beyondintractability.org/essay/peacebuilding (11/06/2014).

Mamdani, M. 2001. *When victims become killers, colonialism, nativism, and the genocide in Rwanda.* Oxford: James Curry.

Martin-Baro, I. 1989. Political violence and wars as causes of psychosocial trauma in El Salvador. *International Journal of Mental health*, 18(1): 3–20.

Mitchels, B. 2003. Healing the wounds of war and more: an integrative approach to peace—the work of Adam Curle and others with Mir i dobro in Zupanja, Croatia. *British Journal of Guidance & Counselling,* 31(4): 403–415.

Neller, D. J., Denney, R. L., Pietz, C. A. and Tomlinson, R. P. 2005. Testing the trauma model of violence. *Journal of Family Violence,* 20(3): 151–159.

Newbury, C. 2002. Ethnicity and the politics of history in Rwanda. In D. E. Lorey and W. H. Beezley (eds.), *Genocide, collective violence, and popular memory: the politics of remembrance in the twentieth century.* Wilmington: S R Books.

Nikondeha, C. 2009. *Transfiguration.* Keynote address at the Amahoro conference, Johannesburg, South Africa.

Papadopoulos, R. 2000. A matter of shades: trauma and psychosocial work in Kosovo. In C. Becker (ed.), *Psychosocial and trauma response in war-torn societies: the case of Kosovo.* Psychosocial Notebook, Vol. 1, IOM. 261

Papadopoulos, R. K. 2007. Refugees, trauma and adversity-activated development. *European Journal of Psychology and Counselling,* 9(3): 301–312.

Pintar, J. 2000. Anticipating consequences: what Bosnia taught us about healing the wounds of war. *Human Rights Review,* January–March: 56–66.

Robben, A. C. G. M. 2000. The assault on basic trust: disappearance, protest, and reburial in Argentina. In A. C. G. M. Robben and M. M. Suárez-Orozco (eds.), *Cultures under siege: collective violence and trauma.* Cambridge: Cambridge University Press.

Saul, J. 2000. Mapping trauma. In C. Becker (ed.), *Psychosocial and trauma response in war-torn societies: the case of Kosovo.* Psychosocial Notebook, Vol. 1, IOM.

Shriver, D. 1999. The long road to reconciliation: some moral stepping stones. In R. Rothstein (ed.), *After the peace: resistance and reconciliation.* Boulder, Co: Lynne Rienner.

Sorabji, C. 2006. Managing memories in the post-war Sarajevo: individuals, bad memories, and new wars. *Journal of Royal Anthropological Institute,* 12: 1–18.

Staub, E. and Pearlman, L. 2001. Healing, reconciliation and forgiving after genocide and other collective violence. In R. Helmick and R. Peterson (eds.), *Forgiveness and reconciliation: religion, public policy and conflict transformation.* Radnor, Philadelphia: Templeton Foundation.

Staub, E., Pearlman, L. A., Gubin, A. and Hagengimana, A. 2005. Healing, reconciliation, forgiving and the prevention of violence after genocide or mass killings: an intervention and its Experimental Evaluation in Rwanda. *Journal of Social and Clinical Psychology,* 24(3): 297–334.

Summerfield, D. 1996. *Impact of war and atrocity on civilian populations: basic principles for NGO interventions and a critique of psychosocial trauma projects.* Relief and Rehabilitation Network. London: Overseas Development Institute.

Summerfield, D. 1999. A critique of seven assumptions behind psychological trauma programmes in war-affected areas. *Social Science & Medicine,* 48: 1449–1462.

Timerman, J. 1981. *Prisoner without a name, a cell without a number.* New York: Alfred A. Knopf.

Uehara, E. S., Farwell, N., Yamashiro, G. and Smukler, M. 2002. The place of ethnographic understanding in the assessment of Asian American mental health. In K. Kurasuki, S. Okazaki, and S. Sue (eds.), *Asian American mental health: assessment, theories and methods.* Cham, Springer.

Warren, M. P. 2006. *From trauma to transformation.* Carmarthen, Wales: Crown House.

Zelizer, C. December, 2008. Trauma-sensitive peacebuilding: lessons for theory and practice. *Africa Peace and Conflict Journal,* 1(1): 81–94.

Zorbas, E. 2004. Reconciliation in post-genocide Rwanda. *African Journal of Legal Studies,* 1(1): 29–35.

# Chapter 4
# Community Trauma Healing—Theory and Practice

*The wounds of trauma are real. They never disappear. Those wounds can be healed, but one never returns to the state in which s/he was before the injury.*
Raymond Finch (2006, p. 29)

*The story of forgiveness begins with the story of trauma.*
Pumla Gobodo-Madikizela (2008, p. 173)

*Those who cannot let go of the hatred of their enemies risk sowing the seeds of hatred within their own communities.*
President Bill Clinton (6 November 1995, funeral speech)

## 4.1 Introduction

*Countries emerging from long-term violent conflict are troubled societies that may develop destructive societal and political patterns. In such cases, fundamental psychological adjustment in individual and group identity—aided by reconstruction—are essential for reconciliation.*
Judy Barsalou (2005, p. 4)

This chapter explores healing in the aftermath of war, violence or genocide, paying particular attention to how healing applies to communities who have suffered from these. The term 'healing' will be defined and we will examine what makes for ideal conditions for healing. The concepts of reconciliation and forgiveness, justice and truth-telling which are often seen as the backbone of any healing process—be it individual or communal—will be discussed (Tutu 1999; Gobodo-Madikizela 2008; Staub et al. 2005). The chapter will explore the concepts of thick and thin approaches to reconciliation. I will propose the adoption of reconciliation as an overarching concept that is underpinned by justice, forgiveness, healing and truth-telling. The case studies of how other communities have dealt with the issue of healing where there has not been an official healing programme—particularly the experiences of Chile, Northern Ireland and Rwanda—will be investigated.



D. Ngwenya, *Healing the Wounds of Gukurahundi in Zimbabwe*,
The Anthropocene: Politik—Economics—Society—Science 19,
https://doi.org/10.1007/978-3-319-66818-5_4

## 4.2 The Meaning of Healing After Traumatic Experiences

> *Recovery can take place only within the context of relationships; it cannot occur in isolation.*
>
> Judith Herman (1992, p. 176)

> *If we are in part who we are because we are embedded in a nexus of relations that make others part of ourselves, then we cannot be properly healed without our relationships being healed too.*
>
> Miroslav Volf (2001, p. 40)

In Chap. 3, we discussed how contemporary political violence tends to rip into the social fabric and leave communities and individuals bearing 'wounds' (Farwell/Cole 2002, p. 22). We noted that, in as much as individuals might sustain emotional wounds, a community can also experience injury to its collective emotions. Relationships and trust between the antagonistic communities are damaged by the violence and this leaves communities in need of 'healing'. Collective healing of memories is crucial where collective traumatisation has taken place. As Pintar (2000, p. 64) has said, 'Men, women, and children in traumatized communities must heal together, if they are to heal at all, because their lives are bound up with one another' (see also Bar-Tal et al. 2007, p. 451).

To better understand the concept of 'community healing', we first need to appreciate what is meant by community in the first place. Often community is perceived in geographical terms, as a place or a physical location where a group of people reside. However, as Farwell/Cole (2002, p. 24) suggest, it is more useful to conceive community as a collective of interests, values, and norms that organise activities and interactions. A community shares a notion of togetherness, united around a common history or goals and might share and participate in activities, culture and ideology.

> Although community can exist within the context of place or function, in order to regard it as a medium for meeting the needs of individuals recovering from psychosocial trauma, we need to consider the community in an affective context, in terms of a 'sense of community' (Farwell/Cole 2002, p. 24).

This notion of community is linked to the concepts of 'collective emotions' and 'group-based emotions' as discussed in Sect. 3.6. In terms of this research, not only do the communities of Matabeleland share the abovementioned characteristics but, since 1982, they have also shared in the 'community of the wounded'.

Hamber (2003, p. 77) has defined healing as 'any strategy, process or activity that improves the psychological health of individuals following excessive violent conflict'. He further states that

> Strategies, processes, or activities aimed at rehabilitating and reconstructing local and national communities more broadly are also integrally linked to this process. As such, healing is not only about assisting individuals to address their psychological health needs in an isolated way, but is dependent upon and integrally linked to repairing and rebuilding

> communities and the social context. This implies restoring a normalised everyday life that can recreate people's sense of being and belonging (Hamber 2003, p. 77).

It is evident from this definition that the healing of community and individual is intricately intertwined. A successful community healing process should result in individual community members who also have been made whole. As indicated in Sect. 2.4, violence done to an individual in contemporary political conflicts is not just aimed at that particular individual but is designed to disrupt the normal everyday function of that individual's community (see also Farwell/Cole 2002, p. 20). Hence the socio-political context is a vital element in the recovery process and healing should utilise the many individual, political, social and cultural responses to a traumatic situation and its aftermath (Hamber 2003, p. 78). In other words, healing is multidimensional and multifaceted. Holistic healing processes will therefore need to address both the causes of the pain and the symptoms. Hamber further states that the traumatic event is not the only thing that needs to be dealt with. What is even more important when deciding on a strategy for the healing process, is the way in which the individual or his/her community interprets the event. This is because different violent political acts can have distinctive cultural meanings and specific impacts (Hamber 2003, p. 78). That is to say, how a community or individual reacts to or is affected by a particular act of violence depends very much on cultural context, beliefs and practices. In Zimbabwe, as in many other Southern African countries, culture and spiritual dimensions are intertwined and this applies to practitioners of both traditional and Christian faiths. Any meaningful and effective healing programme will therefore need to find ways to address these elements (Wessells 1999; Minow 1998; Coban 2007).

In terms of the socio-political aspect, Wessells (1999, 2008) questions the logic of only addressing the psychological and emotional effects of violence, while ignoring underlying causes of violence. As he says:

> No amount of counselling will correct the structural violence, human rights violations and systems of state oppression that produce many forms of trauma. Furthermore, problems such as distrust and low social cohesion often stem from a host of political, economic and social factors (Wessells 2008, p. 11).

Wessells finds it unacceptable that a healing process in a context of political oppression should address traumas solely, without also working to support human rights and constructive political change. He contends that, when we fail to improve the human wellbeing of the victims of political violence, then our interventions 'serve to heal lambs for the slaughter, to enable people to endure oppression without ending it, or to silence rebellion in the face of tyranny' (Wessells 1999, p. 6). While I agree with Wessells in principle, I believe there are times when it is important to mitigate the emotional and psychological suffering of the victims, without tackling the causal elements directly, desirable though this might be. I believe this to be the case with the *Gukurahundi* victims, who since 1983 have been carrying immense feelings of hurt, pain, hatred and mistrust and who are dying with unhealed memories.

Currently the political environment does not allow for the direct challenge of the socio-political causes of the Matabeleland violence of the 1980s. It is still taboo in officialdom to talk publicly about these incidents. For example, a young artist and the director of the National Art Gallery in Bulawayo were, at one point, arrested and arraigned before the courts for exhibiting paintings that depicted scenes from the *Gukurahundi* era. They were charged with causing offence to persons of a particular race or religion (*The Chronicle*, March 30 2010). Charges against the director were withdrawn before plea on 28th January 2011,[1] while the artist appealed to the High Court for infringement of his rights to freedom of expression. At the time of writing, the case was still pending.

The choice seems to be between providing a measure of relief to these elderly people and insisting on taking on the structural causes, which as we saw (in Sect. 1.4), are still perceived to be functional even today. A good healing process should leave the participants with a certain amount of socio-political emancipation and empowerment, even if it does not necessarily address the external conditions surrounding the victims' communities. The work done by psychologists in Chile during the years of dictatorship, as we shall see, illustrates this fact well. By focusing on the victims' pains and 'conscientising' them about the state terrorism strategies, they were able to build up their resistance levels and political consciousness. While the practitioners were not themselves directly involved in challenging the status quo, their work was instrumental in empowering victims to shed their feelings of helplessness and to assume a certain degree of responsibility for their future (Agger/Jensen 1996).

## 4.3 Components of the Healing Process

Dealing with individual and community wounds caused by armed conflicts and atrocities is a complex and delicate process that requires tact, sensitivity and patience. It is necessary to cultivate the healing process in order to create a conducive environment that allows for the creation of the trust needed to heal the torn social fabric. This process is both complex and protracted and requires long-term commitment from both the practitioner and the communities in conflict. As Desmond Tutu, has stated in his forward to the International IDEA handbook:

> There is no short cut or simple prescription for healing the wounds and divisions of a society in the aftermath of sustained violence. Creating trust and understanding between former enemies is a supremely difficult challenge. It is, however, an essential one to address in the process of building a lasting peace. Examining the painful past, acknowledging it and understanding it, above all transcending it together, is the best way to guarantee that it does not-and cannot happen again (Bloomfield et al. 2003, p. 4).

[1]This information was communicated directly to the researcher by the Gallery Director.

Healing is necessary not just for the relief of wounded communities. It is also strategic for the prevention of future violence which might be caused by the victim community's desire to revenge. If not dealt with, the past will continue to haunt the present and to some degree influence the future.

> Hatred and the search for vengeance can consume people, turning them into mirror images of those they hate. Unless people manage to forsake their determination to 'get even', there can be no new beginning, no transformation of relationships. Everyone will remain imprisoned in a particular history or mythology, recycling old crimes and hatreds (Rigby 2001, p. 2).

Justice—in the sense of accountability of the perpetrators of violence—is also highly desirable. Pintar (2000) makes this point quite clear:

> If we recognize trauma as ongoing, as social, as relational, it becomes very stark that while the international community fails to carry through our promises of care and protection, while Mafiosi continue to control local governments, while war criminals sit openly in cafes, the war is not over, the trauma does not end. If perpetrators are not brought to justice, or even worse, if they continue to prosper or retain power as a result of their crimes, the prospects for healing are very poor, for individuals, for villages, for nation (Pintar 2000, p. 63).

People need to feel safe if healing is to occur. Where their lives are still under constant threat and the environment around them continues to remind them of their traumatic experiences, the wounds will remain open (Staub et al. 2005, p. 302). Part of the safety of the environment is created by the 'bringing to book' of the major instigators of violence (Pintar 2000, p. 64). The role of justice in healing and reconciliation is dealt with below (Sect. 4.4), though, as with addressing structural violence, it may not be on offer.

Even in situations where it is not possible for members of victim and perpetrator groups to reconcile or forgive each other, it is still highly desirable that those who have experienced violence and suffering be given an opportunity to heal for *their own sakes* so they can move on with their lives. People who have been traumatised by extreme violence tend to be 'caught up' in a moment of time. Time freezes at the time of the violence for the victims and unless they are helped to deal with the pain and trauma, they can be stuck emotionally at that point. However, as Charles Villa-Vicencio has pointed out, this does not entail the forgetting of horrible acts committed, nor does it mean they should become friends with those who have wronged them. It does mean 'dealing with the "ball of anger", that prevents one from moving on with life.' For, the ultimate revenge for victims is not the trial but that ability to move on with life (Villa-Vicencio 2004, p. 202).

Conversely, perpetrators (and members of the perpetrator group who may not have committed any violence) also need healing. As Staub et al. (2005) have noted: in most cases, perpetrators might have experienced victimisation or some other traumatic experiences themselves, as part of the cycle of violence. Their actions are fuelled in part by their unhealed wounds. Sometimes past traumas may develop into chosen traumas which help shape that particular community's psychology and behaviour. In addition, it is clear that people who take part in extreme violence against others are affected by their own actions, for in order to kill another human being, they have to turn off part of their own humanity, resulting in 'psychological and spiritual woundedness'. Of necessity, such persons must shut down their empathy and compassion towards their victims and possibly to other people as well (Staub et al. 2005, p. 302).

## 4.4 Approaches to Healing

> *A wounded society cannot afford to underplay its tragedy and apply ineffectual remedies any more than it can afford to be overwhelmed by the trauma it has suffered.*
>
> David Bloomfield (2003, p. 41)

It is important to note that the individual and social ramifications of extreme violence and the consequent social disruptions usually have long-lasting effects which go on for decades. The healing process is a lengthy one which demands long-term strategies. There is no one healing process; what works best is what Hamber (2003, p. 80) calls 'a blend of facilitating transformation of the social world that causes distress'. The psychological impact of this violence is rarely ever dealt with completely; some effects will last a lifetime and may well affect the next generation.

Hamber (2003) has proposed three broad principles that those involved in healing programmes need to consider. Firstly, there is a need to understand the victims' context. An effective strategy is best developed when the social and cultural context is acknowledged. In the African context, the individual needs to be addressed as part of the whole. The understanding is not done so that practitioners can adapt a certain approach to fit the context but in order to develop a strategy that is relevant for that particular situation. 'Context is not a minor variable whose influence on a programme needs to be considered and accommodated; rather it is the major variable which should be the starting point when developing the healing strategy in the first place' (Hamber 2003, p. 80). Secondly, it is best to use local resources. Communities have their own traditional coping mechanisms and, even though these may have been damaged, they can be utilised in the healing process. However, we need to guard against either placing too much value on local resources or dismissing external strategies out of hand. Hamber's final suggestion is that healing should be linked with broader reconstruction programmes. Issues of truth, acknowledgement and justice cannot be separated from the healing process. It is very difficult for victims to experience complete healing, while the truth of what happened to them or their loved ones is still unknown and unacknowledged. An effective healing process should therefore be holistic in its approach (Hamber 2003, pp. 80–81).

Such a holistic approach has been adopted by Minow (1998), who has suggested 12 goals that a society or nation needs to consider in addressing any post-atrocity situation. Nine of these are pertinent to our discussion here:

1. Overcome communal and official denial of the atrocity; gain public acknowledgement.
2. Obtain the facts in an account as full as possible in order to meet victims' need to know, to build a record for history, and to ensure minimal accountability of perpetrators.
3. End and prevent violence; transform human activity from violence—and violent responses to violence—into words and institutional practices of equal respect and dignity.
4. Forge basis for a domestic democratic order that respects and enforces human rights.
5. Promote reconciliation across social divisions; reconstruct the moral and social systems devastated by violence.
6. Promote psychological healing for individuals, groups, victims, bystanders and offenders.
7. Restore dignity to victims.
8. Punish, exclude, shame, and diminish offenders for their offences.
9. Accomplish these goals in ways that render them compatible rather than antagonistic with the other goals (Minow 1998, p. 88).

Such an institutional framework could encourage both individual and communal healing and stimulate and strengthen the resolve to work for peace, rather than a desire for vengeance, assuming that there is political will for healing and reconciliation within officialdom. However, even where a government is well-intentioned, the outcomes are often less than what was hoped for. Even the highly-esteemed TRC in South Africa left many victims unhealed and still desiring vengeance, although it laid a foundation that could be built upon at communal and individual levels (Minow 1998, pp. 68–83; Adam/Adam 2000, p. 41). In the case of Matabeleland, not even this opportunity exists, as there has been no acknowledgement of what happened by those responsible.

Walsh's (2007) approach is perhaps relevant to such a context. This process is meant to facilitate healing by encouraging individuals, families and communities to engage in a shared process, designed to heal the social fabric torn by violence. To encourage healing, Walsh (2007, p. 210) argues that the process must include:

1. A shared acknowledgement of the reality of the traumatic event and losses experienced. Facts about the incidents, circumstances and any ambiguities surrounding the event must be clarified. People who have experienced traumatic events are left with a lot of questions and confusion in their minds and sorting these as a communal experience aids the healing process.
2. Shared experience of loss and victimhood. This calls for communities to actively participate in memorial rituals, memorialisation and to share in meaning

making.[2] Spirituality and emotional expression are also important components in this process. This is creating a community which shares a common experience so that individuals can draw strength from each other.

3. The reorganisation of family and community by planning for survivors' well-being. The restabilisation of the community is necessary to foster continuity and change. It might also be necessary to realign relationships which have been disrupted by the traumatic event and to reallocate roles and functions. Often, women and children find themselves playing unfamiliar roles left vacant by men and older brothers who have either been killed or dislocated from their communities and families. Then there is the arduous task of rebuilding lives, homes, livelihood, kinship and community; all of which require a concerted effort from a debilitated community.
4. The final task is the reinvestment in relationships and life pursuits. This is a task connected to the above and is about constructing new hopes and dreams. It might also be necessary to revise life plans and aspirations in view of the new realities. From the ashes of tragic losses new purposes must be found.

The purpose of political violence is to disempower and fragment communities and individuals and the process above is important in working towards reestablishment of the community fabric and healing.

## 4.5 Some Necessary Conditions for Healing

We now turn our attention to what makes healing possible. In doing this we must keep in mind that the process does not follow a straightforward path and healing is not easily attainable. Various schools of thought have placed emphasis on different facets of the healing trajectory for communities emerging from violent conflict. Minow (1998) and Chapman (2001) see truth commissions as being useful in the healing process, while Murphy (2007) talks about the rule of law based on the Fullerian concept of mutual respect for the rule of law (see also Elshtain 2003). On the other hand, Volf (2001), Lederach (1997) and Tutu (1999), among others, put more emphasis on forgiveness, reconciliation, and restorative justice. I believe all

[2]*Grace to Heal* has been involved in a process which Eppel (2006) calls 'healing the dead'. The process involves working with the family and relatives of those murdered during *Gukurahundi* who more often lie in mass shallow graves. Some of the graves are said to contain up to 40 individuals. After working with families in counselling and premortem data collection, the graves are built up properly (in most cases one would never tell there is a grave unless informed by those who know) and the names of those buried there inscribed, after which a memorial ceremony is held as a last step towards the healing process. Depending on the family, this could be a Christian or an African traditional ceremony. Other organisations have done similar work; however due to the current political environment, GTH seems to be the only one still doing this at the moment.

these are necessary aspects in the long road to healing, with the emphasis placed on particular aspects dependent on what a particular situation demands. In this chapter, we focus on issues around forgiveness, truth, justice and reconciliation.

### 4.5.1 *Justice*

Those whose lives have been devastated by atrocities and the practitioners who purport to fight for their rights, have often emphasised justice as an integral component in the healing process. It is argued that, without justice, the processes of reconciliation and healing cannot be attained (Chapman 2001; Theissen 2004). According to Huyse (2003b, p. 97), 'the search for peaceful coexistence, trust, empathy and democratic power sharing demands that justice be done'. However, this term 'justice' is a problematic one, because 'all accounts of what is "just" are to some extent relative to a particular person or group and are invariably contested by that person's or group's rivals' (Volf 2001, pp. 38–39). No matter how just or fair we might try to be in administering due process of the law, whatever action taken is likely to be seen as unjust by the recipient. To quote Volf again:

> Any action we undertake now is inescapably ambiguous, at best partially just and therefore partially unjust. No peace is possible within the over-arching framework of strict justice for the simple reason that strict justice is not possible. Enough justice never gets done because more justice is always possible than in fact gets done (Volf 2001, pp. 38–39).

It is helpful to keep the above statement in mind as we discuss the role played by justice in the healing process. Huyse has helpfully suggested that there are several different forms of justice: retributive, which is based on punishment and prosecutions; restorative, which seeks to bring together the victim, perpetrator and the community; historic, which comes as a result of a truth commission; and compensatory, brought about by reparations (Huyse 2003b, p. 39). We will discuss some of the above-mentioned briefly.

According to the proponents of retributive justice, criminal trials may aid the healing process, insofar as they serve to satisfy the victims' need for justice and prevents them from what Huyse (2003b, p. 98) calls 'self-help' justice. That is to say, victims might be tempted to carry out acts of vengeance if they perceive that the wrong-doers have not been brought to account over their atrocities. According to Theissen (2004, p. 3) and Huyse (2003b, pp. 97–103), criminal trials have the potential of breaking the culture of impunity, and increase awareness of human rights and humanitarian law, sending a clear message that such atrocities are criminal acts and not legitimate actions. In addition, because this process publicly acknowledges who was right and who was wrong, victims' wounds can be healed and their self-confidence restored. Another important perceived benefit of criminal trials is that it individualises accountability and guilt. In a court of law, those responsible for specific atrocities are brought to book and 'appropriate' punishments meted out. In the process, members of the perpetrator community who are innocent will be freed from the collective blame and thus be reintegrated. As has been pointed out, this process is 'crucial in the eradication of the dangerous perception that the whole community is responsible for the violence and atrocities' and that the 'idea of collective guilt is often a source of negative stereotypes, which may provide more violence in turn' (Huyse 2003b, p. 98).

There is however a downside to criminal justice in that, victims might not have confidence in the criminal justice system or be afraid to bring charges. Cases might take too long to come to court, leaving the victims disillusioned and bitter. High-profile suspects might not be found guilty because of lack of evidence or procedural errors, which might be taken to mean that certain people are still above the law. The biggest problem with criminal justice is that it focuses too much public attention on the perpetrators and is of limited use in helping victims heal from the wounds inflicted upon them.

In addition, it is often difficult to strike a balance between the need for justice and practical political considerations. It may be that, for a society coming out of a violent period, other issues may be regarded as more important and more urgent than justice. At times an aggressive pursuit of justice too early in the recovery process might prompt the resumption of violence or a return to the status quo, as perpetrators try to avoid prosecution (Rigby 2001, p. 4; Huyse 2003b, p. 103).

Along similar lines, Murphy (2007) has suggested that the establishment or re-establishment of Fullerian mutual respect for the law better serves the healing process. She objects to the equating of political reconciliation with forgiveness, which she says belongs to the realm of interpersonal relationships. According to her, 'Interpersonal relationships differ from impersonal relations characteristic of members of a society in general,' whereas 'Political relationships are fundamentally relationships among strangers, whose interactions are defined and shaped by economic, political and legal institutions' (Murphy 2007, p. 855). As such, political reconciliation does not entail or require forgiveness. Instead, people should strive to achieve a situation where all are committed to respect and observe the rule of law. She points out that in the Fullerian view, a social order that is brought about by law is conducive to substantive justice. For her, respect for the rule of law assists one to know that injustice exists and its practice encourages a systematic pursuit of injustice. Murphy sees little value in trying to overcome negative emotions as a way of building or repairing political relationships. To her, what is important is to change interactions so that anger, hatred and resentment are prevented from developing.

While I agree that the mutual respect of the rule of law is an important part of the process of healing, I do not concur that it is all that is needed for a successful process. Future negative emotions might be prevented from developing, but what about the existing ones? How does holding on to the rule of law actually deal with these? Further, it is not always true that political relationships are strictly impersonal. One only needs to look at Rwanda, the Balkans and indeed, Zimbabwe, to realise just how intertwined these relationships are. Victims live in the same neighbourhood as perpetrators or, at the very least, members of the perpetrator group. Invariably, interpersonal dynamics will come to play. Miroslav Volf also seems to perceive the limitations of an approach based only on mutual respect for the law:

> The enforcement of justice would rectify past wrongs but would not create communion between victims and perpetrators… Personal and group identities are not defined simply from within individual or group, apart from relationships with their near and distant neighbours. If we are in part who we are because we are embedded in a nexus of relations that make other parts of ourselves then we cannot be properly healed without our relationships being healed too. The pursuit of justice, even if per possible fully successful, would satisfy our sense of what is right but would not heal us (Volf 2001, p. 40).

Restorative justice, it can be argued, better serves the ideals of grassroots peacebuilding and community healing. Restorative justice can be described as 'a problem-solving approach to crime which involves the parties, themselves, and the community generally, in an active relationship with statutory agencies' (Marshall 2003, p. 28). Usually, parties with a stake in a particular offence, decide collectively how to deal with its outcome and its implications for the future, their collective future. This entails 'identifying and addressing the harms, needs and obligations', a process designed to 'heal and to put things as right as possible' (Zehr 2008, p. 3). Sometimes this might mean direct assistance to the victims, like finances or some other forms of material assistance. Alternatively, it could be symbolic forms of reparations, such as setting up facilities to benefit the whole community or affirmative community development, as oppression is usually tied to both economic and political marginalisation of the victim communities.

The goal of restorative justice is above all to restore, as far as possible, relations between the victim and the offender in the context of their community (Huyse 2003b, p. 110). In restorative justice processes, the victim is given centre stage, unlike in criminal or retributive justice where, by default, the perpetrator has prominence. According to Howard Zehr (2008, p. 3), restorative justice has three assumptions, these being that crime is a 'violation of people and of interpersonal relationships', and that they 'create obligations' on the part of the perpetrator, the central obligation being to right the wrongs done.

The following have been suggested as summarising the basic tenets of restorative justice:

- Restorative justice is concerned far more about restoration of the victim and the victimised community than the costly punishment of offenders.
- It elevates the importance of the victim in the criminal justice process through increased involvement, input and services.
- It requires that offenders be held directly accountable to the person or community they have victimised.
- It encourages the entire community to be involved in holding the offender accountable and promoting a healing response to the needs of victims and offenders.
- More emphasis is placed on getting offenders to accept responsibility for their behaviour and make amendments, wherever possible, than on severity of punishment.

- It recognises a community responsibility for the social conditions that contribute to offender behaviour (Huyse 2003b, p. 111).

This process has the potential to better create a more enabling environment for both individual and community healing than does retributive justice or the Fullerian mutual respect for law because, as we have argued, justice by and of itself does not fully satisfy the needs of the victims. The physical and psychological damage caused by violent conflict, more often than not, cannot be fully repaired so 'justice will therefore always be justice only in a limited sense, as it will be impossible to do justice comprehensively' (Theissen 2004, p. 16).

### *4.5.2 Truth and Truth-telling*

*In the name of reconciliation, some ask that we sacrifice truth. The burden of truth will not disappear—we demand to know. This much is not negotiable.*

Father Michael Lapsley (in Rothstein 1999, p. 210)

*Not to know is a terrible thing.*

Elshtain (2003, p. 57)

Truth-telling is another important step in the trajectory of healing. As is so often the case, especially in state oppression of its citizens, much information is concealed from the public eye. For instance, in Argentina, South Africa, Zimbabwe and Chile, authorities caused the disappearance of many of their opponents, while others died under mysterious circumstances, leaving their families without any clear understanding of what took place. It becomes paramount therefore that the truth of what happened in the dark days be exposed to facilitate healing and reconciliation (Staub/Pearlman 2001, p. 207).

Knowing the truth of what happened to one's loved ones is necessary at both the individual and community levels. At an individual level, those who have lost relatives need to know the truth of what happened to their loved ones, so that they can no longer continue to be imprisoned by uncertainty. When one does not know for certain whether a loved one is dead or alive, it is traumatic. Should one accept that that person is dead, or continue to hope for the best? To accept without specific evidence that the person is dead is like a betrayal of that person. Even when the chances are high that the person is dead, accepting the inevitable, especially for parents and spouses, creates an existential dilemma for the living. People will tend to hold on to that thin hope that maybe, just maybe, their loved one is alive. What if the son or daughter comes home tomorrow and finds that he/she has already been written off (Agger/Jensen 1996, pp. 1137–1138)?

Even if people were to get official confirmation that their loved ones are dead, if they do not know where they lie and in what state, they do not get peace of mind. This is particularly so for Africans. It is important to bury the dead in an acceptable manner and to know where they are buried. There are rituals that are performed annually at the grave, especially that of an adult. It is also believed that the spirits of the dead would never rest if they have not been buried according to cultural practices. Such spirits would roam the earth and bring a curse upon the family because they are angry. A happy spirit brings blessings to the living (on which, see Eppel 2006). In situations like this the living will never have peace of mind, not knowing how their loved ones died and where they are buried.

Further, when the truth of what happened to victims is spoken about publicly and accurately, it acknowledges the pain and suffering of those affected and can provide a basis for healing and reconciliation. In addition to validating the victims' stories, it also helps them overcome the tendency to feel that something must be wrong with them, which frequently accompanies such experiences (Staub/Pearlman 2001, p. 207). When victims are given the opportunity to tell their stories in a safe and affirming environment, the process can be restorative for them. The story of trauma, shame and humiliation is transformed, through the process of testimony, to a story of courage, hope and a recovery of self and all that was lost through the traumatic experience. When a victim has to confront once more the painful events and re-experience the emotions they felt, then it allows for grief and mourning and gives him/her the opportunity to clarify in their minds the events and their chronology. As Martha Minow points out:

> By confronting the past, the traumatised individuals can learn to distinguish the past, present and the future. When the work of knowing and telling the story has come to an end, the trauma then belongs to the past; the survivor can face the work of building a future. Coming to know that one's suffering is not solely a private experience, best forgotten, but instead an indictment of a social cataclysm, can permit individuals to move beyond trauma, hopelessness, numbness, and preoccupation with loss and injury… Holding in the account of what happened exacerbates the trauma. In contrast, speaking in a setting where the experience is acknowledged can be restorative (Minow 1998, p. 67).

The poignancy of this fact is brought home by the testimony of one of the victims who participated in the proceedings of the South African TRC: 'I feel what… has brought my sight back, my eyesight back, is to come here and tell the story. I feel what has been making me sick all the time is the fact that I couldn't tell my story. But now… it feels like I have my sight back by coming here and telling my story' (Tutu 1999, p. 167). When the story which the authorities were trying to suppress is no longer the victim's alone, it grants one a certain amount of justice and freedom (Shriver 2003, p. 31). There are, however, other authors who urge caution in the use of formal mechanisms of truth-telling, arguing that the efficacy of this particular process is ambiguous. They point out that there have been cases where the cathartic effect of the testimonies has been short-lived and, at times, victims have been retraumatised after giving their testimonies in a public place (McGrew 2006; Mendeloff 2004; Laplante/Theidon 2007). There is therefore a need to balance the formal and public mechanisms with those that are more personal, in smaller groups and in an environment that honours, empathises and offers the story-tellers support in the aftermath of their testimonies.

However, the whole process of truth finding can sometimes be divisive. The truth of what happened in people's histories is often contestable, more so if that truth implicates one group as perpetrators of violence and oppression. Hearing or recording victims' stories is one thing but trying to come up with a truth palatable to all parties concerned is another. It is a complex process, fraught with many pitfalls and requires very careful handling if it is to have the healing effect it is meant to have.

### *4.5.3 Forgiveness as Healing*

*The question of whether a society should forgive certain wrongs is distinct from the question of whether individual victims should.*

T. Forsberg (2003, p. 69)

*Human forgiveness does not remove guilt.*

Miroslav Volf (2001, p. 24)

While, for a long time, the concept of forgiveness has been viewed as strictly belonging to the religious arena, it has recently found itself in the political (e.g. Rigby 2001; Shriver 1999, 2003; Staub/Pearlman 2001) and scientific arenas (Enright et al. 1998; North 1998; Worthington 2001; Yandell 1998). However, the acceptance of this concept is not without its controversy, particularly in politics where there is a debate raging about its relevancy, especially at communal or group level. People like Couper (1998), Shriver (2003) and Elshtain (2003) see an active role for forgiveness in politics and society, while Minow (1998) and Chapman (2001) argue that forgiveness occurs at the individual rather than communal level.

Worthington (2001) defines forgiveness as the replacement of the coldness of unforgiveness with strong positive emotions, in such a way that unforgiveness is totally overwhelmed by it. He defines unforgiveness as a cold emotional mixture, 'consisting of resentment, bitterness, hatred, hostility, residual anger and fear' (Worthington 2001, pp. 162–163). Forgiveness is the 'willingness to abandon one's right to resentment, negative judgement, and indifferent behaviour toward one who unjustly injured us, while fostering the underserved qualities of compassion, generosity and even love toward him/her' (Enright et al. 1998, pp. 46–47). Staub et al. (2005, p. 301) simply describe it as the 'letting go of anger and desire for revenge' (see also Tutu 1999, p. 273).

Forgiveness therefore implies that a community or an individual chooses to forego its right to revenge in favour of some form of peaceful coexistence and a willingness on both sides to reconstruct a new political community. It could be described as the acceptance of the other, although not necessarily requiring warm feelings or emotions towards them (Chapman 2001, p. 253). Botcharova (2001, p. 271) sees forgiveness as occurring when a group's 'sense of victimhood is understood, respected, and properly addressed'. This is a crucial step in the process of forgiveness because it validates the victims' experiences and feelings, accepts that wrong has been done against them, acknowledges the harm done by the perpetrator and creates a conducive environment in which this can happen.

When a larger portion of the community, particularly the critical mass of the medium and top grassroots levels of society, has managed to heal its traumas and processed its sense of victimhood, it gives hope that a different environment from the war atmosphere can be created that fosters peace and reconciliation (Botcharova 2001, p. 273). Part of this process requires that the past be honestly confronted and dealt with in ways that engender the spirit of forgiveness within a community. As Tutu has said:

> True forgiveness deals with the past, all of the past, to make the future possible. We cannot go on nursing grudges even vicariously for those who cannot speak for themselves any longer. We have to accept that what we do, we do for generations past, present and yet to come. This is what makes a community a community or a people a people - for better or for worse (Tutu 1999, p. 279).

Addressing the past is an important step in the process of forgiveness for a community or individuals as the undealt-with past can hinder healing as it remains ensconced in the collective memory of a community. Michael Ignatieff illustrates this phenomenon well:

> What seems apparent in the former Yugoslavia is that the past continues to torment because it is not in the past. These places are not living in a serial order of time but in a simultaneous one, in which the past and present are a continuous, agglutinated mass of fantasies, distortions, myths, and lies… Crimes can never safely be fixed in the historical past; they remain locked in the internal present, crying out for vengeance (in Minow 1998, pp. 13–14).

Actively and sincerely working through this past makes forgiving a possibility. However, the balance between excessive remembering and what Elshtain (2003) calls, 'knowing forgetting' is extremely important. If the concern for remembering the past is excessive, then the conflicts and divisions of the past will live on, making the healing of wounds impossible. The past then, will continue to dominate the present and will 'overwhelm' the future. In this case:

> Hatred and the search for vengeance can consume people, turning them into mirror images of those they hate. Unless the people manage to forsake their determination to 'get even', there can be no new beginning, no transformation of relationships. Everyone will remain imprisoned in a particular history or mythology, recycling old crimes and hatreds (Rigby 2001, p. 2).

On the other hand, too little remembering of the past results in collective amnesia, and 'empties the future or the selves we carry into the future' (Elshtain 2003, p. 48). The past forms part of our identity and, trying to pretend that horrible things have not happened in our past, is an exercise in futility. This approach often results in authorities repressing any discussion of past atrocities (Adam/Adam 2000, p. 37). This does not contribute to the creation of ideal conditions for forgiveness, but instead perpetuates anger, resentment, hatred, pain and the desire to revenge.

What is needed is a 'knowing forgetting', which is described as 'a way to release present-day agents from the burden of the past, in order that they may not be weighed down by it utterly' (Elshtain 2003, p. 48). This does not require the forgetting of the past altogether but rather requires that the past be kept alive 'as a tradition that must be continuously engaged' (Elshtain 2003, p. 50). The past must be recollected, but people must not be entirely defined by it so that they come to be seen as perpetrator or victim, rather than as 'an accountable human agent' (Elshtain 2003, p. 51).

The onus to forgive is the prerogative of the victim, and the victim only, and should not be required of them or forced upon them (Rigby 2001; Minow 1998). Forgiveness has a moral value and is not done primarily for one's own benefit. It is an 'outward-looking response and other directed' (North 1998, p. 19). There are however some benefits that accrue to the one who forgives, even in the absence of the ideal conditions discussed in Sect. 4.4.

Wrongs done against an individual, if not dealt with, are likely to affect the person and their relationships with those around them. Forgiveness by the victim has the effect of preventing the harm done from continuing to damage their psyche and self-esteem and thus distorting their relationships. It also has the power to release the victim from being haunted by the perpetrator, often long after the incident. Unforgiveness continues to bind the victim to the wrongdoer, in thoughts and emotionally. The victim continues to feel anxiety, nervousness, depression, suspicion and mistrust; by allowing this to persist, the victim has allowed his very existence to be dominated and defined by the perpetrator (North 1998, p. 18). The victim is still in his attackers' grasp. Not only did they violate and harm him in the past, but as long as he holds on to the unforgiveness, his present and future has also been stolen. This is not to say that forgiveness will necessarily change all the harm done; indeed, 'there are wrongs that can never be put right' (Elshtain 2003, p. 49). What the act of forgiveness does is to liberate the person emotionally and psychologically (Gobodo-Madikizela 2008, p. 97; Yandell 1998, p. 39). I believe it is acceptable to feel anger, hatred, hurt, and a desire for revenge for a time but, if one's painful memories are consumed with these intense feelings perennially, then one has become the victimizer's prisoner (see Jaeger 1998, p. 14; Agger/Jensen 1996, p. 204). By letting go of these negative emotions, one frees oneself from being the perpetual victim of the perpetrator (Jaeger 1998, p. 18; Smedes 1996, pp. 78–81). By forgiving, individuals are freed from a condition of stress created by unforgiveness and the past is not allowed to continue to dominate their lives (Worthington 2001; North 1998, p. 18). Forgiveness can heal memories. It can cleanse bitter and aggressive emotions and allow individuals to focus on making themselves better and happier people (Muller-Fahrenholz 1997, p. 38).

However, while admitting that victims indeed have a lot to gain from letting go of hatred and vengeance, even when the perpetrators are unrepentant, Minow (1998) asserts that forgiveness is not necessarily the vehicle for this. She believes victims can find relief through professional and psychological help, without having to forgive. She says that 'learning to manage or extinguish pain and resentment, becoming able to sleep and get on with life, to coexist with former enemies, are valuable; but they do not require, entail, nor necessarily accompany grants of forgiveness' (Minow 1998, p. 20). She seems to favour truth-telling as the best way to bring about healing to the victims of atrocities.

The biggest argument against forgiving is that some see it as requiring victims and their families to give up the pursuit for justice (Minow 1998; Enright et al. 1998). However, as Volf (2001) points out, forgiveness is not found outside of justice.

> Forgiveness is possible only against a backdrop of a tacit affirmation of justice. Forgiveness always entails blame… To offer forgiveness is at the same time to condemn the deed and accuse the doer; to receive forgiveness is at the same time to admit the deed and accept the blame (Volf 2001, p. 45).

So, forgiveness does not mean an acceptance or tolerance of injustice; it is possible to forgive a person and still take legal action if required (Enright et al. 1998, pp. 48–490). Forgiveness does not cross out the crime itself but the effects of the distortions it has on relations with the wrongdoer and sometimes with others as well (North 1998, p. 17). A priest working with victims of state repression in Chile put it this way:

> …I tell them it is not necessary to renounce the demand for justice in order to forgive. Justice is something positive, because, in a way, justice also liberates the criminal. He needs justice to be able to become conscious of what he has done… to forgive is not to renounce justice (Agger/Jensen 1996, p. 204).

However, in practice, more often than not, victims find themselves having to give up a big part of their claim for justice, as Martha Minow has pointed out. Her fear stems from the fact that governmental bodies mandated with the task of dealing with the painful past, tend to understand forgiveness to mean granting amnesty to offenders and encouraging forgetfulness, with no recourse for the victims (Minow 1998, pp. 15–17).

To conclude this discussion on forgiveness, we need to note that there is a difference between individual and socio-political forgiveness. According to Montiel (2002), forgiveness happens on two planes: the individual/private and the socio-political/public levels. At the private level, it happens within an individual and might be expressed between two people. Socio-political forgiveness is between and among large groups of people; it happens when a whole group of those who have been hurt by the actions of another group engages that group in the process of addressing the harm done. It happens in the realm of the conflictual intergroup relationship and not necessarily at an interpersonal level. On the other hand, where individuals have been personally hurt by a particular action that happened during the conflict, the forgiveness process is a private experience that depends on the psychological readiness of the person concerned and, in this case, only the victim can offer forgiveness (Montiel 2002, pp. 271–272). As Forsberg (2003, p. 69) points outs, socio-political forgiveness is not a substitute for individual forgiveness. Societal forgiveness in my view serves to create the right conditions for people to work on forgiveness at an individual and private level.

## 4.6 Reconciliation

While reconciliation has become an important concept in the peacebuilding field, it nevertheless is still a controversial term, understood and defined differently by various people (Bloomfield 2006, p. 3). However, there is general agreement on its importance in the process of the socio-political healing of communities after atrocities. It is '… an essential (and essentially political) ingredient in peacebuilding, just as central and necessary as economic reconstruction, legal reform and all other post-violence reconstructive and preventative measures' (Bloomfield 2006, p. 9).

### *4.6.1 Thin and Thick Approaches to Reconciliation*

The process of reconciliation ranges between what has been called the 'thin' to the 'thick' frameworks. A thin conception of reconciliation would be seen as those processes that focus on impersonal aspects such as the ending of violence, the creation of democratic state institutions, retributive justice and the (re)establishing of mutual respect for the rule of law (Hoogenboom/Vielle 2008, p. 17; Adelman 2004; see also Murphy 2007). The focus is on minimal conditions for simple co-existence and the avoidance of dealing with conflicts violently. Thick approaches are understood to be more intimate and interpersonal and would include developing a shared vision, mutual healing and restoration; the focus is on relationships (Borer 2004; Nagy 2002; Crocker 1999). This thin/thick continuum is best illustrated by the matrix below (Fig. 4.1):

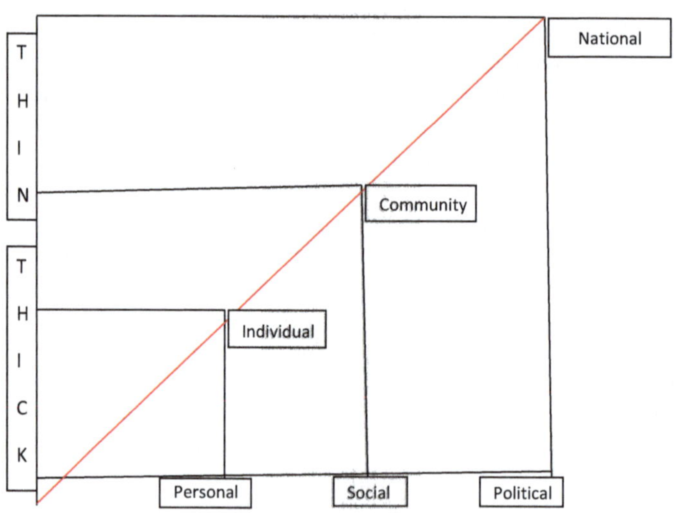


**Fig. 4.1** Reconciliation matrix adapted from F. Du Toit. *Source* Du Toit (2011) interview. Permission was granted by Fanie Du Toit, South Africa, 19 April 2017

According to this matrix, thick reconciliation is at the lower end of the social order. It happens at an individual level, and involves forgiving the 'enemy' at a personal level, seeking to deal with the relationship that was affected by the wrong done. The emphasis is on dealing with the negative emotions of hurt, hatred, resentment, anger and the desire for revenge. In between the two poles lies a zone of moderation and reconciliation at a communal level. Here, collective identity and memory are the focus. Adversaries engage in a dialogue to seek a compromise, a way to co-exist peacefully and to (re)establish some form of relationship that recognises that there is interdependence between the two groups (Lederach 1997, p. 27). At the top end, the thin approach happens at a national level and is primarily political, focusing on the rule of law. Issues of forgiveness are not a concern of this approach, and reconciliation is not about interpersonal relationships but political ones. The concern is about the rule of law (the Fullerian mutual respect for the rule of law), criminal justice and trials, and to an extent truth commissions are the means used to achieve the goal. This is the approach advocated by Murphy (2007) and Minow (1998), among others. These approaches within different societal levels are not necessarily opposed to each other, nor is one better than the other. However, if reconciliation is to be effective it must not be restricted to only a narrow level of society; rather, following Lederach's (1997, pp. 45–46) pyramid, a holistic approach that will deal with the top, middle and bottom strata must be adopted.

### 4.6.2 *Towards a Common Understanding of Reconciliation*

According to the IDEA Handbook (2003), reconciliation is the process of finding a way in which former adversaries learn to live alongside each other, without necessarily loving or forgiving each other, nor forgetting the past. It is to co-exist with the 'other' and to develop sufficient cooperation in that order that the parties have better lives together than they might have separately. Reconciliation therefore is 'a process through which a society moves from a divided past to a shared future' (IDEA 2003, p. 12). For Dawson (2001, p. 219), reconciliation takes place 'when you and I (sic) begin to enjoy intimate fellowship with our previous enemies, people who have tempted us to bitterness by hurting us'. In a social context, intimacy might not necessarily take the same form as in interpersonal relations, nor might it be possible. Slabbert's (2000, p. 70) definition probably better portrays the reality of communal forgiveness. He says it is 'a relationship that is restored to the extent that the parties can move on in peace while accepting each other's integrity'. This view is supported by Staub et al. (2005) who see reconciliation occurring when members of the formerly hostile groups 'mutually accept' each other. This acceptance should be accompanied by not only positive attitudes but also positive actions whenever possible. For them, the most important element in reconciliation is the change of 'psychological orientation' toward the other. Structures and institutions that promote and serve reconciliation are important, but they need to be accompanied by this positive attitude. The primary aim of any reconciliation effort is to create instruments that allow the two sides to engage each other on the level of their humanness. In fact, the word reconciliation implies a pre-existing relationship that has been interrupted by the violence and is therefore in need of a conciliatory effort to restore it.

Kelman (1999) suggests three conditions that are needed for reconciliation and mutual acceptance to occur. Firstly, the parties in a conflict must mutually accept each other's national identity; as we noted in (Sect. 2.4), the modern intra-state violent conflicts are aimed at disenfranchising a particular identity group. This process of trying to dominate the other often means that the targeted group's members are treated as if they are foreigners in their country. Accepting the other then, entails the acknowledgement of the each other's legitimate right to be who they are and the fact that they belong to the same nation. People might have different ethnic identities, but have one national identity.

Secondly, there needs to be an acceptance of the other's basic humanity, and a respect for their life, welfare and dignity. It calls for the rejection of 'extreme acts of dehumanization' such as indiscriminate killing, torture and similar acts. On the positive side, it requires the cultivation of new attitudes that are inclusive and respectful of the other. For Elshtain, it means that:

> One no longer begins with the deadly a priori that the majority or a sizeable proportion of one's fellow country men and women are outsiders and enemies. Rather we are all enclosed within a single socio-political frame and enfolded within a common political-ethical horizon (Elshtain 2003, p. 59).

Finally, acceptance requires a cultivation of a sense of security and dignity for both communities; this is the essence of transformed relationships (Kelman 1999, pp. 198–199).

There is another school of thought that sees different dynamics at play in national reconciliation as opposed to individual reconciliation. Given that the contexts and demands of the two are different, they demand different 'ingredients' in addressing them. In the political process, the concern is about the bigger picture and, as noted above, it is less ambitious about the intimate issues of forgiveness, healing and apology (Bloomfield 2006, p. 10). According to Charles Villa-Vicencio:

> Political reconciliation is not dependent on the kind of intimacy that religions and some forms of individual reconciliation may demand. Rather, statecraft and politics require peaceful co-existence… Forgiveness may come later, after the creation of confidence and building of trust (Villa-Vicencio 2004, p. 4).

While agreeing about the necessity of reconciliation Theissen (2004) insists that ensuring peaceful coexistence should be the priority. What is important for her is the creation of structures that allow for the cessation of the pillars of violence (see also Dwyer 2003, p. 108).

Huyse (2003a) sees reconciliation as having two dimensions: the backward-looking and forward-looking dimensions. The backward-looking process consists of personal healing for survivors, compensation, (re)building of nonviolent relationships between individuals and communities and an acceptance of a common vision for the future as well as understanding of the past. The forward-looking aspect seeks to enable both victims and perpetrators to move on with their lives and the establishment of a civilised political dialogue and equitable power sharing (Huyse 2003a, p. 19). This two-pronged perspective is succinctly summed by Lederach's statement that reconciliation

> Represents a place, the point of encounter where concerns about both the past and the future can meet. Reconciliation-as-encounter suggests that space for the acknowledging of the past and envisioning of the future is the necessary ingredient for reframing the present. For this to happen, people must find ways to encounter themselves and their enemies, their hopes and their fears (Lederach 1997, p. 27).

It is worth noting, however, that in practice this is not a simple and straight forward process. When a society is trying to deal with the experiences of a painful and sordid past, the search for peace is a complex and delicate work. Reconciliation is not a linear process but rather a see-saw activity which is long, unpredictable and difficult (Huyse 2003a).

Perhaps a useful approach would be to see reconciliation as the 'over-arching process which includes the search for truth, justice, forgiveness, healing and so on' (Bloomfield 2003, p. 12). These become the 'instruments' that together work towards the attainment of reconciliation, rather than being antagonistic to it. This approach takes care of the debate about the incompatibility of reconciliation and justice, or truth and justice and so on. Reconciliation becomes then, 'the overall relationship-oriented process within which these diverse instruments are the constitutive parts' (Bloomfield 2006, p. 11). Reconciliation is made possible by the working in unison of truth-telling, restorative justice, healing and reparation (Huyse 2003a, p. 24).

## 4.7 Case Studies of Community-Driven Healing Processes

There has been limited documentation of examples of healing efforts of communities that have dealt, or are seeking to deal with their painful memories, in the face of active governmental resistance or lack of support. Chile's healing programme started during the days of repression, while another two grassroots-based programmes—Rwanda and Ireland—had support from the government or at the very least were not prevented from operating. Nevertheless, these community-based programmes hold valuable lessons for activities for this research.

### *4.7.1 Chile*

In their book, *Trauma and Healing under State Terrorism*, Agger/Jensen (1996) describe the trauma healing strategies carried out in Chile by the human rights movements during the years of dictatorship (1970s and early 1980s). Many Chilean people had suffered physical, psychological and social injuries; others had family members who had disappeared; and some survivors had 'confessed' under torture, resulting in guilt and shame. An interesting aspect of this intervention is that it was going on during the years of violence and suppression, whereas, in most cases, such interventions tend to happen afterwards. According to the authors, those that had been traumatised were unlikely to find professional help and had to find ways of self-healing. Participation in the human rights groups of the movements opposed to the state was one way of dealing with the hurts. Groups such as, the *Association of Ex-Political Prisoners* and groups of witnesses from the various torture houses in Chile were helpful in this regard. Involvement in pro-social actions and self-disclosure in these groups facilitated the healing process. Helping other survivors who had suffered the trauma also counteracted the feelings of being a victim. However, the authors note that at times this self-help was not enough and those who had disclosed information under duress or torture would have to hide their shame and the guilt of having betrayed the movement.

Over time, psychologists and psychiatrists became involved in the interventions and offered psychotherapy. The three pillars of this healing work were *denunciation, investigation* and *treatment.* One of the methods used was what is called 'de-privatisation', a consciousness-raising procedure which allowed survivors to see their traumatic experiences from a broader political perspective. The use of testimonies as part of therapy became one of the important methods devised in the healing process. Started as a way to document the atrocities in order to expose the regime, it was found that the therapeutic value of having people record their stories on tape was an important tool. While it was painful to tell the stories, it helped the survivors to confirm their experiences.

Another aspect of the healing process was to help people redevelop trust in others, since torture tends to destroy trust. Tortured people tend to suffer disruptions in some cognitive self-schemes involving beliefs, assumptions and expectations about self and the world. The most important schemes are those that are related to one's frame of reference and psychological needs for safety, trust, esteem, independence, power and intimacy. Accordingly, Chilean psychotherapists developed new models for their work which involved the following steps:

1. Catharsis and reconstruction of the traumatic experience.
2. Alleviation of symptoms.
3. Emotional elaboration of the traumatic experience.
4. Linking the traumatic experience to the existential meaning of the subject's life.
5. Recovery of his or her role.
6. Reframing of the traumatic experience in the context of the subject's life experiences.
7. Reorganisation of the existential project: continuity between the past, the present and the future.
8. Recovery of collective links.
9. Confrontation of marital problems and problems in relationships with other family members because of the torture experience (Agger/Jensen 1996, pp. 109–110).

Another relevant aspect of the Chilean healing processes was the work with families of those who had disappeared. The *Association of Family Members of the Disappeared* was formed during the dictatorship by families whose loved ones had disappeared at the hands of the oppressors. Participants were encouraged to join others on the streets to protest the disappearances. Although this exposed them to the dangers of the regime, it nevertheless resulted in first steps towards the connection of private and political pain. The survivors' groups enabled families to deprivatise their pain, at least partly. The disappearance was no longer seen as a suffering inflicted on their specific family, but as a political act intended to suppress the collective by those in power.

At a psychotherapeutic level, family members were helped to deal with the reality of living without the knowledge of what happened to a family member, not knowing whether they were dead or alive and whether to 'move on' or 'hold on'. Patients were helped through a therapeutic process that aimed to facilitate the assimilation of the contradictions. That is, it is possible to be both weak and strong, both to mourn and to fight. These people also took part in the testimony element, where families together, in the presence of a counsellor, spoke about their loss and pain. Survivors were also helped to link their traumatic experiences within the social and political context of their time in order to reframe the events. The damage was seen as affecting the whole society and hence a new societal context became an important element in the healing process. These groups held collective mass ritual purification meetings at stadiums, which contributed to the families' healing processes. Ultimately, the recognition of their situations by the Truth Commission established by the new government contributed immensely to their healing process as well (Agger/Jensen 1996, pp. 146–149). Much of the Chilean intervention was carried out by professional psychologists and psychiatrists, whose sole concern was their clients' wellbeing. Issues of forgiveness and reconciliation were hardly ever discussed and the principles of peacebuilding were not the motivating drive. Theirs was a clinical approach carried out in a community setting. However, the environment of fear and terror created by the state has similarities with the Matabeleland situation, as well as the fact that there was no government acknowledgement or involvement. In fact, if anything, both the participants and the practitioners faced certain danger from the state.

### 4.7.2 Rwanda

Staub et al. (2005) describe a healing, reconciliation and forgiveness programme they designed for local practitioners in Rwanda. All four of the authors are professional psychologists but their approach is a peacebuilding one. A peacebuilding approach seeks to deal not only with the victim's trauma, but also addresses the root causes of the violent conflict, as well as issues of forgiveness and reconciliation in the context of wider community relationships. The programme was designed to reach large groups so as to bring communal healing and involved a nine-day training programme for selected practitioners from various local initiatives already involved in peacebuilding programmes. The programme's approach was both psycho-educational and experiential and addressed five issues:

(i) *Understanding genocide* gave the participants an insight into the dynamics of the causes of genocide, helping them appreciate why human beings would engage in such unthinkable acts.
(ii) *Understanding the effects of trauma and victimisation and paths to healing* enabled participants to better deal with their trauma. The framework used was a constructivist self-development theory which suggests that the wide range of psychological, behavioural, somatic and spiritual responses to violence are in fact normal consequences of victimisation and the symptoms are presented as adaptations. This framework offers hope which is a basic aspect of healing. The core concepts of this framework, which are essential for recovery, are respect, information, connection and hope. They also tried as much as possible to normalise the experience of traumatic stress, to depathologise the vast problems faced by people in recovery and to empower the survivors to become active in their own healing process.
(iii) *Understanding basic psychological needs*; these being security, trust, esteem, positive identity, feelings of effectiveness and control, positive connections to other people, and comprehension of reality and of one's place in the world and spiritual needs.
These first three topics were done through brief interactive lectures, large group discussions and small group discussions of ideas from the lectures as they applied to individuals' personal experiences during and after the genocide.
(iv) *Sharing of painful experiences in an empathetic context* was an experiential activity, where participants expressed themselves in writing, drawing and thinking about one's painful experiences during the genocide. This was followed by sharing of the experiences in small groups with group members responding empathically to each other's stories.
(v) *The dangers of vicarious traumatisation* involved one session spent alerting the participants to the dangers of this. Sometimes helpers get traumatised through prolonged exposure to the stories of the survivors. This was so that they could understand themselves and know how to care for themselves.

Other groups like the African Great Lakes Initiative have carried out similar projects in Rwanda (Mahler et al. 2007; Denborough et al. 2008).

### 4.7.3 Northern Ireland

LIVE (Let's Involve the Victims' Experience) was set up in 1999, designed and run by a non-governmental organisation (Glencree Centre for Reconciliation) to facilitate healing and reconciliation amongst and between victims/survivors and perpetrators of the long and intractable conflict, from the 1960s to late 1990s, (de Vries/de Paor 2005, p. 330). This programme was established to build relationships between the victim/survivor communities and to facilitate dialogue between victims/survivors and former combatants willing to engage (White 2003). The programme claims to be addressing healing and reconciliation at grassroots level, which is done through giving participants opportunities to share experiences in a safe environment with people who have had similar experiences (de Vries/de Paor 2005, p. 333). This was done through a process of 10 three-day workshops (mostly on weekends) spread over 12 months. The workshops had three components, which involved structured opportunities for discussion and telling of their stories. Professionals and therapists then provided input on issues that related directly to PTSD and there were social activities designed to build relationships and exchange experiences in an informal environment.

The programme had three stages:

- Stage one consisted of what they called single-identity participants, i.e. victims/survivors who came from one region, with some commonality of history, jurisdiction and so on. This was meant to allow for easier trust building, derived from a sense of safety and familiarity. It also allowed programme staff to listen to and make provision for expectations and fears.
- Stage two was the bilateral and multilateral workshops, involving people either from two or all the three regions of Northern Ireland. Some of the participants were drawn from the single-identity workshops, allowing for continuity and familiarity and making it considerably easier for the participants to feel safe and comfortable, and thus to participate freely.
- Stage three involved dialogue sessions between victims and former members of paramilitary groups. Each session was about four hours long and allowed both sides to come face to face and explore their experiences with the hope of bringing some closure, for the victims in particular (White 2003).

Table 4.1 summarises the stages and steps involved:

**Table 4.1** A composite hierarchy of confrontation and gradual exposure as experienced by participants during a LIVE workshop. *Source* de Vries/de Paor (2005, p. 342)

| |
|---|
| **Level 1: Single identity groups** |
| Step 1: Thinking about attending a LIVE weekend |
| Step 2: Attending the first LIVE weekend |
| Step 3: Being able to relax in the company of other victims/survivors in Glencree |
| Step 4: Listening to other victims/survivors speak about their trauma and thinking about one's own grief or trauma in the presence of others |
| Step 5: Sharing one's own experiences and hurt with other victims/survivors outside the sessions |
| Step 6: Sharing one's own experiences and hurt with other victims/survivors within sessions |
| **Level 2: Dual and multiple identity groups** |
| Step 7: Sharing one's experiences and hurt with victims/survivors from other communities |
| (We may expect that for some people, steps 2–6 will need to be repeated. Others see all victims/survivors in general as allies in their plight. They may not need to go through each of the preceding steps again.) |
| **Level 3: Victims/survivors + ex-combatants of different communities** |
| Step 8: Being at the Glencree Centre with ex-combatants |
| Step 9: Being in the same room with ex-combatants |
| Step 10: Interacting with ex-combatants inside/outside sessions |
| Step 11: Sharing experiences with ex-combatants |
| Step 12: Coming to a mutual understanding and acknowledgement of positions on the basis of sharing and interaction that have taken place |

### 4.7.4 *The International Centre for Conciliation (ICfC) Project*

ICfC is a US-based, non-profit organisation which runs a programme called *Historical Conciliation and Peacemaking* in Israel, Cambodia, Western Europe and some other Asian countries. According to its website, the organisation works with communities that share 'a protracted history of conflict and in which the early signs of volatility express not only current issues but conflicts that transpired at specified and unspecified times.' The historical conciliation process allows groups at loggerheads to conjointly examine collective memory, identity and history, so as to create a shared future that is peaceful, productive and prosperous. They further describe their working environment thus:

> In some inter-group conflicts, members represent ancestors who have transmitted their pained memories of past conflicts. The descendant generation, having internalized their ancestors' pained memories and with their concern to zealously guard their parents' dignity, these descendants are incited to new provocations, resentments, and renewed conflict as a statement of revenge. http://www.centerforconciliation.org (12 June 2010).

This particular description in some ways matches the situation in Matabeleland, where the painful memories of *Gukurahundi* have been, and are being, transmitted to the younger generation who are gradually becoming vocal about it. However, there is a large percentage of primary victims still alive.

The goal of ICfC in dealing with the pained memories is to 'tame the power of the past' but not through repression nor by agreeing to let 'bygones be bygones'. Their approach is to seek what they have described as 'elusive dimensions of parallel histories preserved in those memories that can lead to identification rather than perpetuating the resentment and risking the occasions of volatility and violence'.

The historical conciliation process brings together the members of the different groups involved in a conflict in a safe and conducive environment so they can learn about each other's past; including the suffering that one side might blame the other for inflicting. The strategy is to focus on each side's pain, fears and hopes, and to help participants to appreciate the complexities of the events that have created their painful memories. They are also taught to use the memories of the painful past, to relate them to present problems in the hope of making a better future possible for people on all sides of the conflict. In most cases, although these embattled groups might live close to each other, they have never really had a constructive engagement about what matters most to them. Therefore, this process involves strengthening dialogue and improving listening skills, so that they can engage in a sustained dialogue as a way of problem solving. Initially, trained facilitators lead the groups in this process but, when the group is trained and empowered with the skills to manage their own process, the facilitators withdraw. Through joint decision-making processes the groups may decide to be involved in joint projects, as a way of increasing communication and interaction in order to build confidence and trust amongst themselves, and to help them learn how to live peacefully with each other again.

The process involves five steps as follows:

- Firstly, the conflict in question is *assessed*. It must be determined whether the situation has roots in historical or collective memory, and thus whether the approach of Historical Conciliation is appropriate.
- Secondly, the parties to the conflict in question must be *identified*. Which groups from the community will need to be at the table and who will continue to carry this work forward?
- Thirdly, an intensive *weekend workshop* is held, where sides' hopes, fears, pains and concerns are explored.
- Fourthly, over a period of several months, a *series of eight to ten dialogues* are held, where the groups come together regularly to do the work of sharing and listening. Trained facilitators guide the discussions.
- Lastly, once a level of narrative acknowledgement and understanding has been reached in the dialogue stage, the groups make a plan to undertake a *joint action*. This may be a youth project, an after-school programme, a discussion forum or even plans to hold monthly dinners. Joint action solidifies relationships, builds trust, increases the probability of continued dialogue, and promotes lasting community change.

While this might seem an appropriate model for the Matabeleland situation, there are two things that currently militate against it. Firstly, as already noted in Sect. 3.2, the current environment does not seem conducive for this sort of process. In addition, there has not been a clear admission of any wrongs done and therefore one side might not be willing to participate, notwithstanding the risks involved in engaging in this process at a community level. Secondly, relationships across ethnic lines are complex (see Sect. 1.4). There seems to be a clear distinction, especially among the Ndebele, between hating the Shona in general as a group and having good and often strong relationships with individual Shona neighbours, colleagues etc. It would not therefore be acceptable to a lot of victims to have proxies to engage with. While people hate 'Shona' they know who the masterminds of the atrocities are and this is where they want it to start. In 2007, Grace to Heal took 16 pastors from Mashonaland to one community in Tsholotsho to hear and see first-hand what happened during *Gukurahundi*. During the meeting, some of the pastors tried to offer an apology on behalf of the Shona speaking people. While there can be no doubt that this event was beneficial to the visitors, the benefit to the locals is debatable. One member of a Ndebele pressure group expressed his strong reservations to the author. He felt that all this did was to open more space for the Shonas to 'invade' Matabeleland under licence. So, such approaches might actually affect the integrity of the whole process.

Of these four case studies, the two that seem more applicable to the Matabeleland situation are the Chilean experience and the historical conciliation work done by ICfC. Given the right sort of conditions prevailing, it is possible that the ICfC approach could be adapted to our situation, while the environment in which the Chilean practitioners worked bears resemblance to what is currently prevailing in Zimbabwe concerning *Gukurahundi*.

## 4.8 Conclusion

In this chapter, we have explored the need for healing after extreme violence has occurred in a community. We discussed the fact that collective traumatisation requires the healing of the memories of communities and individuals. It is necessary to create an environment conducive to the creation of trust and reconciliation in a post violence community and this can be achieved through healing the community from its hurts, hate and anger.

Some of the conditions needed for healing to occur are justice, truth-telling, forgiveness and reconciliation. We argued that the best form of justice in community healing is restorative justice, rather than criminal or retributive justice. We also saw that truth-telling can be a form of justice for the victim/survivor community and individuals, because so often people have disappeared and many acts of violence have been committed clandestinely. The telling of the truth helps the community to know what really happened. By sharing their stories, the pain and suffering of individuals is validated. In addition, those with loved ones who have disappeared have a chance to find out what happened and where they might be buried, affording them the prospect of closure.

We discussed the controversy surrounding the issue of forgiveness in politics and described it as the setting aside of negative feelings, such as hatred and the desire for revenge toward the perpetrator. The fact that forgiveness does not mean forgetting or giving up on justice was emphasised. Forgiveness also has important benefits for the forgiver, particularly in being no longer emotionally under the perpetual control of the offender. However, we pointed out that people like Minow (1998) and Murphy (2007) see forgiveness as not being necessary in terms of political forgiveness because they argue that victims/survivors can be helped to deal with negative emotions outside of forgiveness.

Finally, this chapter considered case studies of community-based healing programmes in three countries—Rwanda, Chile, Northern Ireland as well as the US-based ICfC. We noted that, of the three, the Chilean example is the closest to the Zimbabwean situation in that it was carried out under a repressive environment and with no government involvement.

Chapter 5 will review literature on the methodology to be used in this research. This is a participatory action research project, where both the researcher and participants are co-researchers. Participatory action research is not just about the creation of new knowledge; it carries with it the potential for transformation at both social and individual levels.

## References


Adam, H. and Adam, K. 2000. The politics of memory in divided societies. In W. James and L. Van de Vijver (eds.), *After the TRC: reflections on truth and reconciliation in South Africa*. Cape Town: David Philip.

Adelman, H. 2004. *Rule-based reconciliation, roads to reconciliation*. At: http://www.humiliationstudies.org/documents/AdelmanReconciliation.pdf (28 March 2010).

Agger, I. and Jensen, S. B. 1996. *Trauma and healing under state terrorism*. London: Zed.

Aldana, R. 2006. A victim-centred reflection of Truth Commissions and prosecutions as a response to mass atrocities. *Journal of Human Rights*, 5: 106–126.

Bar-Tal, D., Halperin, E. and de Rivera, J. 2007. Collective emotions in conflict situations: societal implications. *Journal of Social Issues*, 63(2): 441–460.

Bloomfield, D. 2003. The context of reconciliation. In D. Bloomfield, T. Barnes, and L. Huyse (eds.), *Reconciliation after violence: a hand book*. IDEA, Stockholm, Sweden.

Bloomfield, D. 2006. *On good terms: clarifying reconciliation*. At: www.berghof-foundation.org/fileadmin/redaktion/Publications/Papers/Reports/br14e.pdf (28 March 2010).

Borer, T. A. 2004. Reconciling South Africa or South Africans? Cautionary notes from the TRC. *African Studies Quarterly*, 8(1): 19–38.

Botcharova, O. 2001. Implementation of track two diplomacy: developing a model for forgiveness. In R. Helmick and R. Petersen (eds.), *Forgiveness and reconciliation: religion, public policy and conflict transformation*. Radnor, PA: Templeton Foundation Press.

Chapman, A. 2001. Truth commissions as instruments of forgiveness and reconciliation. In R. Helmick and R. Peterson (eds.), *Forgiveness and reconciliation: religion, public policy and conflict transformation*. Radnor, Philadelphia: Templeton Foundation.

Cobban, H. 2007. *Amnesty after atrocity? Healing nations after genocide and war crimes.* Boulder, US: A Paradigm.

Couper, D. 1998. Forgiveness in community: views from an Episcopal priest and former chief of police. In R. D. Enright and J. North (eds.), *Exploring forgiveness.* Madison: University of Wisconsin Press.

Crocker, D. 1999. Reckoning with past wrongs: a normative framework. *Ethics and International Affairs*, 13: 43–64.

Dawson, J. 2001. Hatred's end: a Christian proposal to peacemaking in a new century. In R. Helmick and R. Peterson (eds.), *Forgiveness and reconciliation: religion, public policy and conflict transformation.* Radnor, PA: Templeton Foundation.

Denborough, D., Freedman, J. and White, S. 2008. *Strengthening resistance: the use of narrative practices in working with genocide survivors.* Adelaide: Dulwich Centre Foundation

de Vries, J. M. A. and de Paor, J. 2005. Healing and reconciliation in the L.I.V.E. program in Ireland. *Peace and Change*, 30(3): 329–358.

Dwyer, S. 2003. Reconciliation for realists. In C. A. L. Prager and T. Govier (eds.), *Dilemmas of reconciliation: cases and concepts.* Waterloo, Ontario: Wilfrid Laurier University Press.

Elshtain, J. B. 2003. Politics and forgiveness. In N. Biggar (ed.), *Burying the past: making peace and doing justice after civil conflict.* Georgetown: Georgetown University Press.

Enright, R. D., Freedman, S. and Rique, J. 1998. The psychology of interpersonal forgiveness. In R. D. Enright and J. North (eds.), *Exploring forgiveness.* Madison: University of Wisconsin Press.

Eppel, S. 2006. 'Healing the dead': exhumation and burial as truth-telling and peace-building activities in rural Zimbabwe. In T. A. Borer (ed.), *Telling the truths: truth telling and peace building in post-conflict societies.* Notre Dame, Indiana: University of Notre Dame Press.

Farwell, N. and Cole, J. B. 2002. Community as context of healing: psychosocial recovery of children affected by war and political violence. *International Journal of Mental Health,* 30(4): 19–41.

Finch, R. 2006. Trauma and forgiveness: a spiritual inquiry. *Journal of Spirituality in Mental Health,* 9(2): 27–42. At: http://www.tandfonline.com/doi/abs/10.1300/J515v09n02_03 (13 February 2009).

Forsberg, T. 2003. The philosophy and practice of dealing with the past: some conceptual and normative issues. In R. D. Enright and J. North (eds.), *Exploring forgiveness.* Madison: University of Wisconsin Press.

Gobodo-Madikizela, P. 2008. Trauma, forgiveness and the witnessing dance: making public spaces intimate. *Journal of Analytical Psychology,* 53: 169–188.

Hamber, B. 2003. Healing. In D. Bloomfield, T. Barnes, and L. Huyse (eds.), *Reconciliation after violence: a hand book.* Stockholm: International IDEA.

Hoogenboom, D. and Vielle, S. 2008. Rebuilding social fabric in failed states: examining transitional justice in Bosnia. Conference paper, Canadian Political Scientists annual meeting, Vancouver, BC.

Huyse, L. 2003a. The process of reconciliation. In D. Bloomfield, T. Barnes, and L. Huyse (eds.), *Reconciliation after violent conflict, a handbook.* IDEA, Stockholm.

Huyse, L. 2003b. Justice. In D. Bloomfield, T. Barnes, and L. Huyse (eds.), *Reconciliation after violence: a hand book.* Stockholm: IDEA.

Jaeger, M. 1998. The power and reality of forgiveness: forgiving the murderer of one's child. In R. D. Enright and J. North (eds.), *Exploring forgiveness.* Madison: University of Wisconsin Press.

Kelman, H. 1999. Transforming the relationship between former enemies: a social-psychological analysis. In: In R. L. Rothstein (ed.), *After the peace: resistance and reconciliation.* Boulder, CO, and London: Lynne Rienner.

Laplante, L. J. and Theidon, K. 2007. Truth with consequences: justice and reparations in post-truth commission Peru. *Human Right Quarterly,* 29(1): 228–250. At: http://www.jstor.org/stable/20072794 (29 May 2014).

Lederach, J. P. 1997. *Building peace: sustainable reconciliation in divided societies.* Washington, DC: USIP.

Mahler, B., Ntakarutimana, F. and Niyongabo, A. 2007. Now I am human: testimonies from the healing companions program in Rwanda and Burundi. *Peace Ways AGLI,* 2(2): 4–23.
Marshall, T. 2003. Restorative justice: an overview. In G. Johnstone (ed.), *A restorative justice reader: texts, sources, context.* Willan, Cullompton: Devon.
Mendeloff, D. 2004. Truth-telling, and post conflict peacebuilding: curb the enthusiasm? *International Studies Review*, 6: 355–380. At: http://jstor.org/stable/3699695 (28 May 2014).
Minow, M. 1998. Between vengeance and forgiveness: facing history after genocide and mass violence. Boston: Beacon Press.
Montiel, C. J. 2002. Sociopolitical forgiveness. *Peace Review*, 14(3): 271–277.
McGrew, L. 2006. Justice and reconciliation? Can the trails for the Khmer Rouge bring reconciliation and healing in Cambodia? *NIAS Nytt*, 3: 8–11.
Muller-Fahrenholz, G. 1997. *The art of forgiveness: theological reflections on healing and reconciliation*. Geneva: WCC.
Murphy, C. 2007. Political reconciliation, the rule of law, and genocide. *European Legacy*, 12(7): 853–856.
Nagy, R. 2002. Reconciliation in post-commission South Africa: thick and thin accounts of solidarity. At: http://restorativejustice.org/rj-library/reconciliation-in-post-commission-south-africa-thick-and-thin-accounts-of-solidarity/6294/#sthash.8mrEb644.dpbs (28 March 2010).
North, J. 1998. The 'ideal' of forgiveness: a philosopher's exploration. In R. D. Enright and J. North (eds.), *Exploring forgiveness.* Madison, Wisconsin: University of Wisconsin.
Pintar, J. 2000. Anticipating consequences: what Bosnia taught us about healing the wounds of war. *Human Rights Review*, January–March: 56–66.
Rigby, A. 2001. *Justice and reconciliation: after the violence*. Boulder, Colorado: Lynne Rienner.
Shriver, D. W. 2003. Where and when in political life is justice served by forgiveness? In N. Biggar (eds.), *Burying the past: making peace doing justice after civil conflict.* Georgetown: Georgetown University Press.
Slabbert, F. 2000. Truth without reconciliation, reconciliation without truth. In W. James and L. van de Vijver (eds.), *After the TRC: reflections on truth and reconciliation in South Africa.* Cape Town: David Philips.
Smedes, L. B. 1996. *Forgive and forget: healing the hurts we don't deserve.* San Francisco: Harper.
Staub, E. and Pearlman, L. 2001. Healing, reconciliation and forgiving after genocide and other collective violence. In R. Helmick and R. Peterson (eds.), *Forgiveness and reconciliation: religion, public policy and conflict transformation.* Radnor, Philadelphia: Templeton Foundation.
Staub, E., Pearlman, L. A., Gubin, A. and Hagengimana, A. 2005. Healing, reconciliation, forgiving and the prevention of violence after genocide or mass killings: an intervention and its experimental evaluation in Rwanda. *Journal of Social and Clinical Psychology,* 24(3): 297–334.
Theissen, G. 2004. Supporting justice, co-existence and reconciliation after armed conflict: strategies for dealing with the past. Berghof Research Centre for Constructive Conflict Management. At: www.berghof-foundation.org/fileadmin/redaktion/Publications/Handbook/Articles/theissen_handbook.pdf (20 November 2010).
Tutu, D. M. 1999. *No future without forgiveness.* New York: Doubleday.
Villa-Vicencio, C. 2004. 'Reconciliation.' In C. Villa-Vicencio and E. Doxtader (eds.), *Pieces of the puzzle.* Cape Town: IJR.
Walsh, F. 2007. Traumatic loss and major disasters: strengthening family and community resilience. *Family Process*, 46: 207–227.
Wessells, M. G. 1999. Culture, power, and community: intercultural approaches to psychosocial assistance and healing. In K. Nader, N. Dubrow, and B. Stamm (eds.), *Honouring differences: cultural issues in the treatment of trauma and loss.* New York: Taylor & Francis.
Wessells, M. 2008. Trauma, peacebuilding and development: an African region perspective. At: www.incore.ulst.ac.uk/research/projects/trauma/ (17 July 2010).

White, I. 2003. Victim-combatant dialogue in Northern Ireland. In D. Bloomfield, T. Barnes, and L. Huyse (eds.), *Reconciliation after violence: a hand book.* Stockholm: IDEA.

Worthington, E. L. 2001. Unforgiveness, forgiveness, and reconciliation and their implications for societal interventions. In R. Helmick and R. Peterson (eds.), *Forgiveness and reconciliation: religion, public policy and conflict transformation.* Radnor, Philadelphia: R Templeton.

Yandell, K. E. 1998. The Metaphysics and morality of forgiveness. In R. D. Enright and J. North (eds.), *Exploring forgiveness.* Madison: University of Wisconsin Press.

Zehr, H. 2008. Doing justice, healing trauma-the role of restorative justice in peacebuilding. *Peace Prints: South Asia Journal of Peacebuilding,* 1(1) Spring. At: http://citeseerx.ist.psu.edu/viewdoc/download;jsessionid=E12FA9D67F6DC614E602036FF2ECD646?doi=10.1.1.424.2068&rep=rep1&type=pdf (09 September 2009).

# Chapter 5
# Participatory Action Research

*The definition of action, in terms of how it is expressed in both scope and focus, is essentially limitless. Any concerted effort to remove some impediment that hampers the growth of a group of people, be it structural or ideological, could be defined as action within the framework of PAR*

Kidd/Kralik (2005, p. 89)

## 5.1 Introduction

*Apart from inquiry, apart from the praxis, individuals cannot be truly human. Knowledge emerges only through invention and re-invention, through the restless, impatient, continuing, hopeful inquiry human beings pursue in the world, with the world, and with each other.*

Paulo Freire (1970, p. 72)

*Action research is participative research and all participative research must be action research.*

Reason/Bradbury (2008, p. 4)

In this chapter, I review participatory action research (PAR), what it is, where and when it is used and why I chose it as my research framework. I will also discuss some examples of PAR case studies to illustrate its relevance to a research project of this nature.

## 5.2 What Is Participatory Action Research?

Participatory action research belongs to a fairly new methodology of research used mostly in social sciences. Action research is said to be part of a family of 'practices of living inquiry that aims, in a great variety of ways, to link practice and ideas in



D. Ngwenya, *Healing the Wounds of Gukurahundi in Zimbabwe*,
The Anthropocene: Politik—Economics—Society—Science 19,
https://doi.org/10.1007/978-3-319-66818-5_5

the service of human flourishing' (Reason/Bradbury 2008, p. 1). It is regarded not so much as a methodology but an approach to inquiry which aims to 'create participative communities of inquiry in which qualities of engagement, curiosity, and question posing are brought to bear on significant practical issues' (Reason/Bradbury 2008, p. 1). In other words, this approach is concerned with more than knowledge creation, in the sense that it seeks to address the social problems brought to light by the inquiry. Most importantly, this approach moves away from the traditional practice of viewing researched individuals and communities as sources from which information can be extracted; rather, they participate in the research as co-researchers. Some of the well-known proponents of this approach include Kurt Lewin, Paulo Freire, Robin McTaggart, Jack Whitehead & Jean McNiff.

While action research is carried out by a researcher to improve his/her own practice with the focus on self-improvement, PAR involves all the relevant parties coming together to study a common problem, devise plans to deal with it and implement these plans. This is a collaborative inquiry in which, as Cahill (2007, p. 268) says, 'Those typically 'studied' are involved as decision-makers and co-researchers in some or all the stages of the research.' Rather than being 'studied' by an outsider, this approach encourages the researcher to become an outsider-insider and to treat the participants as research partners rather than just information sources. According to Guishard (2009, p. 86) there is a continuum of research activities between the community-based entities and academic researchers, which have varying levels of participation and control. Participants could be involved in every decision, from deciding the research focus, through to the dissemination of the findings; or they could be involved to a lesser extent in some of the activities of the research project. Whatever their degree of involvement, the non-academic participants are viewed as important members of the research team:

> Ideally, participatory action research aspires to initiate transparent, democratic inquiry; that is collaboratively designed, conducted, analysed and disseminated in the context of equal partnerships with university scientists and members of the disempowered groups. Non-academic research partners are not viewed as passive, unintelligent subjects, but as people who possess valuable insight and experiential knowledge into the conditions and problems that affect their lives; expertise that is parallel and as legitimate as academic knowledge (Guishard 2009, p. 87).

According to Bagnoli/Clark (2010, p. 102), there are four levels at which co-researchers can be involved in a research project. These are:

- Contractual—whereby participants are contracted to take part in a research.
- Consultative—participants are consulted on their opinions.
- Collaborative—participants work with academic researchers on projects devised and controlled by the latter.
- Collegiate—participants work alongside academic researchers.

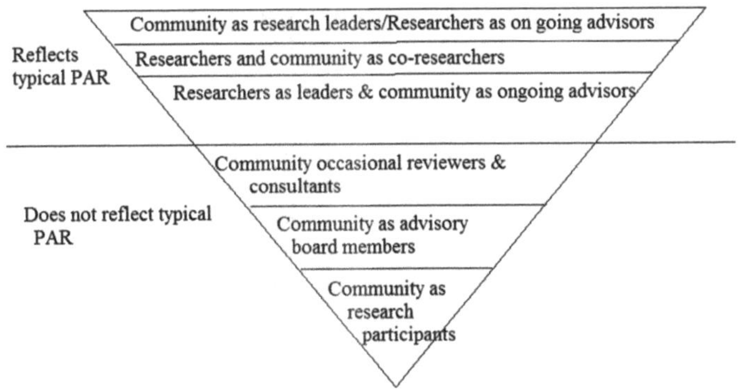


**Fig. 5.1** Levels of participation in research. *Source* Adapted from Weaver/Stark (2006). Permission was granted by the Copyright Clearance Center Inc (CCC) on Taylor and Francis's behalf

Figure 5.1 illustrates the broad spectrum of the levels of participation research. The bottom half of the triangle shows those processes which are at times engaged in by researchers, which are often claimed to be PAR, but in reality, are not, as the community's involvement is only token. This corresponds with Bagnoli and Clark's first two categories above. The top half reflects more authentic approaches to PAR; but even there, there are different levels of community involvement in the research process.

## 5.3 The Practicality of Participatory Action Research

What sets PAR (and other action research approaches) apart from other social sciences research approaches, is that it is not just research, but research which is hoped will be followed by action. It is:

> Action which is researched, changed and re-researched, within the research process by participants… [I]t aims to be an active co-research, by and for those to be helped. Nor can it be used by one group of people to get another group of people to do what is thought best for them—whether that is to implement a central policy or an organisational or service change. Instead it tries to be a genuinely democratic or non-coercive process, whereby those to be helped determine the purposes and outcomes of their own inquiry (Wadsworth 1998, p. 19).

PAR is ideally done by the local people and for themselves. Specific issues to be addressed should be identified by the local people, or in collaboration with them, and the results of the research applied directly to the issue at hand. When ideas are linked to action in this manner, then the potential of participatory action research to contribute to the increased wellbeing (i.e. economic, political, psychological and spiritual) of people and their communities becomes real. PAR, then, works towards the creation of practical outcomes, as well as creating new forms of understanding (Reason/Bradbury 2008, pp. 4–5).

## 5.4 Participatory Action Research and Social Transformation

An important facet of PAR is its emphasis on addressing pertinent issues raised by the inquiry, as opposed to traditional social sciences approaches, which make suggestions for changes that are hardly ever carried out. We have noted from the definition that the goal in participatory action research is not only just to describe reality but to change it (Cahill 2007, p. 268). As Janet Moore points out, 'definitions of participatory research often embody values and ideologies that create a vision of a methodology that goes far beyond a method of obtaining information and data from research subjects to include social change and participant empowerment' (Moore 2004, p. 149).

This approach is intentionally political. It is especially relevant for communities under oppression and tries to make action the catalyst for social change. Grant et al. (2008, p. 589) identify the goals of PAR as being emancipation, empowerment, participatory democracy, and the elimination of social problems:

> Participatory action research has as one of its tenets the importance of addressing power inequities in society. It endeavours to begin the process within the research relationship. Power, as we define it, is a potential which is created within the interaction of relationships and which can be used *over* others as domination or *with* others to make positive change (Grant et al. 2008, p. 592 italics added).

The process itself of deciding to interrogate an existing situation and taking action in order to improve it, is political in the sense that, what one person does, inevitably has consequences for the next person. In questioning the current and historical contexts of a situation, practitioners may discover that there are injustices and must decide whether to try to influence the situation according to what they believe or to go along with the status quo (McNiff/Whitehead 2010). There is no attempt by the researcher(s) for objectivity by distancing oneself/themselves from the situation. (See Sect. 5.4 below for more on subjectivity and values in PAR). The very selection of PAR as a research approach is an indication of the nature of outcome expected by the researchers. Proponents of the approach firmly believe that social change is best determined and achieved by those individuals who are involved in a particular activity. It is also important to note that PAR projects are not started or done solely for the benefit of those who actually participate in the research process. The focus is, or should be, to provide opportunities for the local people to develop strategies and find resources to change their situations for the better (McIntyre 2008). Generally, PAR tries to create what Ghaye et al. (2008) call 'self-critical communities' of people who participate and collaborate in a change process. These communities are committed to learning about the relationship between the situation they find themselves in, the action taken to improve it and the consequences of this. So 'PAR has an emancipating intention, one where participants liberate themselves from the institutional and personal constraints which limit their power to live by their legitimate and freely chosen social values' (Ghaye et al. 2008, p. 363).

According to McIntyre (2008), the range of participant-generated actions varies from changing public policy, to making recommendations to government agencies, to making informal changes in the community that benefit the people who live there, to organising a local event or to simply increasing awareness about an issue that is native to a particular locality. In other words, PAR offers people an opportunity to address events that affect them directly and that contribute to their individual and collective wellbeing. In identifying the actions, it is important to choose issues that the group can effectively address, otherwise failure might add to the feelings of disempowerment they seek to change: 'Acting on something that people have control over is exactly the kind of thing that contributes to people's beliefs that they are creative, knowledgeable, and capable of making a difference in their own lives' (McIntyre 2008, p. 33). In this way, people become aware of their capacity to influence the future. But Grant et al. (2008, p. 596) advice is pertinent for practitioners of PAR: 'In social change work, it is important to achieve 'small wins' rather than expecting large-scale change to occur dramatically.'

An integral part of this process is how knowledge is acquired and disseminated. According to Guishard (2009, p. 87), participatory action research specifically seeks to attend to the 'politics of knowledge production' by problematising and being involved in reflective dialogue about views and ideas that have been traditionally privileged or excluded in research. In PAR, researchers and participants co-generate knowledge through collaborative communicative processes in which everyone's contributions are taken seriously (Greenwood/Levin 1998). This view is buttressed by Farnworth when she says:

> A positivist-realist approach to research considers that reality is something 'out there' to be collected, and analysed, interpreted and presented as objective knowledge about the world. [On the other hand], social constructionism suggests that knowledge about the 'world out there' is produced in a complex process of interaction. There is no 'one reality'; rather people perceive the world in a multitude of ways, which gives rise to multiple realities (Farnworth 2007, p. 273).

PAR is therefore revolutionary because it focuses on working with people to achieve a shared, workable understanding of a particular reality and, in the process, rescues research from the tyranny of the monopoly of knowledge production by academic researchers. PAR recognises the fact that all knowledge is socially constructed. It could be said to be democratic because it enables the participation of all people; equitable as it acknowledges that people are equal in worth; liberating because it provides people freedom from restrictive and oppressive conditions; and life-enhancing because it enables people's full human potential to be expressed (Koch/Kralik 2006, p. 28; Reason/Bradbury 2008; Guishard 2009).

Table 5.1 compares the characteristics of PAR to those of traditional social science research:

**Table 5.1** Comparison of characteristics of traditional social science research and participatory action research. *Source* Moore (2004, p. 148)

| | Traditional social science research | Participatory Action research |
|---|---|---|
| Epistemology | Researchers create new knowledge after researching subjects and analysis of data. | Shared, collaborative approaches to knowledge production. Research for the purpose of change- changing perceptions, understandings and creating action. |
| Principles emphasised | Objectivity, reproducible results, after researching subjects and generalisability. | Participatory, life enhancing, equitable empowerment and action oriented (Stringer 1996). Conscientisation (Freire 1970) and transformation (Hall 1992). |
| Tensions and dichotomies methods | Subjectivity and rigour. Science and social science. | Rigour and social action. Generalisability. Academic status. |
| | A range of methods are used including, surveys, interviews, focus groups, ethnography, case studies, etc. | A wider array of methods is used including surveys, interviews, focus groups, ethnography, case studies, film, autobiography, documentary, drama, storytelling, photo-novels, oral history, community meetings. |
| Relationships and naming | Distance between researcher and researched. Named subjects or research participants. | Active involvement of participants in design and dissemination of results. Named participants, community, collaborators or co-researchers. |
| Level of participation | Subjects participate in research project but rarely in writing, analysis or formulation of research questions. | Participants create research questions, design the study, analyse and interpret, implement and disseminate new knowledge. |
| Power and relationships | Power-oriented: seeking truth, objectivity, universal laws and knowledge (Joyappa/Martin 1996). | Empower-oriented: conscious attempts to balance power (Joyappa/Martin 1996). |
| Control | Researcher has control of research process, research questions and research findings. | Community (includes participants and researcher) has control of research process, research questions, and research findings. |
| Decision-making | Individual or team of researchers make decisions about direction of research. | Group activity: usually a large group, collaborative approach to problem-solving and research directions. |
| Goals | Create new knowledge, seek truth via the objective researcher. | Democratisation of knowledge creation, social change (Stoecker/Bonacich 1992) action and implementation. |

## 5.5 Subjectivity in Participatory Action Research

According to McNiff/Whitehead (2006), positivist forms of research are notionally value- free. That is to say, the researcher tries to stay out of the research, so as not to 'contaminate' it. Even research reports are written in the third person so as to reduce bias and enhance the claim to objectivity. In PAR and related approaches, subjectivity is not only accepted but taken for granted. By subjectivity is meant the 'conscious and unconscious thoughts and notions of an individual, one's sense of oneself and way of understanding one's relation with the world' (Cahill 2007, p. 269). PAR is value-laden and does not try to be neutral, as required by the traditional forms of research; it is accepted that one's values and experiences influence how issues are perceived and research carried out. It begins with the understanding that people—more so those who have experienced historic oppression—have a deep knowledge of their lives and experiences and should help shape the questions and frame the interpretation of research. The participants' individual values come to act as guiding principles in the research (Cahill 2007; McNiff/Whitehead 2006). This does not therefore mean that PAR is unscientific and lacks vigour. On the contrary, it is realistic in the sense that it accepts human realities and that one cannot separate oneself from one's environment and one's values in research. As Schratz/Walker (1995, pp. 60–61) note:

> Social science has only recently come to realise that subjectivity, rather than threatening claims to scientific status, actually marks claims to disciplinary uniqueness. The task of social research has to involve both the exploration of the subjective nature of knowing and the mapping of the world as it is experienced by others. However, this does not mean that research is therapy. What is at stake is the complex interrelationship of the personal/individual with the social, and the ways of thinking about subjectivity as it is expressed in specific social contexts, involving ways of thinking about the self, that are socially rather than individualistically located.

In PAR, the researcher's understanding of reality contributes significantly to the selection and use of research tools and the way results are analysed and interpreted. This approach has the potential to empower 'ordinary people' and address their questions, rather than only those of the academic researcher. Should the respondents participate in devising strategies that address their concerns, based on the findings of a shared research process, the process itself could be said to play a pivotal role in helping the participants work towards attaining improvements in their own quality of life (Farnworth 2007).

Unlike conventional research, which tends to be linear, participatory action research works on a concept of a cycle of action and reflection (incorporating planning, doing, observing and reflecting on changes affected by the action). During the action phase, co-researchers test practice and gather evidence; during the reflection stage, they try to make sense of the evidence and plan for further action as determined by the group. Since this process integrates both knowing and acting,

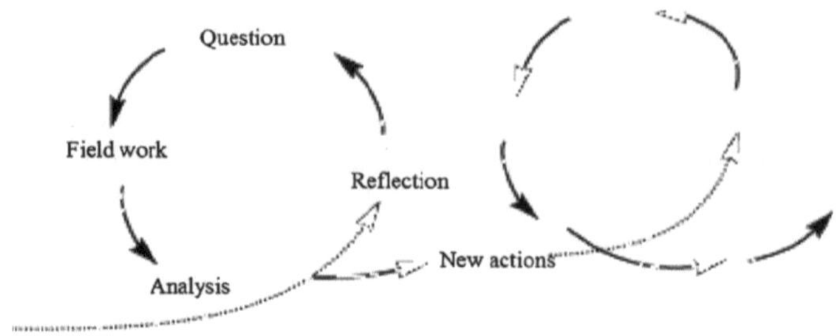


**Fig. 5.2** Cyclical nature of PAR. *Source* Wadsworth (1998). Permission was granted by Yoland Wadsworth and the Action Research Issues Organization Inc., Richmond, Victoria, Australia on 12 April 2017

there is no gap between knowing and doing (Reason/Bradbury 2008, p. 1). Each cycle spirals into more cycles of action, (see Fig. 5.1) 'in which, at each twist of the spiral, the view is both the same and different' (Walker 1998, p. 244). Continuous reflection results in the modification of the action throughout the life of the research project in a recursive rather than linear pattern (Fig. 5.2).

Druckman suggests eight stages that are generally involved in most of the researches of this nature and these are:

- Describe the inquiry: What are the issues? Who are the participants? When and where will it happen?
- Describe the situation: What are we trying to do? Why are we doing this?
- Collect evaluative data and analyse them: What do the participants understand about what is happening in this situation? Which methods are appropriate for gathering this information?
- Review the data and look for contradictions: What are some divergences between what is happening and what we would like to see happen?
- Tackle a contradiction by introducing change by reflecting on the divergences: What changes can we introduce that might be beneficial?
- Monitor the change: What happens over time after the change is introduced?
- Analyse evaluative data about the change: How are the monitored changes through time to be interpreted? Which research methods are most useful for detecting and interpreting the changes?
- Review the change and decide what do to next: What do we think about the change? Is it sufficient in terms of accomplishing our goals set at the beginning of the project? Have our goals changed? Will the change be sustained over time? What should we do next, if anything? (Druckman 2005, p. 315; see also McNiff/Whitehead 2006, pp. 8, 22)

Table 5.2 compares two lists of the main stages of PAR (Kemmis/McTaggart 2008; Weaver/Stark 2006). The slight variations to each approach reveal how

**Table 5.2** Comparison of Weaver & Stark and Kemmis & McTaggart's approaches. *Source* The author

| Stages of PAR (Weaver/Stark 2006) | Key features of PAR (Kemmis/McTaggart 2008) |
|---|---|
| Delineating Problem | Planning a change |
| Choosing action | Acting and observing the process & consequences of the change |
| Design and assessment | Reflecting on these processes & consequences |
| Engaging in action | Re-planning |
| Gathering data | Acting and observing again |
| Reflexive knowledge | Reflecting again, and so on |

varied and numerous the schools of thought in PAR or action-oriented research are. However, what is common in each is the analysis—reflection—action—reflection cycle. The nature and context of the project also contributes to which tasks are undertaken and in which order. What is of note is that practitioners of this approach want to bring about change, to evaluate that change and to interpret its meaning in order to determine future directions.

## 5.6 Validity in Participatory Action Research

In his article, *Is validity really an issue for participatory action research?* McTaggart (1998) suggests that PAR could be viewed as being not valid according to the conventional definition of validity in social science research. He argues an expansion of the meaning of validity to accommodate the aspirations of participatory action research. The focus of traditional social inquiry regarding validity is on two issues—generalisation and causality—which is basically the quest for prediction and control of events. From this perspective, research is seen as valid if the researcher can make defensible general causal inferences. As can be seen from Table 5.1, this is not the emphasis of participatory action research. McTaggart (1998, p. 214) notes that, like all sciences, PAR must submit to the testing of arguments, evidence and conceptual coherence, but a consensus on how these knowledge claims are to be examined needs to be arrived at through negotiation. Another point is that social science aims to be educative. The production of knowledge only is not enough; it must also have a pedagogical purpose as well, and it must also address what McTaggart calls 'political efficacy and prudence'. The last is perhaps what PAR does better than other approaches because it is intentional in seeking change as the key to enhanced understanding as well as enhanced practice. According to Habermas

> The mediation of theory and practice can only be clarified if to begin with we distinguish three functions, which are measured in terms of different criteria: the formation extension of critical theorems, which can stand up to scientific discourse; the organisation of process of enlightenment, in which such theorems are applied and can be tested in a unique manner by

> the initiation of a process of reflection carried on within certain groups toward which these processes have been directed; and the selection of appropriate strategies, the solution of tactical questions, and the conduct of the political struggle. On the first level, the aim is true statements, on the second, authentic insights, and on the third prudent decisions (in McTaggart 1998, p. 214).

Furthermore, McTaggart asserts that the focus of participatory action research and its reporting is how things changed because of the relationships between participants and their shared work. He sees the reporting and understanding of how things changed or were resisted as a more appropriate and useful focus for researchers interested in concrete improvements in people's lives as opposed to just giving voice to people's experiences, gratifications and painp. For him 'validity implies *content. It requires thinking about how a social practice has changed*' (McTaggart 1998, p. 222, emphasis original). The research must demonstrate that its actions have contributed to identifiable enhancements to the situation of the people or community concerned. He suggests that, for participatory action research findings to be more defensible and withstand the validity criteria, five points of reference need to be considered:

- *The establishment of credibility among participants and informants:*
  This is about the way in which the participants are useful and helpful to each other. Ways of achieving this may include the 'professional researcher' providing information about the research process or topic, which might not be easily available or known by the participants, such as theoretical perspectives and other conceptual resources. At times, this might include other services that might be indirectly relevant to the research. McTaggart points out that the goal for participatory action researchers is to bring about constructive change. However, the research act by itself is unlikely to achieve credibility. Other actions that help build trust among the participants need to be encouraged and these are about helping each other in a wide variety of ways throughout the process. The whole purpose is to encourage 'mutual commitment to thoughtfully planned changes in practice, individual and collective' (McTaggart 1998, p. 223).
- *Triangulation of observations and interpretations*:
  He describes triangulation as the comprehending of how oneself and others are situated theoretically, politically and practically. In addition, it takes into account the many and varied perspectives that the group might hold and the fact that viewpoints change over time. This process, for McTaggart, means the juxtaposition of points of view and theoretical interpretive resources; not trying to come up with one common point of view or fitting all outcomes into one interpretive frame. The intent is to ensure that difference is recognised, expressed and understood. By interpretive is meant the seeking out of the meanings people have for their actions or situations.

- *Participant 'confirmation' and 'release' of research 'reporting' of all kinds*: This is about allowing all participants to tell of their experiences of the research process, but to do so with the approval of those whose lives are being portrayed. Participants need to come up with agreed criteria that allow all to be able to tell their stories. While the individuals will report or write about the work of the project, the process of confirmation has to be collective. In other words, members of the research group must have an input into the accuracy, fairness and relevancy of the report.
- *Establishing of audit trail and shared archive of data and interpretations:* This has to do with the obligation to share with the PAR group the 'products' of data collection at all levels of the project. The sharing of data and dialogue about its meaning is an important element in validation as it helps reduce subjectivity.
- *Testing the coherence of arguments, the authenticity of evidence and prudence of action*: This is done, first, within the group itself and then with an external group of people who might have an interest in the work, usually referred to as 'the critical community'. A group of friends could be the critical community (McTaggart 1998, pp. 223–225).

In short, validation in this approach is a process of dialogue and is not necessarily done by observing a set procedure. There needs to be proper communication structures at the research and action stages, which allow the participants to identify and continue to be part of the project collectively. A valid participatory action research project, then, should exhibit the principles that define it, as well as the debates around the principles (McTaggart 1998).

An important point made by McTaggart is that validity is based on the interpretations and conclusions people make regarding information and the theoretical frameworks which guide its collection and use. In PAR, it is generally accepted that, in the process of inquiry, inferences will consider values, ethics, education etc. and play an important role. These inferences are not just those of the researcher but should include a thick description of voices, observations and interpretive position, so that readers can generate their own conclusions.

Greenwood/Levin (1998, pp. 255–256) suggest four categories to determine the validity and credibility of PAR research. By credibility they mean 'the arguments and processes necessary for achieving the goal of making someone trust the research results':

- *Internal credibility:* The group generating the knowledge should itself trust the findings of the research. This category is important because of the collaborative nature of PAR. If the process results directly in altered patterns of social action, then this can be viewed as a clear test of credibility. Locals or organisations with an interest in the research outcomes will find it difficult to accept 'as credible the 'objective' theories of outsiders on the grounds that they cannot recognise the connection to the local situation or because local knowledge makes it clear that the frameworks are either too abstract or simply wrong for the specific context' (Greenwood/Levin 1998, p. 225). It is therefore important in PAR that researchers' findings, the knowledge generated and resultant actions are not only viewed as genuine but also acceptable and recognisable to the members of the communities or organisations being worked with, for it to claim validity. Put simply: it must be credible to them (see also Kemmis/McTaggart 2008, p. 295).

- *External credibility:*
  This regards knowledge that is capable of convincing someone who was not part of the research process that the results are believable. However, because this approach depends on the combination of reflection and action, with the co-generation of knowledge in specific contexts, it becomes a challenge as to how to effectively communicate the credibility of the findings to outsiders. PAR compensates for this by using case narratives, which are often frowned upon by traditional researchers. It needs to be noted though, that if one case narrative contradicts a general social theory, it demands that new interpretations and investigations be undertaken so as to account for this particular case. The oddity of one particular case, then, puts into question all the conclusions reached and the actions taken. 'Viable theories do not have exceptions; they must be formulated to include the exceptions in a coherent way or they must be discarded and replaced by new ones' (Greenwood/Levin 1998, p. 255).
- *Workability.*
  It must be determined whether the actions undertaken in the inquiry have resulted in the solution of the problem and increased the participants' control over their own situation. The inquiry process must be understood as an integration of action and reflection, with workability being the tangible test for the outcome (see also Greenwood/Levin 1998, p. 252).

According to McTaggart (1998, p. 232), 'Participatory action research is not valid unless it meets criteria of defensibility, educative value, and political efficacy and moral appropriateness.'

Change is an important factor in PAR and, as we have observed, without constructive change, credibility is unlikely to be achieved. However, Druckman (2005) is concerned that PAR should be distinct from other forms of practice that do not claim to be research. According to him, many PAR projects 'have been criticised for adopting a naive conception of social change that does not consider bureaucratic processes, anti-democratic values and inertia or lack of a desire for institutional (macro level) change' (Druckman 2005, p. 316). He further suggests that, for researchers to counter any possible barriers to change, they need to think 'systematically' about the change envisaged and to do that, he offers a list of questions that researchers need to work through to help ensure that PAR succeeds:

- What specifically is to be changed? The distinction between micro-level (the group participating in the research) and macro-level (the larger society or culture) change is useful.
- To what extent do participants agree on those particular changes? Participant agreement is essential in action research designs.
- What are some ways to bring about changes? This discussion occurs during the second stage of the action cycle, referred to in step 2 (see Sect. 5.4 Druckmans' eight stages) as 'Describe the situation'.
- What are the roles of research and fact finding in the change design? This should neither be taken for granted nor imposed by the investigator. Ideas should emerge from the discussion during the second stage.
- What are the respective roles of participants and researchers in the change research design? The idea of collaboration in action research is often vague. It would be helpful to clarify roles even in a collaborative process.
- What are some institutional and logistical barriers to implementation? This discussion should alert participants and researchers to the difficulties of changing institutions, leading perhaps to a change strategy at macro-level.
- What are some possible ethical barriers to change? The implications of change for people not involved in the project, and therefore not part of the decision making, need to be discussed. Consent of unwitting members of the community is an issue in change designs.
- How much time and resources are available to implement the change plan? The temptation to implement ambitious plans should be tempered by the reality of available resources to pull it off.
- What criteria should be developed for evaluating whether or not change has occurred? Different criteria may be needed for evaluating short- and long-term change as well as changes that occur in the participants versus those that occur outside the research group. These criteria are discussed in stage 3 of the action research cycle and revisited at a later stage.
- What follow-up activities are needed to sustain the changes? What can the research group do to ensure that the changes last? This entails a discussion of how to create a normative climate (or culture) that will reinforce the changes after the group has concluded its work.
- How should the research be reviewed and reported for dissemination? These are important questions for several reasons. One is the importance of making a contribution to the research literature and influencing the way others develop action research designs. And a third is the importance of encouraging change in other communities by demonstrating the value of this project (Druckman 2005, p. 17).

Moore (2004) draws attention to the fact that PAR is not only about changing social structures and people 'out there', but that researchers also need to be open to the possibilities of the transformation of the self and their relationships with others.

## 5.7 Principles and Features of Participatory Action Research

From the above discussion, the following can be deduced as being the key principles or characteristics of participatory action research:

Firstly, PAR is a social process. It seeks to interrogate the relationship between the individual and the social. It recognises the importance of viewing community as a unit of identification. A community could be identified by a geographic area or as a community whose members are united by a sense of common identity and shared fate, even though they might be geographically dispersed. PAR takes into account the interrelatedness of individuation and socialisation and that these two processes continually shape individual and social relationships in whatever settings people may find themselves in. The participatory action process is therefore achieved if people, individually and collectively, endeavour to understand how they are 'formed and reformed as individuals, and in relation to one another in a variety of settings' (Kemmis/McTaggart 2008, p. 280). In other words, PAR methods could have direct effect on the beliefs and vision of those involved in the research as well as the community at large.

Secondly, it draws from and builds on strengths and resources within the community. It engages the concerned people in interrogating their knowledge (and by this is meant, their understandings, skills and values) and the ways in which they interpret themselves and their actions in their social and material contexts; what Kemmis/McTaggart (2008, p. 281) call 'interpretive categories'. PAR should therefore actively promote the identification, support and reinforcement of social structures and processes as well as knowledge that already exist in a community that might help them work together in improving their lives.

Thirdly, it aims to facilitate collaboration among all project stakeholders at all phases of the research. Community members should be involved in every phase in which they may want to participate. This could include, among other things, definition or identification of the problem, data collection, interpretation of the results and the application of the results in addressing community concerns. It is therefore practical, in the sense that it encourages participants to explore how to improve their interactions by trying to change the acts that make up these interactions; the aim being to mitigate the extent to which participants experience them. This process may entail applying skills from outside the community. Nevertheless, it should focus on issues that the community has identified and allow for a situation where all parties can truly influence the whole project.

Fourthly, it is emancipatory in the sense that it attends to social inequalities and aims to help people deal with and release themselves from 'the constraints of irrational, unproductive, unjust and unsatisfying social structures that limit their self-development and self-determination' (Kemmis/McTaggart 2008, p. 281). This is achieved partly by emphasising community members' knowledge and sharing information, resources and decision-making power. Another way is through people examining how their practices are either shaped or constrained by wider social structures, such as culture, economics and politics, and finding out whether it is possible to set themselves free from these constraints; or if need be how they can adjust to living creatively within and around them. To quote Kemmis/McTaggart (2008, p. 282):

> [It] aims to help people recover and release themselves from, the constraints embedded in the social media through which they interact—their language (discourses), their mode of work, and their social relationships of power (in which they experience affiliation and difference, inclusion and exclusion-relationships in which, grammatically speaking, they interact with others in the 3rd, 2nd and 1st person). It is a process in which people deliberately set out to contest and reconstitute irrational, unproductive (or inefficient), unjust, and/or unsatisfying (alienating) ways of interpreting and describing their world (e.g. language, discourses), ways of working (work), and ways of relating to others (power).

Fifthly, PAR involves a cyclical and interactive process through which people deliberately try to transform their practices. The process is reflexive in that it encourages critical and self-critical action and reflection through the spiral of cycles. In transforming their environment, the participants understand more about the nature of the recursive relationships in the four suggested areas:

- Their (individual and social) practices (the work)
- Their knowledge of their practices (the workers)
- The social structures that shape and constrain their practices (the workplace)
- The social media in which their practices are expressed (the discourses in which their work is represented and misrepresented). (McTaggart 2008, p. 283; see also Moore 2004, p. 150).

## 5.8 Data Collection in Participatory Action Research

PAR utilises a range of data collection methods. Koch/Kralik (2006, p. 25) have suggested the following as the most common:

- Direct observation: where the researcher goes into the situation to see and experience for him/herself so as to understand the context of the situation. Researchers need to be critically aware of their biases resulting from past

education, culture and experiences, which may influence their perceptions and interpretations.
- Collecting stories: asking people questions in a way that prompts them to tell their stories. One seeks to know about their experiences in the past, the things they think worked, what didn't work and the reasons why.
- Group discussions: with community members or a special interest group of people with common features, concerns or issues.
- Timelines and change analysis: involving listing major events and experiences with approximate dates, as well as people's accounts of the past, of how customs, practices and things close to them have changed.
- Shared presentations and analysis: with participants and researchers together sharing the responsibility of presenting the processes and findings of the research project.

As can be observed from this list, the natural bent of PAR is toward inclusiveness in the construction of knowledge that results in action. Participation is the common thread in each point. What each does is to prompt practitioners to weigh their intentions and behaviours and 'the taken-for-granted assumptions, structures and relations that shape the way we live and work' (Koch/Kralik 2006, p. 25).

## 5.9 Some Participatory Action Research Case Studies

I chose PAR for my research because my intention was not only to inquire into the subject topic but to try out actions that might possibly bring healing to the communities affected by the *Gukurahundi* atrocities. I delve more into the rationale of this approach in the following chapters.

Table 5.3 summarises six examples of studies which used PAR and illustrate its diverse contexts and uses. The evidence is striking, but the various levels of involvement of the participants each reflects certain aspects that make them qualify to be participatory action research. As has been said:

> What makes participatory action research 'research' is not the machinery of research techniques. Rather… research in the context of PAR is more about building a relationship between theory and practice. As important, it involves learning about real, material, concrete, and particular practices of particular people in particular places (McIntyre 2008, pp. 58–59).

These examples show that PAR can and has been used in diverse contexts and that, while the involvement of participants is central, the nature and extent of this varies between particular studies:

**Table 5.3** Examples of PAR case studies. *Source* The Author

| References | Target group | Description of research |
|---|---|---|
| Cahill (2007) | Six young women of colour, New York City | This project was a self-exploration and discovery by these women to address stereotypes of young urban women of colour prevalent in that society. The focus of the study was on how lack of resources feeds into both stereotyping and young women's wellbeing and self-understanding. The project was a challenge to both themselves and other women like them to examine the accepted norm and to seek ways to liberate themselves and others by confronting the given stereotypes and to take charge of their identification through self-definition. Actions to challenge the stereotypes were formulated around picture posters challenging the false perceptions about the young urban women of colour. The group also set up two websites, wrote a book chapter, a report, conducted workshops in schools and community-based organisations as well as presenting their research at academic conferences |
| McIntyre (2008) | 24 young adolescents of colour, ages 12–13 years, Bridgeport, Connecticut | These young people came from a similar background as Cahill's study. This was a three-year project and explored what it meant to live in the Bridgeport community and how they experienced multiple forms of violence that characterised their lives. They articulated how violence is produced, reproduced and experienced. They implemented action plans that addressed issues specific to them individually and collectively. This involved participating in a range of activities aimed at furthering the young people's goal of informing their community about the effects of violence on themselves, their schools and environment. The young people created a photo-text book, organised a clean-up of the Blair School community, conducted several school wide activities and presented aspects of their project to Bridgeport City Council and other community groups. |

(continued)

**Table 5.3** (continued)

| References | Target group | Description of research |
|---|---|---|
| McIntyre (2008) | Group of 9 women. Monument Road Community, Belfast North Ireland, 24–40 years | These were females affected by the violence of civil war. In this one community, 50 residents had been murdered; many others injured, imprisoned or forced to leave the area. The women worked to bring to light the gendered violence that occurred during the 35-year war. By engaging in dialogue and participating in a wide range of consciousness raising activities, the women constructed new ways of viewing their lives and new strategies for communicating their experiences to others. They used a photo-text exhibition to present their stories of their realities to the outside community |
| Koch/ Kralik (2006) | Group of nine People living with HIV, South Australia, 33–62 years | The aim of this study was to explore the experience of fatigue and self-care strategies with adults living with HIV. The researchers and the participants explored self-care strategies and identified the catalysts and constraints to self-management of their conditions. The project started with one-on-one interviews of 15 people living with fatigue. A composite story of the 15 stories was created and sent to the interviewees who were then invited to participate in PAR groups to share their stories and discuss fatigue self-management. They were encouraged to come with their partners or friends. Nine people agreed to be part of a PAR group to develop action plans to incorporate alternative strategies into the day to day management of fatigue. The information learnt and the stories were shared with selected government and non-governmental agencies providing services to people with HIV |
| Strydom/ Freek (2008) | Mozambican migrant labourers and their families, Mpumalanga, SA | This project is thin on methodological details but its aim was to address the impact of Mozambican migrants on the South African situation. According to the brief description of the project it would appear that it falls somewhere between level b and c of Bagnoli and Clark's (2010) levels of participation (see Sect. 5.1). The researchers spent time in |

(continued)

**Table 5.3** (continued)

| References | Target group | Description of research |
|---|---|---|
| | | the farming areas trying to understand the situation and building relationships with the farming community. Discussions were had with all stakeholders in an effort to synchronise the community needs with those of the migrants. Through consultations, surveys and personal interviews, needs assessment was carried out. A training programme was drawn up to cover the themes identified from the findings. An evaluation of the programme outcome was planned but there was no indication of the extent of the participants' involvement in the evaluation process |
| Dickson (1997) | Aboriginal 'grandmothers' 50 years and above, Canada | The health assessment research was done within a larger project. The aim was to examine the health needs of these women and to respond through health promoting programmes. The research was pre-determined by planners and funders after an initial needs assessment. Funders wanted the research to be a participatory one and participatory action research was eventually deemed to be the desirable approach. The grandmothers were extensively involved in all crucial decisions of the research. Data was analysed by the researcher but reviewed and used by the grandmothers. The final report was reviewed and used by the grandmothers, the staff and the researcher, individually and in a group. The findings were used by the grandmothers for personal information and as a resource document for a workshop and staff used them at workshops and to communicate the project's work to relevant agencies |
| Babbie (2007) | Xerox Cooperation | Management and union leaders instigated a PAR project under the guidance of an external consultant. The goal of the study was to improve the quality of working life, while lowering manufacturing costs and increasing productivity. Eight workers were appointed to the 'cost study team' (CST), including workers from the wire harness department, where outsourcing and |

(continued)

**Table 5.3** (continued)

| References | Target group | Description of research |
|---|---|---|
| | | laying the off, of 180 workers was being discussed. At the end of six months the goal of saving $3, 2 million and the 180 jobs was achieved. The programme was extended to three other departments with similar results. PAR created a powerful organisational learning process, where leaders of labour and management learnt from each other and from the consultant who also learnt from them |
| Greenwood/ Levin (2007) | Village development in Stongfjorden, Norway | This was a restoration project of a village that had deteriorated due to deindustrialisation. Levin and a team of academics were asked to help the community which had plans to restore this village. After holding a search conference with the villagers, teams of different interests were formed to tackle various areas of the village that needed to be renovated. Periodic conferences for follow-up were held where the different teams shared with each other progress, challenges and reflection on the work being done. This is an interesting type of PAR project because it involved the whole community and, although learning and reflection took place, it was not in the 'normal' academic sense. However, the community moved from being just activists and learnt how to research issues related to mobilisation of resources effectively |

## 5.10 Conclusion

This chapter has discussed what makes PAR unique from positivist social sciences qualitative research. We noted its characteristics, principles and issues surrounding validity and credibility and the fact that it is about changing both theory and practice through the joint participation of the researcher and the researched. PAR confronts the assumption of traditional research—that discovering the facts and making them known will bring about social change. It recognises that desired social change needs to be planned, implemented, evaluated and planned again; in a cyclical fashion and perhaps many times. This demands persistence and energy, which is more likely to be found in the relevant community than in outside researchers.

Chapter 6 will discuss the research design, methodology and data collection methods used in this research and offers a 'thick' description of the research process.

## References


Babbie, E. 2007. *The practice of social research* (11th ed.). Belmont, CA: Thompson learning.

Bagnoli, A. and Clark, A. 2010. Focus groups with young people: a participatory approach to research planning. *Journal for Youth Studies,* 13(1): 101–119.

Cahill, C. 2007. The personal is political: developing new subjectivities through participatory action research. *Gender, Place and Culture*, 14(3) June: 267–292.

Dickson, G. 1997. Participatory action research and health promotion: the grandmothers' story. PhD Thesis, University of Saskatchewan.

Druckman, D. 2005. *Doing research: methods of inquiry for conflict analysis*. London: Sage.

Dwyer, S. 2003. Reconciliation for realists. In C. A. L. Prager and T. Govier (eds.), *Dilemmas of reconciliation: cases and concepts.* Waterloo, Ontario: Wilfrid Laurier University Press.

Farnworth, C. 2007. Achieving respondent-led research in Madagascar. *Gender & Development,* 15(2): 271–284.

Freire, P. (1970) 1993. *Pedagogy of the oppressed.* New York: Continuum.

Ghaye, T., et al. 2008. Participatory and appreciative action and reflection (PAAR)—democratizing reflective practices. *Reflective Practice,* 9(4): 361–397.

Grant, J., Nelson, G. and Mitchell, T. 2008. Negotiating challenges of participatory action research: relationships, power, participation, challenges and credibility. In P. Reason and H. Bradbury (eds.), *The SAGE handbook of action research: participative inquiry and practice*. London: Sage.

Greenwood, D. J. and Levin, M. 1998. Action research, science and the co-optation of social research. *Studies in Cultures, Organization, and Societies*, 4: 237–261.

Greenwood, D. J. and Levin, M. 2007. *Introduction to action research: social research for social change* (2nd ed.). Thousand Oaks: Sage.

Guishard, M. 2009. The false paths, the endless labors, the turns now this way and now that: participatory action research, mutual vulnerability, and the politics of inquiry. *Urban Review,* 41: 85–105.

Kemmis, S. and McTaggart, R. 2008. PAR: communicative action and the public sphere. In N. K. Denzin and Y. S. Lincoln (eds.), *Strategies of qualitative inquiry* (3rd ed.). London: Sage Publication.

Koch, T. and Kralik, D. 2006. *Participatory action research in Healthcare.* Oxford, UK: Blackwell Publishing.

McIntyre, A. 2008. *Participatory action research.* Los Angeles: SAGE Publications.

McNiff, J. and Whitehead, J. 2006. *All you need to know about action research.* London: Sage Publications.

McNiff, J. and Whitehead, J. 2010. *You and your action research project.* London: Routledge.

McTaggart, R. 1998. Is validity really an issue for participatory action research? *Studies in Culture, Organisations and Societies*, 4: 211–236.

Moore, J. 2004. Living in the basement of the ivory tower: a graduate student's perspective of participatory action research within academic institutions. *Educational Action Research,* 12(1): 145–162.

Reason, P. and Bradbury, H. 2008. Introduction. In P. Reason and H. Bradbury (eds.), *The SAGE handbook of action research: participative inquiry and practice*. London: Sage.

Schratz, M. and Walker, R. 1995. *Research as social change.* London: Routledge.

Strydom, H. and Freek, C. 2008. A participatory action research approach in dealing with Mozambican migrant labourers to South Africa. *TILTAI,* 4: 87–98.
Wadsworth, Y. 1998. What is participatory action research? At: http://www.aral.com.au/ari/p-ywadsworth98.html (22 August 2013).
Walker, M. 1998. Action research and participatory research in South Africa. In J. Muller, J. Mouton, T. Sono, and P. Frank (eds.), *Theory and method in South African human sciences research: advances and innovations*. South Africa: HSRC Press.
Weaver, A. and Stark, B. J. 2006. *Making it real: participatory action research in UCEDDs: building the UCEDD of tomorrow*. Council on Community Advocacy, Oregon Health and Science University. At: www.powershow.com/view/ac365-ZjQxO/Making_It_Real_Participatory_Action_Research_in_UCEDDs_powerpoint_ppt_presentation (19 September 2013).

# Chapter 6
# Research Design, Methodology and Data Collection Methods

## 6.1 Introduction

This chapter discusses the research design, research methodology, data collection methods and methods of analysis used in this project, these being the terms used in the standard South African research methods text (Mouton 2001). In addition, the ethical considerations that guided this research are stated. The chapter will also tell the story of the research process—my story of discovery and learning through often unfamiliar territory and the unintended development of a sub-research design.

## 6.2 Research Design

I chose to use participatory action research methodology as the basis of this study. This methodology is a 'systematic inquiry with the collaboration of those affected by the issue being studied, for the purposes of education and taking action or effecting change' (Goto et al. 2008, p. 301). According to Mouton (1996, p. 175), the research design shows how the researcher plans to execute the research problem that has been formulated. The design helps the researcher to plan, structure and carry out the project in a way that maximises the validity of the findings. The design also provides a full account of how the research has been structured, planned and executed.

Prior to commencing this study, I had no knowledge of PAR. When this research topic was approved by my supervisor, he introduced me to PAR and suggested that it might suit my research aims. After reading and considering the relevance and practicability of PAR regarding my topic, I felt that it made sense to adopt this



D. Ngwenya, *Healing the Wounds of Gukurahundi in Zimbabwe*,
The Anthropocene: Politik—Economics—Society—Science 19,
https://doi.org/10.1007/978-3-319-66818-5_6

research design for several reasons. Firstly, by being personally involved in the process over time, I would be able to get first-hand information on how the research would affect the lives of my co-researchers (Francis 2005, p. 16). Secondly, the end purpose of this study was not just to fulfil academic requirements but is closely linked to my work responsibilities (see Sect. 1.6) and was meant to help build the effectiveness of our organisation's work by contributing to our knowledge and praxis. Thirdly, this approach is designed to break down the distinction between the 'researcher' and the 'researched', the subjects and objects of knowledge production, by allowing the people themselves to participate in the process of gaining and creating the knowledge (Collins 1998, p. 3). Fourthly, my own need for transformation and healing might benefit, given that the research would reveal insights as to how self-healing can be best practised and resiliencies developed in order to cope with trauma. Fifthly, the combination of knowledge generation with action appealed to me as a practitioner-researcher as it bridges the gap between research recommendations and the implementation of suggested actions, which in most instances do not have a life beyond the thesis document. As discussed in chapter five, action is carried out and evaluated during the life of the research project (see also Babbie/Mouton 2001, p. 314). Sixthly, while there have been several research projects around the topic of *Gukurahundi* (e.g. Stauffer 2009; Motsi 2010), I was not aware of any that had utilised a participatory action research design.

This participatory action research project is also exploratory and descriptive. It is descriptive in the sense that it seeks to provide a 'thick' description of both the process of the research and the participants' and researcher's responses to it, and to discover and explain in detail the context within which the action occurs. 'Thick' description involves more than just the compilation of relevant detail; it includes the interpretation of circumstances, meanings, motivations, and intentions. It also tries to determine the significance an experience or sequence of events have for the concerned individual[s]. That is to say, it also carries explanatory elements (Schwandt 2001; Holloway 1997; Babbie/Mouton 2001).

As has been noted in chapter five, PAR ideally requires that participants be involved in all stages of the research, from the identification of the problem to the dissemination of the findings. However, this was only partly the case with this study, due to the way my university leans towards the traditional science research paradigm and demands that a proposal be submitted before one's research topic is approved. The resulting dilemma has been described by Janet Moore;

> I want to practice PAR for the principles it espouses and yet I fear that I will create paradigmatic battles in my doctoral research with this type of direction in my research. I am also aware that I do not have the time (and perhaps patience) for engaging in a truly participatory study. *I am required to write a research proposal with research questions, research problems and a direction for the research—none of which involves the participants of the study. If I were to wait until this stage were completed I would risk not completing my doctoral programme within a reasonable timeframe* (Moore 2004, p. 158 italics added).

So, this study already had its research questions and general direction defined. However, efforts were made to discuss this aspect of the research extensively with the participants to create buy-in and a sense of ownership from them. A significant amount of time was spent during the first two dialogue sessions discussing these issues and, while I explained how and what I hoped we could do, I was careful not to present the study plan in a dogmatic way that shut out any input from the group. Thus—the participants had an opportunity to interrogate the plan I presented to them. Fortunately, this was an issue that they were interested in as they had been targets during *Gukurahundi* (see Sect. 2.2). In addition, the members participated in determining the specific direction of the research: they had a large say as to who would be part of the group, the pace and rules of the research, the actions to be undertaken and the analysis of the actions carried out. I believe that there was true ownership of the project and that the research was as democratic as could be in the given reality.

### *6.2.1 The Participatory Action Research Group*

Originally, the ten participants were to be drawn from a community in Tsholotsho, one of the areas most affected by the atrocities. However, due to circumstances beyond my control, participants were eventually drawn from members of the ZIPRA Veterans Trust based in Bulawayo. I faced two major obstacles in the process of trying to identify participants for the research. Firstly, I relied heavily on a Grace to Heal (GTH) volunteer staff member based at Tsholotsho centre to identify and invite potential participants on my behalf. The idea was that, once these had been identified, I would then meet with them to explain the whole process and to find out if they would be interested in being part of the research. The volunteer kept informing me that he was making progress but nothing materialised for almost the whole of 2010. By November, I knew that this was going to be a futile exercise, as the period between November and April is the busiest time for rural people. I realised that, having to wait till May of 2011, would affect my schedule adversely. Secondly, this period also coincided with a time of personal financial difficulty so I was unable to travel to Tsholotsho to organise for the research personally. I then made the decision to work instead with the ZIPRA Veterans Trust, whom I had considered as a second group in order to observe the dynamics of the two groups. This move was fortuitous because, in October 2012, GTH encountered a problem with the police in Tsholotsho over its work there and had to suspend operations for a period. This would have also affected the research had I been successful in recruiting participants there.

From the case studies listed in Table 5.3, it is clear that the numbers of participants vary from one study to another, depending on the availability and interest of the participants and the nature of the research. For this study, a group of ten people was ideal as it allowed for intimacy and trust to be created more easily than in a larger group. It also was big enough for people not to feel too exposed but small enough to allow for participation by all group members within the normal time of 120 min per session. The research group met over a period of two years and eight months in which the various action research steps were undertaken following an adaptation of Denscombe's Action Research Model (Costello 2003, p. 9), as follows:

- The discussion and adoption of the issue of inquiry; in our case, 'How can the community of the hurting actively participate in its own healing?'
- Critical reflection on what has been done to promote healing of memories and the benefits (or lack of) to the victims. This involved the sampling and evaluation of various healing models made available to the group.
- A plan of action and activities to be drawn up based on the models sampled.
- Implementation of various activities agreed upon by the group.
- An evaluation exercise at the end of the specified period to assess the usefulness of the programme, and whether it could be beneficial to the wider community.

This group of ex-combatants can still be defined as a community (see Sect. 4.1 for a discussion of what constitutes community), and I see no contradiction between it and my stated goal of working with a rural community. There are, however, fundamental differences between the two communities in terms of group dynamics because of the locations and levels of political consciousness, as well as education. In addition, I would surmise that rural people would have exhibited higher levels of fear and therefore be more inhibited than the ex-combatants. This would have resulted in a very different set of group dynamics and participation, which would have produced different results from the ones obtained from the ZIPRA Veterans Trust.

### *6.2.2 Healing Power of Narratives: A Sub-research Design*

An unintended consequence of the dialogue sessions was the move towards a group narrative research design within the PAR research design. The discussions on the concepts and theories of healing, forgiveness and trauma often resulted in the telling of personal stories of the participants' struggles with their realities. In addition, the healing workshop and the writing of their life histories, which they chose as their actions, had a cathartic effect on the participants. This agrees with Kearney's (2007, p. 51) assertion that one of the long-lasting functions of stories is catharsis (see also Wimberly 2011; Banks-Wallace 1998 and Sect. 4.5.2). However, it is not just a matter of 'revealing is healing'. There must be a correct approach and space to undertake this in a manner that can produce healing for the survivors (Staub et al. 2005, p. 305; Mitchels 2003, p. 412). 'Stories become cathartic to the extent that they combine empathic imagination with a certain acknowledgement of the cause and extent of the suffering, thereby offering a wider lens to review one's own suffering' (Kearney 2007, p. 61). And so, it was that, because of the trustworthy and emphatic 'community of listeners' (Kaminer 2006, p. 488) created by the common story that bound the group, participants found it natural and inviting to share their stories of suffering in this safe space we had created.

## 6.3 Research Methodology

Since this was an action-oriented research project, the basic aim of which was to seek social and individual transformation, a qualitative methodology was used. This PAR project naturally lends itself to this approach and Babbie/Mouton's (2001, p. 279) key features of qualitative research apply here:

- Qualitative research is conducted in the natural setting of the social actors.
- The focus is on process rather than outcome. (This does not mean that outcomes are not important but that the research is process oriented).
- The actor's perspective (the 'insider' or 'emic' view) is emphasised. As has been discussed in Chap. 5, PAR considers knowledge generated by participants an essential element in the research process.
- The primary aim of qualitative research is in-depth or 'thick' descriptions and understandings of actions and events.
- The main concern is to understand social action in terms of its specific context rather than attempting to generalise to some theoretical population. This study sought to examine actions and responses, of communities in Matabeleland affected by the 1980s atrocities, resulting from attempts to stimulate self-healing.

Table 6.1 summarises the features of the qualitative methodology that influenced me to choose this approach:

The qualitative approach was therefore the most suitable for this study, since the research sought to identify and understand attitudes and behaviours which are best understood within their natural settings, unlike the artificial settings of experiments and surveys (Mouton 2001, p. 194). This research is 'live' in the sense that the process, events and actions were observed as they were experienced, rather than being reconstructed in retrospect. It sought to study the participants according to their own definitions of their world and, as such, it focused on the subjective experiences of the participants as individuals and also tried to be conscious of the contexts in which the participants interacted with each other (Mouton 2001). As has been pointed out (Sect. 6.2.1) these individuals already had relationships outside the research setting because of their history and current activities. Hence the use of a qualitative research methodology was the most appropriate.

**Table 6.1** Key differences between quantitative and qualitative research methodologies. *Source* Suter (2012, pp. 347–348). The permission to use this table weas granted by Michelle Binur, Contract Administrator, SAGE, Thouand Oaks, CA, USA, 21 April 2017

| Quantitative research | Qualitative research |
|---|---|
| Favours standardised tests and instruments that measure constructs | Favours interviews, observations, and documents |
| Generalises from a sample to the population | Applies ideas across contexts |
| Focuses on control to establish cause or permit prediction | Focuses on interpreting and understanding a social construction of meaning in a natural setting |
| Attends to precise measurements and objective data collection | Attends to accurate description of process via words, texts, etc., and observations |
| Favours parsimony and seeks a single truth | Appreciates complexity and multiple realities |
| Conducts analysis that yields a significance level | Conducts analysis that seeks insight and metaphor |
| Faces statistical complexity | Faces conceptual complexity |
| Conducts analysis after data collection | Conducts analysis along with data collection |
| Favours the laboratory | Favours fieldwork |
| Uses instruments with psychometric properties | Relies on researchers who have become skilled at observing, recording, and coding (researcher as instrument) |
| Generates a report that follows a standardised format | Generates a report of findings that includes expressive language and a personal voice |
| Uses designs that are fixed prior to data collection | Allows designs to emerge during study |
| Often measures a single-criterion outcome (albeit multidimensional) | Offers multiple sources of evidence (triangulation) |
| Often uses large sample sizes determined by power analysis or acceptable margins of error | Often studies single cases or small groups that build arguments for the study's confirmability |
| Uses statistical scales as data | Uses text as data |
| Favours standardised tests and instruments that measure constructs | Favours interviews, observations, and documents |
| Performs data analysis in a prescribed, standardised, linear fashion | Performs data analysis in a creative, iterative, nonlinear, holistic fashion |
| Uses reliable and valid data | Uses trustworthy, credible, coherent data |

## 6.4 Data Collection Methods

I sought to understand the subjective experiences of the participants' situation as well as trying to give working accounts of the contexts from which their meanings are derived. This is congruent with both PAR and qualitative research methodology's reliance on local knowledge. According to Babbie/Mouton (2001, p. 326), any of the data-collection methods PAR might use derive from the vernacular traditions of communication and dissemination of knowledge and, as such, these methods are more compatible with qualitative data-collection methods. Qualitative data allow for the preservation of the chronological flow of the processes and enable the researcher to see more easily which events are the results of which consequences. Furthermore, good qualitative data help the researcher to go beyond initial conceptions and to generate or revise the conceptual framework.

Dialogue sessions, which included group discussions, argumentation and consensus meetings, were the prime tool for data collection (McTaggart 1998, p. 326). Dialogue plays a critical part in PAR because, through it, participants can learn about their own reality through the critical analysis of their own particular situations and problems. Participants engaged in informative, reflective and interrogative discussions concerning their experiences and actions during these dialogue sessions and were able to devise solutions or actions.

With the permission of the participants, these dialogue sessions were audio-taped to provide an accurate record of the proceedings, which were then transcribed for subsequent analysis. I recorded directly onto my laptop or tablet. Each audio file was labelled with the date on which the particular session occurred. The sessions were conducted in both English and siNdebele and the transcription was done by student interns attached to GTH at various times during the life of the project. The first three sessions were transcribed entirely into English. When going through them I felt that the vernacular expressions were losing their richness through translation because, although the English translation was technically correct, the meaning was not necessarily the same outside of the context in which it was said. I then requested that subsequent sessions be transcribed verbatim and I would do the translation where necessary for the purposes of direct quotes for the write-up. I listened through each session, checking the transcripts for accuracy, correcting the translation and filling in gaps left as 'inaudible'. However, not all sections deemed inaudible could be corrected as I was not always able to recall the conversations. I also added the identity of the speaker to each portion of dialogue through voice recognition—something which the transcribers couldn't do as they were not present during the discussions and knew none of the participants. One limitation of this way of capturing data is the loss of the nonverbal aspects of the conversations which usually add a critical dimension to the understanding (Gibson/ Brown 2009). Having a transcribed record of the discussions was important because I could share these with the participants, not only for their records and use (as required by PAR) but also for verification purposes.

To address the question of rigour, of which action research has sometimes been accused of lacking: multiple data collection tools and sources were used. Open-ended questions were used whenever necessary to appraise me of an individual participant's progress and in seeking clarity on any aspect of the study. Critical recovery of history was also used as a data-collection method. Witness accounts were gathered through the personal stories of the participants. The primary goal for this process, according to Babbie/Mouton (2001, p. 328) is the discovery of data and facts which 'help correct, complement or clarify official or academic accounts written with other class interests or biases in mind'. In this respect, we saw in Chap. 2 that the history of te Matabeleland region and, in particular, the period between 1982 and 1987, has been suppressed and/or distorted by the government.

In addition to taped recordings, I made use of field notes to record observations of the group dynamics and learning process, as well as a diary to record personal action and reflection of the action and the learning occurring from it. An attempt was made to get the group members to keep journals or diaries in which they would record their own personal reflections on their individual and group actions (McNiff/Whitehead 2010). However, none of the participants took this up. I attribute this largely to the lack of clarity on my part in trying to explain how to do this. Reflexivity is a difficult exercise requiring discipline and practise.

Table 6.2 shows some of the tools used in the data collection process during the project.

As can be noted, the final data-collection tools are different from the ones I had originally proposed to use (see Sect. 1.1). This was influenced mainly by the final format that the study took after negotiations with the research participants, given that one of the characteristics of PAR is that it allows for democratic and genuine cooperation between the researcher and the participants (McIntyre 2007, 2008; Gaventa/Cornwell 2006). PAR recognises and is concerned about oppressed communities and seeks to emancipate and empower participants. This must not only apply to their environment but also throughout the process of the research itself (Grant et al. 2008; Harding 2003, p. 11, see also Sect. 5.3). At the time when I envisaged the research process during the proposal development stage, the suggested tools seemed appropriate. This experience made me realise why PAR emphasises the need to involve participants as much as is possible. At a practical level, had I been dogmatic and insisted on sticking to the chosen tools, the outcome might have been very different, as well as being frustrating to all involved.

The data-gathering process was aided by the following questions:

- What happens to us when somebody deliberately goes out of their way to harm us, especially if that person is supposed to be protecting us?
- How has the issue of *Gukurahundi* affected collective memory?
- What can we do to help ourselves to heal/how can we help others to heal?
- Is healing necessarily tied to forgiveness?

**Table 6.2** Data collection tools. *Source* The author

| Tool | Purpose |
|---|---|
| Dialogue sessions | Group discussion<br>Argumentation<br>Consensus building |
| Open-ended interviews | Appraisal of myself on individual participant's progress.<br>Clarification of any aspect of study |
| Field notes | Recording observations of group dynamics and learning processes |
| Journal | Reflection on personal action and learning |
| Audio recording | Preserving integrity and accuracy of data collection.<br>Allowing ease of transcription of dialogue sessions |

- Is it possible to heal without forgiveness?
- Is there a role for justice in forgiveness and healing?
- What is healing?

However, since this was a discussion as opposed to a focus group discussion, these questions acted as a guide and were more iterative than linear. Right up to the last session, the group was still interacting with these questions and others that arose out of them.

## 6.5 Data Analysis

Qualitative data analysis can involve different and sometimes opposing methods (Braun/Clarke 2006). The research sought to discover whether communities that have experienced violence at the hands of a government could heal in the absence of an official healing programme, and the study was approached from a peacebuilding theoretical framework, with particular focus on the conflict transformation context. The discussion in Chap. 3 on trauma and peacebuilding influenced my data analysis methodology. This participatory action research differed from conventional focus group discussion in the sense that I worked with one group throughout the research, whereas, in conventional qualitative research, one would have worked with several groups to allow for data comparison across them (Harding 2003). Working with one group was preferred because it involved not only the generation of knowledge but also the transformation of certain aspects of the participants' environment they were not happy with. Therefore, data saturation, in the sense of trying to discover from as many groups as is possible concerning the topic of study (Onwuegbuzie et al. 2009), was not a concern for this study.

Following Braun/Clarke (2006), I decided to carry out the data analysis process manually, instead of using a computer-based analysis programme, because it was important that I interacted directly with the data in order to gain the experience of working with it first-hand. A thematic approach was used to accomplish three tasks:

- To examine commonalities in data, finding ways to bring together all the examples across the data set which can then be categorised.
- To examine the distinctive features across the data set, so as to find and analyse peculiarities and contrasts within any given data set.
- To explore relationships between the various elements of analysis, that is, to look at ways in which the different code categories relate to each other and how particular individual characteristics or differences relate to the general themes (Gibson/Brown 2009, pp. 128–129).

Although an inductive content analysis was used, my *a priori* theoretical framework and personal interests and preconceptions influenced my approach to the analysis. Because of the amount of data (150 pages of transcripts) generated by the research, I felt overwhelmed. I realised that a strictly line-by-line or word-by-word analysis would certainly cause what Bazeley (2013) calls 'death by data asphyxiation' on my part. I then decided to code for meaningful qualitative elements by identifying chunks or undivided units of data that demonstrated some commonalities and assigned them relevant codes. There were times, however, when certain words and lines frequently stood out and it made sense to code them as such. Initially, I thought that everything on the transcripts was important and was worried I might leave out something crucial. It was good to learn from people like Auerbach/Silverstein (2003), Saldana (2009) and Bazeley (2013), that there is no one right way of doing coding, but that my way was one of several 'right ways'.

The coding process itself started during the discussions themselves, as certain expressions and phrases caught my attention. As I listened to the recordings and corrected the transcripts, more of these interesting data kept popping up. I highlighted these for further attention (at the time, I was not aware that this was part of the coding process). After correcting the transcripts, they were printed out and read through several times, before embarking on coding. Using the printed versions of the transcripts, key paragraphs, phrases and words were highlighted and comments written in the margins using coloured pens. Codes and categories were developed from these as a way of attempting to summarise our discussions. To assist in the identification of possible data sets, I followed Gibson/Brown's (2009, p. 134) guide, which includes watching for things that occur more than once, things said with intensity or strong emphasis, and instances when people readily agree or disagree on something.

## 6.6 Validity and Reliability

According to Babbie/Mouton (2001, p. 122), validity refers to 'the extent to which an empirical measure adequately reflects the real meaning of the concept under consideration'. In reality, it is impossible to determine this and researchers have to depend on set criteria to measure pre-agreed concepts and terms. Among the suggested criteria for validity are three which I found useful:

- Criterion-related or predictive validity, which is based on an external standard and depends on certain behaviours that could be used to measure relationships between variables.
- Construct validity, which is based on social relationships among the variables and requires the development of a measure to be used, as well as theoretical expectations about the way the variable relates to other variables. These tests provide a weight of evidence (but not definitive proof) as to whether a measure does or does not highlight the quality to be measured.
- Content validity, which refers to how much a certain measure covers the scope of meanings within a concept. Babbie/Mouton (2001, p. 123) suggest that researchers ought to take note of the agreements which participants may

consider as most useful, a point which resonates well with participatory action research.

Reliability may be viewed as a function of consistency; that is, it is a matter of whether a particular technique, when applied repeatedly to the same object, would produce the same results each time (Babbie/Mouton 2001, p. 119). However, McTaggart (1998, p. 225) says that, validity in PAR is a clear process of dialogue that is 'not achieved by adherence to a fixed "procedure"'. Rather, he views validity as being achieved 'if there are appropriate communicative structures in place throughout the research and action which allow participants to continue to associate with and identify with the work of the collective project change'. In the final analysis, the extent to which the participants identify and feel they truly own and recognise both the process and the final product is the crucial indicator of validity (see Sect. 5.5 for further discussion).

Another indicator for validity and reliability was how the project had changed the lives and/or the participants' social environment. These questions were used to determine to what extent the process had informed and influenced social transformation:

- How have things changed?
- What has not changed?
- What has been confirmed?
- What has been ignored?
- What has been made problematic? (McTaggart 1998, p. 228)

Triangulation, using multiple data sources, was also used to improve the validity of the research. Recordings of the dialogue sessions, field notes or my personal reflections, group reflections on actions and interviews were the major sources of data.

## 6.7 Ethical Considerations

The research followed the university's research ethics guidelines. Participants were informed that participation was voluntary and signed consent forms to that effect. The researcher was constantly mindful of not pressuring anyone to speak about or do anything they were not comfortable with. In fact, the group together formulated ground rules which were to govern the research process. One of these had to do with being free to take 'time out' if anyone felt things were getting too emotional—a freedom exercised by one of the participants at our second dialogue session as illustrated below:

> J: Okay, my name is J, I was involved in the war and I served in the ZNA (Zimbabwe National army), I am a *Gukurahundi* victim…(pause) are you going to give it another session for us to talk again? Because as it is…

Dumie: Yes, one of our rules is that when uncomfortable one is free to take time off.

J: Yah, I think I won't talk.

Dumie: Okay, it's fine. What we could look at is, what are some of the things that you might benefit from this?

This was one of the measures meant to mitigate the possibility of re-traumatisation during the research. In addition, two people with experience working with victims of violence were available, when and if needed, to provide expert counselling for the affected individuals. Thankfully, the need never arose and the issue of trauma-processing was addressed by one of the actions chosen by the participants (Sect. 6.8). Participants were given letters that explained in detail what the research was about and the requirements involved and were asked to sign an informed consent form. All efforts were made to observe the 'do no harm' principle, by not revealing information that might embarrass or endanger the participants' lives, homes and friendships. The identities of the participants are disguised using an initial which cannot be linked to any participant in order to strengthen confidentiality.

It was important that I made every effort to include the participants in every aspect of this research as far as was possible. A conscious decision was made to make sure their participation was not token by honestly engaging them and taking their input seriously, even when it meant changing some aspects of the plan. Even though some aspects were already set, to fulfil university requirements, I discussed these with them as well and made compromises wherever necessary (Sect. 5.2).

Although the PAR process tends to address power inequities, I still needed to be aware that this does exist by virtue of positions in life and the fact that the level of studies I was engaged with is normally given high status, while those engaged in them are held in high esteem. I was also wary that PAR does not erase the inequities but only reduces them and that they were still a factor to be worked on. This issue was also raised by a colleague who I had asked to review one of our dialogue sessions.

> I think it is very important that you stressed the fact that there are different forms of knowledge, those based on study and books and those based on experience and that you would like to collaborate with the people in focus groups on an equal basis. In my experience this is easier done than said. Do you have the feeling that you have achieved this goal? I also feel that to make this work one has to demonstrate that one is at an equal basis, that words alone are not enough. How do you make the people in the focus groups feel you are on equal footing (email: 25/06/2012)?

In my reply to her I stated the following:

> The equality issue continues to be a problem. I am not entirely sure if I have reached it, but I have tried particularly not to 'display' the power knowledge. I mean that I try to minimise the use of my academic knowledge and try to listen to them in order to learn. I have avoided even being the source of information that some in the group might not know and instead would seek for us to tease the issue to its logical conclusion… The good thing with this group is that most of these guys have held senior position in the army during and after the liberation war, so there is a certain amount of balance in as far as power influence is concerned. I think I try to give them as much ownership and control over the project as is

> possible… But I believe I do genuinely see them as equals and their opinions, decisions and wishes receive as much consideration as what I contribute… bearing in mind that I myself am 'feeling' my way around this approach, so from that view I guess I might appear to them as the 'expert' on this, however the reality is that what I know doesn't set me much apart from them in practice (email: 28/06/2012).

Another thing we did at the first meeting was to agree on a set of principles that would guide the conduct of the group during our time together. These were democratically discussed and adopted by the whole group. I felt this was necessary as a way to further cede power to the group. In addition, data collected during the research, the transcripts and any other works produced during the action phases were made available to the group and they had the liberty to use them to meet their own objectives as individuals or as a group, with the consent of other members. Where possible and necessary, the opinion of the group members was sought on the relevant parts of the final document, through providing them with summaries of the findings.

I also tried to make sure that the actions undertaken were geared towards the overall transformation of their situation, rather than solely for the benefit of my goals and objectives. I believe I was honest, ethical and forthright in my interactions with the participants and above all tried to remember that I was as much a learner as the participants and that in this research, we stood at the same level.

## 6.8 The Research Story

### *6.8.1 The Context*

The ZIPRA Veterans Trust (ZVT) is a nongovernmental organisation established in 2009 to spearhead the welfare of the former ZAPU military wing, the Zimbabwe People's Revolutionary Army (see Sect. 2.1.3). Although initially they belonged to the state-supported Zimbabwe Liberation War Veterans Association (ZNLWVA), which brought together former ZANLA and ZIPRA fighters, most of the former ZIPRA who had been commanders and trainers during the liberation struggle decided to establish the trust because they felt their welfare was not being taken care of. They also felt that the violent nature of the ZNLWVA did not correspond with the ethos of their former party and liberation army. ZVT is a membership-based organisation with about 10 000 members across the whole country and membership is open to all former ZIPRA combatants. The organisation is run by a committee and reports to the membership at the annual general meeting.

While it was moving around the country mobilising the ZIPRA veterans, members met with chiefs and other traditional leaders who complained to them about the violence they were experiencing at the hands of their comrades. The sheer volume of complaints drove them to want to bring about peace between the communities and their members and so peacebuilding and community healing was added as a component of their programme. They approached GTH in 2010 with a request to collaborate with them in this aspect of their programme and the two organisations have continued to work together as and when necessary. The research participants were drawn from this committee. I was involved in the training of their provincial committee members across the country over a period of six months and we also facilitated funding for their initial community healing activities. Over the years, I had grown to know most of them and had also established relationships with many of them. This relationship made it easier to involve them in the research project and helped reduce some of the power issues between them and myself.

In August 2011, I approached the chairman of the ZIPRA Veterans Trust and explained to him what I was trying to do and my desire to work with his members on this project. He tasked the Secretary General to recruit members who were interested in participating. Unfortunately, due to their internal politics, the start of the research was delayed till January 2012. Another person took over and started recruiting also; this resulted in a number of people pulling back causing a long delay of six months. This was eventually sorted out and I met on 26th January 2012 with some of the interested participants. This was a brief meeting to explain the whole concept. We then met on 27th January with ten participants: seven members of the trust, including the vice chairman, and three of their student interns. Initially, I was not very keen to include the students as I felt they could not make a significant contribution to the process and would not be there till the end, as they had to go back to university in the middle of the research. However, in the spirit of PAR, I accepted them, albeit grudgingly. As it turned out, their contribution was excellent as they helped me understand how the younger generation is experiencing the effects of their parents' trauma.

Altogether, a total of 15 people participated in the research at some point. Of these, two attended the first two meetings and then dropped out, one attended one meeting which was a reflection on the workshop we had held. Two joined us for the workshop and stayed to the end. Four were females and the rest male. One of the females was a student intern, which left two females who participated to the end of the research project, as the other only came to one session. The age range for the ex-combatants was mid-50s to late 60s and the students were all in their 20s. The research was conducted at the GTH offices which are within church premises and provided a relaxed and safe space for the participants.

I think it is important to point out that I do not consider any of these individual participants to be suffering from any form of PTSD or any pathological disorder as such (see discussion in Sect. 3.3). I would not classify them as 'victims' but as 'survivors' because, for the past 30 or so years, they have lived life to the best of their ability and led lives that would generally be considered 'normal' in the circumstances under which they live (see Sect. 2.3). However, as their stories reveal, some are definitely hurting and angry, and one or two often spoke about a desire for revenge. Their struggles though, are similar to those of the average person from the communities of Matabeleland.

### 6.8.2 The Research Process

Several dialogue sessions were held before we could decide our first major action (the TOL workshop, see Sect. 6.8.3) took place. We needed to agree on the modalities of the process and develop a common understanding of PAR and conflict transformation theory. This was a bit challenging because I did not want to portray myself as knowing more than the other participants, so, instead of giving out information on the theories, I had to use a lot of questions as a way of teasing out the theories and concepts from the group. I think that, in the end, it worked out well and proved the veracity of PAR's belief in the knowledge co-generative power of participants (Greenwood/Levin 1998; Farnworth 2007), as we were able to engage with theory and concepts in a practical but academic manner. This exploratory process was very valuable as it resulted in learning for all of us, I reflect on my own learning journey below (Sect. 6.9 and Table 6.3).

This summary of our research process serves to illustrate just how different the working out of one participatory action research can be from another (see Sect. 5.8). Each PAR project is unique because 'it is responsive to the particular context, composition of participants, and research question' (Dickson 1997, p. 57).

**Table 6.3** The chronology and steps of the research process. *Source* The author

| Date | Steps | No. of participants (Excluding Researcher) | Purpose |
|---|---|---|---|
| August 2011 | Initial contact | 1 | This involved meeting with the chairman of ZVT and sharing with him the research topic I wanted to explore and the research design I intended to use. Proposal was accepted and an individual assigned to recruit interested people. Internal politics delay start by six months |
| 26/01/12 | Initial meeting | 4 | At this meeting, I explained to the group what I wanted to do and the fact that this was part of my doctoral studies. I also discussed with them what PAR was and how I hoped it would work for us. They expressed interest and suggested meeting the following day for the first dialogue session as some of them had not made it that day |
| 27/01/2012 | 1st dialogue session | 10 | At this meeting, I again explained how and what I was proposing to do. A considerable amount of time was spent negotiating the form and content of the research and the principles to govern our interaction. I explained that, as primary targets of *Gukurahundi*, the research could be of benefit to them and their organisation. Topics discussed included the effects of violence caused by those who are supposed to be our protectors and the effects of trauma in an oppressive environment, |

(continued)

**Table 6.3** (continued)

| Date | Steps | No. of participants (Excluding Researcher) | Purpose |
|---|---|---|---|
| | | | where people are not allowed to talk about their traumatic experiences and forgiveness and healing |
| 2/02/2012 | 2nd dialogue session | 8 | We discussed journaling our research experiences. Most of the time was spent in people telling their experiences of *Gukurahundi* and how they hoped the research would assist them in their pain |
| 23/02/2012 | 3rd dialogue session | 6 | We explored concepts of healing, forgiveness, forgetting and apology. As a small exercise, the group decided to interview other people to find out what they thought needed to be done for them to heal |
| 29/03/2012 | 4th dialogue session | 7 | This occurred after two previous attempts to meet had failed. There was report back from a few participants about finding out what people wanted done in order to heal. Issues of macro vs micro intervention arose during the discussions, as well as individual vs communal healing |
| 26/04/2012 | 5th dialogue session | 6 | Compensation, justice and a lot of 'off topic' discussion took place. Participants consisted of three trust members and the three interns |
| 17/05/2012 | 6th dialogue session | 5 | We looked at the modalities for workshops. Further discussion around the practicalities of trying to heal without an official apology, justice and the passing of the hurts and hates to the next generation |
| 14–16/06 2012 | 1st action (workshop) | 8 | Trauma healing workshop facilitated by Tree of Life (see Sect. 6.8.3) based on a group therapy approach using the analogy of a tree |
| 28/06/2012 | 7th dialogue session | 11 | Reflection on workshop, planning for next action |
| 16/08/2012 | 2nd action (writers' workshop) | 8 | In preparation for the next action—truth telling and critical history recovery—we invited a local renowned author and historian for a half day seminar on writing personal stories for publishing. Writing of life stories began |
| 15 May 2014 | Review of research process | 4 | End of research project, sharing of research findings and their validation. Story writing project for research participants, TOL workshops for other ZVT members continue |

### 6.8.3 Detailed Description of Research Process

Because of the internal politics mentioned in Sect. 6.8.1, the research project almost suffered a still birth, but, after my intervention, it got back on track. The person who had originally been tasked to mobilise participants did not join the group until the TOL workshop. I could not establish why he did not mobilise participants or why he decided to join the group at this late time. As far as I could tell, the group dynamics did not reflect any tensions at any point during the research period. According to Maguire (1993, p. 163),

> Developing caring relationships with people, oppressed or otherwise, takes time for meaningful involvement in each other's lives and nurturance of the relationship... Likewise, it takes that same time to and meaningful involvement for those participating in the project to develop relationships with each other, and not simply the researcher.

The establishment of rapport between the participants and myself was not difficult as I had a working relationship with each of them and because they also had a long history of group cohesion and trust.

Participants did not actively participate during the first meeting, mainly because they were still trying to understand what it was we were trying to do. A greater part of that meeting was spent in discussions about the logistics of the project. A letter requesting the participation of each person was distributed and the contents explained. Informed consent forms were signed by all participants. We then negotiated about the timing and length of meetings as well as the guiding principles for the process. I then attempted to explain what PAR was and how I thought the process would unfold. As this was my first PAR project, explaining to the group the modalities of PAR was difficult to do as I was doing so from what I had read, rather than from practical experience. I felt I left the participants only a little more knowledgeable but, because the topic was of interest and relevance to them, they were eager to take part. Looking back, maybe this was a good thing as I could genuinely say I was not the source of knowledge and this helped in reducing the power inequalities between us.

I was surprised by how our discussions often mirrored the given theories of healing, although we had not explicitly discussed these. By the second session, the participants were actively interacting with each other and the topic, and even the student interns contributed significantly to the discussions and provided great insight into the world of young people struggling with the reality of the effects of *Gukurahundi* in their generation. At the second session, participants shared their individual experiences with *Gukurahundi*. While most could share their stories comfortably, one participant, J, could not go beyond one sentence (see Sect. 6.7), indicating how raw her pain still was. J became my indicator of how successful our search for healing would be and I was disappointed when she failed to come to the TOL workshop with the rest of the group. However, she subsequently attended the next one organised directly by the Trust and I discuss her experience in full in the following chapters.

By the third session, people suggested that, to come up with a relevant healing mechanism, we needed to find out from the people in our communities what they wanted to see happen for them to heal. I did not see the value of this as I felt we all knew already what the people would say and besides, for me, the focus at this stage was internally focused on the group, rather than externally on the community. Nevertheless, participants agreed to carry out an exercise to interview different community members. During their report back, at the fourth session, I realised we had not thought through the exercise enough. We could have better prepared for it by formulating specific questions to be asked. Although some participants had done the exercise, it was done so haphazardly that little benefit was derived from it.

From this point on (February 23rd 2012), it became difficult for the group to maintain our fortnightly meetings, as they became more and more involved with their own programme, which often took them out of town for long periods of time. As can be noted from the above summary, attendance was an issue right from the beginning and only a few participants managed to attend consistently throughout the project. Sometimes, only three people from the previous session would be present at the next session; it was often necessary to repeat issues from the previous meeting as a way of helping other participants catch up. Since I was not paying them or contributing in any way to their expenses for attending the meetings, I was really at the mercy of their convenience. (The dilemma of paying or not paying the participants (Maphosa 2013) never really arose as I simply had no money to do so.) In fact, there were times when we went for months without meeting, as only two or three people would turn up, despite great efforts to invite them in advance and reminding them twice prior to the meeting day. This became worse after the writing workshop as people struggled to keep up with their writing schedule. What participants had been encouraged to do was to work on the framework of their story and then meet to discuss these in a group before writing out the framework in full. I then resorted to meeting them as individuals to assist with the development of their stories and I was also able to assist with the typing of the final scripts which were handwritten. At the close of this research, four of the participants had completed their stories, although they needed polishing up.

#### 6.8.3.1 The Writing Workshop

The life story writing project was one of the actions requested by the group; indeed, throughout our discussions, the need to record their stories as a way to counter the 'false' history espoused by the ZANU PF government, as well as for posterity, kept coming up. After the TOL workshop and the reflection on the workshop, it was decided to embark on the writing exercise. I approached a renowned Ndebele historian and author, who has written extensively about some of the ZIPRA and ZAPU leaders, to teach the group about how to write their stories for publication. He offered us a half-day workshop for which I paid a nominal fee and eight participants attended. He presented us with a simple but effective method which the writers could use as a guide in their story writing, by dividing their lives into four frameworks. Some of the participants found the writing a challenge and gave up along the way. Although I had offered to record their oral stories and transcribe them, no one took up this offer. At least three of them relished the opportunity and did not struggle much with their stories. These stories will not form part of the data analysis here as that is beyond the scope of this thesis. Since PAR is an ongoing cycle of reflection and action (Wadsworth 1998; McNiff/Whitehead 2006), members of the group will be assisted with the publication of their stories outside of this research.

#### 6.8.3.2 The Tree of Life Workshop

After failing to make any meaningful contact with Father Lapsley's Healing of Memories Institute, we turned to Tree of Life which was willing, not only to facilitate the workshop for the group, but also to bear the greater cost of the workshop. The TOL workshop took place in May 2012 and was attended by eight participants, two of whom joined us for the first time. The workshop was held over a two-day period at a camping site on the outskirts of Bulawayo.

The Tree of Life was originally developed in South Africa for unemployed and HIV/AIDS-affected young people. It was later adapted to the needs of Zimbabwean victims of political violence. Based in South Africa and brought into Zimbabwe in 2004 (Reeler et al. 2009; Schweitzer et al. 2014), the process consists of a series of circles and uses the analogy of individuals in a community and a tree in the bush. The parts of the tree are used to discuss the various stages of an individual's life. Participants discuss the roots (their genealogy), the trunk (childhood), leaves (important features) and fruits (family and future plans), and explore the issues of connectedness and diversity.

Participants agree together on a set of rules for the workshop. One of the central circles is a 'trauma circle' where participants share their traumatic experiences in a safe and honouring environment. After an individual shares their story a moment of silence is held in honour of their story. The setting of this circle is such that participants usually find it easier to tell their stories and to express their deep-felt emotions. Another element of this process which our group found inspiring had to do with observing the experiences which a tree has gone through. The facilitators try to find a tree that has had rough treatment by people or nature. It might have cut-off, bent or dry branches etc. A discussion on the resiliency of the tree and what traumatised participants can learn from it takes place around that tree. Basically, 'the Tree of Life is a healing and empowerment workshop that combines the concepts of storytelling, healing of the spirit, reconnecting with the body and re-establishing a sense of self-esteem and community' (Reeler et al. 2009, p. 182). The process does not require clinically-trained counsellors, thus making it viable for use at minimum cost. I examine the effectiveness of the workshop in Sect. 7.2.

## 6.9 Limitations

This study does not offer 'measurable' empirical data in the sense that the research design is less structured and has fewer formal measures of control (Babbie/Mouton 2001). As has been discussed in Chap. 5 and Sect. 6.6, it relies on relationships of trust and participation to mitigate error and establish validity in the research. This approach can be prone to exaggeration and over-simplification and relies heavily on the researcher's interpretation (Dickinson 1997, p. 109). With such small numbers, the findings of this research cannot be said to be representative of the ordinary community members in rural Matabeleland and, as such it is difficult to assert with certainty whether similar outcomes could be achieved in that environment. Another limiting factor is that the actions we carried out during this project did not confer upon the participants the power to change policy (McIntyre 2008, p. 47) and this was a cause for frustration to participants who really wanted to see the transformation at a systemic level.

## 6.10 Reflection on My Learning Journey

One of the important elements of any action research is the need for self-reflexivity on the part of the researcher (Kemmis 2006; McNiff/Whitehead 2006, 2010). In this Sect. 1 briefly reflect on how this research project contributed to my understanding of both the research process itself and the topic under study (Babbie/Mouton 2001, p. 323; Moore 2004, p. 150).

Doing this research was a sharp learning curve for me because my master's degree was module based with a minor research component. As a result, my research skills and knowledge were limited and using PAR as my research design made things more complicated.

Reading through PAR examples, I understood the need to engage the participants in a dialogue as a way of interrogating their situations, to come up with a better understanding of their problem (Greenwood/Lewin 1998; McIntyre 2008; McTaggart 1998). However, the examples I reviewed (see Table 5.3) did not describe the practical steps of doing this particular process. What was particularly missing in most was the transition from reflection to action as, by the fifth session (26 April 2012), we seemed to have lost direction and momentum. There were times when I felt unsure of the path we were taking and thought that at times we were going around in circles. I was not sure how to get the group to the next level, or if we had now gained enough comprehension and appreciation of the issues surrounding our topic (McTaggart 1998, p. 315).

There were times when I felt the group and I were working at cross purposes, given that, while my interest in the healing process focused on the group itself, theirs seemed to be focused outwardly to people 'out there'. As I noted in my reflections:

> I am a bit concerned that we seem to be focusing mostly outside of ourselves—to 'others out there'. My hope was for us to explore this question closer to home, maybe we are not yet ready to get personal? Or will this way we seem to be taking lead back home (personal reflections, 23/02/2012)?

> I feel we are still generalising and still outward focused rather than inward. The sentiment at this point seems to be that, it is difficult to separate individual healing from the systemic (personal reflections 29/03/2012).

In my eagerness to achieve my goals for this research, I almost fell into the trap of the western approach to trauma healing I have argued against (see Sects. 3.3 and 4.1). However, in deference to PAR principles, I did not seek to force the shift, which eventually happened at the TOL workshop where the group was able to look inward and focus on healing themselves.

One of the discouraging things about the research process was the level of the participants' commitment, especially in the doing of the actions the group had identified. McIntyre's warning was apt:

> It is important to remember that daily life and unexpected events 'get in the way' of participants fulfilling project-related obligations. It is one thing for people to talk through an issue and make plans to take action on that issue during a group session: it is quite another for participants to walk out the doors and fulfil project related activities in the midst of their daily lives. It is unlikely that each party, individually or collectively, can or will participate equally in a PAR process (McIntyre 2008, p. 31).

The reality of missed deadlines and postponed meetings caused a certain amount of consternation. I went into this project with a lot of theoretical knowledge and ideas of how the research would proceed, but the reality was different and often off-putting. Maphosa (2013) has deliberated at length about this in his informative article *Thinking creatively about methodological issues in conflict affected societies: a primer from the field,* which offers great insights into the trials and tribulations researchers face in the field.

In short, going through this research was both overwhelming and frustrating. Overwhelming in the sense that half of the time I was not sure of what I was doing. The literature I read did not spell out in detail the practical steps of doing PAR. I was not always confident I was doing the research correctly, did not know how to lead the process or what to expect next. It was frustrating because it was time consuming (Moore 2004, p. 158; Dickinson 1997, p. 34) and I was not able to predict the direction and outcomes of the actions as much as I would have liked to. Transferring the theoretical steps into practice in my research project was my major challenge. However, a visit to the Centre for Conflict and Peace Studies (CCPS) in Cambodia (they offer an MA through Action Research) in March 2013 helped me conceptualise this approach better. It gave me a clearer idea of what I needed to do and how to do it.

I struggled with determining how much data was enough and at what point to end the research process, especially since I felt there was still more to be explored before we could confidently claim to have fully examined the topic satisfactorily. I agree with Greenwood/Levin (1998, p. 245) that, in action research,

> It is difficult to decide when data collection is complete. Deciding how much data is enough, is often a pragmatic matter, not always justifiable in abstract terms. It may be a decision based on fatigue, on exhaustion of financial, physical, or temporal resources or on the sense that there are enough data to say something others will believe about the problem question.

In this case, approaching submission deadline, the apparent loss of interest and busyness of the participants contributed to the decision to end the research. At this point I also felt I had collected enough data (150 pages of transcriptions) and that the two actions completed were enough for the purposes of this research.

My learning through this process was considerable. I learnt about PAR as a research design, how to utilise the dialogue sessions and how, with others, to devise the actions that were carried out. For instance, while reflecting on the research I had done on 'thick' description, I noted the following:

> In reading up I discovered not only what it means but how I can actually use it in analysis and the discussion of the research process… I think I am learning things over and above the research topic. I am learning about the praxis of the methodology also. I still think I am not at a place where I could consider myself to be a competent participatory action researcher, but from where I started, I now understand the issues much more. In addition, I have been in situations where I have not known how the next stage of not only the research project, but its write up as well, would unfold but further reading and interaction has brought me across pertinent information that has bridged the gap (Personal reflections, 30/11/2013).

However, I do think that, because I was hung up on trying to 'get it right', I missed out on the nuanced aspects of PAR. I surmise that because,

> I was preoccupied by the process of trying to do PAR right, I probably missed the intricacies and dynamics I needed to observe during the research project itself. That is, because I was focusing on one aspect of the process other aspects were missed, ignored, or went unnoticed because at that point I didn't know what to look for (Personal reflections, 21/01/2014).

## 6.11 Conclusion

In this chapter, I have explained how this research was carried out. I indicated that PAR is the main research design on which this research was based. I discussed how the healing power of narratives became a sub-research design by default and that the chosen research methodology was premised on qualitative research. The data-collection methods were explained and included dialogue meetings, recording and transcription of discussions, journaling, critical history recovery and interviews where necessary. I described the data analysis process and discussed issues of validity and reliability as well as the ethical considerations that guided the conduct of this research. The chapter has sought to provide a thick description of the whole research process. I have also reflected on my learning process through this research journey.

The discussion in the following chapters in part four will assess to what extent this PAR research project compares with the description of other PAR projects in literature, as reviewed in Chap. 5, and will discuss data analysis and findings.

## References


Auerbach, C. F. and Silverstein, L. B. 2003. *Qualitative data: an introduction to coding and analysis.* N.Y: New York University Press. At: https://nyupress.org/books/9780814706954/ (15 February 2014).

Babbie, E. and Mouton, J. 2001. *The practice of social research.* Cape Town: Oxford Press.

Banks-Wallace, J. 1998. Emancipatory potential of storytelling in a group. *Image: The Journal for Nursing Scholarship,* 30(1): 17–21.

Bazeley, P. 2013. *Qualitative data analysis: practical strategies.* L. A: Sage.

Braun, V. and Clarke, V. 2006. Using thematic analysis in psychology. *Qualitative Research in Psychology,* 3: 77–101.

Collins, K. J. 1998. *Participatory research: a primer.* Cape Town: Prentice Hall.

Costello, P. J. M. 2003. *Action research.* London: Continuum.

Dickson, G. 1997. Participatory action research and health promotion: the grandmothers' story. PhD Thesis, University of Saskatchewan.

Farwell, N. and Cole, J. B. 2002. Community as context of healing: psychosocial recovery of children affected by war and political violence. *International Journal of Mental Health,* 30(4): 19–41.

Francis, D. 2005. *Applied conflict transformation: action research.* UK: RTC.

Gaventa, J. and Cornwall, A. 2006. Power and knowledge. In P. Reason and H. Bradbury (eds.), *Handbook of action research.* London: Sage.

Gibson, W. J. and Brown, A. 2009. *Working with qualitative data.* London, England: SAGE. At: http://dx.doi.org/10.4135/9780857029041 (16 February 2014).

Goto, K., Tiffany, J., Pelto, G. and Pelletier, D. 2008. Use of Q methodology to analyze divergent perspectives on participatory action research as a strategy or HIV/AIDS prevention among Caribbean youth. *AIDS Education and Prevention,* 20(4): 301–311.

Grant, J., Nelson, G. and Mitchell, T. 2008. Negotiating challenges of participatory action research: relationships, power, participation, challenges and credibility. In P. Reason and H. Bradbury (eds.), *The SAGE handbook of action research: participative inquiry and practice.* London: Sage.

Greenwood, D. J. and Levin, M. 1998. Action research, science and the co-optation of social research. *Studies in Cultures, Organization, and Societies,* 4: 237–261.

Harding, J. 2003. *Qualitative data analysis: from start to finish.* L. A: SAGE.

Holloway, I. 1997. *Basic concepts for qualitative inquiry* (2nd ed.). Thousand Oaks, California: Sage.

Kaminer, D. 2006. Healing process in trauma narratives: a review. *South African Journal of Psychology,* 36(3): 481–499.

Kearney, R. 2007. Narrating pain: the power of catharsis. *Paragraph,* 30(1): 51–66.

Kemmis, S. 2006. Exploring the relevancy of critical theory for action research: emancipatory action research in the footsteps of Jurgen Harbemas. In P. Reason and H. Bradbury (eds.), *Handbook of action research.* London: Sage

Maguire, P. 1993. Challenges, contradictions, and celebrations: attempting participatory research as a doctoral student. *Voices of change: participatory research in the United States and Canada,* 157–176.

Maphosa, S. B. 2013. Thinking creatively about methodological issues in conflict-affected societies: a primer from the field. *Journal of Peacebuilding and Development,* 8(2): 91–103. At: http://dx.doi.org/10.1080/15423166.2013.823058 (25 October 2013).

McIntyre, A. 2007. *Participatory action research: qualitative research methods series* 52. L.A: SAGE.

McIntyre, A. 2008. *Participatory action research.* Los Angeles: SAGE Publications.

McNiff, J. and Whitehead, J. 2006. *All you need to know about action research.* London: Sage Publications.

McNiff, J. and Whitehead, J. 2010. *You and your action research project.* London: Routledge

McTaggart, R. 1998. Is validity really an issue for Participatory action research? *Studies in Culture, Organisations and Societies,* 4: 211–236.

Mitchels, B. 2003. Healing the wounds of war and more: an integrative approach to peace—the work of Adam Curle and others with Mir i dobro in Zupanja, Croatia. *British Journal of Guidance & Counselling,* 31(4): 403–415.

Moore, J. 2004. Living in the basement of the ivory tower: a graduate student's perspective of participatory action research within academic institutions. *Educational Action Research,* 12(1): 145–162.

Motsi, R. G. 2010. The trauma caused by the Matabeleland massacre of 1982–1986 in Tsholotsho and how the church can bring transformation using pastoral care. PhD Thesis. University of Pretoria.

Mouton, J. 1996. *Understanding social research.* Pretoria: Van Schaik Publishers.

Mouton, J. 2001. *How to succeed in your Masters and Doctoral studies: a South African guide and resource book.* Pretoria: Van Schaik Publishers.

Onwuegbuzie, A. J., Dickinson, W. B., Leech, N. L. and Zoran, A. N. 2009. A qualitative framework for collecting and analysing data in focus group research. *International Journal of Qualitative Methods,* 8(3): 1–21.

Reeler, T., Chitsike, K., Maizva, F. and Reeler, B. 2009. Tree of Life: a community approach to empowering and healing survivors of torture in Zimbabwe. *Torture,* 19(3): 180–193. At: https://www.ncbi.nlm.nih.gov/pubmed/20065537 (24 March 2014).

Saldana, J. 2009. *The coding manual for qualitative researchers.* L.A: Sage.

Schwandt, T. A. 2001. *Dictionary of qualitative inquiry* (2nd ed.). Thousand Oaks, California: Sage.

Schweitzer, R. D., Vromans, L., Ranke, G. and Griffin, J. 2014. Narratives of healing: a case study of a young Liberian refugee settled in Australia. *The Arts in Psychotherapy,* 41: 98–106. At: http://dx.doi.org/10.1016/j.aip.2013.10.006 (3 February 2014).

Stauffer, C. S. 2009. Acting out the myths: the power of narrative discourse in shaping the Zimbabwe conflict of Matabeleland, 1980–1987. PhD Thesis, University of KwaZulu Natal.

Staub, E., Pearlman, L. A., Gubin, A. and Hagengimana, A. 2005. Healing, reconciliation, forgiving and the prevention of violence after genocide or mass killings: an intervention and its Experimental Evaluation in Rwanda. *Journal of Social and Clinical Psychology,* 24(3): 297–334.

Suter, W. N. 2012. *Introduction to educational research: a critical thinking approach* (2nd ed.). London: Sage.

Wadsworth, Y. 1998. What is participatory action research? At: http://www.aral.com.au/ari/p-ywadsworth98.html (22 August 2013).

Wimberly, E. P. 2011. Storytelling and managing trauma: health and spirituality at work. *Journal of Healthcare for the Poor and Underserved,* 22(3): 48–57.

# Chapter 7
# Evaluating the Participatory Action Research Process

## 7.1 Introduction

This chapter is concerned with the evaluation of the PAR and TOL processes, while Chap. 9 evaluates the outcomes of the entire research. While efforts have been made to stick strictly to process evaluation, it has been difficult in some cases not to comment on outcome where it relates to the process (e.g. Sect. 7.5).

In this sub chapter I evaluate the extent to which the research conformed to standard understandings of PAR and participants' opinions about the process. For the purposes of comparison, I will use a set of qualities, stages and levels of understanding attained by participants, and some general challenges encountered.

### *7.1.1 Qualities of Participatory Action Research*

As indicated in Sect. 5.6, PAR has several distinguishing tenets including the following features: the people being studied participate in the research; popular or local knowledge, personal experiences and any other commonsensical ways of knowing are included; there is a focus on emancipation and power relations, conscientisation and education; and collective or political action takes place (McIntyre 2007, 2008; Greenwood/Levin 1998; Guishard 2009; McTaggart 1998; Dickson 2010). This research exhibited these values in varying degrees.

#### 7.1.1.1 Participation

According to Weaver/Stark's (2006) diagram on the levels of participation, participation in PAR moves from minimum to maximum involvement and from



D. Ngwenya, *Healing the Wounds of Gukurahundi in Zimbabwe*,
The Anthropocene: Politik—Economics—Society—Science 19,
https://doi.org/10.1007/978-3-319-66818-5_7

practical to liberating (see Fig. 5.1). The purpose of this research was to discover non-clinical self-healing methods that could proffer relief to the participants through the healing of their bad memories resulting from their experiences of *Gukurahundi*. It was therefore important for the group members to have as much control as was possible under the circumstances (see Sect. 6.2). It was not just the actions carried out that were meant to bring healing but the whole PAR process. As was discussed in Sect. 5.3, the very nature of PAR challenges the status quo and seeks to equalise power inequities. Despite the inconsistencies in attendance (Sect. 6.8.3), the participants played an active role in the process, making decisions about the direction of the process, questioning certain things, deciding on the actions to be taken and contributing immensely to the discussions during the dialogue sessions. However, I think that the potential for maximum participation was greatly tempered by my limited experience with PAR and their hazy understanding of PAR. In addition, time constraints, competing interests and their life's responsibilities conspired against their full participation. Nevertheless, to a large extent, I was satisfied with the participation levels. Participants, by and large, produced quality participation and enjoyed the whole experience. Several of them commented at various stages of the research on how much they were benefitting from taking part. Even the benefits of the life stories writing exercise, which most found taxing to do, was deemed to have been worthwhile by those who finished it.

#### 7.1.1.2 Indigenous Knowledge

PAR values popular knowledge, personal experiences and feelings, as has been posited by Greenwood/Levin (1998, p. 253): 'Local knowledge, historical consciousness, and everyday experiences of insiders complements the outsider's skills in facilitating learning, technical skills in research procedures, and comparative knowledge of the subject under investigation.' The participants' knowledge was important for me and I believe I genuinely valued the knowledge we generated during the research process. In my attitude and actions, I sought to recognise, validate and honour their knowledge. Our interaction revealed that the participants had thought deeply about their situations and what these meant to their lives. Even in situations where I might have had more knowledge in terms of theories and concepts, I tried to keep in mind Swantz's (2008, p. 38) advice that in PAR,

> The researcher needs to be open to learn from others and to adopt a genuine learner's attitude even in situations in which apparent ignorance tempts her to become a teacher. The researched and the researcher share their knowledge as equals. The researcher genuinely recognises that she does not know the life world, wisdom or meaning of central symbols of the life of the co-researchers.

It was with this in mind, that whenever we were engaged in such discussions, I adopted Freire's 'problem-posing' approach to education (see Sect. 6.8.2). In this way, we could generate useful knowledge and there were instances where terms more appropriate to us and our situations were coined. One such term being 'a measure of relief', which was coined during a discussion on trauma healing.

#### 7.1.1.3 Consciousness-Raising

Consciousness-raising allows individuals to view their problems and situations in relation to larger societal forces and throws a different light on them. The consciousness levels of my participants were quite high: they did not just show a firm grasp of self and their contexts, but they had a wide understanding of the macro context too. In fact, owing to their previous and current stations in life, they possessed inside information that allowed them to easily make connections between their personal problems and the broader politics. In effect, they helped me gain a better appreciation of the dynamics and intricacies of the bigger picture as reviewed in Chap. 2. They all had personally experienced some of the events written about there, and had been victims of many of the conspiracies aimed at ZAPU and ZIPRA, though sometimes I felt that some of their conspiracy theories were too far-fetched to be true. Nevertheless, they possessed a great and present appreciation of how intricate and intertwined with bigger issues their individual problems were. In retrospect, I think this awareness was a source of frustration for them when it came to some of the actions they wanted to carry out. Initially they wanted to tackle the systemic issues related to the causes of their suffering but I felt that this was beyond the scope of this research as we neither had the resources nor the time to take it on. Grant et al. (2008, p. 596) counsel that 'in social change work, it is important to achieve "small wins" rather than expecting large-scale change to occur dramatically'. On this need to be realistic about the expected change, I was able to persuade the group to start with actions that would not overwhelm us before we even started.

#### 7.1.1.4 Political or Collective Action

According to Babbie/Mouton (2001, p. 321), action in PAR should induce positive, remedial and corrective social change or transformation. It focuses on problem solving and involves challenging beliefs, attitudes, structures and systems which perpetuate inequities and injustices. The action, which is undertaken together with the participants, should result in their emancipation. The group undertook two major actions: the TOL workshop which focused on the inner healing for the participants and the writing of their life stories that was aimed at critical recovery of history as a way of challenging the status quo and the suppression of ZAPU and ZIPRA's contributions to the liberation struggle, by presenting an alternative historical discourse (these are discussed in full in Sect. 7.4). The group also carried out an exercise to garner the views of the community on the conditions necessary for healing (see Sect. 6.8.3). The actions performed had to do with knowledge gathering, emancipation through the healing of memories and a challenge to the political system.

To that extent, our research demonstrated adherence to the principles of PAR, albeit in varying degrees. Had the research been longer and well-resourced, I think there could have been an escalation of the magnitude of the actions geared towards challenging the system. The actions undertaken were not actions for their own sake but were relevant and meaningful to the participants and contributed to their wellbeing.

## 7.2 Stages of Participatory Action Research

As described in Sect. 5.4, PAR projects are characterised by four main stages: inquiry, planning, action and reflection. While all PAR projects will reflect these stages in one form or another, these are iterative and cyclical rather than linear, and how they manifest in a particular project will depend on the nature of that project.

### *7.2.1 Inquiry and Planning*

At this stage of the research, participants spent time identifying the problem they wished to study; setting the agenda for the dialogues and prioritising issues that were important for them; reflecting on their experiences; and drawing up actions they considered to be possible and pertinent in the context of their lives (Koch/Kralik 2006). I have included these two stages together because, in our group, from day one, while we were still crystallising the issues and problems, hints and suggestions of actions that could possibly be taken were already being made. Once the initial hesitations of the first dialogue were overcome, participants delved into serious and deep analysis and reflection regarding their situations and tried to construe meaning out of their experiences. Although possible actions were mentioned quite early on in our dialogue, we did not start thinking seriously about the actions to take and plan for at this point; this happened at the 5th meeting, which was four months later. The two activities we eventually settled on meant that I did most of the organising, since I had connections with the facilitators of the TOL and writing workshops. I was also friends with the proprietors of the campsite where we planned to have the TOL workshop and I was meeting some of the costs for the camp. The actual working out of the modalities for the two activities and decisions that needed to be made was a group effort and each participant had as much a say as the next person in the group. I recall that the issue of the timing of the days was debated quite extensively: the TOL facilitators had preferred weekdays but the group felt that a weekend suited them better and this is what we settled for.

### 7.2.2 Action

This aspect of PAR has already been discussed above and I have indicated that three actions were carried out (see Sects. 8.3 and 7.1 for a full discussion). I am including this matter here just to indicate the progression taken by this research. In this section, I merely wish to point out that the inquiry and exploration engaged in resulted in the translation of the knowledge generated into action (Koch/Kralik 2006). The actions were geared to answering the question of self-healing and, in so doing, we were not oblivious of the macro and systemic dimensions that interacted with the participants' situations and experiences, and, as has been stated (Sect. 7.1) and as is discussed below (Sect. 7.4), we were quite sensitive to these. However, given the prevailing conditions around the issue of *Gukurahundi* (see Sect. 4.1), the research had to address what was possible at that point in time and what was possible was addressing the issues of resilience and agency of each participant. The other actions which participants discussed, such as challenging the perpetrators to apologise, large scale truth-telling or *testimonio* sessions and legal action, were beyond the scope of this research as they would have required mass mobilisation and a direct challenge to the political authorities, none of which we had the capacity nor the time to do. The advice that 'PAR participants must be willing to reasonably live with the consequences of the decisions they make, and the actions they take, and the actions that follow from those decisions' (Kemmis/McTaggart 2005, p. 46), weighed heavily on my mind during the discussions about what actions to take. I for one was not sure I was willing to live with the consequences that would result from such action and ethically, I felt it would be wrong to expose the participants to the dangers that result from direct confrontation with the power holders, although they themselves seemed willing to do that. I also had to consider the fact that an important aspect of PAR is that action is not taken on everything that the participants bring to light. Our actions were of course limited because they did not confer on us the power to change or influence policy (McIntyre 2008), but then that was never one of the stated objectives of this research.

### 7.2.3 Reflection

Francis (2007) suggests that reflection should happen at two levels: the evaluation of the action and its impact on future action, and the research itself. Babbie/Mouton (2001) view it as a discussion of the action implications of results, the reviewing of experiences and reflection in general on the nature of the research with the participants. This group could reflect on the TOL workshop two weeks after the event. The reflection process involved members of the group who had not attended the workshop and it was fascinating to observe the difference in the thinking patterns between the two sub-groups (see Sect. 7.4). This was followed 18 months later by an interview with three of the group members to assess the long-term impact of the workshop, as well as by a final dialogue session where reflections on the whole research process and my preliminary findings were discussed.

Periodically we had what I will call 'informal' reflections on the process and other similar healing processes that the group members had taken part in prior to the research. That is, people kept making inferences during the dialogues about what they thought about the research process. However, in our sixth dialogue, when I tried to ask a direct question about what the group thought about the research process so far, the discussion took an unexpected turn: we ended up having a deep conversation about what it was exactly we were trying to accomplish with the research, which led to a discussion on forgiveness, revenge, tolerance and healing. What I had hoped for in asking the question was to hear how the participants found the process, if it was challenging their thinking capacities, whether they were gaining new insights, etc. On hindsight, I think I should have provided questions that allowed the participants to interrogate the various aspects of the process systematically.

## 7.3 Points of Tension

### *7.3.1 Research Knowledge*

At the outset of a PAR project, it is the responsibility of the researcher to make sure the participants understand the values and principles of PAR and how this research approach is carried out. In our case, as already indicated in Sect. 6.8.3, owing to my lack of practical experience and limited knowledge of PAR, I was not confident that participants had a full appreciation of this research design. But, as Kemmis/ McTaggart (1991, p. 290) have counselled, 'What makes PAR "research" is not the machinery of research techniques but rather an abiding concern with the relationships between social and educational theory and practice.' As I have shown in the sections above, we were nevertheless able to abide by the spirit and praxis of PAR by our approach to knowledge generation and consensus building on the direction and actions to be undertaken by the group. Although not explicitly defined, my epistemological assumptions were that we were unlikely to come up with one answer which was devoid of dissonance and ambiguity. What we created, and what was meaningful and effective to us as a group, was the knowledge which guided our theories. We constantly interacted with this knowledge process right through the research process, and, even by the end of the research, answers generated were still being interrogated. A lot of useful knowledge was created. In some cases, it helped to clarify theories and concepts read in literature; at other times, it helped to crystallise issues by the way certain phrases and ideas were framed (I discuss some of these in Chap. 8).

### 7.3.2 Research Resources

For PAR to be effective, adequate resources need to be utilised: namely—time, finance and skills. This is however not unique to PAR as it applies to most forms of research, but it is often overlooked in PAR because of the view that this is a grassroots approach done by local people themselves, and therefore not requiring the same levels of resources as the other mainstream research approaches (Dickson 1997). In most PAR researches, there is a need to allow for sufficient time for building trusting relationships, but this was not necessary for our group as we already had this established (see Sect. 6.8.3). What was problematic was trying to balance the university time-frame with the participants' life demands. As shown by the case studies (Table 5.3), PAR demands a lot of time and the researcher must be willing to commit an extended period of time for the process. The average time for most of them was two and half years, while bigger projects can take up to 10 years.

Funding is often necessary to sustain the longevity of the project; ours relied on my student scholarship which was not enough to prolong the research. I was unable to fund the participants' bus fares to and from the research venue and it is possible that some might have struggled with this challenge silently. I thought our research still had a few more rounds of action to go and, with time and resources; it might have grown to encompass the wider community. One aspect of the research that continued was the TOL workshops, which the participants felt would benefit the rest of the ZVT membership. TOL continues to fund and run these workshops for them and, as of May 2014, between 50 and 60 of the members had attended the workshops.

## 7.4 Evaluation of the Tree of Life Workshop

### 7.4.1 'If the Tree Can Survive Under All Those Conditions, I Can also Live Under All These Conditions'

This subchapter critically examines the impact of the TOL workshop on the participants, based on reflection and interviews with the participants (see Sect. 7.2 on reflection). The life stories writing exercise is not assessed here as, at the close of the project, the stories were not yet edited and published as planned by the group. I could not therefore, effectively evaluate that process as it was incomplete. The proceeds of the dialogue sessions are discussed in the analysis chapter (see Sect. 8.1) and the overall impact of the whole research process is discussed in Chap. 9.

### 7.4.2 *Effectiveness of Tree of Life in Other Contexts*

GTH and TOL belong to the same trauma healing network in Zimbabwe, so I knew its staff and knew about the work they were doing. Although I had met some of their participants I had not yet witnessed their healing approaches. Most of the work they had done involved recent cases of organised violence and torture in the last ten years. Reeler et al. (2009) carried out an assessment of TOL's work in Mashonaland. According to them, a sample of 73 persons who had attended the TOL workshops were surveyed but detailed data was available for only 33, and these revealed that 36% of participants had shown significant clinical improvement, while the sample as a whole showed significant changes in their psychological state. A smaller sample of 19 had more complete data, and from these it was deduced that 39% showed significant improvement. During the follow-up done a few months after the workshops, they found that 56% reported coping better, while 44% were still experiencing difficulties, with most (72%) experiencing economic difficulties. Only 9% reported health problems, while most of the respondents still had connections to the groups in which they had participated in the process. They report that all the participants felt that the process had helped them find new things to focus on in life and had changed the way they felt about their traumatic experiences. They conclude by saying the 'Tree of Life appears to be a useful, cost effective, non-professional method of assisting torture survivors' (Reeler et al. 2009, p. 180).

I was therefore curious to find out if this method would be appropriate and effective for 30-year old trauma experiences. At this stage of the research, our discussions and the current events[1] had confirmed something I already knew: that there was an unofficial system[2] in place to deliberately marginalise and suppress the people from Matabeleland. In addition, I had become wary of programmes that encouraged victims of violence to 'forgive' their perpetrators so as to heal, but fail to deal with the systemic causes of the violence. Such an approach, I now felt, left people vulnerable to further abuse by the state, as such a process simply served 'to heal lambs for the slaughter' (Wessells 1999, p. 6, see also Sect. 4.1). As I pointed out to the participants during the workshop review:

> I am beginning to develop an issue, having listened to what we have been talking about for the past, almost now…I think it's about three months mmm…I have been a bit concerned that I did not want to do something that will make you forget that there is a system that still needs to be dealt with. That we would say ok, fine, let's get healed and let's go on with life, whereas there's a system that is out to actually continue to destabilise, and that to me has been quite an issue that I have been battling with…

I was therefore concerned that the TOL workshop would turn out to be one of those that would be a tonic for continued suppression of the traumatised

[1]As mentioned in Sect. 4.1.

[2]See Appendix A, Progress Review of the 1979 Grand Plan.

communities because of a reckless push for a 'forgive and forget' type of philosophy, at all costs.

### 7.4.3 *Effectiveness of Tree of Life Workshop in the Context of This Study*

I will evaluate the workshop's effectiveness by tracing and comparing some of the sentiments expressed by the participants before and after the workshop. I will discuss the contents of the workshop evaluation meeting and end by reviewing the follow up interviews that took place about 18 months after the workshop with some of the participants.

When we met on 28th June 2012 to analyse the workshop, the atmosphere created by the retreat was still present and people were still excited about their experiences. The first question asked was, 'What had been helpful and what had not been?' While the entire process had been helpful, the one exercise that stood out above the rest was the discussion we had around the tree about its resiliencies (see Sect. 6.8.3). Our discussion was not linear: certain responses triggered reactions that veered the discussion in other directions which connected to previous discussions, after which we would come back to the original question—and so the process went.

### 7.4.4 *Change in Tone of Language and Attitude*

During the dialogue sessions and before the TOL workshop, there seemed to be a general consensus among the participants about the need for revenge. This issue specifically, as well as other similar sentiments, were discussed robustly, and several of the participants appeared to favour and seemed prepared to exert vengeance in one form or another, given an opportunity. They could not see any other way of dealing with the situation besides getting their own back, as one of them succinctly summed up the hopelessness of the situation as they perceived it: 'I *can't* see the way through. The *only* way through is the way in. The way we got in is the way we will come out' (italics added). At the workshop review this tone of language and attitude had changed significantly and the focus had shifted to healthier ways of dealing with the hurts. The discussion indicated that there had been a notably diminished desire for revenge by most participants. T said, 'I for one had that mind that if one day, if I'm given that chance, I would do it. But looking at this workshop, the way things were laid out, I had or maybe I gained a positive attitude…I noticed that after this I just had a positive mind…' He further indicated that, whereas previously he saw nothing good in the offender, which is a step away from the dehumanisation of the offender (see Oelosfen 2009), he now tried to 're-humanise' or, as he put it, 'view the person with a positive mind.' Another one added: '…I think it's what I said before, that the violent manner has left, and in the end, I also realised that for this thing to end I should not solve it violently…'

While a few had specific individuals in mind when it came to the question about, to whom the vengeance would be meted out, by and large the indication was that vengeance would be targeted at ordinary members of the 'offending' ethnic group (see Sect. 2.3). While I had encountered this attitude mostly among countless survivors and Ndebele activists over the years, I found this somewhat disconcerting within the context of the group, because this was coming from people involved in peacebuilding and students studying peace and conflict at a high level. It appears that when people have no outlet to express their hurts and anger, they will channel their revenge or desire for revenge against innocent members of the group from which the offenders originate (see Botcharova 2001). This phenomenon is similar to the displaced aggression theory in psychology, wherein the target of the aggression is not the source of the initial harm, and is usually less powerful than both the initial offender and offended (see Anderson/Bushman 2002; Kramer 2000; Finch 2006).

What was interesting was the contrast in attitudes between those who had attended the workshop and those who did not. One individual, L, who had not attended the workshop and who was one of those with strong views about the need for revenge, was still in the same place, expressing similar sentiments, albeit in a less vehement manner (I discuss the issue of revenge in detail in Sect. 8.3.2).

### *7.4.5 'Our Branches Have Been Broken'*

The workshop introduction is done in such a way that it puts participants at ease and tries to show them that they are interlinked and interdependent, even though they might be strangers. Although we were all familiar with each other, this approach helped to remove whatever inhibitions there might have been, as the participants felt at home with the process and were able to open up from the beginning. In Sect. 6.10, I referred to how I felt the participants and I were working at cross-purposes in terms of the inward and outward focus of the healing process. The workshop solved this issue as its emphasis was on inner healing, and it prioritised building capacity for resilience and agency in individuals through a group-based approach. It helped to demonstrate the need for participants to be healed themselves before they could embark on efforts to heal their communities. As one of the participants, V, put it: 'Tree of Life gave us an insight into how we can heal as individuals and also empowered us in our quest for resources that would obviously sober down and give us a direction of inducing the rest of the communities around to do the same.'

The issues of resilience and agency came up as some of the things participants had gained from the workshop. Resilience could be defined as the ability to bounce back from adversity or, according to Rivas (2007), the 'ability to respond positively to a stressful event or negative conditions' (see Sect. 3.2.5 for a discussion on resilience). On the other hand, agency could be defined as the capacity of human beings to shape the circumstances in which they live, rather than being shaped by them (Emirbayer/Mische 1998; Abele et al. 2008).

In our case, it was closely tied to the tree we spent some time studying. This tree had one of its boughs sawn off, several scars on its trunk and one branch which at one time seemed to have been growing downwards but had managed to grow upwards again. This particular tree presented an excellent analogy of the type of life experiences that participants had gone through. While analysing this tree and comparing it to our lives, it became clear to all just how much adversity the tree had endured and this became an inspiration to the participants for how it was possible to overcome their personal adversities and live victoriously despite their circumstances. The following were some of the attributes of the tree which participants thought were instructive:

Firstly, the tree continues to grow healthily because its roots, which are the centre of its life, are intact. On this B concluded:

> It helped me a lot, because when I observe, the tree won't die if you cut it and leave its roots. That is the first thing I realised that as long as the roots are not removed the tree will not die…As long as it has roots it will always grow, this is one of the things I liked. If I am cut…, but then still you as a human being, how is your nature, it is to continue going forward you must not go back and say I have been cut and then stay there and limp.

V took this analogy further saying:

> People would say but I am more than a tree, you see. If you cut the tree and it continues to live, why can't I be the same? That's the way of trying to forego the past and continue focusing on the future, because the tree has a future, because it's still continuing to…, isn't and to us this is a double advantage that we had, in the sense that we got to yield ourselves as individuals and also, we obtained a vehicle or we acquired a vehicle which we can institute in our quest to develop this, this face, you see which we always have.

In a way, the participants were saying that, although they had been 'cut down', their life's essence had not been snuffed out or completely destroyed. Like the tree, they still had what it takes to regain their agency and live fruitful and fulfilling lives. It gave them hope and a fresh perspective on life as they realised that the scars and the 'woundedness' that had been inflicted on them and which had been hindering their wellbeing, did not necessarily mean the end of a future they might have once dreamt of.

Secondly, the tree has adapted to its adverse environment; that is to say, the conditions under which it is striving have not necessarily changed to favour it, yet it apparently is growing like any of the other trees around it. If it did not have the visible marks of its adversarial experiences, it would not have stood out from the other trees. Here is how T thought it benefited him:

> Looking at the tree, how it is nurtured or how it nurtured itself, uhm… how it gets to adapt to the environment, all those things. I took it upon myself that, that tree resembles my life, how I've managed to go through all those things and found it helpful because this gave me the strength to keep on keeping on, because looking at the challenges that one might face,

> you might never in life get the chance for someone to come and apologise,… but looking at this workshop that we had, I think it is, uhm… I think it was really helpful, a good benefit to me… So, I took it upon myself that if the tree can survive under all those conditions, then I can also live under these conditions that is how, I found this helpful to me.

Lastly, although the tree was 'hurt', because of its nonviolent nature, it did not retaliate.[3] As they saw it:

> …If you take the symbolism of a tree, when we were around that tree. We all stood by it, we touched its branch, we touched its trunk but then we realise that, that tree was non-violent, ok, that tree of course it's not a human being, however it had feelings, it has got feelings because it bled by the time it was cut that other stump which was on it. I'm sure it bled for weeks on end, isn't it? Until that area dried up but then still it didn't go out to retaliate because it's a tree. If we can symbolise ourselves in the feature of that tree we will be able to reconcile with ourselves… If we imagine ourselves in the form of a tree and say he came, he cut, but left us standing, but our lives must go on isn't it?…Now as human beings we have got feelings and we have got motives…But if we re-align our brains as human beings, ah, let us behave like trees so that we can then be able to reconcile with ourselves.

I was intrigued by the deduction they made about the tree being nonviolent by nature. I think it had to do with the fact that the issue of revenge had featured prominently in our dialogues and was an issue that several of the participants struggled with. The tree's apparent inability to react could have also been interpreted negatively under different circumstances. The fact that the group interpreted this positively could be an indication of the effectiveness of the process and the atmosphere under which the workshop was held. While acknowledging the power of their emotions and motives for revenge, they also realised that as human beings they were superior to the tree in the order of creation and, as such, they had a moral obligation to resist reacting violently towards those perceived to be the perpetrators.

## 7.5 Lessons from Tree

### *7.5.1 Facing the Everyday Realities*

Further to the tenets discussed above, a few more lessons were drawn from the tree. The first one, which is related to the tree's ability to adapt mentioned above, was that the tree lived positively with its everyday realities. That is to say, the tree was not in denial about the realities of its situation. E put it this way: 'We have a saying that, when the tree is cut, the axe will forget but the tree won't. It's another lesson, that tree will always have that stump and so even us as people we live with the

[3]This is one of the limitations of the tree analogy in application to human life, in the sense that such analogies can be stretched so far before they become meaningless or even downright ridiculous. However, although I felt that this analogy may have fallen into this category, the participants found it useful.

reality of our stumps, our branches are broken.' This was in reaction to the question I had asked about whether the participants were finding what they had learnt at the workshop helpful in their everyday situations. They agreed that there was still a positive transformation but also acknowledged that they faced real obstacles as they tried to apply lessons learnt. B pointed out:

> Let me say that it's relief, because it is a short-term relief because, yes at that time you will be relieved, but then you come back to the real society now; you come back and as soon as you arrive you realise that you are still part of the system, you are still in the same environment, in the same environment which cut you down.

My summary of the situation after some discussion was as follows:

> When we were there it was almost like a mini paradise. Problems here are not problems there, we are all in solidarity you know, we are crying with you, but then we come back, you come back to the real world and, you still have to struggle with the same environment. Like that tree is still surrounded by the elements that hurt it, but how is it surviving? I think that is where the big challenge is.

To emphasis this point, L used the analogy of a funeral wake. While the bereaved person has people around her to offer support and comfort, she feels fine and can even joke and laugh but the reality comes back when the coffin is being lowered to the ground. With time this person will learn to cope with the situation but there will always be times when thoughts of the deceased will come back and one might find themselves crying and longing for their loved one. His conclusion was: 'So I think he (referring to B) got relief when the TOL process was going on, but as soon as he got out of that, it was all over again' (I must point out that L is one of the participants that had not made it for the workshop and his views had not been challenged by the process).

Having discussed the reality of their struggles, the participants who had attended the workshop nevertheless unanimously agreed that the process had been worthwhile and that they still found it helpful as they tried to adopt a new perspective in their lives. We settled on the analogy of 'positive living' used by persons living with HIV/AIDS. As we expressed it: 'You are not denying the fact that you are infected, but you have ways of living with it, not as a victim of it, but being able to contain it, to have victory over it.' The point was that while our circumstances had not changed and were unlikely to change in the near future, participants had been equipped by the workshop to live, not as victims but as something above that. This process is similar to that described in Sherman et al.'s (2012, p. 263) study of breast cancer survivors who learnt that they had to develop a new mindset which, while not dismissing their experiences of cancer, required a new way of thinking about their experience and its impact on life in terms of relationships with oneself and others. I understood the participants to be saying that, in the same manner as the cancer survivors, they needed to create a 'new normal' they had control over, using the skills learnt at the workshop. This issue also came up in my follow-up interview with the students 18 months after the TOL workshop (I discuss their responses in Sect. 7.6 below).

### 7.5.2 Agency

The second lesson, related to the above point, was the issue of agency—that participants could still take charge of their destiny despite the debilitating circumstances around them. T expressed it this way: 'So the thing I am trying to say is fine, all these things happened, but we should not glue ourselves to those things and say that all those things happened and my life ends here, no, you can still live within that situation…' His point was that being at the TOL workshop had been like receiving counselling and becoming equipped to live through their circumstances. For him, whether a sick person healed or not, depended on that person's attitude. Even if one receives the best medical care, if they have already given up on life, they will not heal. B pointed out that, even though at some point one of the tree's branches had been growing downward, it had found enough resources within itself to grow upward again and, in comparison, he thought that it was important for one to acknowledge one's pain but then decide on the next course of action in order to move forward. This corresponds with Gaventa's (2006) two forms of power necessary for persons to have mastery over their adverse circumstances: the 'power within' which is defined as 'gaining the sense of self identity, confidence, and awareness that is a precondition for action' and the 'power to' which is 'important for the capacity to act; to exercise agency and to realise the potential of rights, citizenship and voice' (Gaventa 2006, p. 24).

### 7.5.3 Reconciling with Self

Another lesson learnt from the tree by the participants was the ability or need to reconcile with oneself. In chapter three, we discussed the traumatic effects caused by organised violence and noted there, the devastation such effects tend to have on people who experience it. Such experiences, tend to leave individuals alienated from both themselves and their community (see Sect. 3.3.3; Gobodo-Madikizela 2008). So, when the participants spoke about the need to be reconciled to the self, I think they were referring to the journey traumatised people must make back to themselves and their community. As V pointed out:

> In our own hearts, we have to be *reconciled with ourselves*. Say yes *Gukurahundi* it happened (long pause) and of course it's not even in a thousand years will Mugabe come back and say sorry…I think it is a departure point where we can look at another window where we can find a correct, *straight path to healing and personal empowerment*, because what we need at the end of the day is for our people to be healed, because as long as we remain with hurt we will not be able to forgive, whether forgiveness is necessary or not, but we may not be able to live with history of the past that which is distorted, that tree trunk that got cut and probably bent on one side (italics added).

This process of 'reconciling with self' is called 'reclaiming life on one's own terms' by Sherman et al. (2012) or 'meaning making' by Casey/Long (2002). According to Sherman et al. (2012, p. 258), the cancer survivors,

> revealed that breast cancer survivorship is a process marked and shaped by time, the perception of support, and *coming to terms* with the trauma of a cancer diagnosis and the aftermath of treatment. The process of survivorship continues by assuming an active role in *self-healing*, gaining a *new perspective and reconciling paradoxes*, creating a new mindset and moving to a new normal, developing a *new way of being in the world on one's own terms*, and experiencing growth through adversity beyond survivorship (italics added).

One way of achieving this is through storytelling as a way of creating meaning out of one's experiences. For the participants, the workshop, dialogue sessions and life stories served this function (refer to Sect. 8.2.2 for a fuller discussion on the participants' views of narratives as healing).

## 7.6 Follow up Interviews

### *7.6.1 The Students*

As indicated, approximately 18 months after the workshop and the initial post-workshop review, I met with two of the students who had taken part in the research as interns with ZVT. I was interested to determine the long-term impact of the TOL process given the hostile environment the participants faced almost daily. So, I wanted to find out how they had been coping and to hear about their experiences in the 'real' world. The sense I got was that overall, they were still finding the workshop experience helpful. They had apparently developed buzz words such as 'moving on', 'positive mind', 'positive attitude', etc. In fact, in a six-page transcript of the interview the phrase 'moving on' and its derivatives was mentioned 17 times. Both participants indicated that they had had to learn to move on. This was said in the context of what it means to heal. N equated moving on with having a 'clean heart' and for her, it meant the application of the life skills learnt during the TOL workshop. B expressed it thus:

> So, that is the most important thing I learnt is that we have to *move on* sometimes. We don't of course; sometimes we don't get an apology from someone who has hurt us but we have to *move on*. We have to go on by ourselves, it's not about the other person, it's about you personally, so that you can move on because, if you don't heal by yourself, you will always be living in the past; and if you hold on too much to the past, you tend not to grow as a person; it causes trauma to you because you will be always be thinking about that event and blaming the event. If only, if only, if only… So, I think the Tree of Life helped me to have that view on life that you have to *move on* after you have been hurt (italics added).

I was then curious to know what they actually meant by this term 'moving on'. I felt that this was perhaps a key concept in the whole process, and their understanding might provide insights into how they made it work in their lives. N's view of this was that:

> … there are some conditions that have to be met for you to like heal; so, those conditions, they are part of like moving on, because when you say you are moving on with life, it's not like just looking forward and going looking ahead. You have to like look back at the past:

> That's ok—this is what went wrong. It was supposed to go like this and if it's possible to change that route to be what it is supposed to be, then you do that; but at some instances it's not possible because that route would include justice being met… so instead of focusing mainly on those parts that pull you down in life, you focus on the positive. You seek to meet up the demands that have to be met by your positive side…and focusing on that thing, it will help you yourself, even if you are thinking at night, you are thinking about your assignment, you are thinking I should do this, you are not thinking about that thing that happened in the past…but you are just moving on in your heart, which is why I said a clean heart. It means you are no longer burdened by those burdens from the past, but then it's looking forward to challenges in the future.

B pointed out that:

> Moving on is not necessarily forgetting what happened in the past, it is being strong to move on: that is healing. Healing for me is that, that wound which has been there shouldn't be a stumbling block to where you want to go; it should give you power to move on to the future. Yes, that thing happened to me, this thing happened like this to me. It should inspire and motivate me to move to the future rather than going back. Because sometimes we tend to focus too much on the wound or the scar, let me say on the scar, that it was like this here (pointing to a scar on himself), but then it's only a scar. That scar shouldn't pull you back; instead it should motivate you to forge to the future to give you strength rather than pull you back.

Their views represent a higher level of perception and mirror Papadopoulos' (2007) Adversity-Activated Development theory (see Sect. 3.3.4 for a discussion on this), what Carver (1998) calls 'thriving' and Tan (2013) 'posttraumatic growth theory'. Basically, what they say is that sometimes adversity can make a person become better after undergoing that particular adverse circumstance than they were before. In fact, that is exactly what I perceived from the conversation with the students. I understood them to be saying that the workshop had helped them to discover the potential of growing everyday through the adversities they faced. Their conclusions about how to deal with stressful situations corresponds with some of Meichenbaum's (2013, p. 6) pathways to resilience and thriving. He suggests that there are several factors that influence how effectively people deal with trauma and adversity in their lives, and I find some of them to be applicable to how the students seem to have ordered their individual coping strategies:

- *The extent of perceived personal control and use of energies and time on activities and circumstances in which they have some effect.*
  The participants revealed that they had learnt 'certain life concepts' at the workshop, which they said gave them the life skills to deal with obstacles encountered. They spoke of having mastery over their circumstances or seeking to exert this mastery as an important aspect in their healing journey. As B described it: 'If you have a victim mentality you will always have a bargaining chip, like, these people are the ones who did this to me. So, whilst you, you are not trying your best, you see,…you won't try your best, you will be knowing that I am a victim, so you won't get to your full potential if you are a victim.' The issue of the currency of victimhood was discussed in Chap. 3, where it was indicated that sometimes practitioners may encourage it for their own selfish ends (Sect. 3.3). B's insight is very perceptive and agrees with the viewpoints of

Papadopoulos (2000) and Lamott (2005), who state that this attitude of self-entitlement and perpetuation of the victim mentality can be addictive and ultimately self-defeating as it prevents the development of the affected individual from victim to survivor. I thought this was a profound pronouncement because the people of Matabeleland have been accused by ZANU PF politicians from the region many times of being 'cry babies', who complain all the time and yet do nothing about their situation (for instance, The Chronicle 4 October 2012; Bulawayo24 News 5 June 2012). It indicated a determination by these students to shake the lethargy and be proactive in their situation in the face of unfavourable circumstances.

- *The extent to which people can have positive emotions and control negative feelings (those who daily experience a 3 to 1 ratio of positive to negative emotions tend to be resilient).*
  Having a positive mind or attitude and focusing on the positive side of things are some of the things that were referred to constantly by the two students, as being important in assisting them to face their daily realities. They emphasised the need not to allow one's circumstances to dictate one's outlook on life. 'If you let a situation change who you are then you are destined to be bitter all your life. You will be bitter because every situation that comes will change you. At least if you are focused then no, you will keep on forging ahead step by step,' posited one participant.
- *The ability to function with cognitive flexibility, using problem-solving and acceptance skills, depending on the situation.*
  I think to a certain extent this also applied to them, as the whole interview indicated their ability to interact with their situations and at least, at that point, they seemed to have found ways of addressing their situations. I think the most important dimension was their acceptance that life is full of obstacles; what matters most is how one approaches those obstacles. Taking 'each day as it comes' and 'approaching each situation that you face with a positive mind', seem to suggest a well-calculated effort to systematically encounter adversities.
- *The ability to be involved in activities that follow their priorities and values in life and for their future.*
  N spoke about focusing on her education in order to secure employment and how this was a priority for her at present. This focus, she said, made her a 'happier person'. For B also, being at university and focusing on the prospects of a better future, was a factor in dealing with the effects of a bad past. As he put it: 'Every day you have to have your own goals, so I set my goals where I want to go. I know where I want to go each and every day. Sometimes if I take one step back or when a situation makes me take a step back, I know where I want to go so that keeps me going.'
- *The ability to face life's adversities and trauma, work through them and share their struggles with others, instead of denying or avoiding negative emotions and pain.*

> They stressed the importance of viewing the negative effects positively and believing that, out of the bad, good could emerge eventually, because 'everything happens for a reason'. For B, it was, 'because every negative aspect teaches you something about life, so in the end you will learn something that will help you in the future later.' N saw it as being 'about learning everyday' (in Tan 2013, p. 358–359).

My deduction of this interview was that a measure of healing was possible but, for it to be holistic or meaningful, it was still necessary for conditions discussed in Sect. 4.4 to be fulfilled to a certain extent. The students also felt that there was still a need to have a dialogue between the Ndebele and the Shona to deal with misperceptions and tensions that exist between the two ethnic groups. While a person could attend the TOL workshop and be able to live and carry on with life, it would be difficult as long as the prevailing conditions exist. However, the big difference would be that person would no longer be living as a victim. They might be living in the same circumstances and struggling with the same circumstances as before, but their outlook towards life and circumstances and how to deal with them would no longer be from a victim mentality perspective.

### 7.6.2 Interview with J

I consider J to be the litmus test for the workshop and an intriguing candidate to interview. As indicated in Sect. 6.7, J was not able to go beyond one sentence in trying to tell her story. She was still very emotional and hurt by her experience. J was unable to attend our workshop due to other commitments but she later attended another one organised for other members of ZVT. I interviewed her in October 2013, about 11 months after the workshop. I was therefore interested to find out what the workshop had done for her.

J exhibited a phenomenon that is very similar to a theory that Romero-Jódar (2012) espouses. According to this theory, after a traumatic experience, which may lead to PTSD, an individual is deprived of the mental defences that normally allow him or her to arrange their past memories and gives him or her, a linear perspective of their life. These memories become dissociated and are stored in the subconscious where they remain buried until another apparently unrelated incident brings them to the fore. Furthermore, this theory posits that there are two types of memory in a traumatised person: a 'narrative memory' and a 'trauma memory'. Narrative memory allows remembrances of past happenings to 'be organised and arranged sequentially, thus granting a narrative, coherent sense of the passing of the subject's time'. On the other hand, trauma memory includes 'the memories of extreme events which cannot be assimilated by the mind, and therefore, surface to the conscious as dissociated images which find no logical place in the lineal structure of the narrative memory'. Consequently, these memories tend to return unexpectedly to afflict a traumatised mind that is unable to integrate them into the structure of the narrative memory. Therefore, these fragmented memories allude to the destruction of the conception of time as a lineal continuum in the individual's daily life. One of the results of this destruction of the linear is a distorted coherent perception of existence. The affected individual struggles to organise their narrative in a linear progression of time, as they have to come to terms with two different timelines: the linear perception of narrative time and the fragmented memories of traumatic time (Romero-Jódar 2012, pp. 1002–1004).

I have witnessed three such similar instances: two in the context of my work and one with J in the context of this research. The first instance was the ascribing of a wrong timeframe to an experienced event. This was during an interview with an elderly lady who had two of her children killed during *Gukurahundi* and who had also been politically active in the 1970s. While telling us the events surrounding their deaths, she also narrated an event that happened in the 1970s, during the liberation war, as if it had happened in the 1980s during *Gukurahundi* and was part of the whole plot. This came to light when we were verifying the story with someone else familiar with the incident from the same area (see Chap. 2). This conflation of time was also observed in victims of violence in the former Yugoslavia, where it was found that, when people told stories of the atrocities experienced, listeners would occasionally be uncertain whether the stories had occurred yesterday, in 1941, in 1841 or in 1441. The conclusion was that 'these people were not living in a serial order of time, but a simultaneous one, in which the past and present are a continuous, agglutinated mass of fantasies' (Minow 1998, p. 13).

The other two incidents bear a very striking resemblance (coincidentally, both ladies were members of the ZVT[4]). The first incident happened during a trauma healing session conducted by a member of staff. The woman's first words were: 'I hate Shonas for the pain they caused me.' She then proceeded to narrate her childhood story, how her mother, who was South African, had been segregated and mistreated by both her father and his family (from a different ethnic group) when she was young and how much this had hurt her.

As already introduced in Sect. 6.7, J informed us that she was a victim of *Gukurahundi* and at that point could not proceed to narrate her story to the group. When interviewing her, I expected to hear a horrific account of what had happened to her during *Gukurahundi*. However, she narrated a different incident that happened to her in the 1970s when she and a number of her school mates were abducted by some ZIPRA guerrillas and forcibly taken to join the war. There were four soldiers and in the group, there happened to be only four girls. The soldiers forced the girls to have sexual relations with them all the way into Botswana and this had severely traumatised her, more so because, although they were taken aside, the other students could guess what was being done to the girls, even if they couldn't talk about it. In contrast, her *Gukurahundi* experience was mild because

[4]I do not read much into the fact that all the individuals happened to be women. I think this is coincidental and does not necessarily mean that women are more prone to this phenomenon.

the most she suffered was being locked up in the army detention barracks for two months. It would appear then that prolonged and sustained traumatic events caused what Lopez-Corvo (2013) calls 'trauma entanglement'. J's two major traumatic experiences had been enmeshed into one another and, because *Gukurahundi* had occurred after her rape incident, she viewed it as her source of pain and hurt, as it had elicited emotions that echoed similar emotions to her previous experience. I think therefore the fragmented nature of her traumatic memory at this point precluded the development of a narrative, sequential account of her experience (Kaminer 2006, p. 485).

J's trauma was compounded by the fact that she was never able to tell her mother and her husband what had happened to her and this affected her marriage in particular, as she noted:

> The pain that I felt, it turned to be, I could say, I was not faithful to my husband. This is the most painful thing, that I should have told him what happened, but I had……… it stayed in my heart for a long time till he died without, aaah, I had not told him, even my mother died without me telling…Can you imagine, even my marriage, Ngwenya, I didn't enjoy it from the beginning anyway. You know that process, as you start you already have that picture, it was so difficult, very, very difficult but I stayed, I stayed like that, always saying aaah, what can I do, but it was stuck in my heart and it did not come out.

Interestingly, when I asked J if she thought her past experience had contributed to her trauma or had any bearing on her current feelings, she said that it had not, and yet it was clear from the interview that it had a profound effect on her. Her reasoning was that, though she had heard what had been happening to the ZANLA female soldiers, where it was an accepted norm that the girls were available for the senior officers' entertainment, in ZIPRA this was forbidden. So, according to her reasoning: 'I told myself that it was probably the normal system.' I find this to be a paradox because, at one level she recognises that her bitterness and pain stem from that particular experience, yet at another she does not seem to see how this connects with the rest of her exhibited behaviour. I say this because, according to Mullet et al. (2013, p. 72), 'We live a personal narrative that is grounded in our past experience, but embodied in our present. As such, it filters what we see and how we interpret events.'

As with other participants, J also found the experience around the tree liberating:

> You know, the thing that made me bold enough, the very day we learnt about the tree, I said, 'So which means everything created by God has what, it has its own issues.' So, that tree was cut and it felt pain but the tree did not dry up, life goes on and so I said, 'I am a human being whatever happened, I too will live my normal life.' For me the thing that did it was the tree. I really looked at it and studied it properly, that oh, the tree also feels pain like a person. It has been cut and all sorts of things done to it, but still have leaves. I said, 'Aah well I am alive, I am alright then I will move on…' So, when we went there and when we were being taught about the tree, I said, 'So it is possible to bury your past and talk about it, and heal.'

More significantly, narrating her story in an environment that both honoured and acknowledged it, had a definite cathartic effect for her and contributed significantly towards her healing (see Sects. 6.2.2 and 8.2). She told me that she was the first to volunteer to narrate her story. During the interview, it was clear that something momentous had happened in her life, as she could narrate her story without breaking down. Her countenance, demeanour and several of her statements during the interview, bore testimony to this. As she pointed out:

> It was as if there was something pushing, saying, 'Just speak, speak out till everything is finished.' Just like that, as if there was a person pushing me saying, 'Talk, talk, talk,' because when I started I didn't stop. I cried until I had finished, but I had courage to say it, you know, eeh... After opening up, you know, it was as if I was a new person.... I cried a lot to the extent that everything came out. Then the following day, I could even talk about it without feeling the pain I used to feel before this day.

This points to the importance of creating a conducive and enabling environment, which Staub et al. (2005) and Mitchels (2003), say is important if narratives are to have a healing effect. The danger of a haphazard approach to narratives is all too real as Kaminer (2006, p. 481) notes: 'In the absence of a clear and coherent theoretical framework to guide trauma reconstruction, re-tellings of the trauma story could create a risk for re-traumatisation of the survivor' (I return to this discussion in Sect. 8.2.). J found the process to be so helpful that she sent her maid, who was in a very abusive relationship, to the next workshop. According to her, this young lady had been so affected by the husband's abuse that she barely ate and looked like she was sick. She claimed that, when her worker came back, she had changed and could open up and for the first time tell J what had happened to her. She even had courage enough to stand up for herself against her abusive husband. Asked about the possibility of a relapse, she responded, 'You think it will recur? Aah, I don't think so, I don't know about others but to me, no, it's now water under the bridge. It went just like that, I am very happy now... it's like someone going for baptism. I don't believe that..., when I came from there I said aah, I'm born again now.'

It would appear therefore, that the participants benefitted variously from the TOL workshop. The workshop, to a great extent, dealt with most of the effects caused by the participants' traumatic experiences, such as feelings of disempowerment, the desire for revenge, misdirected anger and hurts. Participants appear to have been internally fortified and their resilience levels increased and, in some cases, post-traumatic growth had taken place, or at the very least, the foundation for thriving in adversity was laid. What is crucial is that this process did not create a false sense of hope based on intense emotions. The process emancipated the participants and left them with a real sense of freedom. It also gave them the courage to face their daily realities, not as bitter, defeated victims, but as victorious survivors. The workshop did not, however, neatly address all pertinent issues: it problematised some issues which I shall address in Chap. 9, together with other issues from the whole research process.

Virtually all participants said that they thought the workshop was relevant and appropriate and could see the possibility of the process benefitting not only their colleagues, but other people as well. N said, 'I think it is important that from the communities where we come from, there be trauma processing, but then as the issue is being raised, I don't think it should only target the victim communities, but then the communities that side, who don't know what happened…' E thought that they, as ZVT, could incorporate the process into their existing community healing programme. D was more specific on how they could apply the elements of the workshop to their constituencies:

> If you look at that workshop, I think it empowered us so we can have the… at that time we were targeting big groups, but now we can start with small groups. Maybe we call five or six guerrillas; we almost conduct the same thing with them alone. After that we can go within, they can go within their communities and do the same thing, so we can do healing starting with this. I think this is one of the things that benefitted us greatly from that workshop.

At the time of writing this thesis, several TOL workshops have been facilitated by the TOL staff, for the benefit of the other members of the organisation, and between 50 and 60 individuals have attended the workshop. This is likely to continue with the expectation that as many of their members as is possible will be assisted.

## 7.7 Conclusion

In this chapter, we have assessed the degree to which the PAR undertaken during this research conform to other PAR projects. Using several 'bench marks', it can be ascertained that, to a great extent, this research adhered to the spirit and letter of PAR. It has been shown that, by and large, participants formed an integral part of this research. Their involvement in terms of participation, creation of indigenous knowledge and the planning and execution of agreed actions, was high per Weaver and Stark's (2006) scale of levels of involvement in PAR projects (see Fig. 5.1). In addition, the research satisfied all the prerequisite requirements of the various stages of PAR as undertaken by the researcher and the participants. The chapter also evaluated the effectiveness of the TOL workshop, which was part of the actions the group chose. Overall, participants acknowledged the usefulness of the process and, even those followed up some months later, revealed that they still found the skills acquired to be helpful as they tried to negotiate the hazards of their daily realities.

Chapter 8 analyses and discusses the findings of the dialogue sessions.

## References

Abele, A., Rupprecht, T. and Wojciszek, B. 2008. The influences of success and failure experiences on agency. *European Journal of Social Psychology*, 38: 436–448.

Anderson, C. A. and Bushman, B. J. 2002. Human aggression. *Annual Review of Psychology*, 53: 27–51. At: http://www.annualreviews.org/eprint/wZXD4ZASNg4bU/full/10.1146/annurev.psych.53.100901.135231?siteid=arjournals&keytype=ref& (22 April 2014).

Babbie, E. and Mouton, J. 2001. *The practice of social research*. Cape Town: Oxford Press.

Botcharova, O. 2001. Implementation of track two diplomacy: developing a model for forgiveness. In R. Helmick and R. Petersen (eds.), *Forgiveness and reconciliation: religion, public policy and conflict transformation*. Radnor, PA: Templeton Foundation Press.
Carver, C. S. 1998. Resilience and thriving: issues, models, and linkages. *Journal of Social Issues*, 54(2): 254–266. 244
Casey, B. and Long, B. 2002. Reconciling voices. *Journal of Psychiatric and Mental Health Nursing*, 9: 603–610.
Dickson, G. 1997. Participatory action research and health promotion: the grandmothers' story. PhD Thesis, University of Saskatchewan.
Emirbayer, M. and Mische, A. 1998. What is agency? *The American Journal of Sociology*, 103(4): 962–1023.
Finch, R., J. 2006. Trauma and forgiveness: a spiritual inquiry. *Journal of Spirituality in Mental Health*, 9(2): 27–41. At: http://www.tandfonline.com/doi/abs/10.1300/J515v09n02_03 (14 September 2009).
Francis, D. 2007. *Applied conflict transformation: action research* (update). UK: RTC.
Freire, P. (1970) 1993. *Pedagogy of the oppressed*. New York: Continuum.
Gaventa, J. 2006. Finding the spaces for change: a power analysis. *IDS Bulletin* 37(6): 23–33.
Gobodo-Madikizela, P. 2008. Trauma, forgiveness and the witnessing dance: making public spaces intimate. *Journal of Analytical Psychology*, 53: 169–188.
Greenwood, D. J. and Levin, M. 1998. Action research, science and the co-optation of social research. *Studies in Cultures, Organization, and Societies*, 4: 237–261.
Guishard, M. 2009. The false paths, the endless labors, the turns now this way and now that: participatory action research, mutual vulnerability, and the politics of inquiry. *Urban Review*, 41: 85–105.
Kaminer, D. 2006. Healing process in trauma narratives: a review. *South African Journal of Psychology*, 36(3): 481–499.
Kemmis, S. and McTaggart, R. 2005. Participatory action research: communicative action and the public sphere. In N. K. Denzin and Y. S. Lincoln (eds.), *The SAGE handbook of qualitative research*. California: Sage.
Koch, T. and Kralik, D. 2006. *Participatory action research in Health care*. Oxford, UK: Blackwell Publishing.
Kramer, R. C. 2000. Poverty, inequality, and youth violence. *Annals of the American Academy of Political and Social Science*, 567: 123–139.
Lamott, F. 2005. Trauma as a political tool. *Critical Public health*, 15(3): 219–228.
Lopez-Corvo, R. E. 2013. Time distortion between 'conceptual' and 'preconceptual' traumas. *Psychoanalytic Review*, 100(2): 289–310.
McIntyre, A. 2007. *Participatory action research: qualitative research methods series* 52. L.A: SAGE.
McIntyre, A. 2008. *Participatory action research*. Los Angeles: SAGE Publications.
McTaggart, R. 1998. Is validity really an issue for participatory action research? *Studies in Culture, Organisations and Societies*, 4: 211–236.
McTaggart, R. 1991. Principles for participatory action research. *Adult Education Quarterly*, 41(3): 168–187.
Meichenbaum, D. 2013. Ways to bolster resilience across the deployment cycle. *Military Psychologists' Desk Reference*, 325–355.
Minow, M. 1998. *Between vengeance and forgiveness: facing history after genocide and mass violence*. Boston: Beacon Press.
Mitchels, B. 2003. Healing the wounds of war and more: an integrative approach to peace—the work of Adam Curle and others with Mir i dobro in Zupanja, Croatia. *British Journal of Guidance & Counselling*, 31(4): 403–415.
Mullet, J. H., Akerson, N. M. K. and Turman, B. A. 2013. Healing the past through story. *Adult Learning*, 24(2): 72–77.
Oelosfen, R. 2009. De- and rehumanisation in the wake of atrocities. *South African Journal of Philosophy*, 28 (2): 178–188.

Papadopoulos, R. 2000. A matter of shades: trauma and psychosocial work in Kosovo. In C. Becker (ed.), *Psychosocial and trauma response in war-torn societies: the case of Kosovo.* Psychosocial Notebook, Vol. 1, IOM. 261.

Papadopoulos, R. K. 2007. Refugees, trauma and adversity-activated development. *European Journal of Psychology and Counselling*, 9(3): 301–312.

Reeler, T., Chitsike, K., Maizva, F. and Reeler, B. 2009. Tree of life: a community approach to empowering and healing survivors of torture in Zimbabwe. *Torture*, 19(3): 180–193. At: https://www.ncbi.nlm.nih.gov/pubmed/20065537 (24 March 2014).

Rivas, B. 2007. *Modelling your resilience and finding it in your students.* Presentation at Safe schools unit offices, San Diego. August 27th, 2007.

Romero-Jódar, A. 2012. 'When the life giver dies, all around is laid waste.' Structural trauma and the splitting of time in *Signal to Noise,* a graphic novel. *Journal of Popular Culture*, 45(5): 1000–1019.

Sherman, D. W., Rosedale M. and Haber S. 2012. Reclaiming life on one's own terms: a grounded theory of the process of breast cancer survivorship. *Oncology Nursing Forum*, 39(3): 258–268.

Staub, E., Pearlman, L. A., Gubin, A. and Hagengimana, A. 2005. Healing, reconciliation, forgiving and the prevention of violence after genocide or mass killings: an intervention and its Experimental Evaluation in Rwanda. *Journal of Social and Clinical Psychology,* 24(3): 297–334.

Swantz, M. L. 2008. Participatory action research as practice. In P. Reason and H. Bradbury (eds.), *The SAGE handbook of action research: participative inquiry and practice.* London: Sage.

Tan, S. Y. 2013. Resilience and posttraumatic growth: empirical evidence and clinical applications from a Christian perspective. *Journal of Psychology and Christianity*, 32(4): 358–364.

Weaver, A. and Stark, B. J. 2006. *Making it real: participatory action research in UCEDDs: building the UCEDD of tomorrow*. Council on Community Advocacy, Oregon Health and Science University. At: www.powershow.com/view/ac365-ZjQxO/Making_It_Real_Participatory_Action_Research_in_UCEDDs_powerpoint_ppt_presentation (19 September 2013).

Wessells, M. G. 1999. Culture, power, and community: intercultural approaches to psychosocial assistance and healing. In K. Nader, N. Dubrow, and B. Stamm (eds.), *Honouring differences: cultural issues in the treatment of trauma and loss.* New York: Taylor & Francis.

# Chapter 8
# Findings and Discussion

*To be human is to have a story to tell.*
Isak Dinesen (in Parry and Doan 1996, p. 6)

*The past is never dead. It's not even past.*
Faulkner (1951, p. 85)

## 8.1 The Road to Healing

This chapter presents the analysis and discusses the findings of data gleaned from the dialogue sessions under three main themes, each with several sub-themes. The major themes are: sharing our stories, hindrances to healing and the consequences of an unhealed past. It also reviews participants' views about the usefulness of the research process to them. The data set is based on a series of dialogues with the same group of participants over a period of time.

## 8.2 Sharing the Stories of Suffering

While acknowledging the extent of suffering and loss for the participants and their families, the researcher explored with the group their ideas on strategies to facilitate healing for themselves and for their communities. This part of the discussion elicited several ideas and suggestions which are discussed hereafter:

### *8.2.1 Speaking*

Throughout the discussions, participants constantly expressed the need, not only to tell their stories, but also to know that they were being listened to. One participant suggested that, 'People talk about their past experiences as talking helps.' This idea was



D. Ngwenya, *Healing the Wounds of Gukurahundi in Zimbabwe*,
The Anthropocene: Politik—Economics—Society—Science 19,
https://doi.org/10.1007/978-3-319-66818-5_8

strongly supported by others in the group. Engaging in discussions with other people was associated with positive outcomes such as 'feeling healthy', 'feeling relieved', 'getting help with handling issues' and 'finding answers. For instance, G said:

> To me this thing still lingers and I am also part of those who need healing. At times, when we discuss like this, I always realize that this thing that troubles me like this, I am not the only one affected but we are many. When you find people with similar issues and you discuss you feel relieved.

A few issues arise from G's statement, including the efficacy of talking about one's experiences with others—especially those who have had similar experiences—and the comfort derived from realising that one's reaction to these experiences is not unique to oneself; that others share it and therefore one is not abnormal. This suggests that the sharing of the story with a community of sympathetic and empathetic listeners, who acknowledge both the pain and the reality of the experience, offers validation and comfort to the storyteller. Minow (1998, p. 67) states: 'Coming to know that one's suffering is not solely a private experience, best forgotten, but instead an indictment of a social cataclysm, can permit individuals to move beyond trauma, hopelessness, numbness, and preoccupation with loss and injury.' Her premise was amplified by V's comment that,

> If I can share with the group what has happened to me, myself, it *lessens the severity of the problem*, because a problem shared is a problem relieved, so to say. It may not go away completely, but the fact that you now all know about my problem, I *feel consoled.* I don't know whether it happens to other people, unless if it is a secret I don't want you people to know, but if it is something that hurt me really and probably something that amputated my leg, it has to be known how I lost my leg, and for you people to be able to *feel for me*, I should tell it to (inaudible) By this act of telling to other people, it reduces the severity of the problem that I carry (italics added).

Sharing the story of one's pain in a conducive environment therefore, provides relief and restoration to the hurting individual (see Sect. 6.2.2) However, just as conflict has different effects on people, so too talking about it (or truth-telling) is beneficial for some, while other individuals or even cultures may prefer not to, believing that it is best not to revisit painful pasts. That is, rather than being cathartic, for them it is re-traumatising, and may lead to further conflict as well as psychological damage, particularly if done inexpertly. There have been some criticisms that the 'don't bottle it up' school is based on just one stream of western psychotherapy, yet it is universally promoted as essential and beneficial. Rosalind Shaw's report *Rethinking Truth and Reconciliation Commissions. Lessons from Sierra Leone* (2005, p. 1), for example, argues that the valorisation of truth telling—a particular kind of memory practice—is 'based on problematic assumptions about the purportedly universal benefits of verbally remembering violence' and that 'ideas concerning the conciliatory and therapeutic efficacy of truth telling are the product of a Western culture of memory deriving from North American and European historical processes.' She adds that '[i]n northern Sierra Leone, social forgetting is a cornerstone of established processes of reintegration and healing for child and adult ex-combatants. Speaking of the war in public often undermines these processes, and many believe it encourages violence'.

The consensus, however, seems to be that people in post war/conflict situations experience some measure of healing from telling their stories. However, McKinney (2007) urges caution here, as she argues that this approach might be a particular cultural and historical notion and not necessarily a universal or timeless one. To my mind this approach is particularly suited to the African culture because we are an oral society and from time immemorial stories have been used to communicate various truths, lessons and history. While it is true that storytelling, in the context of trauma and healing is prone to exaggeration, romanticising and memory failure, it nevertheless holds great value for victims seeking relief. Writing about South Africa, apartheid and the Truth and Reconciliation Commission, Wieder (2004, p. 23) observed that,

> Storytelling becomes a form of testimony as oral history in South Africa with political and cultural dimensions since the stories of both the horrors of apartheid and the struggles of the people who fought the government finally have come into the public arena and offer both personal meaning and counter narratives to the official historical record.

In my view, his observation is equally applicable to the ZIPRA veterans who not only suffered greatly at the hands of ZANU PF but have also been denied an opportunity (with the rest of the people of Matabeleland) to tell the stories of both their role in the liberation struggle and their suffering during *Gukurahundi*. A certain amount of justice and freedom is gained when once the victim's story, which authorities would be trying to suppress, no longer belongs to that individual alone (Shriver 2003). As Farwell/Cole (2002, p. 32) have affirmed: 'Establishing an accurate understanding of objective conditions validates all survivors, even those whose story has not been told, through individual assertions of self-worth and guiltlessness on behalf of the entire victimised community' (see also Lederach 1997, p. 26).

It is important to note that the storytelling is happening within the context of a community, because I believe there is a great difference between this type of approach and a clinical approach where therapy takes place between a practitioner and a single individual. The focus and the dynamics between the two are very different: one aims to heal an individual and the other to heal a community through healing of individuals in a group setting (Pia 2013, p. 483). We have already discussed how organised violence is designed to disrupt community and people's support systems, and that there is therefore a need for healing to also focus on the healing of the social fabric (see discussion in Chaps. 3 and 4).

As suggested by Cobham et al. (2012), Mullet et al. (2013) and Pia (2013), repetitive storytelling is a powerful method of facilitating healing in victims of trauma. This need, to tell one's story repetitively, was aptly summed up by V when he said:

> I think eh something has got to be *discussed over and over, and over and over repeatedly* such that then it dawns into you to say, well I can forgo, but otherwise *I think that it is very difficult that we can quickly forgo things by the first encounter, or second or third,* it should

> be a dream, a dream eventually is like a transformation, you change completely. I think honestly speaking we need to indulge more in trauma healing and talking about forgiveness as a topic in its own right (italics added).

His sentiment resonates well with one aspect of most black people's cultures in Zimbabwe: when a person dies, people visit the bereaved person(s) and usually each person who comes will ask about the circumstances leading to the death. For each person who comes, the bereaved person will have to narrate what, how and when it happened.[1] The person will keep on narrating the same story as long as there are people asking. Initially, I used to think this practice was insensitive to a person who had just lost a loved one as I thought the person would not want to relive the excruciating details of the sad event. However, on close examination, I realised that, unconsciously, this process actually helped the bereaved individual to make the transition quickly from denial to acceptance; thus, embarking on the journey to recovery. I think this act also allows the person to clear any confusion and fantasies that might linger in the mind. I have observed that, after retelling the story several times, most individuals are soon able to do so with less emotion and more clarity. It therefore does seem as if there is real value in this practice.

Fooladi (2005) and Bylsma et al. (2008) are some of the authors who have highlighted the health benefits of such victims being provided with a space to talk and express emotion. They particularly view crying as being cathartic for those hurting. Likewise, the participants in this study elaborated on the need to express emotions, to have a shoulder to cry on and to deal with deep feelings of hurt. As G explained:

> …because of such things people will always feel pain but people will work together and they still need a shoulder to cry on. It is always said that if a person is hurt by someone, he or she cries so that at the end he or she gets relieved. The victims did not get a shoulder to cry on because it is why, even if you approached them today, they will still cry. They did not get an opportunity to mourn. When they get the opportunity to expose what they hold in their mind and hearts they will cry. At the end, maybe they may feel much better.

These statements bring to the fore the power of talking to effect attitudinal/emotional change in individuals. We have already noted in Sect. 7.6 how J described the expression of her emotions as having brought her release from her pain, which she had bottled up within for many years. When she cried at the workshop, 'everything came out' and the following morning she felt relieved, much as the Roman poet Ovid postulated: 'It is a relief to weep; grief is satisfied and carried off by tears' (quoted in Bylsma et al. 2008, p. 1166). However, as the authors point out, the cathartic effect of tears depends, to a greater degree, on the extent to which the individual feels safe and secure during this event. Cathartic crying therefore, occurs when 'an unresolved emotional distress is reawakened in a

[1]This is usually done by people who are close to the surviving family members, such as relatives, friends, neighbours, colleagues, etc. I doubt that when people do this, there is a reasoned method and intention to it other than simply wanting to know what happened, just for their information's sake.

properly distanced context, in which there is an appropriate balance of distress and security' (Bylsma et al. 2008, p. 1167). The benefits of crying therefore operate through a social mechanism. That is to say, the crier derives benefits from the crying if it happens in an environment that elicits empathy, sympathy, pity and comfort from those in whose presence the crying happens.

### 8.2.2 *Writing*

Closely related to the catharsis of telling of trauma stories, is writing about one's experiences. The use of writing for therapeutic purposes has been extensively written about, with subjects ranging from traumatised children (Van der Oord et al. 2010), to women (Adams 1999), to couples (Jordan 1998), to lab experiments (Pennebaker 1997) and to community groups (Lieblich 2013; Adams 1999). All these studies attest to the transformational qualities of what Van der Oord (2010) calls 'cognitive behavioural writing therapy', and although the traumatic experiences written about by these authors differ from our group's experiences, the outcome of any traumatic experience is more or less similar and, as such, these experiments offer insights regarding our situation. Participants mentioned several times throughout the dialogues the need to write down their stories and those of their communities, as a way of preserving history. They wished to correct what they perceived as the distorted history of the facts about the *Gukurahundi* era and their role during the armed struggle, currently touted by government. This resulted in the group deciding to adopt the writing of their life stories as one of the actions undertaken during the research (see Sects. 6.8.3 and 7.1). Participants viewed this as an important process on their road to healing. They felt that getting their stories out could contribute to their healing, as their voices would no longer be silent, since their stories would become public knowledge. G's suggestion was that,

> People should be taught to stand up for themselves and it should be agreed upon and there should be ways of writing it. This is history. As it is, it is now 10:45 for us. We will die. Those left behind have to know that such things once happened… If people can get an opportunity to say out what they feel and people be told that it will not end, even if their names will not be written in the books as individuals, but their experiences will be exposed, it is now part of history.

V had a more comprehensive idea as to how this process could be carried out: he viewed it as a three-phase process, which would include them recording their experiences and sharing them with other people; then approaching other victims they knew personally to do the same; and lastly, soliciting stories from others in their communities:

> True, I believe it is possible it can contribute because there is one documentary that was done on *Gukurahundi,* and everywhere I have shown that documentary at first people cry. It makes them feel very angry, but if you ask them, I believe they find it helpful. The purposes of this is [to say to people], what do you think we should do, then people be given a chance to say whatever it is they want to speak about. At least if a person talks about their pain,

they will be able to slowly release the pain. This should be on three levels that we embark on: First of all, our team here, we should be able to record these things, our own personal stories and tell them to the public so that the public know that even if we were in the army, I was also a victim. While I was in uniform I was also a victim of *Gukurahundi,* and then tell each other that the feeling that you had I too, I was also quite hurt inside here. Then, on the other level, I know somebody who was a victim. That person we go out to them, we record, I know of course for several reasons (inaudible) but for the purposes of publishing, may be having another layer over what we are doing here, would also be an addition. If necessary, the third layer would be community engagement. Let's suppose we identify one community, may be that place where the eight teachers were killed, what do you call that place? We go into that community we ask those people to relive what they saw that time and then tell the world how they felt at that time and how they feel now and how they want other people to feel in the next or future generations. I think this is very important that… probably this will augment our position and reinforce this process which we are doing. There should be an element of truth telling. There also should be recorded that people are given to replay those feelings but in a free environment.

Participants also felt that it was also important for them to record the experiences of *Gukurahundi,* so that they could preserve a legacy for posterity. Concerning this idea, one participant had this to say:

We live on expecting that one day, may be even when we are gone there be even some recordings… the truth will come out eventually. So, you see that, maybe we can do something and it be recorded, that might be advantageous to the next generation, because as long as this regime is in power we will live in fear.

L advanced a long hypothesis of why he thought it was important to have a record of their experiences with *Gukurahundi*:

Ehh… you know what Mr Ngwenya? …five years, ten years ago, we could not sit down and talk about this, but things are opening up, we are getting closer. We are getting closer and it's not the victims now who are making the loudest noise. Today in the paper we have got one of the perpetrators making the loudest noise there… [T]he perpetrator has done, he has committed a lot of crime. He has forgotten the crime that he committed earlier you see, and if you get into the media, you get into the electronic, it's not the perpetrators who are talking about this *Gukura*, ah… it's not the victims who are talking about the *Gukurahundi* issue, but the people in Harare who were not affected, are making the loudest noise on behalf of the, what call? Now how do we take advantage of that situation now, you know. A lot of guys in Harare who have never been in Bulawayo, they are very bitter about this thing, because the system of governance that they are fighting. We cannot have a government that goes and kills twenty thousand people. Last time I was talking to some young people here in Bulawayo, I wanted to buy a car from them. They picked me up from ZAPU offices, and when they asked me, 'So old man what are you people up to? So old man, tell us, is it true that twenty thousand people died?' *No, they can't believe it; the young guys cannot believe it.* It doesn't make sense now that people were killed, for what? *The new generation is now at hand. The older generations are getting fewer, and the majority generation now they don't accept that. They don't want to accept it.* Now I think we've got to make use of that. This is why we are seated here. I don't know how safe your offices are. Are they bugged or not (laughter), because POSA does not allow this, POTRAZ does not allow this, but it is opening up. This is the opening up we are talking about and how do we manipulate and this time, because to make this thing heard is to tell those people with loud mouths. Give them the information to talk about. *I think I want to go back to say, let's record. Ah… let's record what really transpired and pass it on to the next person or to the next generation* (italics added).

By recording or writing, their stories would permanently be in the public domain, despite the authorities' efforts to stifle their truth. As such, their private stories would no longer be hidden; they would now be accessible to the greater public. Participants also thought that such information could be used in the future to prosecute the perpetrators. They referred to precedents that have been set in other countries. Answering a question on what the end result of the process should be, F offered this explanation:

> The end, you know if you try to go deep, this end of course, we are trying to do something, but our generation maybe will not see this through. If there were resources, these facts could be written down, or somebody publishes a big book, even 20. This would help the next generation. Some [perpetrators] will still be alive, even if they are 90 years old. For instance, a week ago, I saw this other Nazi dragged from Argentina. So, if you observe this thing it doesn't end. Just imagine that World War II ended in 1945, but they are still hunting them down. When they catch one, he tells them we were 20 or 100. So, if there is a book, people should write books so that this crime doesn't disappear, because things will not always be like it is now. Look at Turkey now. There is a similar situation. Some people in Turkey want to sue for something that happened 50 years ago.

L was even more explicit about what he thought the writings should be used for:

> Now, if the Government is hostile as it is, there is always a window. The Government is a signatory to the AU Charters, to the SADC Charters, to the United Nations Charters. *I think what we can do is to record all evidence and make it known to the world that we have got this problem,* through the relevant channels. They must know. How much does SADC know about our case? How much does AU know about our case…? I think we have to record all the evidence and push it. If the Government is hostile, you always use the international window to let your case to be known. Smith suppressed us here and then we opened the window to build international, and then we went to the international community and they helped us and this is what we can do. *Let's make our case to be known. Let's make the world know about this. Let's give them the correct evidence of what really transpired, and give names of the perpetrators* (italics added).

These sentiments seem to be, in part, tied to the desire for justice (Sect. 8.3.2). While perhaps some of the things suggested by participants seem far-fetched, the writing of the stories had a positive effect on those who undertook that particular action (see Chap. 9) for participants' comments on the writing exercise). As has been explained by Farwell/Cole (2002), this process allows private pain to be transformed into political dignity, as well as alleviating the human tendency to internalise blame. Furthermore, 'establishing an accurate understanding of objective conditions validates all survivors, even those whose story has not been told, through individual assertions of self-worth and guiltlessness on behalf of the entire victimised community' (Farwell/Cole 2002, p. 32).

## 8.3 Hindrances to Healing

While participants acknowledged the benefits of the research in terms of setting them on the road to recovery, they nevertheless identified several obstacles that made it difficult to attain a fuller healing. As indicated in Sect. 7.5, participants faced real everyday challenges in trying to live out the life skills learnt from the workshop.

### 8.3.1 Repressing the Truth

> *Denial is an integral part of atrocity, and it's a natural part after a society has committed genocide. First you kill, and then the memory of killing is killed*
>
> Iris Chang 1997 (in the *New York Times*, 20 May 1999).

The most difficult thing for the participants to accept was not being allowed, by default or by design, to talk publicly about their experiences and about *Gukurahundi* in general. We discussed at length the consequences of the effects of harm deliberately caused by a government that was supposed to be protecting them, and they expressed frustration at this inability to openly tell their stories because of the state-imposed silence. They spoke of an 'internalised pressure', 'fear factor' and a 'powerful police system' as some of the issues contributing to this 'conspiracy of silence'. Fear seemed to be the driving force behind most of the frustrations and reactions; in fact, during our six dialogue sessions, fear was mentioned 22 times and, in addition, several actions or lack of, were directly attributed to fear. V pointed out that

> Of course, what we discover is that people are afraid of going out and talk about *Gukurahundi* because we have been publicly threatened that *Gukurahundi* is a closed chapter. But within our families we keep on asking ourselves questions and get asked questions—'But Dad, what happened?'

He also spoke about 'the threat outside that makes us not to talk'. Another participant added: 'The state does not want us to talk about it. The state says let's not open old wounds now.' These were references to newspaper articles where ZANU PF politicians had been quoted as uttering such statements (see The Chronicle 19 July 2011 and 22 June 2011). Such utterances, while they might not be overt threats or prohibitions, nevertheless communicate that message in no uncertain terms. Participants surmised that the reason for this suppression was that the government hoped that, by silencing talk about *Gukurahundi* for as long as possible, people would eventually forget about it, with the death of the primary victims. This is a strategy that regimes, that have perpetrated violence against their citizens and are still in power, tend to use to suppress discussion of their past crimes. Adam/Adam's (2000, p. 6) pronouncement that, 'All nations depend on forgetting: on forging myths of unity and identity that allow a society to forget its founding crimes, its hidden injuries and divisions, its unhealed wounds,' confirms the group's observation (see also Chang's quote above).

This inability to talk about their experiences is counterproductive for victim communities, because, as has been discussed in Sect. 8.2.2, for victims of organised violence, being able to talk about such experiences in public and in an accepting and empathetic environment plays a major role in the healing process (see Sect. 4.3). When this does not happen, the 'old wounds', no matter how long the period of suppression, will continue to fester until they are attended to. Participants agreed that 'instead of people forgetting about *Gukurahundi,* they are thinking even more about it' and that the wounds would never heal because the pain and hurts had already been passed to the next generation (see Sect. 8.3.1). As one of them pointed out:

> There are certain documents. For instance, the Dumbutshena Commission and Chihambakwe Commission reports, which were commissioned by the government to study into the disturbances in Matabeleland; it was not called genocide at that time. If we got access of those documents and be made public consumption, but as you have rightly said, I think those documents are under lock and key. Obviously, there is information on those documents that is incriminating against what they did and what they think, if it will be known to the public, will make them worry—just to know that they did something and believe that, if it gets known, they will not be at ease; it makes it not easy for people to forget. *We will not forget because you refuse with the truth, if you came out clean and explained it was going to be better* (italics added).

The 'internalised pressure' due to the inability to talk only served to keep the wounds fresh, and with time, this pressure might force the next generation to consider taking drastic measures on behalf of their parents. The mixture of desperation and desire to speak out was poignantly captured in this statement from a participant:

> Naturally that's what it means, the reason why they are promoted is that, then they can shut this thing out completely. To us it will remain a big wound and *I cannot keep quiet, I cannot.* I have said to myself over the years this thing must be said out, but alright, *who will listen to me?* This is a problem you see (italics added).

This statement portrays the dilemma that participants faced, very well: the great need to talk but realising that there is no one, at least among the authorities, who is willing or prepared to listen. It also demonstrates a sense of helplessness which victims often experience in such situations. If the very institution that is meant to protect them is the same one that caused harm and now prevents the victims from even talking about it, it disempowers and only serves to aggravate the pain. Often, the rise in the internalised pressure may lead to victims using violent means to have their voices heard. However, the example of the Mothers of La Plaza de Mayo (a central square in Buenos Aires, Argentina, where the government house is situated), offers a nonviolent solution, which is effective and augurs well for healing through peacebuilding: When the military junta in Argentina tried to suppress information about the whereabouts of disappeared young people, their mothers came together to demand to know where their children were. Meeting at the Plaza de Mayo every week, they wore placards with the names, photos and dates their children disappeared. While initially, the authorities may have ignored them, the sheer size of the group and the persistence of the mothers brought about action on the part of the government. These women managed to create a public voice and in so doing were able to 'speak' and be 'listened to' by the authorities, albeit involuntarily (Abreu Hernandez 2002; Goddard 2007).

Related to the inability to talk was a great desire to know the reason why these things were done to them. Participants felt strongly that knowing why, would assist in the healing process. The desire to know concerned two stages: the planning and implementation stages of *Gukurahundi*. Regarding the implementation stage, the need to know why the foot soldiers did what they did to them was pointed out by L:

> I think we need to establish, or we have some bits and pieces of facts for the reason why they launched that operation. And if we know the aim why they launched this operation, did they achieve their aim or they achieved part of their aim? Because if somebody apologises and then he will give us a bit of why they did it because if you apologise you will say why you did it.

Hayner (2001, p. 157) says victims are not ready to engage in a reconciliation process unless they know more about what happened. While they might be ready to forgive, they need to know who to forgive and what it is they are forgiving them for.

From the participants' statements, there appeared to be a desire to humanise the perpetrator, to find a redeeming trait in them that could perhaps make it easier for the victim to forgive. This focuses primarily on individualising the guilt; not in order to excuse, but to understand, what Kliman (2002) calls 'humanising conversations'. According to Botcharova (2001, p. 289), when victims seek to rehumanise the perpetrator by asking 'Why them?', it is possible that victims might 'recognise their own fears, shame, and hopelessness in the perpetrators, and understand that the perpetrators' aggressions were driven by feelings and concerns as unbearable as their own.' According to the above statement, I think participants might have found it easier to deal with their 'ball of anger' and move on, understanding a situation where they felt the perpetrator might have killed or tortured under duress, although discerning the perpetrators' motives and intentions would be extremely difficult.

The second aspect of knowing had to do with the intentions of the whole operation. That is to say, what really was the aim of *Gukurahundi*? L's comments above speak clearly about this issue. F also reiterated this point when he said:

> It is very difficult, forgiveness most of the time. You can do it, only if your perpetrator comes into terms to understand the reason why they did it. Maybe they did it because they were ordered to, then maybe you can say in your heart I will not retaliate on this person… The perpetrator did not come out in the open to say why they did this. If only the perpetrator had come out in the open to explain the reason for their plan of action. Because the root cause of *Gukurahundi*… we can't just say they killed people without finding out the reason why *Gukurahundi* was formed…

I think this had to do with the fear that, if the aims were not fully accomplished, then the perpetrator could still seek other means to fulfil their goals and objectives. This sentiment was prevalent throughout our dialogues—the participants frequently referred to incidents which they saw as indications that the perpetrators were still working towards their aim. Their primary conclusions about the reasons for *Gukurahundi*, from the examples they referred to, had to do with political and ethnic domination (see Appendix A). However, since there is no official explanation of why it happened, this had created a siege mentality among the participants and increased their sense of insecurity. It would appear that, in some situations where perpetrators have offered a fuller picture of an event, explanation has played an important role in the survivors' healing process (Moon 2009; McGrew 2006). However, in our case and as far as the participants were concerned, the intention to cause harm still existed and, as long as the truth regarding these two stages remained unknown, it was difficult for participants to experience healing.

Participants referred to several incidents, which they felt vindicated their belief that the intentions and purpose of *Gukurahundi* were not over. In my opinion, their concerns were not politicking but appeared genuine. L was the one most vocal on this. In one dialogue, he said:

> I am saying, the people who are talking the loudest right now, they are not particularly the people who are victims (inaudible)… The writers in Harare, the researchers in Harare, they are very worried about this act and they are the ones who are speaking louder now, accusing their kith and kin that why did they do it, because it will cause problems in the future, because any sane-minded person can see that there is a problem here. The recent event in Nkayi: these are signals on what's going on—a simple policeman who is a beer reveller, and then erupts a tribal warfare, a tribal conflict and memories had to break that *Gukurahundi* has started, you see, so this will never end.

He then narrated a story of how, during the war, their camp in Zambia had been bombed by the Smith regime. When this raid was not announced on the radio, he told his comrades that the raid was not over and, for sure, the second wave of bombing started soon after. He continued:

> I am in the shelter with this young man and I said, 'This operation has not been reported in the news and the whites will enter just now.' The guy who brought the radio, while trying to communicate with other units threw the radio inside. We asked why he did so, and he then said, 'The whites have already entered.' Yah, that's why this operation has not ended, so I am likening this thing to that operation, that if it is still continuing, why will they apologise? And besides there are these circulars which are still circulating for the Grand Plan (see Appendix A), which we do not know the originator but we know who it is.

G was also equally convinced that *Gukurahundi* was still continuing, albeit in other forms:

> There is a difficulty, and the way I view it, yes, we call it *Gukurahundi* because it was that time, but I would like to say *Gukurahundi* is still experienced in many ways. The question is, what was it about and why did it happen? To destroy people, are people still not dying? They are… If it gets difficult to understand that we are all human beings, *Gukurahundi* will not end. *Gukurahundi* is still there. As we are talking about *Gukurahundi*, we will find that

> we will create boundaries and have Matabeleland, Midlands. Alright, but those people from the other side have also seen it, a similar thing, like *Gukurahundi.* That is why I am saying it's continuing…

Later on, while narrating the story of her encounter with *Gukurahundi*, she added:

> To me this *Gukurahundi* issue starts from this incident going forward and I feel that it is continuing and it hasn't finished. I am one of the people who, even now if people run and say there is unity, I don't like it. I was so angry and was even angry against Nkomo,[2] that if he had not done that. I remember when people were mourning for him at Barbourfields [stadium], I just went there, but could not cry with others. People asked me why I wasn't crying and I said, 'Cry for what?' I think this anger made my heart to be hard.

Generally, all participants were agreed on this hypothesis and even the young people in the group felt the same. N noted: 'When there is violence, the parents at home feel angry and they would say, "This was done before and it's continuing." As G mentioned, *Gukurahundi* is still continuing so the hatred is still there.'

The question of the continued effects of *Gukurahundi* cannot be doubted and, as has been observed in Sect. 2.3, participants' views mirror those found within the broader communities of Matabeleland. What is of interest here is that participants believe that *Gukurahundi* continues in other forms and that, generally, all incidents of violence perpetrated by state security organs is interpreted within the context of a continued pogrom represented by *Gukurahundi.* Again, the continued existence of documents, such as the various versions of The Grand Plan (see Appendix A), that clearly outline a purported Shona plan to dominate the Ndebele people, leads many to hold on to these beliefs (see discussion of historical injustices and enduring injustices in Sect. 8.4.4). This inevitably contributes significantly to the continued fear and feelings of insecurity discussed below.

### 8.3.2 Deep Seated Feelings of Insecurity

The pervasive nature of fear in victims of *Gukurahundi* was well illustrated by members of our group, at least in as far as identifying it as a factor within the victim communities in Matabeleland. I perceived this insecurity to be of two types: the fear of what the state's repressive machinery might do currently and the fear of what did not happen then during *Gukurahundi.* Regarding the fear of what might happen, participants pointed out that this was preventing most people from engaging in activities or rituals that might heal them. So, apart from the fear of speaking, which we have already discussed above, most people, according to the participants, were

---

[2]This was a reference to the Unity Accord of 1987 between PF ZAPU and ZANU, which resulted in the merger of the two former liberation movements. Many people in Matebeleland blame Joshua Nkomo, the leader of PF ZAPU for having capitulated easily to ZANU PF, as they say this pact was an elitist pact which brought very little to their lives (see Sect. 2.4.2).

afraid to do things (even in the relative comfort of their communities) to alleviate their pain. The fear of a 'powerful police system' or 'monitoring system' is so pervasive that it has become self-perpetuating, and the fear of the unknown now hangs over the heads of the people, even where there might be no reason to fear. For instance, H pointed out:

> I would like to say about this *Gukurahundi* issue: In the communities… for example, I come from Tsholotsho, people who were killed are known where they were buried, and they are not allowed to temper with these places…, but someone might know where their uncle is buried, but they can't even go there and perform rituals, it's difficult. There might be a child who needs a birth certificate, because he didn't get a birth certificate. For a person to have it, he or she is supposed to have a death certificate. These people do not have death certificates. Obviously if this child is being asked, the child does not have a birth certificate because my father died. People will tell this child the reason…, because it is not said that these people died. If they died, they should be having death certificates, it is known where they were buried. So, to the communities, as long as such is not addressed, hurt is still there.

This inability to attend to their loved ones means that there is no closure and conversely there is no moving on and no healing (see Eppel 2006). We noted previously how the sharing of stories validates the victims. Conversely, being prevented from talking (actively or otherwise) means that the victims' reality is being denied and treated as if it never happened, thereby stunting the healing process (see Hayner 2001, p. 164).

The second element of insecurity—the fear of what did not happen—has to do with the psychological state of the individual. In our case, the participants, as ex-ZIPRA combatants, were among the primary targets of *Gukurahundi*. It is the realisation that, had the circumstances been different, they would have been killed. V captured this notion very well in his remarks:

> It begins to be painful now because, if you really sense that members of the family, maybe the entire family in some instances, was wiped down and you could be the few who are remaining. Suppose you were at home that time when the others were being killed, you would also have died isn't, because people were being killed that time. I believe that already opens up wounds and forgiveness can't be there, because you would then begin to imagine that I would have died if I was there.

In another similar discussion during the sixth dialogue session, a similar statement came up again, emphasising intention to kill and the difficulty of simply accepting this fact and moving on:

> But it happened; the truth is that it happened. They wanted to wipe you out completely, isn't? If you read "The Year of the People's Storm" authored in 1979 by president Robert Mugabe, he said they were going to remove all the barriers, the stumps, uproot even the roots and come and till anew the land, so that meant that they reap, *Gukurahundi* is the year of the people, we need to go back to the philosophy of *Gukurahundi* itself. So, you can't say they wanted to spare me. They wanted to obliterate, completely remove you from the face of the earth and how can you TO-LE-RA-TE that kind of thing?

The thought of what might have been, induced a sense of incredulity, terror and outrage within the participants. I would liken this phenomenon to a person who survives a serious accident: later, when they ruminate on the accident, there is a sudden rush of horror and fright about what might have happened. According to Isserman (2009, p. 25), there are two types of threats that feed into this insecurity: the sociotropic threat which is 'a generalised anxiety and sense of threat to society, the country as a whole or the regions where one lives and a threat to one's community, group, or way of life', and the egocentric threat which is a 'threat to oneself or one's family'. This 'terrifying existential crisis' faced by the participants is as a result of the realisation of the magnitude of the intentions of the state to 'obliterate' not just them but everything that makes for their very existence (Zorbas 2004, p. 30). When these two threats combine, as with the research group, it created deep suspicions and high levels of mistrust that made it very difficult for some members of the group to view the perpetrators in any positive light, thus making it difficult for them to address the issue of healing in their own lives. Staub/Pearlman's (2001, p. 196) comment about the necessity of security in healing is very pertinent here. According to them, 'Traumatised people require at least a rudimentary feeling of security for healing to begin. When there is continued threat from the other, depending on circumstances, healing may be difficult or even impossible.' In his article, 'The land of murderers: Jewish survivors in post-war Germany', Kupferberg (1997) describes his struggle with the insecurity of living briefly (six months) in Germany as a Jewish Swede. Although this was in 1994, the struggle was nevertheless real for him, due to the subtle and sometimes not-so-subtle anti-Semitic attitudes perpetuated by a minority. The fascinating aspect of his experience is that his insecurities happened in a modern and law-abiding state, almost 50 years after the holocaust. One can then imagine how the victims of *Gukurahundi*, who still live under the rule of the perpetrator state, must struggle with this issue of insecurity, and how difficult it must be for them to work on their healing under such circumstances.

### *8.3.3 Impunity*

What exasperated the participants even more was the fact that, some of the architects of *Gukurahundi* known to them seemed to be living large, while they struggled through life. Participants felt that the issue of status disparity was a major stumbling block in their healing process. First of all, they complained about their treatment when they were in the Zimbabwe National Army (ZNA), that there was a ceiling on promotions for ex-ZIPRAs. Most in the group had only gone up to the rank of major, while they felt they were more qualified than their ex-ZANLA counterparts. As one of them stated, 'We just stayed in the army without being promoted' (See Sect. 2.2.1). Some indicated that they had been forced to retire from the army prematurely because of the unfair treatment they received. Another expressed the following sentiments:

> …currently, as ZIPRA we still feel *dehumanised* because we have been abused by ZANU PF and you know we are *substandard*… but until we are *at par* with those in power, those who did it, I think I would rather be a bit close to making a revenge of some sort,

> where we will then revenge and be at par with them, that is not necessarily causing harm as it were, but being *at par* with them… (Italics added).

What they could not deal with was the fact that it seemed that the perpetrators had been rewarded for their part in *Gukurahundi*. One participant pointed out that the problem was that the real perpetrators were still alive and enjoying life. V commented:

> The people who could have killed me are these ones and they are still eating *sadza* (pap, thick porridge) today. Yet there is nothing that has been done to them today. Thirty years on, let's say 28 years on, these people have been promoted in their ranks. I know for instance D N was promoted major general only last month…But when I met D N in Jotsholo, Lupane, and I had witnessed a real situation and today it's still a log piercing in me.

V went on to relate how an ex-ZIPRA colleague of his who was subsequently a civilian nurse during the *Gukurahundi* period, was brutally murdered at the command of D N and described how he was powerless to intervene and save him and all he could do was to watch helplessly. He ended by saying '…That in itself will never go out and D N who was responsible for that, today he is major general, he is happy and he is enjoying himself.' These statements revealed a person who was greatly pained and struggling with the issue of impunity, which evidently was preventing his recovery. Talking about the people he had interviewed as part of the group exercise we did, B told us that people indicated that they wanted the perpetrators to be brought to justice one way or another because, 'We know these people and we see them and they are driving cars. They are enjoying their lives whilst we are hurting, we have scars inside us. Every day we see these people enjoying their lives whilst we are hurting.'

Participants also felt that another obstacle to healing was the fact that their lives are still dominated by the perpetrators, who are still in power, as was emphatically expressed by L:

> I am already in that environment right now. I am living that life, in my life without that, I need it now, I want to place it as a process because at the end of the day, I want this process to come to an end with a normalisation of this process. This life is not normal—living with my perpetrator, my perpetrator in charge of almost all of my life. The perpetrator is in charge and I am an underdog. It's like a person steps on you and you say, 'Please may I remove my foot from under yours (laughter)'. So I would like to [] a process because we have to live through and hope time, or hope for a miracle to come, because it cannot continue like this… It's not fair…. At the end of the day there must be a cut off, come to an end. It's a fake life I am living; I am living a fake life. It's not me.

The participants' sentiments and experience cohere with Pinta's (2000) assertion that, as long as perpetrators continue to prosper or retain power as a result of their crimes, the prospects for healing are diminished, for individuals and communities (see Sect. 4.2; Staub et al. 2005; Opotow 2001).

### 8.3.4 Lack of an Apology

While it was perfectly clear to the participants that no apology was ever likely to come from the perpetrators of *Gukurahundi*, they nevertheless indicated their preference for it. This was actually the central theme of this research—how to find alternative approaches to healing in the absence of an official apology from the perpetrator. In a conflict, an apology is always desirable as it enhances the possibility of the offended party's healing and restoration of the broken relationship (Lederach 1997; Tatt 2014; La Caze 2006). As Lazare (2004, p. 1) has postulated: 'Apologies have the power to heal humiliations and grudges, remove the desire for vengeance, and generate forgiveness on the part of the offended parties' (See also Goldwater 2004; Hayner 2001). Lazare's statement is aptly demonstrated by this conversation that ensued among the participants when discussing the issue of forgiveness and what they saw as necessary for the perpetrators to do in order to qualify for forgiveness:

V: Are you suggesting that they should show a sign of contrition?
F: Yah, that little sign (pause).
V: Will soften people's hearts?
F: Maybe, but they are hard core (reference to victims), not all, we can say a small percentage, let's say 45%.
V: How would you feel it personally?
F: To me, I think it, this thing affected me personally. Of course, the tragedies started in our family in 1980…

It was the participants' view that, had there been an apology, perhaps that would have addressed the needs of a significant number of victims. Sentiments such as these: 'As long as there is no apology for what they did, it's difficult. There will need to be formulated a way that can make the issue public, maybe these people be humiliated, maybe internationally,' and 'We can't forgive them without their apology,' and 'People can forgive their hurts but without official apology, it is going to be difficult to talk about this lightly,' indicated how strongly they felt about the issue of an apology.

They were however also keenly aware of what Tatt (2014) calls an apology with impunity. This is an insincere apology given on the sly while the perpetrator continues unrepentant. In desiring an apology, they were not under any illusion about the sort of apology that could come from the perpetrators, and J's observation was quite astute:

> This apology, Ngwenya, I really don't see what kind of an apology it would be. You come and stand in front of me and say, 'Mrs J, I apologise, really for what I did, bla, bla.' Then it's over—life goes on. I don't know what kind of thing this apology is going to be, and then you can say, 'I apologise, I have apologised.' Then the next thing, the following day you are abusing other people, but you say you have just come from apologising elsewhere.

Tatt (2014, p. 1013) has observed that an apology is an integral aspect of reconciliation, which, if performed authentically, can induce forgiveness and reconciliation between an injured party and the offender. The key here though regards how genuine and sincere the apology is perceived to be by the injured party. Feeling as they did, participants would have been sceptical of any apology that would have been proffered to them at that point. They also knew that no apology would be forthcoming and their opinions of this were quite strong.

An important ingredient in this apology is how one offers it; that is, the perpetrator needs to assume the blame for the offense committed. According to Newman/Kraynak (2013), an apology can elicit empathy from the victim if the transgressor acknowledges personal responsibility for the wrong done and includes the thoughts and feelings that led to the transgression. For instance, saying, 'I was under pressure,' is quite different from saying, 'I was thoughtless and irresponsible.' One deflects blame to circumstances and the other reflects the assumption of responsibility and acknowledges guilt or remorse. The latter is more likely to elicit the type of response Tatt talks about (see also Lazare 2004; Murphy 2011; Weyeneth 2001). Participants identified this as one of the things that would have probably redeemed President Mugabe had he been bold enough to accept responsibility for *Gukurahundi*. As one participant correctly observed:

> When we started talking about the issue of *Gukurahundi,* I am one of the people who said there was at one stage a record in the newspapers where the head of state admitted that 'It was a moment of madness.' He just fell short of accepting the entire blame because, as the head of state, he would have signed into action all these activities. The deployment of the army could not go out without his consent. After all he is the key author of "The Year of the People's Storm" in 1979. He should have come out clearly to say. 'I was responsible for a moment of madness.' If he had come out like that people would think that, 'He is a gentleman,' because he admits. If he refuses, what about P S, D N, and all the young men who did some dirty work in the field? They will not admit but we know all of them.

This variance between the desire for an apology and the realisation that none would be forthcoming, created a real tension within the participants and created a dilemma between their ideal and their reality. In the end, they grudgingly accepted that they had to 'continue living normally without an apology'. I could not ascertain whether this was resigned acceptance of their fate or a positive pragmatism—a determination to make the best of the situation (see Sect. 3.3.4)—as this dialogue took place before the TOL workshop.

## 8.4 Consequences of an Unhealed Past

It was clear from the participants' discussions that a lack of healing carried negative consequences for an individual, their community and the country in general. From the discussions, I identified several issues which resulted from a failure to meet the healing needs of the participants and, by extension, the communities in Matabeleland. These included the intergenerational transmission of trauma, a desire for revenge, a struggle to forgive, a mistrust of the government and a sense of guilt for 'failing' the people, which was coupled with a sense that their respective communities had questions about participants' roles during *Gukurahundi.*

### 8.4.1 Intergenerational Transmission of Trauma

As indicated in Sect. 6.8.1, our group had three university students who were interns with ZVT. This provided me with the unique opportunity of having two generations (the ex-combatants being the primary victims and the students being the next generation) in the same study, and to better appreciate the dynamics of the transmission of the victims' trauma to the next generation and how this manifested itself therein. From the discussions, it was clear that the participants were aware of this concept and I was also able to pick up sentiments from the student interns that indicated that they had been affected by the hurts of the older generation. Volkan (2001, p. 87) says:

> Within virtually every large group there exists a shared mental representation of a traumatic past event during which the large group suffered loss and/or experienced helplessness, shame and humiliation in a conflict with another large group. The transgenerational transmission of such a shared traumatic event is linked to the past generation's inability to mourn losses of people, land or prestige, and indicates the large group's failure to reverse… humiliation inflicted by another group, usually, a neighbour, but in some cases, between ethnic or religious groups within the same countries.

Volkan's statement can be held to pertain, not only to the participants in the research, but to the communities of Matabeleland in general. Studies in the trans-generational transmission of trauma in holocaust survivors has helped shed some light on this subject and has increased our understanding of trauma transmission in current incidents of political violence (see Connolly 2011; de Vinar 2012; Kellermann 2001; Fromm 2012).

According to Kogan (2012, p. 6), there are two mechanisms by which trans-generational trauma is transmitted, the first being 'primitive identification', which refers to the child's unconscious introjection and assimilation of the damaged parent's self-images through interaction with that parent. That is to say, the child unconsciously incorporates into its own psyche the parent's ideas. This is apparently an attempt to heal the parent and to help him/her recover. However, this identification leads to a loss of the child's separate sense of self and to an inability to differentiate between the self and the damaged parent. The second mechanism is 'deposited representation', which emphasises the role of the parent, who unconsciously, and sometimes even consciously, forces certain aspects of themselves on to the child. In so doing, the parent affects the child's sense of identity and passes to the child certain specific tasks to perform. In a sense the children become 'reservoirs for the deposited images connected to the trauma' and as a result, 'the children are compelled to deal with the shame, rage, helplessness, and guilt that the parents have been unable to work through for themselves' (Kogan 2012, p. 7). I found that the group tended to lean towards the second method. It appeared that, for the students in particular, parents had shared their stories together with the pains that go with them. Whether there was a deliberate attempt, on the part of their parents, to deposit their representation or not, would be difficult to determine. Nevertheless, the end result was the same as that described by Kogan. Statements such as, 'It becomes painful for us when our parents tell us of their experiences during *Gukurahundi,'* and 'It has an effect when our parents narrate how it took place,' or 'Sometimes you also end up feeling the pain,' seem to confirm Kogan's hypothesis.

In addition, their assertions also concurred with Kogan regarding the children being compelled to act on behalf of their parents. Describing his feelings, T, a male student intern, put it this way: 'I feel pained and my heart struggles. I fail to think as a human being. I become evil in a way.' B, another male student, added: 'It becomes a cycle of violence if there is no healing. The youth are now taking it as family honour to avenge their parents.' Later on, during the same discussion, B went further, saying, 'The anger which is transferred will be from my father or mother to me. It's not one time, it's two times. It is no longer the same; it becomes worse than my parents.' Their observations concur with Weingarten (2004, p. 52) who says that 'children who see, know, or intuit that their parents or grandparents have been humiliated are particularly vulnerable to developing retaliatory fantasies. When one generation fails to restore social and political equality, this failure forms the next generation's legacy' (See also Fromm 2012; Belnap 2012).

On the part of the older generation (the ex-combatants), there seems to have been a conflict between the desire not to taper the pain and hurt, and the realisation of the negative impact the transmission process might have on the next generation. The dichotomy between the urge to deposit their failed retaliatory fantasies on their children, and the desire to spare them pain, was fascinating to observe. For instance, in one discussion L declared: 'It is painful if we can't get an apology, but we will pass that to the next generation. We will not bury it; we will pass it to the next generation.' In another discussion, he seemed concerned about the negativity of burdening the next generation with their issues when he said, 'As I was reading Bill Clinton's quote in your office, I identified with it.[3]' Yet, a short while later, in the same conversation, he was once more adamantly saying, 'Let's pass it to the next generation. If we can't do anything now, maybe the next generation can…'

There then ensued a three-way discussion between L, V and myself, in which I pointed out that, while I had no problems with the passing on of the history of *Gukurahundi* to the next generation, my concern was that it should be done in a way that did not cause much trauma in the younger generation, to which L interjected saying, 'No, no, no, we have to pass it with the correct tempo, so that when they approach it, they approach it with the necessary strength, because if you polish it up, if someone wants to kill you…' At this point V entered the conversation to agree with L that indeed someone was really out to kill them at that time and such

---

[3]The Bill Clinton quote reads: 'Those who cannot let go of the hatred of their enemies risk sowing the seeds of hatred within own their communities.'.

people should not be tolerated, but then added: 'We are saying we shouldn't inspire anger and hatred in the lives of future generations.' L interjected wanting to know why not, to which V answered that it would leave the whole country in continuous turmoil and he ended by saying, 'You want to tolerate, at the same time you want to recriminate, but I think we need to find *space in between the two approaches*' (italics added). I think this was a genuine struggle caused by this dilemma among the participants.

### *8.4.2 Desire for Vengeance*

As indicated in Sect. 7.4, most participants were not reticent about talking about their desire to exact some form of revenge upon their perpetrators. These desires were stated quite forcefully through statements like, 'We need revenge,' and, 'Given a chance I would also inflict the same pain' and, 'The best is to do the worst.' Participants' stated desire for revenge appeared to encompass both the desire for private revenge, as exhibited by utterances such as, 'I for one, I am looking for revenge. Personally, I think I need revenge' or, 'I am prepared to bring down D. N…,' and for public revenge typified by statements such as, 'These people must face retribution, they must face the law' and, '…so that perpetrators…face justice.[4]' However, participants seem to have not made a clear distinction between revenge, justice and punishment; these terms were used interchangeably. There seems to be no consensus among scholars on the definition of revenge and it is perhaps prudent at this point to offer some of the definitions which I thought made sense to me and my understanding of the term. Rosebury (2009, p. 4) defines revenge as 'a deliberate injurious act against another person which is motivated by resentment of an injurious act or acts performed by the other person against the revenger (sic), or against some other persons whose injury the revenger resents'. While Gollwitzer et al. (2011, p. 364) describe it as 'an act designed to harm someone else or social group, in response to feeling that oneself has been harmed by that person or group'. Finally, Stillwell et al. (2008, p. 253) say it is 'an aggressive act that is often justified by the pursuit of equity'.

These definitions are included here because they somewhat reflect elements of what the participants mentioned in our discussion on revenge. First of all, there is the issue of resenting the wrong done to the participants. This has to do with a person's sense of right and wrong. As Gollwitzer et al. (2011, p. 364) explain, the desire to avenge is 'directly tied to our moral intuitions and our subjective notions of justice and deservingness'. Participants certainly exhibited a sense of indignation and unfairness regarding the wrongs visited upon them by the perpetrators of

[4]Private revenge does not necessarily refer to an act done in secrecy, but revenge carried out by individuals or groups outside of the justice system, while public revenge refers to acts carried out by the state through its law enforcement organs such as the courts (see Rosebury 2009, for a fuller discussion of the modes of revenge).

*Gukurahundi*. Certainly, their sense of justice seemed to have been assaulted by the fact that this transgression was committed by a government that was meant to protect them, and by people with whom they had fought to liberate Zimbabwe. They also strongly felt that they had done nothing to deserve the treatment they got and, as such, these acts were not only injurious to them but were also morally unjustifiable.

When one examines this discussion on revenge closely, three things stand out as possible reasons why participants would be drawn towards the need to avenge their suffering: The first is what Worthington (2006) calls the 'injustice gap and its appraisal'. Participants have had a long time to ruminate and stew over the wrongs that were done to them, and the more a person does this, the more the actions seem unjust and the angrier they become. Naturally, people who have a healthy self-respect, tend to resent moral injuries done to them. In that regard, 'retributive feelings can be synonymous with self-respect because they demonstrate that victims take their rights seriously' (Aldna 2006, p. 117). One who fails to be at least offended by such acts, is almost necessarily lacking in self-respect. It wasn't therefore surprising that participants harboured these feelings. For the younger participants, their desire for revenge seemed to have been premised on their 'affronted sense of honour' (Rosebury 2009), because of their parents' suffering (see Sect. 8.3.1). Secondly, participants' comments seemed to indicate that they felt that there was an 'emotional asymmetry' caused by the fact that the perpetrator is enjoying life while the victims are suffering (see Sect. 8.3.3). According to Gollwitzer et al. 2011, the offense causes an imbalance between the perpetrator and the victims, which the victims try to reduce by wanting the perpetrator to also experience an appropriate amount of harm or suffering. Hence the statements at the beginning of this section indicating the participants' desire to 'get their own back' (see also Stillwell et al. 2008, p. 253; Jackson/Gerber 2013). Thirdly, I noted a certain level of humiliation felt by most participants, more so because the ZIPRA ex-combatants have always viewed themselves as having been better trained, and possessing superior skills than their ZANLA counterparts. So, their suffering at the hands of 'ill-trained' soldiers, only served to 'rub salt into the wound' as it were (see Sect. 8.3.3). This point coheres with Goldwater (2004, p. 25) who points out that feelings of humiliation or shame are powerful motivators of reprisal and that it is harder to forgive an injury to one's pride than any other form of injury to oneself. Weingarten (2004, p. 52) also says, 'When groups are humiliated and must swallow their resentment, the desire for revenge builds.' For the younger participants, their desire for revenge was tied to the obligation they felt to avenge their parents' humiliation. This is because 'children who see, know or intuit that their parents or grandparents have been humiliated, are particularly vulnerable to developing retaliatory fantasies. When one generation fails to restore social and political equality, this failure forms the next generation's legacy' (Weingarten 2004, p. 52, see Sect. 8.3.1). In addition, the mourning mechanisms of the previous generation, which are necessary for the repair of loss, no longer provide relief to the younger generation and leads to them experiencing all life as loss. This contributes to the transfer of destructive aggression from the older to the younger generation. It therefore is no surprise that participants felt quite strongly about the need for revenge.

It was not very clear what participants expected the end result of revenge to be, and from the data analysed, I deduced a dual purpose in their desire for revenge: One had to do with trying to restore a sense of justice through proportional compensation from the perpetrator, what Jackson/Gerber (2013), have termed 'just deserts'. Participants expressed it this way: 'If you kill someone and then you are sentenced to death, that's a sort of revenge' and, 'I think we need retributive justice whereby a criminal should go through the same pain I went through.' At the same time, they also seemed to express vindictiveness and a desire to 'get back' at the offender and make him suffer for the offense. This was exemplified by a participant who said, 'I would love to see these people punished… The best is to have this thing solved by punishment… First, they must be punished. Secondly there must be a retribution of some kind.'

Because of the injustice gap, the desire for revenge seems to be the default response to any act deemed to be unjust by the recipient of that act. Indeed, this desire to retaliate is a universal phenomenon found in both human and non-human primates across all ages and cultures (Gollwitzer et al. 2011), and it probably is the reason why God instituted the laws governing revenge in the Old Testament. In Numbers 35, God instructed the Israelites to set up cities of refuge to where those who killed another person accidentally could run and, once there, the avenger of blood would not touch the person who had sought refuge in that city. The 'eye for an eye' principle set out in Leviticus 24 verse 20, is not God necessarily endorsing revenge, but an acknowledgement of this tendency and an attempt to provide an equitable and fair way to execute vengeance.

I am inclined to wonder what any of the participants would have done, had they indeed been given an opportunity to take revenge. Placing the discussion on revenge within the larger context of the whole research, I did not find much that suggested seriously that most of the participants would actually retaliate given the opportunity to do so. This led me to hypothesise that these manifestations were perhaps an expression of frustration at their feelings of helplessness and powerlessness. Another hypothesis, as advanced by Goldberg (2004) and Gower (2013), is that these desires, while real, remain in the realm of fantasy. According to these scholars, vengefulness maintains the balance of the destructive drive by directing it away from the self. They see wanting revenge as part of the healing process of hurt and anger (Goldberg 2004, pp. 5–6). So, when our desire for revenge remains on the level of fantasy, it actually serves several constructive psychological functions as it allows us to work with and to master the feelings of revenge. 'Being able to fantasise the ways in which one might redress and avenge hurtful acts is a great outlet and a discharge for aggression: a way of acting w*ithout acting*' (Gower 2013, p. 115, italics added). At the same time, the inability to imagine and fantasise can be very problematic and might lead to action in order to release aggression and get relief. In my view, in our case this would probably apply more to the younger generation because of the pressure of expectations placed upon them. This was highlighted by one participant when he said, 'It will happen…people get educated nowadays at schools and start asking questions on the reasons for *Gukurahundi*. When they look for information, it makes them feel angry… People will stand up at one stage and say, "come on man, let's confront this system."'

The last observation I wish to make in this discussion has to do with the 'magnitude gap', the problem of quantifying the proportionate measure of revenge. I perceive a problem with both forms of revenge—the 'just deserts' and the 'get even' or vindictive retribution—on the basis that what might seem fair to the original victim may seem grossly unfair to the original perpetrator. Statements by participants as discussed above appear to show a desire not to go beyond the pain inflicted on them in their quest for revenge. We have already described how they wanted to do only what was done to them, to make the perpetrators 'feel the same pain' or for the courts to impose the death penalty on those who inflicted pain on them, for example. However, it will always be difficult to satisfy both parties in terms of the restoration of equity. Even when the 'eye-for-an-eye' principle is legalistically applied, there will always be discrepancies, since different people perceive the same event quite differently. If one depends on precision to accomplish their work (a surgeon for example), one is bound to place a higher premium on being precise than that of a general worker whose work does not require the same level of precision. In this case the surgeon is going to likely view any discrepancy as a miscarriage of justice, and this will lead to feelings of having been victimised, leading to a desire for revenge, which might, in turn, result in a vicious cycle of revenge and counter revenge (see also Stillwell et al. 2008).

While participants desired some form of revenge, they nevertheless seemed to have been caught between two minds: wanting to revenge and realising the negative results of revenge. I found this dynamic fascinating because this dichotomy was not just intrapersonal, it was also interpersonal. The intrapersonal dilemma was illustrated well by T a male student intern:

> What I see is that this thing will never ever get out of my mind and if everyone had the same thinking like me it was going to be something else but, thank God that we are different, *because if they had the same mind like me, this is the recipe for a civil war but we are not ready for that because I know it's got more impact further on, but let's rather try to talk over things because 'an eye for an eye' will leave everyone blind. I am no longer sure who said that.* I think that we need retributive justice whereby a criminal should go through that same pain that I went through. Given a chance I would also inflict that same pain that I have to the next person, but I would not want to do that because of the way I was raised and the way I believe things should be… (italics added).

A conversation we had on day six illustrates the interpersonal aspect of this dichotomy:

> L: A case in point is [Minister] Mzila's.[5] Two days ago in Hwange, a lot of people went in support… They could not fit in the court room, they were pushed away and they remained singing emotional songs outside, saying we were killed, when we try and talk about it we

[5]Moses Mzila was one of the three co-ministers of the Organ for National Healing and Reconciliation under the Government of National Unity (2009–2013). He was arrested in Lupane while attending a *Gukurahundi* event organised by a community in Lupane, Matebeleland North.

get arrested. You know it stings a part of the body, people in Mat North—they are very angry right now about it…This thing is a problem. We are living a fake life. We are living on borrowed time. We need revenge

Dumie: What form of revenge, should we also go and kill someone?

L: No, no, in the form of a civilised court so that the perpetrator they face justice, because this was a crime, a crime was committed. If you kill someone and then you are sentenced to death that's a sort of revenge. The victims they feel consoled…

V: Retributive

L: Yes, if that person comes out clean (pause), that's why people go and look for African medicines so that…

V: to make them disappear, feel the pain, equitably?

L: Yah, A tooth for a tooth and an eye for an eye.

V: But it will make Zimbabwe blind! (laughs)

L: Right there must be people like Ngwenya somewhere, to control this anger (laughter), to say, no, no, L don't kill. I for one, I am looking for revenge, personally, I think I need revenge. If I can get hold of some of the perpetrators and do the same to them, my community, the community I come from would be very excited and probably make them forget as they would say, we in the end, we dealt with them and generally in my community the feeling is there should be revenge because the state does not want us to talk about it. The state says let's not open old wounds now…

In this case V acted as the external voice of reason, but what is interesting is that V himself, in one of the previous dialogues, had indicated his willingness to 'bring down' a certain individual who had not only caused him personal grief, but had also presided over the death of a friend while he watched helplessly. Perhaps it is easier to appreciate the negativity of revenge from a distance, but somewhat difficult if it concerns one personally. It seems that pain might to some extent cloud one's moral judgement as one becomes consumed by the injustice of the act perpetrated against him/her. For T, it would seem that the dilemma was raised by his belief system and upbringing: he indicated that he was a Christian.

### *8.4.3 Dysfunctional Relationships*

I will now address some minor themes which, although not extensively discussed, were still important enough to be highlighted as some of the consequences of an unhealed past. I have also chosen to address the issue of forgiveness, not here, but under the next topic, because it was a contentious issue for the group. Participants, the ex-combatants to be specific, expressed concern that, because of the silence around *Gukurahundi*, people in the communities were suspicious of the possible role they too might have played in the atrocities. L elaborated the concern saying, 'They know I was a soldier so they would ask, "Where were you? Were you killing people somewhere?"...Obviously, they think I was doing something similar somewhere.' G amplified this concern further when she added:

> The fifth brigade used to come to Gwanda with people who knew how to speak isiNdebele, so the elders now don't know whether these people were Ndebele people or people who only knew how to speak it. What L was saying, they are no longer sure, they say, 'Maybe while you were not here, you were also somewhere else doing the same.' Last year we visited Tsholotsho. A certain lady said, 'Amongst you, there might be one of them because they are still there but we no longer know them.'

Although they made light of this concern, it seemed it was a real issue because they mentioned that, according to their training in ZIPRA, they had been taught to respect civilians as they were their lifeline.

These suspicions and accusations levelled against them by some community members, led to some of them developing a sense of guilt for having failed their parents and their communities. Again, L expressed this concern succinctly when he told the group that, whenever he visits, people in his home area ask: 'Why did you let our people be killed whilst you were there?' He further said, 'I don't know how to answer that, I feel I betrayed them.'

Behnia (2004) posits that most survivors of war and torture often feel guilty from thinking that they are alive, safe and well. He further points out that the extreme situations that are caused by war and torture, also call into question connections such as kinship, friendship and a sense of community that link individuals to each other. What this indicates is that, even without any accusations being levelled against them, the participants, most of whom are survivors of war and torture already, carried a burden of guilt, and having their communities accuse them in this manner, only served to increase these negative feelings. Endreß/Pabst (2013, p. 90) explain that 'violence captures the experience of human vulnerability and the power to violate others. Being violated affects one's capacity to encounter others and the world as well as one's self-understanding and potentiality to act, experiences of violence lead to a fundamental shattering of trust' (See Sects. 3.3 and 4.1; Fisher/Zimina 2009). This mistrust is not only held within an affected community, but is also strongly experienced towards the perpetrators. The discussion revealed just how pervasive mistrust towards the ZANU PF government is. This has led most people in Matabeleland to dissociate themselves from anything to do with the government. L observed: 'They are now isolated... They have found solace in South Africa. They don't want anything to do with the government. They don't want to join the army. They don't want to join the police.' Ross (2011) says that this attitude is driven by the belief that it is safer to keep a distance from others. For Ross, 'Mistrust makes sense where threats abound, particularly for those who feel powerless to prevent harm or cope with consequences of being victimised or exploited.' We noted in Sect. 7.5 that this is the sort of environment in which participants felt they lived in on a daily basis (see also Sect. 8.3.3).

Unfortunately, this mistrust runs so deep that just about everything that happens to the victims is treated with suspicion. Participants seemed to connect and interpret every action associated with the government within the framework of the *Gukurahundi* discourse, as demonstrated by N's observation that

> Trust has also been affected by those past experiences. The police have become enemies and they are no longer protecting our lives. Why? Because most police speak Shona and they have been used to perpetrate violence, especially during elections. When there is violence, the parents at home feel angry and would say, 'This used to happen before and it's continuing.' As G has mentioned, *Gukurahundi* is continuing so hatred is still there.

Mistrust is self-fulfilling, in the sense that people will always find evidence that justifies why they should never trust their perpetrators again.

## 8.5 Participants' Overall Assessment of the Research Project

Participants' comments throughout the research process and during the evaluation of the research session indicated that the issue I had independently selected was pertinent to them. The statements below are some of the comments they expressed in regards to its usefulness at different stages of the research. In regards to its relevancy to themselves, participants said the following:

> I think I feel healthy when we discuss about *Gukurahundi.* I feel healed discussing these things about *Gukurahundi.* If I am here I am comfortable, I feel I am with comrades who talk like me and have problems like me and I am happy. (L)

> If I think of these things, there is a lot of things that come to my mind and when I am here I think I am in the right place because a problem shared is a problem half solved in a way. So, I am in this group, I believe there is a common ground and all of us we have got the same problem that we are sharing and we are trying to help each other to recover from it… I think that as I am also participating in this programme, maybe my mind will change and I will think differently. (T)

> I believe to us…, to me as an individual first, it will help me to come out with some ideas on how we can come up with solutions individually to cope with *Gukurahundi.* (V)

> I am happy that we are discussing such issues because I still believe that I will get a way that will help me to forgive as we keep talking together. (G)

During our last dialogue session, when we were evaluating the overall impact of the research, participants reiterated their belief that they had benefitted from the research process. Naturally, different people found certain aspects of the research more beneficial than others. One participant, G, had not found the TOL process very helpful to her because she felt as if they had just talked and left things hanging.[6] She had benefitted more from the writing workshop. However, she is one

[6] G attended one of the subsequent workshops as she had not been able to attend the one specifically meant for research participants. However, these workshops are standard. What might differ is perhaps the group dynamics. So we can assume that she might have felt the same way, even if she had attended the research participants' workshop.

of the participants who, although they started writing their stories, did not finish. She also indicated that she had no intention of completing it but would not proffer any reasons for her decision. Participants also indicated that they felt they had been fully involved in the process and felt their opinions had been respected. J commented that the reason they had kept attending was because they felt the process had been useful to them, otherwise they would not have continued coming had they felt excluded.

Participants also viewed the research process as something that would also have a positive influence on how they carried out their own peacebuilding activities in the communities they work with. V thought that the research 'can equip us also to have the ideas and strategies of resolving the conflicts that exist among the people and particularly on healing the trauma that we find interned in people's feelings right now within the communities,' while G commented:

> What I like and what makes me part of this discussion is that, as part of our work, we as ZVT, is that when we go out and try to talk to people on the issue of reconciliation, you can't go far before people start talking about *Gukurahundi* and asking, 'How can you come and tell us about forgiveness when we were killed so much?'

She further said, 'I hope that I will get help during these discussions that will help me and give me answers to give to people.'

The above comments indicate that, although participants might not have participated in the formulation and identification of the research question, they nevertheless found it pertinent, not only for their lives, but their work as well. As such, it can be assumed that this PAR principle was adequately met.

As noted in Sect. 6.8.3, the existence of previous relationships between the ZVT members and myself and amongst themselves, helped significantly in creating a level of caring relationships within the research process. It also allowed us to become a community, if only for the duration of the research, which helped to focus the research purpose. V expressed it thus:

> It's ground breaking now in the sense that, we are now the community and, collectively and individually, we have had our own experiences of *Gukurahundi*, directly and indirectly. It is quite a benefit to our community here, and of course those we represent externally, to come up with reasoned approaches to these discussions which are going to be worthwhile and a benefit for the research, and also equip and arm ourselves of the general understanding of issues of *Gukurahundi*, particularly where there is an absence of an official apology.

We therefore did not spend much time in the creation of a conducive and enabling environment for the research. It also helped that they, as a group, were already part of an organisation that sought to recreate some of the camaraderie they had had previously.

Another way to assess the validity of the research is to evaluate how useful the exercise has been to the participants: whether the practical knowledge that is useful to people in the everyday conduct of their lives has been produced, and how much this practical knowledge has contributed to the wellbeing of participants and their communities, be it psychologically, politically, economically and spiritually (Reason/Bradbury 2008, see also Sects. 5.5 and 6.6). In other words, how much has the research been able to bring about meaningful change to the participants and their communities? According to McTaggart (1998), it is difficult to do this without referring to its social purpose and to the practices it seeks to inform and transform. Hence, in this section I shall seek to establish how effective this research was in that regard. In doing so, it will be prudent to bear Koch/Kralik's (2006) advice that, change processes can occur slowly; hence, the impact of engaging with a PAR process can resonate long after a researcher has left the field. It is therefore important that outcomes of PAR be not 'judged in terms of the magnitude of the change achieved or action taken, because PAR often makes impact as a process of ongoing learning and awakening' (Koch/Kralik 2006, p. 41). Nevertheless, for the sake of this evaluation, we will assess, to the extent that is feasible, the change process among the participants.

### *8.5.1 Effectiveness of Actions*

A significant amount of chapter seven was spent evaluating the TOL workshop and its impact on the participants (see Sects. 7. 4 and 7. 5). This section will not seek to reproduce that discussion. It was ascertained from that discussion that participants generally found the workshop helpful and, for some, it resulted in significant personal transformation. Most participants' resiliencies and agency were enhanced by the process. Change in attitudes, from a desire for vengeance and clinging to a victimhood mentality, to a positive engagement with their hurts in an effort to 'move on' as best as was possible with their lives, were noted. Participants not only found the experience transformative but also empowering, in the sense that they found life skills to enable them to attain a measure of relief for their pains, despite the intransigency of the perpetrators. Some of them who had participated in similar healing processes thought that the TOL process was more practical compared to these other approaches.

Regarding the critical recovery of history: while the participants' stated desires in wanting to write their stories were to 'preserve history', to 'record what really transpired', 'write facts', and 'to pass it on to the next generation'; the potential therapeutic benefits of this act cannot be ignored, since recovery requires an examination of the truth. What this exercise did was to break the state-imposed silence and bring dignity to the experiences of the participants. As has been mentioned (see Sect. 6.8.3), not much in-depth analysis of the writing process was done, because the stories had not been finalised at the close of the research. However, being able to put their experiences on paper was in itself, for most of them, a liberating experience. This was a great source of comfort and pride, because during the writing workshop, the facilitator had spoken about how important it was to leave one's 'presence' or legacy behind after death, in the form of a written story. The majority feeling was that, finally, they would not be forgotten after death, since they would leave their stories behind to continue bearing testimony on their behalf. C explained the importance of this exercise this way:

> You know that writing workshop? It encouraged me a lot, but there is one thing that I learnt from Phathisa (facilitator): We are all mortal. He is also accepting that he is mortal, he is as mortal as other people, but he is not going to die like us because he will remain forever, because he has got something written about him. It taught and encouraged me that at least I also need to write something, so that people..., we don't want that..., something written down can't be answered in the streets, at a rally. You can only do it by writing, which is something that will endure for long. A rally is here today but soon gone and people soon forget, but writing, whether a book or a pamphlet, it will always be there and people can always refer to it and say 'This one said this and the other said that.'

M said that writing had been therapeutic for him:

> I believe the whole research process was healing to me and the writing exercise added to it. Since I wrote this thing, I had to write it twice because the young lady I asked to type it for me lost all the five exercise books I had written, so I had to rewrite another five books. For me, if I offload something from my mind, I think I get healed because all of it is removed from my mind and I feel as if the heavy burden I was carrying is gone.

The use of writing as a method to promote healing and wellbeing has been well accepted by most helping professionals, and Connolly Baker/Mazza (2004) and Lengelle/Meijers (2009) discuss this in detail in their works. M also mentioned the interest the writing exercise had aroused in his children who were now keen to read about their parent's experiences (see Sect. 8.1.3). However, much like the speaking, the correct procedure and environment are essential if the writing exercise is to be cathartic.

The potential of the writing exercise to correct distorted history was brought home for a number of participants who, on behalf of ZVT, were asked by the National Archives to come and relate the history of ZIPRA and its contribution to the struggle for independence. While narrating their history, the young officials pointed out to them that some of the things they were talking about as having done, ex-ZANLA combatants were also claiming to have done. The following morning one of the young officials telephoned the chairman of ZVT to say that he had gone through the archives and had discovered a newspaper clip of 8 December 1978 which stated that indeed ZIPRA had carried out the attacks. According to C, 'I learnt that things that are written are important. They can unlock some (inaudible) that now we can talk with authority without fearing that someone might say you are lying because it's there written even in the archives.'

### 8.5.2 The Research Process

At the evaluation meeting participants commented about how much they had gained from being part of this research. V's assessment of the whole research process was that PAR is

> a practical way of studying the situation. It gives a direct response to a situation and we were able to enquire and act. It is not theoretical but practical. If people had participated all the time, it would be the best form of research. If we turn our stories into a book that will be the best objective indicator that action was carried out.

V's statement is actually a good definition of what PAR is and what it does and compares well with those given by scholars such as Reason/Bradbury (2008), Cahill (2007), and Guishard (2009), among others (see Sect. 5.1). D said it was 'revealing and reminded us about the past; it taught us to analyse situations.' By 'revealing' he meant that hearing other participants' stories made him gain an understanding of the bigger picture (see Minow 1998). F said that, for him, the lesson was the realisation that, 'If you do not research, who will do it?' An important goal of PAR is to assist 'ordinary' people in gaining the skills and confidence to reflect upon their problems and to be actively involved in seeking solutions to these problems. This process implies improving participants' capacity to solve problems and achieve their objectives, but, most importantly, developing their capacity to conduct their own research. Babbie/Mouton (2001, p. 324) suggest that 'the medium of doing research as a way in which information is imparted to participants is therefore considered to be just as, or even more, important than the message or the product of research'. J said, 'We thank you for opening our eyes. At times, you just exist as a person aimlessly…' M added, 'You would be at your wits' end, not knowing what could heal you. Even now, when we go to the communities, we can see that people are still oppressed and if you, whose eyes have been opened, try to open the people's eyes, you have to contend with the police. You become a bad person.' While acknowledging the difficulty of the task ahead of them, in terms of their community peacebuilding initiative, participants felt they were now better prepared to carry this work out. As a final assessment of the research project, participants were asked to mention how the research had benefitted them.

Table 8.1 is a summary of some of the participants' views about the usefulness of the research process in their lives:

As can be noted from the remarks above, participants believed they had developed or enhanced their subjectivities and critical awareness. While the goal of PAR is not to describe reality but to change it (Cahill 2007), one needs to at least understand this reality. Participants' understanding of their subjectivities developed through the interactions they had with each other. The discussions that we had deepened as the process went on and, as has been reflected in this chapter and Chap. 9, participants could critically analyse their own situations and were aware of the broader issues affecting them.

**Table 8.1** Summary of participants' assessment of the research process. *Source* The author

| | |
|---|---|
| **N** (student intern) | For me as a student and now practitioner in the field of peacebuilding, I gained mostly from the data. It gave me a chance to hear stories I don't hear often, which will help me in my work |
| **B** (student intern) | Having an opportunity to air my views, it gave me an outlet to speak. I was able to vent my anger and frustrations and I got relief from that |
| **M** | You know this country we live in, the research helped me, it set me free. It helped me learn to focus on myself and to try to live my life positively without worrying too much about the circumstances around me |
| **C** | There has been an improvement in the way I view things. I learnt to interpret life and how to handle the things that come my way and to know that this is not just happening to me but that is how life is. I also learnt to accept those things I can't change |
| **E** | Those were progressive meetings, they helped us to interact and engage each other constructively in addressing issues. We have been using the same approach within our programmes. The programme was beneficial not only to us but could also benefit the student interns that come to work with us |

## 8.6 Conclusion

In this chapter, we have discussed the themes based on the data from the dialogue sessions. Essentially, there are three major themes, each with several sub-themes that were highlighted. These are: 'Sharing the stories of suffering', with its sub-themes of writing and speaking; 'Hindrances to healing' with the sub-themes of repressing the truth, deep-seated feelings of insecurity, impunity and lack of an apology; and 'Consequences of an unhealed past', the sub-themes being inter-generational transmission of trauma, the desire for vengeance and dysfunctional relationships. The chapter also discussed participants' views concerning the usefulness of the research process to them.

Chapter 9 discusses some of the issues that were problematised by the research under the title 'Contentious Issues'.

## References


Abreu Hernandez, V. M. 2002. The mothers of La Plaza de Mayo: a peace movement. *Peace & Change*, 27(3): 385–411.

Adam, H. and Adam, K. 2000. The politics of memory in divided societies. In W. James and L. Van de Vijver (eds.), *After the TRC: reflections on truth and reconciliation in South Africa*. Cape Town: David Philip.

Adams, K. 1999. Writing as therapy. *Counselling and Human Development*, 31(5): 1–16.

Aldana, R. 2006. A victim-centred reflection of Truth Commissions and prosecutions as a response to mass atrocities. *Journal of Human Rights*, 5: 106–126.

Babbie, E. and Mouton, J. 2001. *The practice of social research*. Cape Town: Oxford Press.

Behnia, B. 2004. Trust building from the perspective of survivors of war and torture. *Social Services Review*, 1: 26–40. At: http://www.jstor.org/stable/10.1086/380768 (6 June 2014).

Belnap, B. 2012. Turns of a phrase: traumatic learning through the generations. In M. G. Fromm (ed.), *Lost in transmission: studies of trauma across generations*. London: Karnack Books Ltd. At: http://us.karnacbooks.com/product/lost-in-transmission-studies-of-trauma-across-generations/30112/ (29 May 2014).

Botcharova, O. 2001. Implementation of track two diplomacy: developing a model for forgiveness. In R. Helmick and R. Petersen (eds.), *Forgiveness and reconciliation: religion, public policy and conflict transformation*. Radnor, PA: Templeton Foundation Press.

Bylsma, L. M., Vingerhoets, J. J. M. and Rottenberg, J. 2008. When is crying cathartic? An international study. *Journal of Social & Clinical Psychology*, 27(10): 1165–1187.

Cahill, C. 2007. The personal is political: developing new subjectivities through participatory action research. *Gender, Place and Culture*, 14(3) June: 267–292.

Cobham, V. E., March S., De Young, A., Lesson, F., Nixon, R., McDermott, B. and Kenardy J. 2012. Involving parents in indicated early intervention for childhood PTSD following accidental injury (online). *Clinical Child & Family Psychology Review*, 15(4): 345–363. At: https://link.springer.com/article/10.1007/s10567-012-0124-9 (10 May 2014).

Connolly, A. 2011. Healing the wounds of our fathers: intergenerational trauma, memory, symbolisation and narrative. *Journal of Analytical Psychology*, 56: 607–626.

Connolly Baker, K. and Mazza, N. 2004. The healing power of writing: applying the expressive/creative component of poetry to therapy. *Journal of Poetry Therapy: The Interdisciplinary Journal of Practice, Theory, Research and Education*, 12(3): 141–154. At: http://dx.doi.org/10.1080/08893670412331311352 (6 June 2014).

De Viñar, M. U. 2012. Political violence: transgenerational inscription and trauma. *International Journal of Applied Psychoanalytic Studies*, 9(2): 95–108.

Endreß, M. and Pabst, A. 2013. Violence and shattered trust: sociological considerations. *Human Studies*, 36: 89–106.

Eppel, S. 2006. 'Healing the dead': exhumation and burial as truth-telling and peace-building activities in rural Zimbabwe. In T. A. Borer (ed.), *Telling the truths: truth telling and peace building in post-conflict societies*. Notre Dame, Indiana: University of Notre Dame Press.

Farwell, N. and Cole, J. B. 2002. Community as context of healing: psychosocial recovery of children affected by war and political violence. *International Journal of Mental Health*, 30(4): 19–41.

Fisher, S. and Zimina, L. 2009. Just wasting our time? Provocative thoughts for peacebuilders (online). *Berghof handbook*. At: http://citeseerx.ist.psu.edu/viewdoc/download?doi=10.1.1.550.1263&rep=rep1&type=pdf (03 October 2010).

Fooladi, M. M. 2005. The healing effects of crying. *Holistic Nursing Practice*, 19(6): 248–255.

Fromm, M. G. 2012. *Lost in transmission: studies of trauma across generations*. London: Karnack Books Ltd. At: http://us.karnacbooks.com/product/lost-in-transmission-studies-of-trauma-across-generations/30112/ (29 May 2014).

Goddard, V. A. 2007. Demonstrating resistance: politics and participation in the marches of the Mothers of Plaza de Mayo. *European Journal of Anthropology*, 50: 81–101.

Goldberg, J. G. 2004. Fantasies of revenge and the stabilisation of the ego: acts of revenge and the ascension of Thanatos. *Modern Psychoanalysis*, 29(1): 13–21.

Goldwater, E. 2004. Getting mad and getting even. *Modern Psychoanalysis*, 9(1): 23–36. 250

Gollwitzer, M., Meder, M. and Schmitt, M. 2011. What gives victims satisfaction when they seek revenge? *European Journal of Social Psychology*, 41: 364–374.

Gower, M. 2013. Revenge: interplay of creative and destructive forces. *Clinical Social Work Journal*, 41: 112–118.

Guishard, M. 2009. The false paths, the endless labors, the turns now this way and now that: participatory action research, mutual vulnerability, and the politics of inquiry. *Urban Review*, 41: 85–105.

Hayner, P. 2001. *Unspeakable truths: confronting state terror and atrocity*. London: Routledge.

Isserman, N. 2009. Political tolerance and intolerance: using qualitative interviews to understand the attitudes of holocaust survivors. *Contemporary Jewry*, 29(1): 21–47.

Jackson, J. and Gerber M. M. 2013. Retribution as revenge and retribution as just deserts. *Social Justice Research*, 26: 61–80.
Jordan, J. B. 1998. Writing and therapy with conflictual couples. *Journal of Family Psychotherapy*, 9(2): 27–39. At: http://dx.doi.org/10.1300/J085V09N02_03 (21 May 2014).
Kellermann, N. P. F. 2001. Transmission of Holocaust trauma: an intergretive view. *Psychiatry*, 64 (3): 256–264.
Kliman, J. and Llerena-Quinn, R. 2002. Dehumanising and rehumanising responses to September 11. *Journal of Systematic Therapies*, 21(3): 8–18.
Koch, T. and Kralik, D. 2006. *Participatory action research in Healthcare.* Oxford, UK: Blackwell Publishing.
Kogan, I. 2012. The second generation in the shadow of terror. In M. G. Fromm (ed.), *Lost in transmission: studies of trauma across generations*. London: Karnack Books Ltd. At: http://us.karnacbooks.com/product/lost-in-transmission-studies-of-trauma-across-generations/30112/ (29 May 2014).
Kupferberg, F. 1997. The land of murderers: Jewish survivors in post-war Germany. *Innovation*, 10(1): 85–102.
La Caze, M. 2006. The asymmetry between apology and forgiveness. *Contemporary Political Theory,* 5: 447–468
Lazare, A. 2004. *On apology*. New York: Oxford University Press.
Lederach, J. P. 1997. *Building peace: sustainable reconciliation in divided societies*. Washington, DC: USIP.
Lengelle, R. and Meijers, F. 2009. Mystery and mastery: an exploitation of what happens in the black box of writing and healing. *Journal of Poetry Therapy: The Interdisciplinary Journal of Practice, Theory, Research and Education*, 22(2): 57–75. At: https://doi.org/10.1080/08893670903072935 (6 June 2014).
Lieblich, A. 2013. Healing plots; writing and reading in life-stories groups. *Qualitative Inquiry*, 19: 46–52. At: http://qix.sagepub.com/content/19/1/46 (20 May 14).
McGrew, L. 2006. Justice and reconciliation? Can the trails for the Khmer Rouge bring reconciliation and healing in Cambodia? *NIAS Nytt*, 3: 8–11.
Mckinney, K. 2007. 'Breaking the conspiracy of silence': testimony, traumatic memory, and psychotherapy with survivors of political violence. *Ethos*, 35(3): 265–295.
McTaggart, R. 1998. Is validity really an issue for Participatory action research? *Studies in Culture, Organisations and Societies*, 4: 211–236.
Minow, M. 1998. *Between vengeance and forgiveness: facing history after genocide and mass violence*. Boston: Beacon Press.
Moon, C. 2009. Healing past violence: traumatic assumptions and therapeutic interventions in war and reconciliation. *Journal of Human Rights*, 8: 71–91. At: https://doi.org/10.1080/14754830902717726 (28 May 2014).
Mullet, J. H., Akerson, N. M. K. and Turman, B. A. 2013. Healing the past through story. *Adult Learning*, 24(2): 72–77.
Murphy, M. 2011. Apology, recognition, and reconciliation. *Human Rights Review*, 12: 47–69.
Newman, L. S. and Kraynak, L. R. 2013. The ambiguity of a transgression and the type of apology influence immediate reactions. *Social Behaviour and Personality*, 41(1): 31–46.
Opotow, S. 2001. Reconciliation in times of impunity challenges for social justice. *Social Justice Research*, 14(2): 149–170.
Pennebaker, J. W. 1997. Writing about emotional experiences as a therapeutic process. *Psychological Science,* 8(3): 162–166. At: http://www.jstor.org/stable/40063169?origin=JSTOR-pdf. (20 May 2014)
Pia, E. 2013. Narrative therapy and peacebuilding. *Journal of Intervention and Statebuilding,* 7(4): 476–491. At: http://dx.doi.org/10.1080/17502977.2012.727538 (10 May 2014).
Pintar, J. 2000. Anticipating consequences: what Bosnia taught us about healing the wounds of war. *Human Rights Review*, January–March: 56–66.
Reason, P. and Bradbury, H. 2008. Introduction. In P. Reason and H. Bradbury (eds.), *The SAGE handbook of action research: participative inquiry and practice*. London: Sage.

Rosebury, B. 2009. Private revenge and its relation to punishment. *Utilitas*, 21(1): 1–22. 263

Ross, C. E. 2011. Collective threat, trust, and the sense of personal control. *Journal of Health and Social Behaviour*, 52(3): 287–296.

Shriver, D. W. 2003. Where and when in political life is justice served by forgiveness? In N. Biggar (ed.), *Burying the past: making peace doing justice after civil conflict.* Georgetown: Georgetown University Press.

Staub, E. and Pearlman, L. 2001. Healing, reconciliation and forgiving after genocide and other collective violence. In R. Helmick and R. Peterson (eds.), *Forgiveness and reconciliation: religion, public policy and conflict transformation.* Radnor, Philadelphia: Templeton Foundation.

Staub, E., Pearlman, L. A., Gubin, A. and Hagengimana, A. 2005. Healing, reconciliation, forgiving and the prevention of violence after genocide or mass killings: an intervention and its Experimental Evaluation in Rwanda. *Journal of Social and Clinical Psychology,* 24(3): 297–334.

Stillwell, A. M., Baumeister, R. F. and Del Priore, R. E. 2008. We're all victims here: toward a psychology of revenge. *Basic and Applied Social Psychology*, 30: 253–263.

Tatt, L. 2014. Apology within a moral dialectic: a reply to Professor Robbennolte. L*aw Review*, 103(5): 1010–1017. At: http://www.jstor.org/stable/30044450 (9 May 2014).

Van der Oord, S., Lucassen, S., Van Emmeril, A. A. P. and Emeelkamp, P. M. G. 2010. Treatment of post-traumatic stress disorder in children using cognitive behavioural writing therapy. *Clinical Psychology and Psychotherapy*, 17: 240–249.

Volkan, V. D. 2001. Transgenerational transmission and chosen traumas: an aspect of large-group identity. *Group Analysis*, 34: 79–97.

Weyeneth, R. R. 2001. History, memory, and reconciliation: the power of apology and the process of historical reconciliation. *The Public Historian*, 23(3): 9–38. At: http://www.jstor.org/stable/10.1525/tph.2001.23.issue-3 (29 May 2014).

Wieder, A. 2004. Testimony as oral history: lessons from South Africa. *Educational Researcher*, 33(6): 23–28.

Weingarten, K. 2004. Witnessing the effects of political violence in families: mechanisms of intergenerational transmission and clinical interventions. *Journal of Marital and Family Therapy*, 30(1): 45–59.

Worthington, E. L. 2006. *Forgiveness and reconciliation: theory and application*. New York: Routledge.

Zorbas, E. 2004. Reconciliation in post-genocide Rwanda. *African Journal of Legal Studies,* 1(1): 29–35.

# Chapter 9
# Contentious Issues

## 9.1 Introduction

This chapter discusses four issues which were points of tension in the research: forgiving and forgetting, what heals and what does not, the dilemma of compensation and whether the past can be corrected or not.

## 9.2 On Forgiving and Forgetting

The issue of forgiveness and forgetting dominated discussions during the third dialogue session. Participants wrestled intensely with both concepts. In some instances, they seemed to view forgetting as a prerequisite for forgiving and yet, at the same time, acknowledged the difficulty of forgetting. Time, extent of trauma and opportunity to talk about transgression freely and continuously, were some of the mitigating factors. For instance, T emphasised this point saying:

> It's hard to just let go of these things, but looking at time, it may heal but to forget and say, 'I'm done with that, I will just let go, it's now water under the bridge,' it's hard to face such a situation. We can try and forgive, but, removing that thing of saying I have forgotten about it, I doubt if it's something that can just happen. I think it is a process that you have to go through, to go through the first stage, the second stage up to a level of saying "I have really forgiven you and I have forgotten about it." You can never, you can never.

His sentiments were echoed by V also felt that

> It is not easy just to forego things and then you say, 'I am forgiving.' You will realise that it is not something easy to let go and trauma will always remain, but I believe, with a lot of deliberations, discussions on the same thing, drumming on it over and over again, maybe



D. Ngwenya, *Healing the Wounds of Gukurahundi in Zimbabwe*,
The Anthropocene: Politik—Economics—Society—Science 19,
https://doi.org/10.1007/978-3-319-66818-5_9

> we may forget; but I know, I am saying 'Maybe,' qualified. I am saying 'MAYBE' but I feel it. It is very difficult.

Although participants acknowledged that it was difficult to forget, they somehow still felt it was necessary to do so if one was to forgive. We then explored what we meant by forgetting and whether it really was possible to forget. Most participants agreed that this was near impossible. As one of them put it, 'To forget is like erasing something from the mind.' T offered this explanation:

> *It's like formatting the brains of which we cannot do that* (laughs), because you are still living. The brain can be formatted when a person is dead. They cannot just forget as long as they are living. A person can end up writing it in a diary that 'Such a thing happened in such a day.' The moment it is written down it means that they cannot easily forget that thing… (Italics added).

However, a few felt that it was possible to forget; and this forgetting they felt was based on the willingness of the offender to acknowledge the wrong and show signs of remorse. As one of them put it; 'If he shows some signs to be forgiven then I can forgive and forget. We can still be friends. I have forgotten that aspect of what they did.'

This issue of forgiving and forgetting has been discussed extensively by scholars from various disciplines, including religion (Krondorfer 2008; Smedes 1996), psychology (Enright et al. 1998; Cosgrove/Konstam 2008; Worthington 2001) and peacebuilding (Elshtain 2003; Biggar 2003) among others. Participants' views pretty much mirror the ongoing debate among scholars. For instance, Krondorfer (2003) seems to agree with those participants who viewed forgetting as an essential part of forgiving. Writing on the holocaust, his premise is that forgetting might not be as reprehensible as it has been made to be and that perhaps the 'We shall forgive, but we will never forget' mantra needs to be revisited, in order to find other ways of dealing with memory around the holocaust.

The rest of the participants, while acknowledging that it was impossible to forget an act as gross as *Gukurahundi,* advocated for what Elshtain (2003) has called 'knowing forgetting', but not a collective amnesia where the past is totally relegated from memory. What these participants wanted was a situation where the past is recollected without the people being entirely defined by it (see Sect. 4.5.3). The statements by G who said, 'Forgiveness' can be there. Why? Because those people cannot revenge and kill that person even if you introduce him today, but they can accept to work with him for the future, but it's not possible to forget' and N who indicated that, while people could not forget, what was necessary was 'realising that when memories come back, we talk about it lightly, as if it's a past that has been forgiven,' offer a practical way of dealing with the problem of forgetting in forgiveness. Their suggestions resonate well with Cosgrove/Kostam's (2008) assertions. They suggest that some victims may be empowered by letting the memory of the transgression recede. The forgetting they suggest allows the victim to have a future with the transgressor that is not tainted by unresolved emotions. This kind of forgiving puts the past behind in such a way that it permits the continuation of the relationship, even though the relationship dynamics have changed, and I think this is what G was alluding to by saying people could accept to work with the perpetrator for the future, even if they could not forget. This perspective is well expressed by Cosgrove/Kostam (2008, pp. 7–8) when they explain that the relationship between the two is best 'described in terms of transcending the negative affect incurred by the hurtful incident thereby allowing the individuals to focus on the future rather than dwell on the past' as well as being understood 'in terms of the importance of the ability to refrain from rumination about the offense'—what N described as 'talking lightly' about it, as if the past has been forgiven. What this means is that, although it might not be possible to wipe out the transgressions from one's mind completely, one chooses to put those thoughts aside in order to continue with the relationship, albeit an altered one.

There was also a strong discussion on the role of trust and forgetting in the healing process. Some of them felt that forgetting contributed to the building of trust, while others said that forgetting was not necessary for healing. I think this disagreement was caused in part by the fact that, although asked, the question of what forgetting meant was never answered, although from the discussions it seemed that different types of forgetting were being referred to. Below are snippets of that discussion:

> Dumie: Okay, so what I'm saying is that, really, is forgetting part of the healing process? Should it be part of the healing process?
>
> V: No, No, It should not! No, it should not… the element of forgetting is not part of the healing process. But the element of forgiving, yes, is part of the healing process. So, I can forgive but I cannot forget… Those things that are painful will always stick out like a pin in your mind and ehh, in the flesh and they will always haunt you sort of…
>
> B: Then forgetting isn't it, you say is not applicable in the healing process. So then where is the element of trust? Because if you cannot forget what this guy has done to me, I will not trust him in the next assignment… We will always be divided. I will not forget what he did. Next time when he comes so that we unite, I won't trust this guy.
>
> V: I don't think it's necessary for you to forget what he did (inaudible).
>
> B: Yes, I understand. I am just posing a question. That in the way forward of this country, with this thing, your trust will never be there.
>
> V: Trust, trust can only, ehh, exist when there is a positive reaction from the other partner isn't it? Without you having forgotten but his actions, ehh, his positive contribution towards you will create the trust, he acknowledges… from the sincerity that he expresses, you can even smell the sincerity, isn't it? You can even touch it, you can even feel the sincerity, uhh, that okay, this person is right down to earth sincere about what he is saying. And that's how trust can be built. otherwise it will be perfunctory just to say, 'I'm sorry, I'm sorry, I'm sorry,' and then you look at the outsider and say, 'I've fixed him' you know and that trust

> will never exist, even if you would have wanted to accept me, but the moment he sees me looking at the other side and laughing about what I would have just said then that trust will never stick on.
>
> N: I would like to differ a bit: I think forgiveness, yes, it's difficult to forgive but then for healing, forgetting has to be necessary because, take for instance, let's say T wronged me. Right, but then we are still together in the industry—we have to work together for the sake of the future. I have to forget about that wrong so that we can work together like willingly, because I can work with him but in the mind, say that, 'No this person did this, he might do this.'

As can be seen from the above conversation, it was difficult to find common ground on this issue. However, it seems to me that there was a general agreement about the need not to allow memory to hinder healing, and that the repair of a relationship was desirable. Forgiveness was therefore problematised in this research because no conclusive meeting of the minds on this issue was possible, and maybe not even necessary. However, perhaps Cosgrove/Konstam's (2008, p. 8) insightful comment that 'forgetting may, under some conditions, be experienced by an individual as an *active decision* about when to *remember* and when to let *memory recede* (italics added)' could be taken as an accurate conclusion of the discussion.

This discussion raised the issue of trust, which is vital in the restoration of relationships after a conflict. Some participants felt that forgetting aided in the building of trust, as N said:

> I think there comes back the element of trust. When you have forgiven someone and you have forgone that process you need to be able to trust them that they will not repeat that mistake but then, if they had not asked for forgiveness and (they) just forgave them, you know it's difficult—they have to work with them.

B earlier on had also raised this issue of trust. V pointed out that trust did not depend on forgetting but on the perpetrator's response and their sincerity. He spoke about 'smelling', 'touching', and 'feeling' the sincerity as it were. In other words, while forgiveness was undeserved, trust had to be earned and this was done by how the individuals conducted themselves after repenting of the transgression committed. Trust building might be a long process that depends on the perpetrator exhibiting signs that they are remorseful and are taking steps to avoid causing deliberate harm to the victim. Perhaps one might say that trust building is necessary if the continuation of the relationship is both desirable and inevitable, but might not be a big factor where the relationship is not.

## 9.3 What Heals and What Does not?

Another contentious topic that arose during the dialogues (particularly during the seventh dialogue), had to do with the issue of emotional or memory healing. While narrating his experiences of *Gukurahundi,* F spoke about how he sometimes would have nightmares related to his experiences:

> Most people of my age and older later died as a result of having been beaten. That creation *will haunt us because it haunted some of us physically, it will haunt us.* Like me, I used to say I fought for this country, now I am being hunted again. One of these things happened in front of my sister… A young man came… He cocked his gun. You know when someone does that, and, you know, it's very painful when someone cocks their gun for you. He said, 'Open your mouth,' and I did. He said. 'You know I can pump five bullets into your brainless head? Go and become a dissident and you will see what we will do to you. You are lucky because there is someone here with a small baby. Your brain is dead. We were going to shoot you and throw away your grey matter…' *This thing stays... you can't stop dreaming about it. I would dream about it some days, only to wake up to find that you are in your house and my mother would ask, 'What were you doing?' I would just say, 'I was just dreaming about something.' This thing will not come out of the mind; this hallucination about Gukurahundi will never go away* (italics added).

Participants agreed that it was difficult for them to talk about complete healing because they felt that there were too many reminders of the past for them to experience the kind of healing they expected (see Sect. 7.5). They then settled on calling what they had experienced 'relief' as opposed to 'healing'. This term was attractive because, while acknowledging the difficulty in which daily life is lived, it also recognised that something had shifted within the participants. L commented:

> You know, these emotions, ehh, life will continue but, there are moments when that person (deceased) will come back, and you might say, 'Hey, if only my father was alive,' you see. Sometimes, someone, while alone in the bedroom, you just see tears dropping. So I think in a way, he [B] got relief when actually this process was going on at Tree of Life, but as soon as he got out of that, what do you call that? By the time he got home, it was all over again. Just like what I was saying that people can console you, that you lost someone. Now there is the body viewing, it all starts again (laughter) you see. It's very… emotions, emotions, they are difficult to heal. I don't know how to put it; if we are really talking about healing, its, how do we heal an emotion? It's very difficult. Which part of the emotions can get healed? *We learn to live with what hurt us. We get used to it* and stay with our enemies as our neighbours. We live with them and give a dog smile. (Italics added)

Another one added:

> Another thing, L has touched on it, that you notice in life. Let me say that you have a wound, ah, even a big scar. Let me take L's wound here. This wound healed a long time ago, isn't it, but the scar is still there, he lives with it. So what I am trying to express here is that healing is a process; it is not a thing that can happen overnight. Looking at the workshop that we had, it was trying to equip us so we can go through, because if you get relieved now and again tomorrow, the pain will be lessening, but that thing is still there.

Kaminer (2006) calls this process 'habituation', where one is exposed to the feared stimulus (the trauma memory in our case) repeatedly until the physiological anxiety associated with the stimulus is reduced. L's last statement is very deep and insightful and resonates with Seligman (2007) who has suggested that there are certain conditions that will never be totally cured and that people must be taught how best to live with those conditions. He mentions PTSD and depression among those conditions that cannot be totally cured. While I do not necessarily agree with all his conclusions, there is nevertheless wisdom in his overall assertion. It was during these discussions that participants coined the word 'relief' to refer to the kind of healing possible under such conditions.

I think what participants were acknowledging and advocating for was a 'good enough' healing; one that was best and possible under the prevailing political dispensation in Zimbabwe.

## 9.4 The Dilemma of Reparations

The issue of compensation is another one that participants grappled with, but also did not entirely resolve. Some participants felt that restitution needed to be considered as one of the things that would aid the healing process for the victims and survivors of *Gukurahundi*. The feeling was that because of *Gukurahundi*, Matabeleland lagged behind in development (see also Sect. 2.3.1). The real debate was about the appropriateness and the kind of compensation to be given, and who was to be compensated. This debate is like what scholars such as Meyer (2006), Perez (2011), Boxhill (2003) and Sher (2005), among others, have been having over the past decade, with little agreement on the issue. Unlike these scholars' debate, which discusses transgenerational compensation, in the case of *Gukurahundi*, there are still a fair number of both the primary offenders and the victims alive; so, the premise of our discussion was slightly different from theirs. Participants talked about community compensation, whereby the government would improve the wellbeing of the communities in Matabeleland through infrastructural and economic development of the region; what Spinner-Halev (2007) calls 'collective compensation'. Participants also agreed that the compensation of individuals was a difficult proposition. Nevertheless, some felt that, where there was evidence that people had lost property, then individual compensation was necessary. Some participants strongly objected to the paying of compensation for the dead. The strongest objection came from J who said:

> …if they took your goats or whatever, then there is a possibility that they can compensate your 10 goats. What if they killed your loved ones? Even if they pay you, will they resurrect those people? Even if they pay me, but the pain, aah, it will still be there. Even when I use their money, really, aah, what will I be saying the money is for? It is paying for my brother's death, and paying that my mother was murdered, aah! I would, instead, I would be adding pain because that person would then boast, saying. 'There is nothing you can do to me, because I killed whoever, then I paid you, and they used that money.'

V added: 'For restitution purposes, or for compensation purposes, that we are talking about, the people that were killed will never be replaced, even if he pays a billion dollars…those lives will never come back.' L, while agreeing that compensating the dead was impossible, argued thus:

> I would love a scenario where…all the places that were affected by *Gukurahundi,* be given a development plan, roll out a development plan to cushion the people from poverty, because this caused poverty after building homes. Our home was built in 1903. My father's elder brother was born in 1903. Our home was built in 1903 and was burnt in 1983 you see. A home is a lifetime move in the rural areas and now they have started to build other homes and these people are old and do not have strength. *Now we would like to roll out a development plan. They should build us schools, roads, dams, as compensation because you can't compensate the dead, but if they can compensate in a development plan that will compensate in the building of roads, dams, so people can live* (italics added).

Boxhill (2003) says the family of the murdered person can receive reparation for the loss suffered because of the person's death, but they cannot receive compensation for his death. He agrees that no reparation can compensate for murder. The participants, on the other hand found the idea of receiving 'death' money, for whatever reason, reprehensible, and therefore would probably not agree with Boxhill on this one. As V concluded: 'Those people who will enjoy that money, like J has said, would obviously have, every time they use that money, they will have a sub-conscience that says, "I am eating from the dead because of *Gukurahundi.*" I should say that this debate reflected debates that are ongoing wherever and whenever the issue of *Gukurahundi* is brought up and it has been difficult for people to reach consensus on the reparations issue. Part of the argument (of scholars and participants) against individual reparations is around what is to be done for those who lost limbs. If property can be compensated, surely, they too should be. But how does one quantify loss of limbs in monetary terms?

## 9.5 Correcting the Past

The final issue of contention that the group wrestled with was whether it was possible to correct the past. Although this discussion was very brief, I think the issue it raised was pertinent enough to be included here and I also see a connection with the above discussion. This conversation took place within the context of evaluating the TOL workshop and specifically while discussing lessons from the tree. It started with T's statement that history determines the present and the future, which, Bevernage (2008) appears to agree with by saying that 'the past is not merely the precondition of the present but a condition of it'. T went on to argue:

> So, if we look at that thing that we need to try to empower others and heal others without the official apology. The thing that we need to notice first is that we need to know our history well. If we know it very well, we will know where we are coming from and where we are going. The current situation that we now have is because of the past, so what we need to do is to correct the past by making sure that all those things that happened in the past should not happen again and then our future will be brighter. If we just look at this history and say, 'Well all these things happened to us,' and then what? But what we need to realise is that from that history we should learn something. From that tree, you learn

something. The tree had all these challenges but it managed to grow. With us, fine, our history had ABCD but what did we do about it?

At this point V interjected and wanted to know if the past could be corrected or what was needed was to acknowledge it. His argument was that we could not really go back into the past to correct it, but we could certainly reflect on the past, acknowledge it and realise our mistakes. He said:

Can we really correct the past or we need to learn from the past (pause)? *Can we really correct the past or we need to acknowledge what happened in the past so that at least*? It is of necessity, correctly so, rightly so, what you said, it is of necessity because for one to understand where he stands now, he must reflect to the past and be able to focus forward. It is of necessity, *but I doubt very much if we can really go back and correct the past but if we can acknowledge what happened in the past and realise the mistakes*, who the perpetrator was, what motivated him, what were his strengths and weaknesses, and what opportunities may arise, may arise now, in the future for us to be able to, with the focus in the front, be able to review what happened in the past, and say, this is what happened and therefore what we need to look at and guard against is this. In the same vein, it empowers us in, in, I very much appreciate the way you have put it because you want that thing to be corrected, but who will bear the axe? (Speaks in ChiShona) *Ndiyani achasungirira kati beru?* [Who will tie the bell to the cat?] (Speaks in SiNdebele) *Ngubani ozabophela umakiti iklogwe?* [same English translation]). In this case, it is our group here. We are the vehicle that should bring in the victim and the perpetrator in this place and then suggest that…, the past the present, and future are aligned, are synchronised as it were, as we go. And I think your proposition is correct. However, I have this point to say—*we might not be able to correct the past but we may need to acknowledge the issues of the past with a view of correcting the future.* (Italics added)

At the time, my understanding of what T was saying, which I shared with the group, was that he was talking about correcting the distorted facts of our history, but looking at that conversation now, he seems to have been talking at a deeper level than that. L, who seemed to have better understood what T meant, joined the conversation at this point and there was a short interchange between him and V:

L: I think yes, we can correct the past for a better future. If you look at quite a lot of wrongs that happened or that have happened before, what this young man has just said that, he who speaks of the past has the future in mind. And he who speaks of the future has no right to forget the past. They are interlocked; the mistakes that you did yesterday you correct it tomorrow; you correct those mistakes of yesterday, tomorrow. You will not do the same mistakes. So yes, you can correct the past…

V: Or (inaudible) or history, I think it's not clearer there.

L: The past is all the archives of everything! (laughs). Now you can pluck out one by one whatever you want to correct. If there was ethnism(sic) you correct that and say, 'No! No! Let's live together.' If there was marginalisation, you correct, well if you killed people, you stop killing the people … (laughs)

V: But you can't resurrect them… (laughs)

L: Well that goes to justice (laughter) because the past is filled up with a lot of crimes, and with a lot of anomalies which may not be crimes, to an individual, because let's say marginalisation, you can't attribute that to an individual. It was the system but you correct the system and you correct those actions that were done by stopping them …

At the time, this discussion sounded trivial and superficial, but having reviewed some literature on the topic, I find that this was indeed a profound and philosophical discussion, which, perhaps, should have been afforded more time. Bevernage's (2008) article, *Time, Presence and Historical Injustices*, offers an in-depth and complex discussion on the 'presence' of the past in the present and how to address it. Michael Ignatieff argues for the importance of attending to the past, in post conflict countries because,

> ...what seems to be apparent, in the former Yugoslavia, in Rwanda and in South Africa is that the past continues to torment because it is not past. These places are not living in a serial order of time, but in a simultaneous one, in which the past and the present are a continuous, agglutinated mass of fantasies, distortion, myths and lies... Crimes can never be safely fixed in the historical past; they remain locked in the eternal present, crying out for vengeance (in Bevernage 2008, p. 149, see also Sect. 7.6).

Furthermore, Spinner-Halev (2007), talks about 'enduring injustices' which he says have their roots in the past but continue to the present day. They are more than historical, because those injustices are still being perpetuated in the present. Therefore, I think the bottom line of this discussion was that the injustices of the past need to be addressed because they continue to influence the present negatively, and that the continuation of the enduring injustices needs to be halted.

## 9.6 Structural Violence

I include this issue here, which served to create a backdrop to the environment in which participants live. During the dialogue sessions, participants could identify the nuanced and subtle forms of structural violence which they felt were being perpetuated by the state and were linked to the overall objectives of 'The Grand Plan' (see Appendix A). They identified the subtle intimidatory tactics and the systemic marginalisation practised by the state. Apart from repressive laws and the utterances by ZANU PF regarding the undesirability of openly discussing *Gukurahundi*, the role played by the state security agents in intimidation was discussed. For instance, during one of our dialogue sections, V received a phone call from a person who claimed he worked in the president's office (that is how the members of the Central Intelligence Organisation [CIO] choose to identify themselves to people). Coincidentally, we were in the middle of discussing the issue of forgiveness and forgetting (see Sect. 9.1) when the call came through and when he came back he was arguing about the impossibility of forgetting when there were so many reminders around. He said:

> As it is, you see, right now the phone that I'm getting outside there, somebody is reminding me saying, 'Is that V?' I say, 'Yes.' He says, 'We once met at the Baptist Church and talked about *Gukurahundi* issues.' Coincidentally I get this, you see and I ask him, 'Where are you?' He says, 'I am in the president's office.' You know what that does to me to my

> kidneys? It sends adrenaline straight into my ears and I hear them, hiii… I can't forget that because I said something here, isn't it? And this person could be tying me to that statement that I said…

This person did not need to say much more. The mere fact that he had identified himself as a member of the CIO who was there when V participated in a *Gukurahundi* event and had spoken there was enough to cause anxiety. This was a subtle kind of intimidation because they were probably letting him know that they knew things about him. By such tactics, they have managed to project an image of having 'eyes and ears' everywhere, which in turn has created this fear of the unknown which hangs invisibly in people's subconscious.

Participants also identified incidences of systemic marginalisation, which they felt justified the existence of 'The Grand Plan'. F narrated his observation of how this 'policy' manifested itself within the banking system:

> I agree with you, young man because I always (inaudible) in the banks, you will find that once the lady [bank employee] tries to help you, maybe you might have met in church and she tells people to come and she would help them access loans. If she is unlucky and may be gives 30 people from this region projects or loans, next time you visit the bank, that lady is no longer there. I have witnessed this with two different banks. The person might have been fired, when you ask her she will say, 'I was fired because there was this programme and I gave people from this side,' even though there was nothing wrong she did. This instils fear. She was genuinely trying to help people but now she is fired or transferred back to Harare. Maybe the person was the regional manager; they make her a bank teller. This is the reality.

V, who happens to be Shona, corroborated F's assertion by narrating a conversation he had once had with a Shona lady who was the regional manager of some firm in Bulawayo. His whole speech here demonstrates the level of critical understanding on his part and offers a tangible example of how systemic the structural violence is. I think that quoting only a segment of this statement would rob it of its poignancy and clarity.

> I can confirm on that, the reality and the potential aspect (inaudible). There is a regional manager of an influential institution. She confessed she is Shona and she is from just below Nyanga, Mutasa area, from Bonda mission. She said, 'You people seem not to realise, why don't you carry out a survey and check, how many regional managers are there in Matabeleland who are MaNdebele. You can't be in regional management of an institution of any sort. If you carry out that survey you will discover that there are nil. The best you can find is maybe a supervisor. If you find that Ndebele being a regional manager of a system, he has got an *accommodation with ZANU*, not anybody else, otherwise there is no Ndebele who will be a regional manager forever, in this region.' I said, 'But why?' She said, 'But you forget the purpose of *Gukurahundi*. The purpose of *Gukurahundi* was here so that they level these places and grow the MaShona culture. That is why you find a lot of us are deployed from there to *come here and dominate over them.*' I said, 'But that's tribalising (sic) the country.' She said, 'But it's a weapon that is being used,' and sure, it's a weapon that galvanises power and the power of these people who are ruling us. They want to be so

> dominant and sit over us until each one of us agrees to be ZANU or agrees to be Shona or agrees to be whatever, but me I am of the Shona stock. I am saying this with a feeling of nostalgia but I am of the Shona stock. It's not really the Shona who are hitting the MaNdebele. It is somebody, one person with a shrewd mind a philosophy that he is applying and twisting things around hitting people's emotions from the backside, so that they make a lot of noise and cause them to sit on the line, because if you go back into our organisation *ZIPRA, you will find there is no difference between Ndebele and Shona, but we are one and we are sharing one and the same thing.* What is bad are the ills, the ills that were caused by *Gukurahundi.* It is because they wanted to sustain themselves in positions of power that they thought about all these divisive [things] that they could apply, and they had to twist around the mentalities, and twist around the feeling of the people and subjugate them…, but then we need to find a formula of pacifying that and that *formula has got to do with power. In my view, it has to do with powe*r until such day when the current rulers' power dissipates or is reduced and there is an equation that could balance that will match them, I think then we will begin to feel good, at least there will be a feel good situation of some sort… (italics added).

The above statements are but a few that show how well participants understood, and were conscious of, their environment. Participants developed a social analysis that knitted together stories of pain, marginalisation, of Shona elite privileges and suppression. In the process, they not only defined the problem but also developed a better understanding of who they were. These moments of reflection allowed them to redevelop a sense of pride in their identity. Cahill (2007, p. 283) says, 'If to tell one's story is to know one's story, it is also to take control over one's representation.'

The existence of structural violence contributed to the difficulty of attaining a sustainable result from the healing process. In Sect. 7.5 we discussed some of the daily realities that participants struggled with on their journey towards healing, and this structural violence underpins those negative realities.

## 9.7 Conclusion

This brief chapter has examined issues of tension which were raised by this research: whether forgetting is necessary in forgiveness; the dilemma of reparations; what heals and what doesn't; and whether the past can be corrected. It also gives an example of how, through critical analysis, participants could see their context for what it really was. As noted in the discussion, participants wrestled to find answers to these questions. We also noted that, although some discussion had initially appeared trivial, they were nevertheless important themes which have raised a lot of debate among scholars.

Chapter 10 offers a summary, conclusions and final reflections of this research project.

## References

Bevernage, B. 2008. Time, presence, and historical injustice. *History and Theory*, 47(2): 149–167. At: http://www.jstor.org/stable/i25478740 (11 June 2014).
Biggar, N. (ed.). 2003. *Burying the past: making peace doing justice after civil conflict*. Georgetown: Georgetown University Press.
Boxhill, B. R. 2003. A Lockean argument for Bleck reparations. *The Journal of Ethics*, 7(1): 63–91. At: http://www.jstor.org/stable/25115749 (10 June 2014).
Cahill, C. 2007. The personal is political: developing new subjectivities through participatory action research. *Gender, Place and Culture*, 14(3) June: 267–292.
Cosgrove, L. and Konstam, V. 2008. Forgiveness and forgetting: clinical implication for mental health counsellors. *Journal of Mental Health Counselling,* 30(1): 1–13.
Elden, M. and Levin, M. 1991. Cogenerative learning: bringing participation into action research. In W. Foote Whyte (ed.), *Participatory action research.* California: Sage.
Enright, R. D., Freedman, S. and Rique, J. 1998. The psychology of interpersonal forgiveness. In R. D. Enright and J. North (eds.), *Exploring forgiveness.* Madison: University of Wisconsin Press.
Kaminer, D. 2006. Healing process in trauma narratives: a review. *South African Journal of Psychology*, 36(3): 481–499.
Krondorfer, B. 2008. Is forgetting reprehensible? Holocaust remembrance and the task of oblivion. *The Journal of Religious Ethics*, 36(2): 232–267. At: http://www.jstor.org/stable/40014887 (6 June 2014).
Meyer, L. H. 2006. Reparations and symbolic restitution. *Journal of Social Philosophy*, 37(3): 406–422.
Perez, N. 2011. On compensation and return: can the 'continuing justice argument' for compensating for historical injustices justify compensation for such injustices or the return of property? *Journal of Applied Philosophy*, 28(2): 151–167.
Seligman, M. E. P. 2007. *What you can change...and what you can't: the complete guide to successful self-improvement.* New York: Vintage Books.
Sher, G. 2005. Transgenerational compensation. *Philosophy and Public Affairs*, 33(2): 181–200.
Smedes, L. B. 1996. *Forgive and forget: healing the hurts we don't deserve.* San Francisco: Harper.
Spinner-Halev, J. 2007. From historical to enduring injustice. *Political Theory,* 35(5): 574–597.
Worthington, E. L. 2001. Unforgiveness, forgiveness, and reconciliation and their implications for societal interventions. In R. Helmick and R. Peterson (eds.), *Forgiveness and reconciliation: religion, public policy and conflict transformation.* Radnor, Philadelphia: R Templeton.

# Chapter 10
# Summary, Conclusions and Reflections

*Liberation is a praxis: the action and reflection of men and women upon their world in order to transform it.*
Freire (1970, 1996. p. 60).

## 10.1 Introduction

Chapter 7 assessed the research process and whether it adhered to the general principles of PAR, as well as reviewing the TOL workshop, while Chap. 8 discussed the results of the findings of the analysed dialogue sessions data. Chapter 9 explored some of the issues that were problematised by the research. This chapter concludes the discussion by reflecting on the whole research process and its outcomes, highlighting some insights and learning derived from it. The research process consisted of the dialogue sessions and actions in the form of the healing workshop and critical recovery of history, which in our case involved participants writing their life stories.

## 10.2 Summary of Findings

The aim of this research was to engage in an action research project with victims of *Gukurahundi* aimed at the healing of memories.

The research objectives were:

(i) To review the recent literature on
   (a) the nature, extent and consequences of trauma following community violence.
   (b) healing processes; with particular reference to healing groups of victims in the absence of an official apology or reconciliation programme.



D. Ngwenya, *Healing the Wounds of Gukurahundi in Zimbabwe*,
The Anthropocene: Politik—Economics—Society—Science 19,
https://doi.org/10.1007/978-3-319-66818-5_10

(ii) Together with a group of victims of *Gukurahundi,* to identify contexts, barriers and issues that may be significant in the healing process for people traumatised by political violence, with specific reference to the *Gukurahundi* violence.
(iii) To develop a sustainable and replicable model that can facilitate self-healing for victims of *Gukurahundi.*
(iv) Together with these victims, to assess the potential of such and the possibility of its widespread usage.

Although not intended, the bringing together of the ZVT members and their three student interns provided me with an opportunity to study the research topic holistically, as I could observe two generations in a single study. This helped to bring certain issues alive and offered me ethnographic insights into the intergenerational effects of trauma.

Chapters 3 and 4 fulfilled the two aspects set out in objective number one. Literature points to the fact that identity-based organised violence, be it political, ethnic or religious, tends to affect not just individuals but also their communities. In fact, the violence is calculated at achieving just that (see Sect. 3.1), and is designed at disrupting the everyday functions of the individual's community, thus robbing individuals of their support systems which are necessary for healing. These chapters described the effects of trauma resulting from such violence and the need to bring healing to the communities and individuals affected. They also discussed the conditions that have been identified as being necessary for this healing to occur. Four case studies of community-based healing programmes, which were not part of official government initiatives, were reviewed (Sect. 4.6) and it was observed that, although most of the contexts in which they were carried out differed from the Matabeleland situation (the Chilean situation was quite similar), they nevertheless offered lessons for our situation. Because I was using a research design that was unfamiliar to me and which is still to gain wider recognition within the academic world, I dedicated a whole chapter to reviewing some of the PAR literature currently available (see Chap. 5). I discovered that the democratic nature of PAR and its principles were not only appealing to me because of its ability to address learning and action simultaneously (what Babbie/Mouton [2001: 320] term 'knowledge for action'), but also that PAR and peacebuilding principles are compatible, both having the teleological goal of social transformation and equitable resolution of power inequalities.

Participants had a comprehensive appreciation of their context and were able to articulate the issues they viewed as barriers and stumbling blocks to their healing. Structural violence, in the form of marginalisation and intimidation, impunity, lack of an apology, feelings of insecurity and the repression of truth, were identified by the participants as being significant issues in their situation. This fulfilled the second objective which was to identify the contexts, barriers and issues which participants saw as important to victims of traumatic political violence (see Sect. 8.2). Participants also identified a desire for vengeance, recognising the transgenerational transmission of trauma and dysfunctional relationships (see Sect. 8.3) as stemming from a lack of healing. Furthermore, they could make a connection between the structural violence that underpinned the various other forms of violence they were experiencing as individuals and as a group (see Sect. 9.5).

The third objective of the research was to create a healing process that could be offered to other victims and communities affected by *Gukurahundi*. Three aspects were found to be useful by the participants. Firstly, the dialogue sessions themselves offered participants an opportunity to share their stories in an environment that was both safe and affirming (see Sect. 8.5). There were seven sessions altogether, which included a review of the TOL workshop. Secondly, most of the participants found the TOL workshop healing as they experienced some relief from their painful memories (see Sects. 7.4, 7.5 and 7.6). Lastly, the writing workshop itself and the actual writing of their life stories also provided a useful avenue for the participants to preserve their history and to counter some of the historical facts that have been deliberately distorted by the state. Those that had completed their stories by the end of the research process found that the exercise had therapeutic effects in their lives as well (see Sects. 8.2.2 and 8.4.1).

Participants evaluated the effectiveness of this approach to healing and its potential for use with other communities affected by *Gukurahundi* (objective iv). The TOL workshop was evaluated a few weeks after it took place and participants indicated that it had given them a new perspective on life and their struggles with the hurts of the past. Some 18 months later, three of the participants were interviewed to determine the long-term effectiveness of the workshop and these three indicated that, although they still faced the same situation, yet they were able to exercise agency and resilience (see Sects. 7.5, 7.6, and 8.4.1). The entire process was evaluated by the participants at the end of the research project and again, participants expressed positive sentiments about its efficacy and how they had benefitted from taking part in the research (see Sect. 8.4). Generally, participants indicated that the process was useful and could benefit other groups too. However, we did not go to the next stage of co-creating and fine-tuning a model from this process that could be used with the broader community. What this process did was to provide definite building blocks that could form the basis of a healing programme which could be adapted to the various contexts that prevail in Matabeleland, approaches that would differ in urban and rural areas and from district to district.

Overall, the research found that, through a broadly-based array of actions, it is possible for traumatised communities to attain a measure of relief from their emotional and psychological wounds. These were actions such as creating safe and empathetic spaces for storytelling, both verbal and written, group-based healing workshops, and a critical analysis of participants' contexts to understand what needs transformation. It was also found that relief could be more sustainable if certain conditions were eliminated.

## 10.3 Validity, Reliability and Limitations

PAR is sensitive to the need of involving participants in research, not as objects but as active co-researchers, with a more-or-less equal say in the formulation of the research problem and the research process. As indicated, it was not possible for this research to adhere to all these principles because of university requirements (see Sects. 5.2, 6.2, and 6.7). It was therefore important to assess how well participants identified with the topic and the extent to which they saw it as relevant to their own lives and situations. I was fortunate in the sense that, although I came to the group with the research problem and question already settled, the issue of *Gukurahundi* and healing resonated well with the participants. The fact that there was a ready acceptance of the research topic indicates just how pertinent and relevant this issue still is, despite the government's efforts to suppress it. I also discovered that this was still an emotive subject, even for people involved in peacebuilding.

McTaggart (1998) sees validation as a process of explicit dialogue, which can only be achieved if appropriate means of communication are present throughout the research and includes actions which allow participants to continually associate and identify with the work of collective project change. I tried to follow this advice and created opportunities for participants to feed back their views about the research process. I think they were frank enough and refused to allow me to take them for granted in the sharing of the findings. This process of inter-subjectivity—the process of the participants challenging, questioning and bringing their reflections to bear on my own observations and experiences—formed an integral part of the validation process for the research project. Participants took this role seriously and wanted to have their opinions heard. This ability in PAR, for participants and researcher to interact constantly, provides a useful 'built in' process that ensures that the research's validity is checked throughout the life of the project. In addition, the summary of my findings was shared with the participants, who validated them and added some aspects they felt had been overlooked. The social actions the group carried out also demonstrated the ability of PAR projects to bring about change in people's situations (see Sects. 7.6 and 8.4.1).

Ultimately, the success of a PAR project does not rely on how one closely follows the methodology, important as that may be. The criterion of the success of the research 'is not whether participants have followed the steps faithfully but rather whether they have a strong and authentic sense of development and evolution in their practices, their understandings of their practices, and the situations in which they practice' (Kemmis/McTaggart 1991, p. 277). In that regard, I think this research fulfilled the criterion satisfactorily. According to Greenwood/Levin (1998), whatever problem participants seek to address, be it social, organisational or material, the results of the research need to be tangible, in that participants should be able to figure out if the solutions they have developed actually resolve the problem they have set themselves. They suggest that workability (whether or not a solution resolves the initial problem) should be the standard by which the solutions arrived at are judged. This evaluation process 'is a matter of collective social judgement about a collective social action and that social judgement is itself the result of a kind of democratic conversation in which the professional researcher in only one voice' (Greenwood/Levin 1998, p. 252). If we use this as the measure of our judgement of the research, then, based on the participants' own conclusions, the research outcome can be regarded as valid in terms of meeting their need for healing.

I think the biggest limitation that this process had in terms of its efficacy to heal the emotional wounds of *Gukurahundi*, was what the participants came to refer to as the measure of 'relief' which it provided. As indicated in Sect 9.2, this did not bring a cure or complete healing, but provided some respite from emotional wounds. There was no doubt that this approach did empower most of the participants with better abilities to function within the abnormal context in which they currently live; but sustainable peace demands that the issues of relationships and the structural/systemic issues which resulted in *Gukurahundi* be addressed.

To enhance validity, PAR scholars encourage the use of a critical reference group as a triangulation technique to assist in maintaining the integrity of the research process. While I had every intention to observe this norm, it was difficult to implement as I could not find people who had knowledge of the research design used. To compensate for that, I consulted colleagues, all of whom are based outside Zimbabwe, via email and when they made the occasional trip to Zimbabwe. Although their input was very useful, they did not have time to go through vast amounts of information. In this regard, I think the research missed out on an important process that could have enhanced its conduct and the collection of the data (see also Sect 6.9).

The issue of time was another limiting factor. As pointed out in Sect. 10.4, a few more cycles could have enhanced the effectiveness of the research project. However, due to the non-availability of most participants and the length of time it took them to write their life stories, it became impractical to continue with the research, thus short-circuiting the lifespan of the project. This in a way also affected the full treatment of objective number iii: to develop a model that would facilitate the self-healing of communities affected by Gukurahundi. However, it is still possible to craft a viable model based on the outcomes of this research. A major difference would be the process of gathering the life stories using alternative methods such as recordings, interviews or photo-text (see Table 5.3). Time also meant that the long-term monitoring and evaluation of the impact of the research could not be fully assessed (Koch/Kralik 2006). While I received feedback after the research, finding out how participants are coping three or five years after the research would be a better indicator of the long-term effectiveness of the process, and would strengthen the validity and credibility of the research.

## 10.4 Summing up—Personal Assessment

At the proposal stage of this research, I had anticipated that during the research the issues of reconciliation and forgiveness would take centre stage in the process. This assumption was based on my personal beliefs and faith, that view reconciliation and forgiveness as central tenets in the healing process and restoration of broken relationships. My views were also greatly influenced by the school of thought in conflict transformation that views these two aspects as being very important for building peace in communities affected by political violence. It was therefore a surprise when these did not feature prominently in the research. Although we discussed forgiveness to an extent, it was never as a requirement for participants to heal within the context of the research, and reconciliation was only mentioned in passing (no more than twice). On reflection, perhaps one need not be surprised, given the purpose of the research, which was to explore if it was possible for victims of *Gukurahundi* to heal in the absence of an official apology or healing process. While it is quite clear that total healing cannot be achieved without addressing other pertinent issues (see Sects. 4.4 and 8.2), what this study has shown is that it is possible for people to be helped to move on, away from what Father Lapsley calls being 'caught in a moment in time', to a situation where people can begin to live again and have hopes and dreams, as it was before their traumatic experiences. This possibility is aptly exemplified by the student interns who found a way of living as survivors and not victims, and especially by J who received a tremendous amount of relief from a debilitating past fraught with guilt, shame and hurt.

PAR is a cyclical process of reflection and action over time (Walker 1998; Gaventa/Cornwall 2006; Sect. 5.4). Although the research project ended in May 2014, ZVT decided that they would continue to offer the TOL workshops to as many members of their organisation as was possible, and by July 2014 five or six workshops had been carried out. TOL has used these workshops as an entry point with the intention of expanding their work into the rest of Matabeleland. The writing project continues beyond the life of this research project. I undertook to assist participants with the typing and editing of their stories as well as finding a publisher for them, as they indicated that they wanted their stories to be published in a book of short stories. When participants indicated that some of their colleagues might be motivated to write their stories too, once they saw the participants' stories in print, I offered to assist by availing them of the template suggested to the group by Mr Nyathi, the author/historian who facilitated the writing workshop.

Several cycles of new actions could have been carried out to make a better and fuller assessment of this project. For instance, it would have been informative to observe what sort of affect the publishing and launch of the participants' book project would have had on them. Cahill's (2007) and McIntyre's (2008) work seem to suggest that such activities can have a profound effect, not only on the participants but on their community as well. Be that as it may, this research proved to me the efficacy and potential that PAR holds as a research process that is best suited to practitioners concerned with social transformation, such as myself. For the participants, themselves, in addition gaining from the actions carried out, the research offered them an opportunity to carry out an academic inquiry into their problems by engaging in informative, reflective and critical dialogue concerning their experiences (McIntyre 2008). Their levels of critical consciousness were raised as they cultivated their abilities to both perceive and deconstruct the dominant ideologies and practices that legitimise inequalities and tried to change the conditions of their lives by reconstructing the skewed power relations (Guishard 2009). As Martin-Baro has said, 'practical knowledge acquired through participatory research should lead toward the people gaining power, a power that allows them to become the protagonists of their own history and to effect change' (in Guishard 2009, p. 91).

## 10.5 Implications

This research confirmed that the wounds of *Gukurahundi* are still very fresh in people's minds. Even though the sample used can never be representative of the communities in Matabeleland, the research indicates that, for most people, time does not heal and, unless healing processes are established, the pains and hurts are likely to continue unhealed. While the transmission of transgenerational trauma might not be universal, enough of it has been passed on to make this issue a problem for the coming generations. This is especially so for those who come from families with members who were direct victims of *Gukurahundi*. While it might be too late to reach the entire older generation, it might be prudent for NGOs to address the issue of the healing of memories for the younger generation. While the current GTH programme, which addresses the issue of mass shallow graves, does address issues of healing for families of those killed during *Gukurahundi*, the experience of my research may offer a prototype programme that could meet this specific need for healing, not only for *Gukurahundi* survivors but survivors of political violence in general.

## 10.6 Conclusion

Overall, it seems the research contributed to participants' knowledge and a betterment of their situations. As a researcher, my understanding of the research question increased, but, apart from the knowledge of the subject matter, I also acquired new research skills and gained a better understanding of PAR. While it is true that, with hindsight, there are aspects of the research I could have done differently, I do not think that the integrity of the research process and data collection was adversely compromised in anyway. I am confident that, by and large, the findings would remain largely unchanged, despite any improvements in the execution of the research process.

## References

Babbie, E. and Mouton, J. 2001. *The practice of social research.* Cape Town: Oxford Press.

Cahill, C. 2007. The personal is political: developing new subjectivities through participatory action research. *Gender, Place and Culture*, 14(3) June: 267–292.

Freire, P. (1970) 1993. *Pedagogy of the oppressed.* New York: Continuum.

Gaventa, J. and Cornwall, A. 2006. Power and knowledge. In P. Reason and H. Bradbury (eds.), *Handbook of action research.* London: Sage.

Greenwood, D. J. and Levin, M. 1998. Action research, science and the co-optation of social research. *Studies in Cultures, Organization, and Societies*, 4: 237–261.

Guishard, M. 2009. The false paths, the endless labors, the turns now this way and now that: participatory action research, mutual vulnerability, and the politics of inquiry. *Urban Review,* 41: 85–105.

Koch, T. and Kralik, D. 2006. *Participatory action research in Healthcare.* Oxford, UK: Blackwell Publishing.

McTaggart, R. 1998. Is validity really an issue for Participatory action research? *Studies in Culture, Organisations and Societies*, 4: 211–236.

McTaggart, R. 1991. Principles for Participatory action research. *Adult Education Quarterly,* 41 (3): 168–187.

Walker, M. 1998. Action research and participatory research in South Africa. In J. Muller, J. Mouton, T. Sono and P. Frank (eds.), *Theory and method in South African human sciences research: advances and Innovations*. South Africa: HSRC Press.

# Appendix A

For Restricted Circulation For The Eyes of the Shona Elite Only, Please Pass To Most Trusted Person!

## Progress Review on the 1979 Grand Plan (Unedited)

### *Gift*

Never before has history given us the majority Shona people, such a precious present than it has done with Robert Gabriel Mugabe. R.G. is simply a perfect embodiment of all our cultural norms and values, our aspirations and expectations, our wants, desires and interests. In his whole life R G has not failed to demonstrate that incredible consciousness of who we are as people. The most vivid imagination of what an ideal Shona person should look like in appearance as well as how he should behave or present himself to the public, finds an exact match in R.G. His presence among us as a leader with and an abundant and compelling inspiration towards the establishment of Shona Nationhood deserves to be honoured and celebrated as a memorable great occasion in the life histories of all the generations of our people.

### *Acknowledgement*

We do not as a matter of obligation, fail to appreciate and acknowledge wonderful achievements, the great valour and the spirit of stubborn resistance against formidable adversaries of all those other great Shona men and women who led our people before. However, without prejudicing fair comparison, it is inarguable though that R.G. stands out distinctly as a cut above the rest among both the dead and the living Shona leaders.



D. Ngwenya, *Healing the Wounds of Gukurahundi in Zimbabwe*,
The Anthropocene: Politik—Economics—Society—Science 19,
https://doi.org/10.1007/978-3-319-66818-5

## *Consistency*

Countless incidents in R.G.'s decorated and exuberant political career testify to the conviction most of us have that the man is a visionary of rare gifts. He is an astoundingly brilliant intellectual as well as being an accomplished academic. Having distinguished himself as the most consistent revolutionary in the fight against colonialism he has gone further to achieve the emancipation of the majority Shona people and consolidated their supremacy. And signs are that he has not reached the pinnacle of his political life yet.

Few would argue that R.G. is endowed with a mesmerising eloquence in speech which together with his subtle charisma captivates and electrifies audiences whenever he stands to speak. Little wonder that he outclassed and turned his political peers into pitiable political dwarfs many of whom have fallen victim to consumptive jealous and betrayal. Several of them rubbished themselves to the political dustbin and personalities like Edgar Tekere and Edson Zvobgo are not exceptions.

## *Envy*

R.G. is an unquestionable source of envy to many, not only amongst ourselves but his foes too, who grudgingly admire him as they learn painfully to accept defeat at his hands. Tony Blair a classic case in point. Blair's clumsy arm twisting political tactics geared to tame this solid and firebrand revolutionary giant, left his finger thoroughly scalded. Mr. Blair must be ruefully licking his wounds at No. 10 Downing Street, having learnt his lesson well, that plagiarising Bush's approach to Saddam would attract serious and perilous consequences to him.

## *Imperialists*

Western leaders are so shamelessly spoilt and conceited to the extent that they throw all caution to the wind when it comes to dealing with Third World political issues. Their naivety often manifests itself whenever there is a lack of agreement on key issues especially those that adversely affect the poor nations such as the land issue in Zimbabwe. They refuse to realise that there is a new breed of leadership who will not ask how high when ordered to jump but will certainly ask WHY. African leaders in particular are regarded by the West as filthy hypocrites who are radicals by day but beggars by night, as well as lacking personal opinion and relevant political sophistication. The tendency is to destroy those who defy imperialist dictatorship. R.G. has resolutely said no to imperialism and this way he must be treated like Saddam Hussein, according to Western opinion.

## *Black Jesus*

Some people have a small problem in understanding why Mugabe is to the Shona people, what Jesus is to the Christians or what Kim il Sung and his Juche idea is to the North Koreans. This status was awarded to R.G. by his people in recognition of political astuteness acquired over many years of experience in the fight against colonialism it is an uncommon achievement to earn the love and respect of one's enemies. R.G. did just that with the descendants of Mzilikazi/Lobhengula—a people with a contemptible history of violence. This did not just happen—it took many years of careful political manoeuvring and scheming. An application of similar tactics to the descendants of Cecil John Rhodes is beginning to yield similar political dividends.

## *Illusions*

For many years both the Ndebeles and Europeans were living under a shameful illusion that the crimes of their forefathers had been forgiven and forgotten. This was not to be as R.G., the illustrious son of the Shone people ensured that the two groups pay daily for the evil deeds of their ancestors. Is it possible that such heinous crimes as those committed by these people against the Shone can just be swept under the carpet because it is political expedient to do so?

## *Legacy*

It costs a daring mind to carve a rich legacy for the good of the general public especially one that restores the dignity of the people at the same time assuring them of eternal dominance over settlers. R.G's legacy brewed in an African pot is unparalleled by any on the continent. Nelson Mandela covertly tried to outshine R.G. by elbowing him off the world political limelight. No Sooner had Mandela started this, did he realise the folly of such an attempt. It dawned on him that he was making an error and that he was too new on the regional political plane.

The twenty-seven years Mandela spent crushing stones in jail did not automatically confer upon him the sort of leadership skills acquired by R.G. in a protracted and arduous struggle for Zimbabwean independence. In fact, jail stunted the growth of Mandela's legal mind—a sad happening indeed. However, his attempt to compensate for the deprivations of that ugly experience by posturing a false image of 'towering African statesman' created by his imperialist jailers, collapsed no sooner than it had started.

## *Betrayal*

Mandela betrayed and deserted the Black majority in South Africa at the most crucial hour. Speculation is rife that he is severely petrified of whites so much that making land demands, for instance, would, in his view, muddy the waters and blemish his political career. As if his political career is more important than the black people in South Africa. At the present moment, the African continent needs genuinely high calibre leadership that is self-assertive and principled, a leadership that is selfless, a leadership that will serve the people's interest.

Mandela simply chickened out and retreated in haste unremorsefully. Praises continue to be piled on him because he did not touch the foundation of white wealth.

## *Privileges*

Future Shona generations will forever enjoy the opportunities and privileges that will at all times flow from the heroic deeds of R.G. We feel strongly encouraged to stand resolutely behind him and will not cease to see an angel where our detractors/enslavers see a devil and we will continue to see a liberator where they see a murderer.

## *Differences*

Such are our differences that must be resolved not in a superficial manner but in practical terms within such a real concrete political context as ours. The redefinition of our relationship with the settlers, black or white, is long overdue! We therefore, salute the launch of the third phase of our struggle (THIRD CHIMURENGA) and invite the reader of this article to join us in celebrating the manner in which this fight is being conducted and its guaranteed success in smashing the white economic infrastructure such as farms which facilitated the exploitation of our people.

## *Dominance*

All the struggles that took place in this country since the 1830s were about dominance. Lessons from these struggles confirm the view that a human social group is either dominant or subordinate when comes to issues of political power, especially in Africa.

## *Mzilikazi*

Mzilikazi fled from Zululand because there was no political space for him to be dominant. He therefore needed to look elsewhere for land where he could exercise power authority and dominance. But because there was no land not belonging to anyone, he targeted militarily weaker societies and found one in the Shona people whom he viciously subdued and forcibly settled in their land, imposing his authority on them.

Now comrades come to think of it—a settler is a settler—PERIOD!! What peaceful coexistence can there be to talk about between the majority indigenous Shona and the occupying force of those of Ndebele extraction? A black settler is as unwelcome as a white settler in our country.

## *Ndebele Crimes*

Mzilikazi's men, in particular under the command of his terrorist successor Lobhengula, wreaked havoc in our country. They raped and kidnapped Shona women, looted grain and stole our cattle. Anyone who disputes that this was conquest needs medical examination. For some sixty long years, the Shona people were brutalised, insulted and abused by the Ndebeles. Their wealth was ravenously plundered and economic life left to bleed to death in the most cruel manner. The Ndebele subjected the Shona people to the worst forms of barbarism and tyranny. They imported violence to Zimbabwe and it is a well-known fact that violence was a virtue in Zulu land and perhaps continues to be to this day. No one doubts the assertion that violence flows in Ndebele blood.

## Lazy

Periodic and incessant waves of cruel raids by Ndebele warriors harvested cattle, women and grain from the Shona to enrich the bogus Ndebele King. The inherently lazy and unintelligent Ndebele anarchist savages preferred to loot and plunder than to learn the skills of the more culturally advanced Shona people who excelled in building epitomised by the Great Zimbabwe as well as in crop farming and the arts such as stone carving and moira music.

## *Complexes*

Subjecting the Shona people to a reign of terror created both an inferiority and persecution complex in them. For instance, the Shona people began to shun the use of their clan names in preference for the totem system such as Dube, Sibanda, Nyoni etc. This was straight forward case of political subjugation of the Shona people.

### *White Settlers*

The carnage viciously unleashed on our people by the Ndebeles was interrupted by the coming of white settlers who were motivated by the same desire to dominate. Cecil John Rhodes men were more advanced in systems of plunder and exploitation than the Ndebeles. The whites dubbed both the Shona and the Ndebeles as African savages of the bush needing to be rescued from the darkness of ignorance.

The white settlers swiftly annexed our country as a colony of Britain. The Shona and Ndebele were, in the view of settlers, identical natives belonging to the same race, totally disregarding the oppressor/oppressed relationship between the Shona and the Ndebele that existed before colonialism. However, this did not alter or erase the crimes committed against our people before by the Ndebeles.

### *Land*

The whites too were in search of land. Back home (UK) they were little known minnows, mostly sons of serfs who were used to expand the horizons of the British Empire by carving colonies in all corners of the world.

Some of them were convicts let off on a new lease of life to prove their usefulness to the Crown. In-so-far as we are concerned the whites removed us from the clutches of Ndebele colonialism onto the rapacious claws of European imperialism a case of Jumping from the pan onto the fire.

Our gallant forefathers put up countless spirited fights against the new settlers but were subdued by the militarily superior invading barbaric force which iced its successs/conquest with the hanging of our great spirit medium. Mbuya Nehanda and others.

## Crimes of the White Man

The conquest of our people by the white men was in itself a criminal act. Having conquered our people they immediately went into an unbridled frenzy of raping Shona women producing a mixed breed that has been behaviourally as confused as the act of rape itself since that time. The breed chronically suffers from an incurable and severely traumatic identity crisis. The white invader too started to steal Shona cattle and wildlife sending trophies to the King enslaving Shona men on the stolen land (horse-pegged farms) and on mines. The savagery was soothed by a crude dosage of religious opium administered by their forerunner imperialist chief-scout, Robert Moffat—a man of the cloth.

The rest of the details of this call1age may be obtained from history texts as well as from the sad oral tales of our people.

## Freedom

An attempt to throw of the colonial yoke in the first half of the twentieth century did not succeed until the entry onto the Zimbabwean political scene in 1963 of a Shona led political party. In this year Zanu was born and excitedly welcomed by those ethnically conscious Shona people who threw their weight unreservedly behind its leadership.

This birth signified the beginning of serious business to wrestle our heritage from the white man. Zanu's moto was 'A fight for Shona Majority Rule', making an instant impact politically by going into an armed struggle a move later mimicked by the Ndebele led Zapu which comprised of mainly semiliterate hero-worshippers of Joshua Nkomo. Nkomo's lieutenants followed him blindly until he committed political suicide on December 22nd, 1987. The only few educated people in Zapu were Shonas like Ariston Chambati and Daniel Madzimbamuto whose true ethnic allegiance ceased to be questionable in 1980.

## *Partnership*

The Majority Shona people had realised that our partnership, with deposed Ndebele savages, to oust the white settler regime from dominance was an extremely complicated affair. This was particularly true in this instance because prior to the birth of Zanu the struggle had been led by Joshua Nkomo, a Ndebele assimilant of very vague, dubious and untraceable ethnic/tribal origins. Nkomo parroted a motto similar to Zanu's, that of Majority Rule but would not commit himself to "Shona Majority Rule", preferring to distort it into 'Black Majority Rule'. Such a distortion flew into the face of the real aggrieved person because Nkomo arrogantly and deliberately missed the point. Black majority could only be

Black Shona Majority Rule. Anyone who stubbornly refuted this rendered themselves an enemy of the Shona people and Nkomo became one. Nevertheless, in the interest of the struggle we in Zanu appreciated the fact that Nkomo had no option but to offer himself for use to achieve Majority Shona Rule. Hence every positive effort he made was on behalf of us the majority Shona, Now and then he needed to be whipped into line because of his conformist tendencies as in the cases of numerous agreements he struck with Ian Smith under the cover of darkness thereby putting the Liberation process in severe stress and jeopardy.

## *Objective*

Zanu sought to regain lost Shona dignity, looted cattle, stolen land and everything else I that accrued to the colonialists as a result of their thuggery by the successive Ndebele and European dominant generations. It makes economic sense to charge interest on money borrowed to someone. Therefore, the development/civilisation which the whites brag about that they brought to Zimbabwe is part of the profit which is due to us and we inherit all that violently or not, without a guilty conscience.

## *White Wealth*

The riches of the white men in Zimbabwe were and still are accumulated through monopoly, exploitation, theft, plunder, murder, rape, corruption, treachery, hypocrisy and lies. Is it possible to correct or reverse such inhuman acts without resorting to similar tactics? Truly, violence begets violence, and for every action there is a reaction.

## *Scavengers*

It is a known fact, though, that ever since its conception Zanu had a double-pronged struggle to wage, that is, on the one hand against the Ndebeles and on the other against the whites. When the Ndebeles and whites fought one another in the 1890s and then in the 1970s, they were like vultures fighting over a carcass of dead prey. One vulture cannot claim ownership of the dead animal on the grounds that it landed there first. It remains a vulture by name and scavenger by habit.

## *Sithole*

The Ndebeles had no legal claim whatsoever upon Zimbabwean sovereignty just like their earlier cousins (followers of Soshangane) later led by Ndabaningi Sithole, that hob goblin who tried to hijack the struggle. Sithole was foiled and summarily ejected from the party—an act he regretted till his grave. The simple question is why would these two black groupings fight for what did not legitimately belong to them. Participating in the struggle only meant that they were offering themselves for use by the majority Shonas.

### *Correction*

Zanu's correction of Sithole's errors left the Shangaans a thoroughly confused group despite the modification of their identity to drift closer to Shona under the guise of a language called Ndau, generally accepted among the ignorant as a dialect of Shona. The truth remains—they are foreigners, unwilling to advance our cause as they huddle around and cling childishly to the 'Ndonga'.

### *Sustenance of Illegal Regime*

For seventeen years of bitter Zanu struggle (2nd Chimurenga) to repossess lost Shona pride and stolen land the whites put up a very stiff but doomed resistance. They were aided and abetted by their British and American kith and kin who today will never forgive R.G. for taking on our behalf what belongs to us. During the struggle, Ian Smith received modern war equipment from the GS such as Gazelle helicopters, UZls, etc, but Zanu received expired medicines through the U.N. There was no doubt in our minds that the point made by such assistance to Smith in violation of UN sanctions was that blood is thicker than water.

### *Strategy*

Now in a struggle, comrades, you must have strategies and develop your own tactics suitable for the environment in which that struggle is being executed. Chairman Mao Ze Dong wrote quite extensively on strategy and tactics. The material is easily accessible to those willing to read and learn. Designing good strategies is not a simple matter—it requires acutely intelligent minds spiced with an unwavering commitment to success and was not found wanting in this regard. Men and women made of the correct political material and with characters made of sterner stuff tempered with resilience, honestly and awesomely high levels of political acumen began to distinguish themselves on the ground. We remember Chitepo and Takawira, at this level with great fondness.

## Reigns

When R.G. took over the reins of power in Zanu tremors of fears in the hearts whites were heard throughout the country. R.G. immediately proved to be good quality leadership material through the manner in which he meticulously and incisively executed the revolutionary fight for the restoration of our hallowed independence and Shona democracy. Revolution means a violent overthrow of the status quo. R.G. did precisely that. As we all know the fight is far from being over.

## *Flag Independence*

As long as the white community remained economically dominant beyond Independence Day of April 18, 1980, then the battle is certainly not over yet. Flag independence remains meaningless until the transfer of wealth into the hands of its rightful owners. No one understands this position in Zanu better than the amazingly resilient and conscientious strategist R.G.

## *Impediment*

Because of the Lancaster House Constitutional trappings, R.G. put the issue of white economic dominance in a political freezer which he safely locked with the word "Reconciliation". This earned him boundless praises such as "brilliant politician" by his former tormentors who could not believe their ears when the policy or (sic) reconciliation was announced. R.G. knew how to leave sleeping dogs to lie. He opted to decisively deal firstly with the Ndebeles once and for all.

## *Zapu and Zipra*

At independence Zapu posed the most difficult challenge to Zanu over the leadership of the country. The threat was not so much in terms of grassroots support as it was in terms of military firepower which ZAPU built over many years with Russian and Cuban support while Zanu sweated it out on the war front fighting Rhodesian forces.

Zipra was strong but inexperienced since they knew no battles of note. Nevertheless, Zipra remained an impediment in desire to conclusively deal with the issue of Ndebeles and their ugly past and the need to pacify Zapu was never greater than in 1980.

## *5th Brigade*

R.G. instantly realised that it would be futile to draw open battle-lines with "vaDumbuguru" preferring to do his homework. He brought into the country super military experts from North Korea. Within eight months, a revered, feared and uncompromising crack force, known as *Gukurahundi* had been trained. This is the

(5th Brigade) which was to strike terror in the hearts of Ndebeles. On one hand R.G. consistently dangled juicy carrot of Government of National Unity and the integration of forces into the National Army. Mugabe always knew that Nkomo was a desperate for power and so he let him have a little of it. The integration of the three armies would help to scatter Zipra far and wide.

## *Dissidents*

On the other hand, R.G. created a small rebel 'force comprising mainly of recruits from Zipra and called them dissidents who were complimented by selected highly trained Zanla forces who would direct operations. The group was put on pay role and then deployed in the Midlands and Matabeleland. Soon the self-styled dissidents were joined by other genuincly aggrieved Ziprns who could not stand the heat generated exclusively for them in the National Army. However, the army deserters and a few notorious Zipras who hated R.G. with a passion, never had a clue that the dissident element was not a Zapu initiative. While Zapu denied sponsoring dissidents, leading to a loss of faith and confidence in their leadership by Zipras, the genuine dissidents remained confused and uncoordinated finally resorting to aimless nomadic movement within the region. It is during this wondering that they got ambushed, killed and displayed at Police Camps until they began to decompose.

The Government-sponsored dissidents straight away went on an orgy of bandit activity such as destroying development project equipment, raping women, demanding food, killing a few Ndebele 'sell-outs' especially those in the Zapu party structures. They cleverly avoided direct contact with the National Army units except a few small skirmishes meant to deflect suspicion.

## *Pretext*

A perfect pretext had been created. The 5th Brigade was then swiftly deployed in the three provinces to "deal with the dissidents under the command of that agile and indestructible Perence Shin. The real targets were Ndebele civilians and Zipra men, whose fathers had committed crimes against the Shona people. The strategy worked well in no time Zapu's political structures were smashed.

## *Liquidation*

Within five years, 25,000 Ndebeles had been exterminated in ways that instilled fear in the survivors, family life was dislocated as members scattered in different directions. The rate of kill was just unbelievable and in spite of rumblings by the minority Zapu in parliament, the exercise carried on undisturbed culminating in the "Head of the Snake" villain fleeing the country to take refuge in a European country where his stay was bankrolled by the same multinationals he had earlier proclaimed to be fighting.

## *Achievements*

The real achievements of such a strategy were much greater than what the numbers of those slaughtered reflect. There is probably roughly 2 million Ndebeles still alive today and therefore the first achievement of the 5th Brigade was redefining Ndebele and Shona relationships so far as to who matters in this country. The Ndebeles now fully know who wields what political clout in this country and this sets the stage for the discussion of other achievements of the 5th Brigade. The achievements include:

(a) **Heritage**

The military offensive in Matabeleland opened new windows of opportunity for the Shonas to reassert themselves in the country as the dominant and numerically superior group, in order to repossess our lost glory and heritage expressed in material, cultural, social and spiritual terms.

(b) **Language**

The Shona language has regained its dominant position in our society. It has become the lingua franca of Zimbabwe in the public sector particularly in government departments such as the army, police, hospitals, schools, immigration, customs throughout the country. One can now authoritatively demand service in the Shona language, even conduct telephonic conversation anywhere in Matabeleland without any need to apologise for the use of Shona or without the burden of having to speak Ndebele. National Z.T.V. is completely Shona and does very well to promote and develop our language. This is as it should be since Zimbabwe is a Shona Nation. We should not give room to languages of the invading groups because our intention is to culturally fracture and dislocate them.

Let us be reminded that language dominance automatically creates many opportunities such as employment which occurs according to the language spread. Shona speakers are now everywhere, in every comer of the country not as vegetable vendors but holders of influential positions. This occurrence is not accidental and the doubting Thomases better get this point straight because it cost careful planning. Ndebele children now realise that ignorance of Shona is a serious handicap and have, therefore, slowly but surely grown to accept the inevitable relegation of their own language to an insignificant and parasitical second class means of communication restricted to their homes or play in the streets. Ndebele can only play a translational role in Zimbabwe and nothing else beyond this—check the Zimbabwe passport, Newspapers etc.

As Shonas, we can now freely traverse the length and breadth of the country armed only with our language for communication. The same cannot be said of Ndebele. We must take note that even when a Shona person makes an effort to utter just a single 'ngca' or 'ka' for 'qa', the Ndebele stupidly get amused or fascinated like we used to when a white men attempted to speak Shona, for instance if the white man in church spoke broken Shona, like 'imwari yedu' you could not miss the excitement and appreciation on the faces of the black congregation who believed in the superiority of the English language.

The sell-out tea-boy Morgan Tsvangirai, rides on this crest of the success of our policy to elevate Shona to undisputed one National official language. We gather that when he roves around denouncing the President in his party's stronghold of Matabeleland he addresses his rallies in Shona. He better be advised that this is filthy opportunism as he exploits R.G.'s deeds at the same time trying to destroy him politically. In any case he is politically a product of Zanu turned prodigal son. The ZCTU which shot him to prominence was established by Zanu in the interest of the oppressed workers and Tea-boy better put his act together. Ziva kwawakabva!! Or else hemlock is ready for you Mr. Chameleon.

### (c) **Jobs**

Roughly 95% of Government jobs in Matabeleland and almost 100% in the rest of the country are held by Shonas. We cited the relevant departments earlier and added to them are parastatals such as Dairy Board (DZ Ltd), Railways, CSC, GMB, where all positions that matter as well as low grade jobs are invariably in Shona hands. Exceedingly heartening is the fact that the private sector went ahead without waiting for directives to implement the policy successfully. This includes factories, banks, construction companies etc. Training in tertiary institutions too has played a very significant role, as it is critical that in manpower development due attention is paid to giving skills to the Majority indigenous Shona who will be able to take up employment opportunities always. Teachers' Colleges, Polytechs, Universities all reflect in their enrolment, Shona dominance regardless of where the institution is located in the country. The most educated people are Shonas consequently.

With time cities such as Bulawayo will be Shona dominated as predicted accurately by the late hero Herbert Ushewekuunze who at some point ill-timed the naming of Mtshabezi dam as Mwanakuridza. It is a well-known fact that the job distribution in the city council of Bulawayo is skewed in favour of Ndebeles. However, it is pleasing that this is the only employer in Matabeleland with a majority of Ndebeles. Efforts must be made to put them in line with the present trend.

The resistance to the teaching of Shona in all schools in Matabeleland will soon fizzle out. More and more teaching posts are being taken up by Shona college graduates and appointments of Shona school heads has already been won. Students/pupils in all schools in that part of the country will in the not too distant future be mostly Shona. We must not forget that Nathan Shamuyarira once observed in the 1979 Grand Plan that 'the only way to weaken the Ndebele is to deprive him of an education'. Shona is taught in all teachers' colleges countywide but Ndebele is confined to Matabeleland colleges and pressure must continue to be applied to limit the teaching of Ndebele to those few who happen to be enrolled.

Some churches too are beginning to realise the trend of the times. They have introduced strictly Shona services—a very pertinent move towards achieving our goal. All churches nation-wide must conduct services in Shona to achieve that national cohesion and singular Zimbabwe national identity. However, there are some Bishops of a known church organisation pretending to be self-anointed champions of a Ndebele lost cause. Their days are certainly numbered as the 4th Chimurenga will leave no stone unturned, even religious stones will roll.

(d) **Culture**

I fact there is no such portion of this country called Matebeleland. This was colonial mischief at its worst, in order to apply the divide and rule barbaric policy.—How could invaders have a place named after their tribe as if they were legitimate inhabitant?

Our culture, robust and durable as ever, is spreading swiftly throughout the country and the agents are known to us all. Shona cultural trends are emerging in areas of 'rowora' traditionally bastardised as Lobola' where astronomical bride prices are now being sought by every Zimbabwean parent. Burial rites like mock drama in imitation-of the deceased's fond habits are now done even where no Shona person is present. Once a trend is self-perpetuating, it ceases to need monitoring as it gets weaned off—from its architect. The drum and dance at funeral wakes and our trust and faith in black magic have all permeated the social value structures of our former masters.

National public addresses at official functions are done in Shona. Being a Shona is now a source of pride particularly in Shona assimilates who in place of that cultural void, have received a reward to fill in the gap as a result of seeking redemption from Shonas.

Marriage partner preferences bear full the testimony to the superiority of Shona. Ndebele girls will without exception opt to marry a Shona man given a choice between men from the two groups. This is not without reason. Ndebele men are often savage and brutal prospective husbands. They are ungiving, unprotective and stingy. Since time immemorial, Shona men have enjoyed the luxury of making Ndebele girls pregnant and then deserting them. There are several benefits from this. The young ladies lose out on education hence on reliable sources of income, eventually resorting to prostitution. In fact, our Shona drama script writers have captured this when invariably all loose female characters playing the role of prostitute or infidelity are given Ndebele names such as MaNcube, MaKhumalo. Secondly, we have managed to dilute the Ndebeles since children fathered and left by our brothers (illegitimates) are Ndebele by name but Shonas by blood. This is a legitimate form of struggle. The end justifies the means. The true Ndebele population is shrinking and we can all be catalysts in this.

(e) **Business opportunities**

The emergence of Shona indigenous black business entrepreneurs is another great achievement towards our goal. Most black owned retail shops in Bulawayo belong to Shona people the Chigumiras, Munyoros, etc. Most black owned firms in manufacturing, communication engineering, clothing, transport, belong to Shonas in the so-called Matabeleland. Names such as Phillip Chiyangwa that whiz-kid who turns anything he touches into gold are now household names especially amongst fighters for black empowerment.

Chiyangwa and others are leading the crusade to funnel every—industrial and commercial asset in Bulawayo and elsewhere into Shona hands. Consumable products such as milk, beef and soups carry Shona labels, the purpose here is to force the die-hard Ndebele families to start using Shona words in their home. Language describes one's surroundings and becoming abundantly clear to the Ndebele that this situation is inescapable and R.G. must take credit for it all.

## Combined Effort

The military, cultural, economic and political assaults complimented one another very well to bring about the sterling achievements cited above. The success of the business enterprise mentioned elsewhere was well calculated. The appointment of a Shona to head the Central Bank (Reserve Bank) ensured that no one else gets a banking licence except Shonas, paving the way for the establishment of indigenous banks with branches all over the country by Shonas only.

We now have a Shona dominated banking sector which used to be a preserve of foreigners and there is no doubt that this development is pivotal to the indigenisation process. Despite serving everyone, regardless of race, colour, creed, tribe, these banks have fulfilled their role in our struggle for Shona dominance and therefore would need to congratulate Julius Makoni of National Merchant Bank (NMB), Leonard Nyemba Trust Bank (Trustfin), Gideon Gono of the Commercial Bank of Zimbabwe (CBZ), Francis Nhema of Zimbabwe Building Society (ZBS), Thaka Mutunhu of Agribank, Nigel Chanakira of Kingdom Bank—the list is endless, Recently one of these banks helped establish a Shona person in the heart of Matabeleland North farming area of Nyamandlovu, on the aquifer—the most valuable land-in this area, The Shona man Tom Gweru was facilitated with a $60 million loan to takeover a highly priced productive dairy enterprise from a Swindells who could only take from the Kershelmar dairies, his personal belongings before he left for Australia. The Tagariras, also Shonas from Bulawayo, have taken over large properties in the same area, thanks to these banks and A2 Resettlement. More and more large properties (farms) in Matabeleland, especially Nyamandlovu, have fallen into Shona hands under the A2 Fast Track Resettlement. Shona workers are employed in these farms. One must be a fool, to fail to realise such political astuteness on the part of our leader.

Most of those who are ungrateful to Zanu for these achievements are ignorant of the fact that the 1979 Grand Plan intended to facilitate funding for budding Shona business enterprises in farming, the hotel industry, the purchase of large industrial complexes being sold by migrating former Rhodesians such as G & G in Bulawayo. We must appreciate that wherever these banks occur in the country, 100% staff is Shona.

R.G. sourced funds from the IMF and World Bank and then channelled them into loan disbursement programmes through these banks. No foreign owned commercial bank could be trusted with such funds lest they fail to apply the relevant discrimination against the Ndebeles. Indigenous banks funnelled the funds into Shona hands. And therefore, our obligation is to ensure that the noises made by IMF & company about non-payment, does not hurt us politically because the money was put to good use. Those young Shonas tempted to shun the party should seek more information on the 1979 Grand Plan of Zanu.

## Land

This brings us to the very sensitive issue of land which has been a bone of contention since the Ndebele occupation of Zimbabwe. Because the majority of people in Bulawayo are Shonas, the rural areas must now be the target. This can only be done through the resettlement programme. The deployment of Shonas in rural Matebeleland will be the last blow to break the spine of the enemy. Because of this vision on our part, political power cannot be allowed to slip into the hands of tyrants. Zapu was an impediment to the realisation of this vision but we managed to destroy it. In the words of the now maverick and controversial Zvobgo being advice to Zapu. 'there is no less painful way for you than to join Zanu.' Nkomo capitulated in 1987 and we all know that the unity accord was a farce or smokescreen face saver for Zanu's one time greatest foe and headache turned tool.

Shona supremacy is not a dream but a reality. Should you stand idle and fail to throw your weight behind the leadership? Ask yourself whether you could be where you are, were it not for Mugabe and Zanu—educationally, economically, etc. Land that is still in white hands must all find its way into Shona hands. The courts can shout until the cows come home. Many of us were sent to the gallows for demanding our independence. The question of compensation is a non-starter. White farmers must go to Australia via the UK to collect their compensation. Zanu is simply returning to the rightful owners what is rightfully theirs. Food shortages will soon be a thing the past we must persevere. Those whites who bought farms are as guilty as their fathers who horse-pegged Zimbabwean land, parcelling out to world war fighters because they received stolen property. The ongoing agrarian revolution must be won or else our independence shall remain hollow. The party will continue to use Nkomo's fighters to further the cause but we must know when and how to dump them so that their presence within our ranks does not unmake our victories in the area of marginalising them.

Fortunately, most of them are not intellectually gifted enough to suspect that we are still guided by the 1979 Grand Plan. Zanu will not change—Zipra should change to accept that they are foreigners and therefore not entitled to enjoy the benefits of being Zimbabweans. So far they have done well in striking terror in the hearts of their MDC colleagues. The struggle is a process—from Mgagau/Morogoro to the establishment of Shona Nationhood onward ever! BACKWARD NEVER!

Great Man must be told while they leave. We need to refocus in view of the presence of the enemy within our ranks.

FROM THE CORE

# References


Abele, A., Rupprecht, T. and Wojciszek, B. 2008. The influences of success and failure experiences on agency. *European Journal of Social Psychology*. 38: 436–448

Abrams, B. E. 2006. Strategy of domination: Zanu-PF's use of ethnic conflict as a means of maintaining political control in Zimbabwe, 1982–2006. MA, Tufts University. At: http://fletcher.tufts.edu (21 May 2009).

Abreu Hernandez, V. M. 2002. The mothers of La Plaza de Mayo: a peace movement. *Peace & Change*, 27(3): 385–411.

Adam, H. and Adam, K. 2000. The politics of memory in divided societies. In W. James and L. Van de Vijver (eds.), *After the TRC: reflections on truth and reconciliation in South Africa.* Cape Town: David Philip.

Adams, K. 1999. Writing as therapy. *Counselling and Human Development*, 31(5): 1–16.

Adelman, H. 2004. *Rule-based reconciliation, roads to reconciliation.* At: http://www.humiliationstudies.org/documents/AdelmanReconciliation.pdf (28 March 2010).

Agger, I. and Jensen, S. B. 1996. Trauma and healing under state terrorism. London: Zed.

Aldana, R. 2006. A victim-centred reflection of Truth Commissions and prosecutions as a response to mass atrocities. *Journal of Human Rights*, 5: 106–126.

Alexander, J. and McGregor, J. 1996. Democracy, development and political conflict: rural institutions in Matabeleland North after independence. *International conference on the Historical Dimensions of Democracy and Human Rights in Zimbabwe*. Harare, September, 1996.

Alexander, J. and McGregor, J. 2004. War stories: guerrilla narratives of Zimbabwe's liberation war. *History Workshop Journal*, 57: 79–100.

Alexander, J., McGregor, J. and Ranger, T. 2000a. *Violence and memory: one hundred years in the 'dark forests' of Matabeleland.* Oxford: James Curry.

Alexander J., McGregor, J. and Ranger, T. 2000b. Ethnicity and the politics of conflict: a case for Matabeleland. In E. W. Nafziger, F. Stewart, and R. Vayrynen (eds.), *War hunger and displacement: the origins of humanitarian emergencies: analysis.* Oxford: University Press, N.Y.

Almqvist, K. and Broberg, A. G. 2003. Young children traumatized by organized violence together with their mothers—the critical effects of damaged internal representation. *Attachment & Human Development*, 5(4): 367–380.

Anderson, J. 2007. Forgiveness—a relational process: research and reflections. *European Journal of Psychotherapy and counselling*, 9(1): 63–76.

Anderson, C. A. and Bushman, B. J. 2002. Human aggression. *Annual Review of Psychology*, 53: 27–51. at: http://www.annualreviews.org/eprint/wZXD4ZASNg4bU/full/10.1146/annurev.psych.53.100901.135231?siteid=arjournals&keytype=ref& (22 April 2014).

Andria, K. 2009. 'Sorry for genocide': how public apology can help promote national reconciliation. At: http://mil.sagepub.com/content/38/1/3 (28 March 2010).


 

D. Ngwenya, *Healing the Wounds of Gukurahundi in Zimbabwe*,
The Anthropocene: Politik—Economics—Society—Science 19,
https://doi.org/10.1007/978-3-319-66818-5

Assefa, H. (nd). The meaning of reconciliation. At: www.gppac.net/documents/pbp/part1/2_reconc.htm (28 March 2011).

Auerbach, C. F. and Silverstein, L. B. 2003. Qualitative data: an introduction to coding and analysis. N.Y: New York University Press. At: https://nyupress.org/books/9780814706954/ (15 February 2014).

Babbie, E. and Mouton, J. 2001. *The Practice of social research.* Cape Town: Oxford Press.

Babbie, E. 2007. *The practice of social research* (11th ed.). Belmont, CA: Thompson learning.

Bagnoli, A. and Clark, A. 2010. Focus groups with young people: a participatory approach to research planning. *Journal for Youth Studies* 13(1): 101–119.

Banks-Wallace, J. 1998. Emancipatory potential of storytelling in a group. *Image: The Journal for Nursing Scholarship.* 30(1): 17–21.

Barsalou, J. 2005. Trauma and transitional justice in divided societies. *United States Institute of Peace,* 135 (Special Report): 1–11. At: www.usip.org (12 June 2009).

Bar-Tal, D., Halperin, E. and de Rivera, J. 2007. Collective emotions in conflict situations: societal implications. *Journal of Social Issues,* 63(2): 441–460.

Bazeley, P. 2013. *Qualitative data analysis: practical strategies.* L. A: SAGE.

Beach, D. N. 1980. *The Shona and Zimbabwe 900–1850.* London: Heinemann Educational Books.

Beach, D. 1994. *The Shona and their neighbours.* Oxford: Blackwell.

Becker, D. 2004. Dealing with the consequences of organised violence in trauma work. In *Berghof Handbook for Conflict Transformation.* At: www.berghof-handbook.net (14 June 2013).

Behnia, B. 2004. Trust building from the perspective of survivors of war and torture. *Social services Review,* 1: 26–40. At: http://www.jstor.org/stable/10.1086/380768 (6 June 2014).

Belnap, B. 2012. Turns of a phrase: traumatic learning through the generations. In M. G. Fromm (ed.), *Lost in transmission: studies of trauma across generations.* London: Karnack Books Ltd. At: http://us.karnacbooks.com/product/lost-in-transmission-studies-of-trauma-across-generations/30112/ (29 May 2014).

Bevernage, B. 2008. Time, presence, and historical injustice. *History and Theory,* 47(2): 149–167. At: http://www.jstor.org/stable/i25478740 (11 June 2014).

Biggar, N. (ed.). 2003. *Burying the past: making peace doing justice after civil conflict.* Georgetown: Georgetown University Press.

Blair, D. 2002. *Degrees in violence: Robert Mugabe and the struggle for power.* London: Continuum.

Bloomfield, D. 2003a. Reconciliation: an introduction. In D. Bloomfield, T. Barnes, and L. Huyse (eds.), *Reconciliation after violence: a hand book.* Stockholm, Sweden: IDEA.

Bloomfield, D. 2003b. The context of reconciliation. In D. Bloomfield, T. Barnes, and L. Huyse (eds.), *Reconciliation after violence: a hand book.* Stockholm, Sweden: IDEA.

Bloomfield, D. 2006. *On good terms: clarifying reconciliation.* At: www.berghof-foundation.org/fileadmin/redaktion/Publications/Papers/Reports/br14e.pdf (28 March 2010).

Borda, F. O. 2000. Participatory (action) research in social theory: origins and challenges. In P. Reason and H. Bradbury (eds.), *Handbook of action research.* London: SAGE.

Borer, T. A. 2004. Reconciling South Africa or South Africans? Cautionary notes from the TRC. *African Studies Quarterly,* 8(1): 19–38.

Botcharova, O. 2001. Implementation of track two diplomacy: developing a model for forgiveness. In R. Helmick and R. Petersen (eds.), *Forgiveness and reconciliation: religion, public policy and conflict transformation.* Radnor, PA: Templeton Foundation Press.

Boutros-Ghali, B. 1992. An agenda for peace; Preventative diplomacy, peacemaking and peace-keeping. At: http://www.un.org/en/sc/repertoire/89-92/Chapter%208/GENERAL%20ISSUES/Item%2029_Agenda%20for%20peace_.pdf (08 March 2007).

Boutros-Ghali, B. 1995. Supplement to an agenda for peace. *New York: United Nations.*

Boxhill, B. R. 2003. A Lockean argument for Bleck reparations. *The Journal of Ethics,* 7(1): 63–91. At: http://www.jstor.org/stable/25115749 (10 June 2014).

Bracken, P. J. and Petty, C. 1998. *Rethinking the trauma of war.* London: Free Association Books.

Bracken P. 2000. Rethinking the trauma of war. In C. Becker (ed.), *Psychosocial and trauma response in war-torn societies: the case of Kosovo.* Psychosocial Notebook, Vol. 1, IOM.

Braithwaite, J. 2003. Restorative justice and a better future. In G. Johnstone (ed.), *A restorative justice reader: texts, sources, context.* Devon, Willan: Cullompton.

Braun, V. and Clarke, V. 2006. Using thematic analysis in psychology. *Qualitative Research in Psychology*, 3: 77–101.

Bylsma, L. M., Vingerhoets, J. J. M. and Rottenberg, J. 2008. When is crying cathartic? An international study. *Journal of Social & Clinical Psychology*, 27(10): 1165–1187.

Cahill, C. 2007. The personal is political: developing new subjectivities through participatory action research. *Gender, Place and Culture*, 14(3) June: 267–292.

Cairns, E. 2005. Healing, reconciliation and the prevention of violence: a comment. *Journal of Social and Clinical Psychology*, 24(3): 335–337.

Caruth, C. 1996. *Unclaimed experience: trauma, narrative, and history.* Baltimore: The John Hopkins University Press.

Carver, C. S. 1998. Resilience and thriving: issues, models, and linkages. *Journal of Social Issues*, 54(2): 254–266.

Casey, B. and Long, B. 2002. Reconciling voices. *Journal of psychiatric and mental health nursing*, 9: 603–610.

CCJP. 2007. *Gukurahundi in Zimbabwe: a report on the disturbances in Matabeleland and the Midlands 1980–1988.* Johannesburg: Jacana Media.

CDA Collaborative learning projects. 2009. *Reflecting on peace practice: participant training manual.* At: http://cdacollaborative.org/wordpress/wp-content/uploads/2016/01/Reflecting-on-Peace-Practice-1-Participant-Training-Manual.pdf (22 April 2011)

Chapman, A. 2001. Truth commissions as instruments of forgiveness and reconciliation. In R. Helmick and R. Peterson (eds.), *Forgiveness and reconciliation: religion, public policy and conflict transformation.* Radnor, Philadelphia: Templeton Foundation.

Chigas, D. and Woodrow, P. 2009. Envisioning and pursuing peace writ large. *Berghof Handbook.* At: http://cdacollaborative.org/wordpress/wp-content/uploads/2016/02/Envisioning-and-Pursuing-Peace-Writ-Large.pdf (28 June 2011).

Chronicle, 22 June 2011. Nkomo calls for dialogue on Gukurahundi. At: www.chronicle.co.zw/nkomo-calls-for-dialogue-on-gukurahundi/ (22 May 2014).

Chronicle, 9 July 2011. We need not open old wounds: Mnangagwa. At: www.chronicle.co.zw/we-need-not-open-old-wounds-mnangagwa/ (22 May 2014).

Clancy, M. A. C. and Humber, B. 2008. Trauma, peacebuilding and development: an overview of key positions and critical questions. At: www.incore.ulst.ac.uk/research/projects/trauma/ (17 July 2010).

Clark, J. N. 2010. 'Reflections on trust and reconciliation: a case study of a central Bosnian Village'. *The International Journal of Human Rights*, December: 239–256. At: http://www.tandfonline.com/doi/abs/10.1080/13642987.2010.528205 (28 March 2010).

Cobban, H. 2007. *Amnesty after atrocity? Healing nations after genocide and war crimes.* Boulder, US: A Paradigm.

Cobham, V. E., March S., De Young, A., Lesson, F., Nixon, R., McDermott, B. and Kenardy J. 2012. Involving parents in indicated early intervention for childhood PTSD following accidental injury. *Clinical Child & Family Psychology Review*, 15(4): 345–363. At: https://link.springer.com/article/10.1007/s10567-012-0124-9 (10 May 2014).

Cockell, J. 2003. Conceptualising peacebuilding: human security and sustainable peace. In M. Pugh (ed.), *Regeneration of war-torn societies.* London: Macmillan.

Cole, R. 1991. Participant observer research: an activist role. In W. Foote Whyte (ed.), *Participatory action research.* California: SAGE.

Cole, J. 2004. Painful memories: ritual and the transformation of community trauma. *Culture, Medicine and Psychiatry*, 28(1): 87–105.

Collins, K. J. 1998. *Participatory research: a primer.* Cape Town: Prentice Hall.

Coloma, M. P. 2006. Eugenio Dittborn: clashes of memory in post-dictatorship Chile. *Hispanic Research Journal*, 7(4): 321–336.

Connolly, A. 2011. Healing the wounds of our fathers: intergenerational trauma, memory, symbolisation and narrative. *Journal of Analytical Psychology*, 56: 607–626.

Connolly Baker, K. and Mazza, N. 2004. The healing power of writing: applying the expressive/creative component of poetry to therapy: *Journal of Poetry Therapy: The interdisciplinary Journal of Practice, Theory, Research and Education*, 12(3): 141–154. At: http://dx.doi.org/10.1080/08893670412331311352 (6 June 2014).

Cosgrove, L. and Konstam, V. 2008. Forgiveness and forgetting: clinical implication for mental health counsellors. *Journal of Mental Health Counselling,* 30(1): 1–13.

Costello, P. J. M. 2003. *Action research*. London: Continuum.

Couper, D. 1998. Forgiveness in community: views from an Episcopal priest and former chief of police. In R. D. Enright and J. North (eds.), *Exploring forgiveness.* Madison: University of Wisconsin Press.

Crocker, D. 1999. Reckoning with past wrongs: a normative framework. *Ethics and International Affairs*, 13: 43–64.

Dawson, J. 2001. Hatred's end: a Christian proposal to peacemaking in a new century. In R. Helmick and R. Peterson (eds.), *Forgiveness and reconciliation: religion, public policy and conflict transformation.* Radnor, PA: Templeton Foundation.

de Jong, K., Mulhern, M., Ford, N., van de Kam, S. and Kleber, R. 2000. The trauma of war in Sierra Leone. *The Lancet,* 355: 2067–2068.

Denborough, D., Freedman, J. and White, S. 2008. *Strengthening resistance: the use of narrative practices in working with genocide survivors.* Adelaide, Australia: Dulwich Centre Foundation.

Denzin, N. K. 1989. *Interpretive interactionism*. Newbury Park, California: SAGE.

Denzin, N. K. and Lincoln, Y. S. 2005. The discipline and practice of qualitative research. In N. K. Denzin and Y. S. Lincoln (eds.), *The SAGE handbook of qualitative research.* California: SAGE.

de Rivera, J. and Paez D. 2007. Emotional climate, human security, and cultures of peace. *Journal of Social Issues,* 63(2): 233–253.

de Vries, J. M. A. and de Paor, J. 2005. Healing and reconciliation in the L.I.V.E. program in Ireland. *Peace and Change*, 30(3): 329–358.

De Viñar, M. U. 2012. Political violence: transgenerational inscription and trauma. *International Journal of Applied Psychoanalytic studies*, 9(2): 95–108.

de Waal, V. 1990. *The politics of reconciliation: Zimbabwe's first decade.* Cape Town: David Philip.

de Zulueta, C. F. 2007. Mass violence and mental health: attachment and trauma. *International Review of Psychiatry*, 19(3): 221–233.

Dickson, G. 1997. Participatory action research and health promotion: the grandmothers' story. PhD thesis, University of Saskatchewan.

Dignan, J. 2005. *Understanding victims and restorative justice.* Berkshire, England: Open University Press.

Dillenburger, K., Akhonzada, R. and Fargas, M. 2006. Post-trauma: is evidence-based practice a fantasy? *International Journal of Behavioral and Consultation Therapy,* 2(1): 95–102.

Druckman, D. 2005. *Doing research: methods of inquiry for conflict analysis.* London: SAGE.

Dwyer, S. 2003. Reconciliation for realists. In C. A. L. Prager and T. Govier (eds.), *Dilemmas of reconciliation: cases and concepts.* Waterloo, Ontario: Wilfrid Laurier University Press.

Ehrenreich, J. H. 2003. Understanding PTSD: forgetting 'trauma'. *Journal of Social Issues*, 3(1): 15–28.

Edkins, J. 2003. *Trauma and the memory of politics*. Cambridge: Cambridge University Press.

Elden, M. and Levin, M. 1991. Cogenerative learning: bringing participation into action research. In W. Foote Whyte (ed.), *Participatory action research.* California: SAGE.

Elshtain, J. B. 2003. Politics and forgiveness. In N. Biggar (ed.), *Burying the past: making peace and doing justice after civil conflict.* Georgetown: Georgetown University Press.

Emirbayer, M. and Mische, A. 1998. What is agency? *The American Journal of sociology,* 103(4): 962–1023.

Emry, M., Radke, B., Newman, D. and Hanson, M. 2004. Using appreciative inquiry in a planning process. At: http://srdc.msstate.edu/trainings/presentations_archive/2004/2004_rcci_emery.doc (August 20 2009).

Endreß, M. and Pabst, A. 2013. Violence and shattered trust: sociological considerations. *Human Studies*, 36: 89–106.

Enright, R. D., Freedman, S. and Rique, J. 1998. The psychology of interpersonal forgiveness. In R. D. Enright and J. North (eds.), *Exploring forgiveness.* Madison: University of Wisconsin Press.

Erickson, K. 1995. Notes on trauma and community. In C. Caruth (ed.), *Trauma: explorations in memory.* Baltimore: The John Hopkinson University Press.

Eppel, S. 2006. 'Healing the dead': exhumation and burial as truth-telling and peace-building activities in rural Zimbabwe. In T. A. Borer (ed.), *Telling the truths: truth telling and peace building in post-conflict societies.* Notre Dame, Indiana: University of Notre Dame Press.

Farnworth, C. 2007. Achieving respondent-led research in Madagascar. *Gender & Development* 15(2): 271–284.

Farwell, N. and Cole, J. B. 2002. Community as context of healing: psychosocial recovery of children affected by war and political violence. *International Journal of Mental Health,* 30(4): 19–41.

Fisher, S. and Zimina, L. 2009. Just wasting our time? Provocative thoughts for peacebuilders. *Berghof handbook.* At: http://citeseerx.ist.psu.edu/viewdoc/download?doi=10.1.1.550.1263&rep=rep1&type=pdf (03 October 2009)

Finch, R. 2006. Trauma and forgiveness: a spiritual inquiry. *Journal of Spirituality in Mental Health,* 9(2): 27–42. At: http://www.tandfonline.com/doi/abs/10.1300/J515v09n02_03 (13 February 2013).

Flood, R. L. 2006. The relationship of 'systems thinking' to action research. In P. Reason and H. Bradbury (eds.), *Handbook of action research.* London: SAGE.

Fooladi, M. M. 2005. The healing effects of crying. *Holistic Nursing Practice*, 19(6): 248–255.

Forsberg, T. 2003. The philosophy and practice of dealing with the past: some conceptual and normative issues. In R. D. Enright and J. North (eds.), *Exploring forgiveness.* Madison: University of Wisconsin Press.

Francis, D. 2005. *Applied conflict transformation: action research.* UK: RTC.

Francis, D. 2007. *Applied conflict transformation: action research* (update). UK: RTC.

Freeman, M. and Hayner, P. B. 2003. Truth-telling. In D. Bloomfield, T. Barnes, and L. Huyse (eds.), *Reconciliation after violence: a hand book.* Stockholm: IDEA.

Freire, P. (1970) 1993. Pedagogy of the oppressed. New York: Continuum.

Fromm, M. G. 2012. *Lost in transmission: studies of trauma across generations.* London: Karnack Books Ltd. At: http://us.karnacbooks.com/product/lost-in-transmission-studies-of-trauma-across-generations/30112/ (29 May 2014).

Fuertes, A. B. 2004. In their own words: discourse of (war) trauma and healing. *Conflict Resolution Quarterly*, 21(4): 491–500.

Galtung, J. 1996. *Peace by peaceful means: peace and conflict, development and civilization.* UK: SAGE.

Gaventa, J. 2006. Finding the spaces for change: a power analysis. *IDS Bulletin* 37(6): 23–33.

Gaventa, J. and Cornwall, A. 2006. Power and Knowledge. In P. Reason and H. Bradbury (eds.), *Handbook of action research.* London: SAGE.

Ghaye, T., et al. 2008. Participatory and appreciative action and reflection (PAAR)- democratizing reflective practices. *Reflective Practice* 9(4):361–397.

Gerzon, M. 2006. *Leading through conflict: how successful leaders transform differences into opportunities.* Boston: Harvard Business School Press.

Gibson, W. J. and Brown, A. 2009. Working with qualitative data. London, England: SAGE. At: http://dx.doi.org/10.4135/9780857029041 (16 February 2014).

Giller, J. 1998. Caring for 'victims of torture' in Uganda: some personal reflections. In P. J. Bracken and C. Petty (eds.), *Rethinking the trauma of war*. London: Free Association Books.

Gilligan, J. 1996. *Violence: reflections on a national epidemic*. New York: Vintage Books.

Gobodo-Madikizela, P. 2003. *A human being died that night: a story of forgiveness*. Cape Town: David Philip.

Gobodo-Madikizela, P. 2008. Trauma, forgiveness and the witnessing dance: making public spaces intimate. *Journal of Analytical Psychology*, 53: 169–188.

Goddard, V. A. 2007. Demonstrating resistance: politics and participation in the marches of the Mothers of Plaza de Mayo. *European Journal of Anthropology*, 50: 81–101.

Goldwater, E. 2004. *Getting mad and getting even*. Modern Psychoanalysis, 9(1): 23–36.

Goldberg, J. G. 2004. Fantasies of revenge and the stabilisation of the ego: acts of revenge and the ascension of Thanatos. *Modern Psychoanalysis* 29(1): 13–21.

Gollwitzer, M., Meder, M. and Schmitt, M. 2011. What gives victims satisfaction when they seek revenge? *European Journal of Social Psychology*, 41: 364–374.

Govier, T. and Verwoerd, W. 2002. Forgiveness: the victim's prerogative. *South African Journal of Philosophy*, 21(1): 97–110.

Goto, K., Tiffany, J., Pelto, G. and Pelletier, D. 2008. Use of Q methodology to analyze divergent perspectives on participatory action research as a strategy or HIV/AIDS prevention among Caribbean youth. *AIDS Education and Prevention*, 20(4): 301–311.

Gower, M. 2013. Revenge: interplay of creative and destructive forces. *Clinical Social Work Journal*, 41: 112–118.

Grant, J., Nelson, G. and Mitchell, T. 2008. Negotiating challenges of participatory action research: relationships, power, participation, challenges and credibility. In P. Reason and H. Bradbury (eds.), *The SAGE handbook of action research: participative inquiry and practice*. London: SAGE.

Grävingholt, J., Ganzle, S. and Ziaja, S. 2009. The convergence of peacebuilding and state building: addressing a common purpose from different perspectives. Briefing Paper 4/2009. Bonn: German Development Institute / Deutsches Institut für Entwicklungspolitik (DIE).

Greenwood, D. J. and Levin, M. 1998. Action research, science and the co-optation of social research. *Studies in Cultures, organization, and Societies*, 4: 237–261.

Greenwood, D. J. and Levin, M. 2007. *Introduction to action research: social research for social change* (2nd ed.). Thousand Oaks: SAGE.

Guess, K. F. 2006. Posttraumatic stress disorder: early detection is key. *The nurse practitioner*, 3 (3): 23-3. At: www.tnpj.com (28 December 2009).

Guishard, M. 2009. The false paths, the endless labors, the turns now this way and now that: participatory action research, mutual vulnerability, and the politics of inquiry. *Urban Review*, 41: 85–105.

Gustavsen, B. 2006. Theory and practice: the mediating discourse. In P. Reason and H. Bradbury (eds.), *Handbook of action research*. London: SAGE.

Hamber, B. 2003. Healing. In D. Bloomfield, T. Barnes, and L. Huyse (eds.), *Reconciliation after violence: a hand book*. Stockholm: International IDEA.

Harding, J. 2003. *Qualitative data analysis: from start to finish*. L. A: SAGE.

Harjula, E. 2002. Trauma lives in speech: the rhythm of speech breaks, words disappear, a hole is torn in speech. *International Forum Psychoanalysis*, 11: 198–201.

Hawkins, K. 2007. Participatory action research, sacred existential epistemology, the eighth moment of qualitative research and beyond. PhD: University of Southern Queensland.

Hayner, P. 2001. *Unspeakable truths: confronting state terror and atrocity*. London: Routledge.

Heathershaw, J. 2007. Peacebuilding as practise: discourses from post-conflict Tajikistan. *International Peacekeeping*, 4(2) April: 219–236.

Herman, J. L. 1992. *Trauma and recovery: from domestic abuse to political terror*. London: Pandura.

Higson-Smith, C. 2002. *Supporting communities affected by violence: a casebook from South Africa.* Oxford: Oxfam.
Hill, G. 2005. *What Happens after Mugabe? Can Zimbabwe rise from the ashes?* Cape Town: Zebra.
Holliday, A. 2007. Doing and writing qualitative research. London: SAGE. At: https://doi.org/10.4135/9781446287958.n3 (7 April 2014).
Holloway, I. 1997. *Basic concepts for qualitative inquiry* (2nd ed.). Thousand Oaks, California: SAGE.
Hoogenboom, D. and Vielle, S. 2008. Rebuilding social fabric in failed states: examining transitional justice in Bosnia. Conference paper, Canadian Political Scientists annual meeting, Vancouver, BC.
Humphrey, M. 2005. Reconciliation and the therapeutic state. *Journal of Intercultural studies,* 26(3): 203–220.
Huyse, L. 2003a. The process of reconciliation. In D. Bloomfield, T. Barnes, and L. Huyse (eds.), *Reconciliation after violent conflict, a handbook.* Stockholm: IDEA.
Huyse, L. 2003b. Justice. In D. Bloomfield, T. Barnes, and L. Huyse (eds.), *Reconciliation after violence: a handbook.* Stockholm: IDEA.
Inter Agency Standing Committee (IASC). 2007. *IASC Guidelines for on mental health and psychosocial support in emergency setting.* Geneva: IASC.
Inter Agency Standing Committee (IASC). 2010. Guidance note for mental health and psychosocial support: Haiti earthquake emergency response. Geneva: IASC. At: https://www.apa.org/international/resources/info/haiti-guidelines.pdf (20 October 2010).
International Centre for Conciliation. At: http://www.centerforconciliation.org (12 June 2010).
Iliff, A. 2010. Transitional justice: sowing the seeds of its grassroots. *Oxford Transitional Justice Working Paper Series.* At: http://africanarguments.org/2010/03/11/root-and-branch-tree-of-life-sowing-the-seeds-of-grassroots-transitional-justice/ (20 March 2014).
Isserman, N. 2009. Political tolerance and intolerance: using qualitative interviews to understand the attitudes of holocaust survivors. *Contemporary Jewry,* 29(1): 21–47.
Jackson, J. and Gerber M. M. 2013. Retribution as revenge and retribution as just deserts. *Social Justice Research,* 26: 61–80.
Jaeger, M. 1998. The power and reality of forgiveness: forgiving the murderer of one's child. In R. D. Enright and J. North (eds.), *Exploring forgiveness.* Madison: University of Wisconsin Press.
Jelin, E. and Kaufman, S. G. 2002. Layers of memories: twenty years after in Argentina. In D. E. Lorey and W. H. Beezley (eds.), *Genocide, collective violence, and popular memory: the politics of remembrance in the twentieth century.* Wilmington, Delaware: SR Books.
Jordan, J. B. 1998. Writing and therapy with conflictual couples. *Journal of Family Psychotherapy,* 9(2): 27–39. At: http://dx.doi.org/10.1300/J085V09N02_03 (21 May 2014).
Kanyangara, P., Rimé, B., Philippot, P. and Yzerbyt, V. 2007. Collective rituals, emotional climate and intergroup perception: participation in 'Gacaca' tribunals and assimilation of the Rwandan genocide. *Journal of social Issues,* 63(2): 387–403.
Kaminer, D. 2006. Healing process in trauma narratives: a review. *South African Journal of Psychology,* 36(3): 481–499.
Kaulemu, D. 2005. Archaeology of violence in Zimbabwe. Unpublished paper.
Kearney, R. 2007. Narrating pain: the power of catharsis. *Paragraph,* 30(1): 51–66.
Kellermann, N. P. F. 2001. Transmission of Holocaust trauma: an intergretive view. *Psychiatry,* 64(3): 256–264.
Kelman, H. 1999. Transforming the relationship between former enemies: a social-psychological analysis. In R. L. Rothstein (ed.), *After the peace: resistance and reconciliation.* Boulder, CO, and London: Lynne Rienner.
Kemmis, S. 2006. Exploring the relevancy of critical theory for action research: emancipatory action research in the footsteps of Jurgen Harbemas. In P. Reason and H. Bradbury (eds.), *Handbook of action research.* London: SAGE.

Kemmis, S. and McTaggart, R. 2005. Participatory action research: communicative action and the public sphere. In N. K. Denzin and Y. S. Lincoln (eds.), *The SAGE handbook of qualitative research.* California: SAGE.

Kemmis, S. and McTaggart, R. 2008. PAR: communicative action and the public sphere. In N. K. Denzin and Y. S. Lincoln (eds.), *Strategies of qualitative inquiry* (3rd ed.). London: SAGE Publication.

Kliman, J. and LLerena-Quinn, R. 2002. Dehumanising and rehumanizing responses to September 11. *Journal of Systematic Therapies*, 21(3): 8–18.

Koch, T. and Kralik, D. 2006. *Participatory action research in Healthcare.* Oxford, UK: Blackwell Publishing.

Kogan, I. 2012. The second generation in the shadow of terror. In M. G. Fromm (ed.), *Lost in transmission: studies of trauma across generations*. London: Karnack Books Ltd. At: http://us.karnacbooks.com/product/lost-in-transmission-studies-of-trauma-across-generations/30112/ (29 May 2014).

Kombanie, S. 2011. The effect of migration on school dropout. MA Dissertation, University of the Free State.

Kramer, R. C. 2000. Poverty, inequality, and youth violence. *Annals of the American Academy of Political and Social Science*. 567: 123–139.

Kringer, N. J. 1992. *Zimbabwe's guerrilla war: peasant voices*. Cambridge: Cambridge University Press.

Krondorfer, B. 2008. Is forgetting reprehensible? Holocaust remembrance and the task of oblivion. *The Journal of Religious Ethics*, 36(2): 232–267. At: http:www.jstor.org/stable/40014887 (6 June 2014).

Kupferberg, F. 1997. The land of murderers: Jewish survivors in post-war Germany. *Innovation*, 10(1): 85–102.

La Caze, M. 2006. The asymmetry between apology and forgiveness. *Contemporary Political Theory*. 5: 447–468.

Lambourne, W. 2004. Post-conflict peacebuilding: meeting human needs for justice and reconciliation. *Peace, Conflict and Development*, 4: 1–24.

Lamott, F. 2005. Trauma as a political tool. *Critical Public health.* 15(3): 219–228.

Lanzmann, C. 1995. The obscenity of understanding: an evening with Claude Lanzmann. In C. Caruth (ed.), *Trauma: explorations in Memory*. Baltimore: The John Hopkinson University Press.

Laplante, L. J. and Theidon, K. 2007. Truth with consequences: justice and reparations in post-truth commission Peru. *Human Right Quarterly,* 29(1): 228–250. At: http://www.jstor.org/stable/20072794 (29 May 2014).

Laub, D. 1995. Truth and testimony: the process and the struggle. In C. Caruth (ed.), *Trauma: explorations in Memory*. Baltimore: The John Hopkinson University Press.

Lazare, A. 2004. On apology. New York: Oxford University Press.

Lederach, J. P. 1997. *Building peace: sustainable reconciliation in divided societies*. Washington, DC: USIP.

Lemaire, J. M. 2000. Disconcerting humanitarian interventions, and the resources of collective healing. In C. Becker (ed.), *Psychological and trauma response in war-torn societies: the case of Kosovo*. Psychological Notebook, Vol.1, November, 2000, IOM.

Lengelle, R. and Meijers, F. 2009. Mystery and mastery: an exploitation of what happens in the black box of writing and healing. *Journal of Poetry Therapy: The Interdisciplinary Journal of Practice, Theory, Research and Education*, 22(2): 57–75. At: https://doi.org/10.1080/08893670903072935 (6 June 2014).

Lieblich, A. 2013. Healing plots; writing and reading in life-stories groups. *Qualitative Inquiry*, 19: 46–52. At: http://qix.sagepub.com/content/19/1/46 (20 May 2014).

Lindner, E. G. 2004. Humiliation in a globalizing world: does humiliation become the most disruptive force? At: http://www.humiliationstudies.org/documents/evelin/HumiliationFearGlobalizingWorld.pdf (6 June 2013).

Losi, N. 2000. Understanding the needs of the displaced: some elements on the Kosovo case. In C. Becker (ed.), *Psychosocial and trauma response in war-torn societies: the case of Kosovo*. Psychosocial Notebook, Vol. 1, IOM.
Lopez-Corvo, R. E. 2013. Time distortion between 'conceptual' and 'preconceptual' traumas. *Psychoanalytic Review*, 100(2): 289–310.
MacDonald, C. 2012. Understanding participatory action research: a qualitative research methodology option. *Canadian Journal of Action Research*, 13(2): 34–50.
Maguire, P. (1993). Challenges, contradictions, and celebrations: Attempting participatory research as a doctoral student. *Voices of change: Participatory research in the United States and Canada*, 157–176.
Mahler, B., Ntakarutimana, F. and Niyongabo, A. 2007. Now I am human: testimonies from the healing companions program in Rwanda and Burundi. *Peace Ways AGLI*, 2(2): 4–23.
Maiese, M. 2003. What it means to building everlasting peace. *Beyond intractability*. At: http://www.beyondintractability.org/essay/peacebuilding (11/06/2014).
Mamdani, M. 2001. *When victims become killers, colonialism, nativism, and the genocide in Rwanda*. Oxford: James Curry.
Maphosa, S. B. 2013. Thinking creatively about methodological issues in conflict-affected societies: a primer from the field. *Journal of Peacebuilding and Development*. 8(2): 91–103. At: http://dx.doi.org/10.1080/15423166.2013.823058 (25 October 2013).
Marshall, T. 2003. Restorative justice: an overview. In G. Johnstone (ed.), *A restorative justice reader: texts, sources, context*. Willan, Cullompton: Devon.
Martin-Baro, I. 1989. Political violence and wars as causes of psychosocial trauma in El Salvador. *International Journal of Mental health*, 18(1): 3–20.
McCaffery, J. 2005. Using transformative models of adult literacy in conflict resolution and peacebuilding process at community level: examples from Guinea, Sierra Leone and Sudan. *Compare*, 35(4): 443–462.
McGrew, L. 2006. Justice and reconciliation? Can the trails for the Khmer Rouge bring reconciliation and healing in Cambodia? *NIAS Nytt*, 3: 8–11.
McIntyre, A. 2007. *Participatory action research: qualitative research methods series* 52. L.A: SAGE.
McIntyre, A. 2008. *Participatory action research*. Los Angeles: SAGE Publications.
Mckinney, K. 2007. 'Breaking the conspiracy of silence': testimony, traumatic memory, and psychotherapy with survivors of political violence. *Ethos*, 35(3): 265–295.
McKnight, A. N. (nd). Historical trauma, the persistence of memory and the pedagogical problems of forgiveness, justice and peace. *Educational Studies*, 36(2): 140–158.
McNiff, J. 1988. *Action research: principles and practice*. London: Routledge.
McNiff, J. and Whitehead, J. 2006. *All you need to know about action research*. London: SAGE Publications.
McNiff, J. and Whitehead, J. 2010. *You and your action research project*. London: Routledge.
McTaggart, R. 1991. Principles for participatory action research. *Adult Education Quarterly*, 41 (3): 168–187.
McTaggart, R. 1998. Is validity really an issue for Participatory action research? *Studies in culture, organisations and societies*, 4: 211–236.
Meichenbaum, D. 2013. Ways to bolster resilience across the deployment cycle. *Military Psychologists' Desk Reference*, 325–355.
Mendeloff, D. 2004. Truth-telling, and post conflict peacebuilding: curb the enthusiasm? *International Studies Review*, 6: 355–380. At: http://jstor.org/stable/3699695 (28 May 2014).
Menkhaus, K. 2004. Impact assessment in post-conflict peacebuilding: challenges and future directions. At: www.interpeace.org/index.php/publications/doc_download/101-i (28 March 2009).
Meredith, M. 2008. *Mugabe: power, plunder and the struggle for Zimbabwe*. Jeppestown, South Africa: Jonathan Ball.

Meyer, L. H. 2006. Reparations and symbolic restitution. *Journal of Social Philosophy*, 37(3): 406–422.

Miall, H. 2006. Conflict transformation: a multi-dimensional task. At: http://www.berghof-handbook.net (10 February 2006).

Minow, M. 1998. *Between vengeance and forgiveness: facing history after genocide and mass violence*. Boston: Beacon Press.

Mitchels, B. 2003. Healing the wounds of war and more: an integrative approach to peace—the work of Adam Curle and others with Mir i dobro in Zupanja, Croatia. *British Journal of Guidance & Counselling,* 31(4): 403–415.

Montiel, C. J. 2002. Sociopolitical forgiveness. *Peace Review*, 14(3): 271–277.

Montero, M. 1998. Psychosocial community work as an alternative mode of political action (the construction and critical transformation of society). *Community, Work & Family,* 1(1): 65–77.

Moon, C. 2009. Healing past violence: traumatic assumptions and therapeutic interventions in war and reconciliation. *Journal of Human Rights*, 8: 71–91 At: https://doi.org/10.1080/14754830902717726 (28 May 2014).

Moore, J. 2004. Living in the basement of the ivory tower: a graduate student's perspective of participatory action research within academic institutions. *Educational Action Research,* 12(1): 145–162.

Morkel, E. 2011. A participatory approach to healing and transformation in South Africa. *Family Process*, 50(4): 486–502.

Motsi, R. G. 2010. The trauma caused by the Matabeleland massacre of 1982–1986 in Tsholotsho and how the church can bring transformation using pastoral care. PhD Thesis. University of Pretoria.

Mouton, J. and Marais, H. C. 1996. *Basic concepts in the methodology of the social sciences* (2nd ed.). Pretoria: HSRC.

Mouton, J. 2001. *How to succeed in your Masters and Doctoral studies: a South African guide and resource book.* Pretoria: Van Schaik Publishers.

Mouton, J. 1996. *Understanding social research.* Pretoria: Van Schaik Publishers.

Msindo, E. 2006. Ethnicity, not class? The 1929 Bulawayo faction fights reconsidered. *Journal of Southern African Studies*, 1(3) September: 429–447.

Mugabe, R. 2003. *Our war of liberation: speeches, articles and interviews 1976–1979.* Gweru: Mambo Press.

Muller-Fahrenholz, G. 1997. *The art of forgiveness: theological reflections on healing and reconciliation.* Geneva: WCC.

Mullet, J. H., Akerson, N. M. K. and Turman, B. A. 2013. Healing the past through story. *Adult learning*, 24 (2): 72–77.

Munyas, B. 2008. Genocide in the mind of Cambodian youth; transmitting (his)stories of genocide to second and third generations in Cambodia. *Journal of Genocide Research,* 10(3): 413–439.

Murphy, C. 2007. Political reconciliation, the rule of law, and genocide. *European Legacy*, 12(7): 853–856.

Murphy, M. 2011. Apology, recognition, and reconciliation. *Human Rights Review*, 12: 47–69.

Nagy, R. 2002. Reconciliation in post-commission South Africa: thick and thin accounts of solidarity. At: http://restorativejustice.org/rj-library/reconciliation-in-post-commission-south-africa-thick-and-thin-accounts-of-solidarity/6294/#sthash.8mrEb644.dpbs (28 March 2010).

Ndlovu-Gatsheni, S. J. (2003). The post-colonial state and Matebeleland: regional perceptions of civil—military relations, 1980–2002.

Ndlovu-Gatsheni, S. J. (2008). Nation-building in Zimbabwe and the challenges of Ndebele particularism. *African Journal of Conflict Resolution,* 8(3): 27–56.

Neller, D. J., Denney, R. L., Pietz, C. A. and Tomlinson, R. P. 2005. Testing the trauma model of violence. *Journal of Family Violence.* 20(3): 151–159.

Neto, F., Da Coneição Pinto, M. and Mullet, E. 2007. Intergroup forgiveness: east Timorese and Angolan perspectives. *Journal of Peace Research,* 44(6): 711–721.

Newberg, A. B., d'Aquili, E. G., Newberg, S. K. and deMarici V. 2000. The neuropsychological correlates of forgiveness. In M. E. McCullough, K. I. Pargament, and C. E. Thoresen (eds.), *Forgiveness, theory, research, and practice*. N.Y: Guilford Press.

Newbury, C. 2002. Ethnicity and the politics of history in Rwanda. In D. E. Lorey and W. H. Beezley (eds.), *Genocide, collective violence, and popular memory: the politics of remembrance in the twentieth century*. Wilmington: S R Books.

Newman, L. S. and Kraynak, L. R. 2013. The ambiguity of a transgression and the type of apology influence immediate reactions. *Social Behaviour and Personality*, 41(1): 31–46.

Nikondeha, C. 2009. *Transfiguration*. Keynote address at the Amahoro conference, Johannesburg, South Africa.

Nkala, P. 2010. Artist in court for 1980s disturbances paintings. *The Chronicle*, March, 30, 2010. At: www.thechronicleonline.co.zw (30 March 2010).

Nkomo, J. M. 1983. *Informative letter to Prime Minister Mugabe*. In *The Zimbabwe Independent*.

Nordstrom, C. 2007. *A different kind of war story*. Pennsylvania: University of Pennsylvania Press.

North, J. 1998. The 'ideal' of forgiveness: a philosopher's exploration. In R. D. Enright and J. North (eds.), *Exploring forgiveness*. Madison, Wisconsin: University of Wisconsin.

O'Brien, R. 1998. *An overview of the methodological approach to action research*. Toronto: University of Toronto.

Odell, M, J. and Mohr, B. J. 2008. The power of a positive lens in peace building and development. *Advances in Appreciative Inquiry*, 2: 307–327.

OECD/DAC. 2005. Preventing conflict and building peace: A manual of issues and entry points. At: https://www.scribd.com/document/248493915/OECD-Preventing-Conflict-and-Building-Peace (16 April 2011).

Oelosfen, R. 2009. De- and rehumanisation in the wake of atrocities. *South African Journal of Philosophy*, 28(2): 178–188.

Okasha, A. 2007. Mental health and violence: WPA Cairo declaration- international perspectives for intervention. *International Review of Psychiatry*, 19(3): 193–200.

Onwuegbuzie, A. J., Dickinson, W. B., Leech, N. L. and Zoran, A. N. 2009. A qualitative framework for collecting and analysing data in focus group research. *International Journal of Qualitative Methods*, 8(3): 1–21.

Opotow, S. 2001. Reconciliation in times of impunity challenges for social justice. *Social Justice research*, 14(2): 149–170.

Parnell, L. 1997. *Transforming trauma: EMDR, the revolutionary new therapy for freeing the mind, clearing the body, and opening the heart*. New York: W. W. Norton & Company.

Papadopoulos, R. 2000. A matter of shades: trauma and psychosocial work in Kosovo. In C. Becker (ed.), *Psychosocial and trauma response in war-torn societies: the case of Kosovo*. Psychosocial Notebook, Vol. 1, IOM.

Papadopoulos, R. K. 2007. Refugees, trauma and adversity- activated development. *European Journal of Psychology and Counselling*, 9(3): 301–312.

Park, P. 2006. Knowledge and participatory research. In P. Reason and H. Bradbury (eds.), *Handbook of action research*. London: SAGE.

Passmore, W. 2006. Action research in the workplace: the socio-technical perspective. In P. Reason and H. Bradbury (eds.), *Handbook of action research*. London: SAGE.

Pennebaker, J. W. 1997. Writing about emotional experiences as a therapeutic process. *Psychological Science*, 8(3): 162–166. At: http://www.jstor.org/stable/40063169?origin=JSTOR-pdf (20 May 2014).

Perez, N. 2011. On compensation and return: can the 'continuing justice argument' for compensating for historical injustices justify compensation for such injustices or the return of property? *Journal of Applied Philosophy*, 28(2): 151–167.

Perry, C. 2002. A structured approach for presenting theses: notes for students and their supervisors. At: http://citeseerx.ist.psu.edu/viewdoc/download?doi=10.1.1.203.2738&rep=rep1&type=pdf (9 April 2014).

Peterson, R. L. 2001. A theology of forgiveness: terminology, rhetoric, & the dialectic of interfaith relationships. In R. G. Helmick and R. L. Peterson (eds.), *Forgiveness and Reconciliation: religion, public policy and conflict transformation.* Radnor, Pennsylvania: Templeton.

Phimister, I. and Van Onselen, C. 1979. The political economy of tribal animosity: a case study of the 1929 Bulawayo 'faction fight'. *Journal of Southern African Studies*, 3(2): 187–206. At: http://www.jstor.org/stable/2636770 (3 July 2014).

Pia, E. 2013. Narrative therapy and peacebuilding. *Journal of Intervention and Statebuilding,* 7(4): 476–491. At: http://dx.doi.org/10.1080/17502977.2012.727538 (10 May 2014).

Pintar, J. 2000. Anticipating consequences: what Bosnia taught us about healing the wounds of war. *Human Rights Review*, January–March: 56–66.

Ponterottto, J. C. 2006. Brief note on the origins, evolution and meaning of qualitative research concept 'Thick description'. *The qualitative Report*, 11(3): 538–549.

Ranger, T. 1992. War, violence and healing in Zimbabwe. *Journal of Southern African Studies*, 13 (3): 698–707.

Reason, P. and Bradbury, H. 2006. Introduction: inquiry and participation in search of a world worthy of human aspiration. In P. Reason and H. Bradbury (eds.), *Handbook of action research.* London: SAGE.

Reason, P. and Bradbury, H. 2008. Introduction. In P. Reason and H. Bradbury (eds.), *The SAGE handbook of action research: participative inquiry and practice.* London: SAGE.

Reeler, T., Chitsike, K., Maizva, F. and Reeler, B. 2009. Tree of Life: a community approach to empowering and healing survivors of torture in Zimbabwe. *Torture* 19(3): 180–193. At: https://www.ncbi.nlm.nih.gov/pubmed/20065537 (24 March 2014).

Rigby, A. 2001. *Justice and reconciliation: after the violence.* Boulder, Colorado: Lynne Rienner.

Rimé, B. 2007. The social sharing of emotion as an interface between individual and collective processes in the construction of emotional climates. *Journal of Social Issues.* 63(2): 307–322.

Rivas, B. 2007. Modelling your resilience and finding it in your students. Presentation at Safe schools unit offices, San Diego. August 27th, 2007.

Robben, A. C. G. M. 2000. The assault on basic trust: disappearance, protest, and reburial in Argentina. In A. C. G. M. Robben and M. M. Suárez-Orozco (eds.), *Cultures under siege: collective violence and trauma.* Cambridge: Cambridge University Press.

Rodden, J. 2004. Forgiveness, education, public policy: the road not yet taken. *Modern Age,* 46(4): 334–341.

Romero-Jódar, A. 2012. 'When the life giver dies, all around is laid waste.' Structural trauma and the splitting of time in *Signal to Noise,* a graphic novel. *Journal of Popular Culture*, 45(5): 1000–1019.

Rosebury, B. 2009. Private revenge and its relation to punishment. *Utilitas*, 21(1): 1–22.

Ross, C. E. 2011. Collective threat, trust, and the sense of personal control. *Journal of Health and Social Behaviour*, 52(3): 287–296.

Rothschild, B. 2000. The body remembers: the psychophysiology and trauma treatment. New York: W.W. Norton and Company.

Rowan, J. 2006. The humanistic approach to action research. In P. Reason and H. Bradbury (eds.), *Handbook of action research.* London: SAGE.

Saldana, J. 2009. The coding manual for qualitative researchers. L.A: SAGE.

Salvatic, S. 2000. The archives of memory, from the experience of the individual to the conscience of the collective. In C. Becker (ed.), *Psychosocial and trauma response in war-torn societies: the case of Kosovo.* Psychosocial Notebook, Vol. 1, IOM.

Sarantakos, S. 2005. Social research, 3rd ed. Hampshire: Palgrave Macmillan.

Saul, J. 2000. Mapping trauma. In C. Becker (ed.), *Psychosocial and trauma response in war-torn societies: the case of Kosovo.* Psychosocial Notebook, Vol. 1, IOM.

Schratz, M. and Walker, R. 1995. Research as social change. London: Routledge.

Schwandt, T. A. 2001. Dictionary of qualitative inquiry (2nd ed.). Thousand Oaks, California: SAGE.

Schweitzer, R. D., Vromans, L., Ranke, G. and Griffin, J. 2014. Narratives of healing: a case study of a young Liberian refugee settled in Australia. *The Arts in Psychotherapy*, 41: 98–106. At: http://dx.doi.org/10.1016/j.aip.2013.10.006 (3 February 2014).

Seligman, M. E. P. 2007. *What you can change...and what you can't: the complete guide to successful self-improvement.* New York: Vintage Books.

Shaw, R. 2005. *Rethinking Truth and Reconciliation Commissions: Lessons from Sierra Leone.* Washington DC: United States Institute for Peace.

Sher, G. 2005. Transgenerational compensation. *Philosophy and Public Affairs*, 33(2): 181–200.

Sherman, D. W., Rosedale M. and Haber S. 2012. Reclaiming life on one's own terms: a grounded theory of the process of breast cancer survivorship. *Oncology Nursing Forum* 39(3): 258–268.

Shriver, D. 1999. The long road to reconciliation: some moral stepping stones. In R. Rothstein (ed.), *After the peace: resistance and reconciliation.* Boulder, Co: Lynne Rienner.

Shriver, D. W. 2003. Where and when in political life is justice served by forgiveness? In N. Biggar (ed.), *Burying the past: making peace doing justice after civil conflict.* Georgetown: Georgetown University Press.

Silverman, D. 1985. *Qualitative methodology and sociology*. Aldershot: Gower.

Slabbert, F. 2000. Truth without reconciliation, reconciliation without truth. In W. James and L. van de Vijver (eds.), *After the TRC: reflections on truth and reconciliation in South Africa.* Cape Town: David Philips.

Smedes, L. B. 1996. *Forgive and forget: healing the hurts we don't deserve.* San Francisco: Harper.

Smedes, L. B. 1998. Stations on the journey from forgiveness to hope. In E. L. Worthington, Jr. (ed.), *Dimensions of forgiveness: psychological research and theological perspectives.* Philadelphia: Templeton.

Sorabji, C. 2006. Managing memories in the post-war Sarajevo: individuals, bad memories, and new wars. *Journal of Royal Anthropological Institute*, 12: 1–18.

Spinner-Halev, J. 2007. From historical to enduring injustice. *Political Theory,* 35(5): 574–597.

Staff reporter. 2012. Marginalisation of Mat'land a myth fuelled by cry babies-Masuku. *The Chronicle*, 4 October. At: http://www.chronicle.co.zw/marginalisation-of-matland-a-myth-fuelled-by-crybabies-masuku/ (7 May 2014).

Staff reporter. 2012. Bulawayo full of cry babies, says Governor Mathema. *Bulawayo24*, 5 June 2012. At: bulawayo24.com/index-id-news-sc-local-byo-16040.html (7 May 2014).

Stauffer, C. S. 2009. Acting out the myths: the power of narrative discourse in shaping the Zimbabwe conflict of Matabeleland, 1980–1987. PhD Thesis, University of KwaZulu Natal.

Staub, E. 2000. Genocide and mass killings: origins, prevention, healing and reconciliation. *Political Psychology*, 21(2): 367–382.

Staub, E. 2006. Reconciliation after genocide, mass killing, or intractable conflict: understanding the roots of violence, psychological recovery, and steps towards a general theory. *Political Psychology*, 27(26): 867–894.

Staub, E. and Pearlman, L. 2001. Healing, reconciliation and forgiving after genocide and other collective violence. In R. Helmick and R. Peterson (eds.), *Forgiveness and reconciliation: religion, public policy and conflict transformation.* Radnor, Philadelphia: Templeton Foundation.

Staub, E., Pearlman, L. A., Gubin, A. and Hagengimana, A. 2005. Healing, reconciliation, forgiving and the prevention of violence after genocide or mass killings: an intervention and its experimental evaluation in Rwanda. *Journal of Social and Clinical Psychology,* 24(3): 297–334.

Staub, E., Pearlman, L. A. and Miller, V. 2003. Healing the roots of genocide in Rwanda. *Peace Review* 15(3): 287–294.

Stewart, F. 2001. Horizontal inequalities: a neglected dimension of development, United Nations University World Institute for Development Economics Research. *WIDER Annual Lectures 5,* UNU/WIDER.

Stillwell, A. M., Baumeister, R. F. and Del Priore, R. E. 2008. We're all victims here: toward a Psychology of revenge. *Basic and Applied Social Psychology*, 30: 253–263.

Strydom, H. and Freek, C. 2008. A participatory action research approach in dealing with Mozambican migrant labourers to South Africa. *TILTAI*, 4: 87–98.

Summerfield, D. 1996. *Impact of war and atrocity on civilian populations: basic principles for NGO interventions and a critique of psychosocial trauma projects*. Relief and Rehabilitation Network. London: Overseas Development Institute.

Summerfield, D. 1999. A critique of seven assumptions behind psychological trauma programmes in war-affected areas. *Social Science & Medicine*, 48: 1449–1462.

Summerfield, D. 2000. Myths over the field of intervention. In C. Becker (ed.), *Psychosocial and trauma response in war-torn societies: the case of Kosovo*. Psychosocial Notebook, Vol. 1, IOM.

Suter, W. N. 2012. *Introduction to educational research: a critical thinking approach* (2nd ed.). London: SAGE.

Swantz, M. L. 2008. Participatory action research as practice. In P. Reason and H. Bradbury (eds.), *The SAGE handbook of Action research: Participative inquiry and practice*. London: SAGE.

Tan, S. Y. 2013. Resilience and posttraumatic growth: empirical evidence and clinical applications from a Christian perspective. *Journal of Psychology and Christianity*, 32(4): 358–364.

Tatt, L. 2014. Apology within a moral dialectic: a reply to Professor Robbennolt. *Law Review*, 103 (5): 1010–1017. At: http://www.jstor.org/stable/30044450 (9 May 2014).

Templer, S. 2010. Integrity of process: how Tree of Life is taking root in Zimbabwe. *Africa Peace and Conflict Journal*, 3(2): 106–112.

The Paul H. Nitze School of Advanced International Studies. (nd). *The conflict management toolkit*. At: https://www.sais-jhu.edu/content/conflict-management (March 2011).

Theissen, G. 2004. Supporting justice, co-existence and reconciliation after armed conflict: strategies for dealing with the past. Berghof Research Centre for Constructive Conflict Management. At: www.berghof-foundation.org/fileadmin/redaktion/Publications/Handbook/Articles/theissen_handbook.pdf (November 2010).

Thesnaar, C. 2003. Facilitating healing and reconciliation with young people living in the aftermath of a political and cultural conflict: the challenge to the church and its youth ministry. *The Journal of Youth Ministry*, 2(1): 8–28.

Timmerman, J. 1981. *Prisoner without a name, a cell without a number.*. New York: Alfred a knopf Inc.

Truth and Reconciliation Commission of South Africa. March 1999. *TRC Report*, Vol.1, Cape Town.

Todd, J. G. 2007. *Through the darkness: a life in Zimbabwe*. Cape Town: Zebra.

Tutu, D. M. 1999. *No future without forgiveness*. New York: Doubleday.

Uehara, E. S., Farwell, N., Yamashiro, G. and Smukler, M. 2002. The place of ethnographic understanding in the assessment of Asian American mental health. In K. Kurasuki, S. Okazaki, and S. Sue (eds.), Asian American mental health: assessment, theories and methods. Cham, Switzerland: Springer.

Van der Merwe, H. 2003. National and community reconciliation: competing agendas in the South African Truth and Reconciliation Commission. In N. Biggar (ed.), *Burying the past: making peace doing justice after civil conflict*. Georgetown: Georgetown University Press.

Van der Oord, S., Lucassen, S., Van Emmeril, A. A. P. and Emeelkamp, P. M. G. 2010. Treatment of Post-Traumatic Stress Disorder in children using Cognitive Behavioural Writing Therapy. *Clinical Psychology and Psychotherapy*, 17: 240–249.

Verwoerd, W. J. 2008. Equity, mercy, forgiveness: interpreting amnesty within the South African Truth and Reconciliation Commission. PhD, University of Johannesburg. At: http://www.peeters-leuven.be/boekoverz_print.asp?nr=8252 (28 March 2010).

Villa-Vicencio, C. 2000. Restorative justice: dealing with the past differently. In C. Villa-Vicencio and W. Verwoerd (eds.), *Looking back, reaching forward: reflections on the Truth and Reconciliation Commission of South Africa*. London: Zed.

Villa-Vicencio, C. 2004. 'Reconciliation,' In C. Villa-Vicencio and E. Doxtader (eds.), *Pieces of the puzzle*. Cape Town: IJR.

Volf, M. 2001. Forgiveness, reconciliation and justice: a Christian contribution to a more peaceful social environment. In R. Helmick and R. Peterson (eds.), *Forgiveness and reconciliation: religion, public policy and conflict transformation.* Radnor, Philadelphia: Templeton.

Volkan, V. D. 2001. Transgenerational transmission and chosen traumas: an aspect of large- group identity. *Group Analysis,* 34: 79–97.

Wadsworth, Y. 1998. What is participatory action research? At: http://www.aral.com.au/ari/p-ywadsworth98.html (22 August 2013).

Walker, M. 1998. Action research and participatory research in South Africa. In J. Muller, J. Mouton, T. Sono, and P. Frank (eds.), *Theory and method in South African human sciences research: advances and Innovations.* South Africa: HSRC Press.

Walsh, F. 2007. Traumatic loss and major disasters: strengthening family and community resilience. *Family Process*, 46: 207–227.

Warren, M. P. 2006. *From trauma to transformation.* Carmarthen, Wales: Crown House.

Weaver, A. and Stark, B. J. 2006. Making it real: Participatory action research in UCEDDs: building the UCEDD of tomorrow. Council on Community Advocacy, Oregon Health and Science University. At: www.powershow.com/view/ac365-ZjQxO/Making_It_Real_Participatory_Action_Research_in_UCEDDs_powerpoint_ppt_presentation (19 September 2013).

Weine, S. M. and Chae, S. 2008. Trauma, disputed knowledge, and storying resilience. At: www.incore.ulst.ac.uk/research/projects/trauma/ (17July 2010).

Wessells, M. G. 1999. Culture, power, and community: intercultural approaches to psychosocial assistance and healing. In K. Nader, N. Dubrow, and B. Stamm (eds.), *Honouring differences: cultural issues in the treatment of trauma and loss.* New York: Taylor & Francis.

Wessells, M. 2008. Trauma, peacebuilding and development: an African region perspective. At: www.incore.ulst.ac.uk/research/projects/trauma/ (17 July 2010).

Weyeneth, R. R. 2001. History, memory, and reconciliation: the power of apology and the process of historical reconciliation. *The Public Historian*, 23(3): 9–38. At: http://www.jstor.org/stable/10.1525/tph.2001.23.issue-3 (29 May 2014).

White, I. 2003. Victim-combatant dialogue in Northern Ireland. In D. Bloomfield, T. Barnes, and L. Huyse (eds.), *Reconciliation after violence: a hand book.* Stockholm: IDEA.

White, L. 2007. 'Whoever saw a country with four armies?' the battle of Bulawayo revisited. *Journal of Southern African Studies*, 33(3) September: 619–631.

Whyte, F. W. 1991. *Participatory action research.* California: SAGE.

Wieder, A. 2004. Testimony as oral history: lessons from South Africa. *Educational Researcher*, 33(6): 23–28.

Weingarten, K. 2004. Witnessing the effects of political violence in families: mechanisms of intergenerational transmission and clinical interventions. *Journal of marital and family Therapy*, 30(1): 45–59.

Wilde, A. 2002. Irruptions of memory: expressive politics in Chile's transition to democracy. In D. E. Lorey and W. H. Beezley (eds.), *Genocide, collective violence, and popular memory: the politics of remembrance in the twentieth century*. Delaware: SR Books, Wilmington.

Williams, S. J. 2008. My story: implementing a grief and loss programme in a remote village in Zambia. *Nursing Forum,* 43(4): 224–237.

Wimberly, E. P. 2011. Storytelling and managing trauma: health and spirituality at work. *Journal of healthcare for the poor and underserved.* 22(3): 48–57.

Worthington, E. L. 2001. Unforgiveness, forgiveness, and reconciliation and their implications for societal interventions. In R. Helmick and R. Peterson (eds.), *Forgiveness and reconciliation: religion, public policy and conflict transformation.* Radnor, Philadelphia: R Templeton.

Worthington, E. L. 2006. *Forgiveness and reconciliation: theory and application.* New York: Routledge.

Yandell, K. E. 1998. The Metaphysics and morality of forgiveness. In R. D. Enright and J. North (eds.), *Exploring forgiveness.* Madison: University of Wisconsin Press.

Zehr, H. 2008. Doing justice, healing trauma-the role of restorative justice in peacebuilding. *Peace Prints: South Asia Journal of Peacebuilding,* 1(1) Spring. At: http://citeseerx.ist.psu.edu/viewdoc/download;jsessionid=E12FA9D67F6DC614E602036FF2ECD646?doi=10.1.1.424.2068&rep=rep1&type=pdf (09 September 2009).

Zelizer, C. December, 2008. Trauma-sensitive peacebuilding: lessons for theory and practice. *Africa Peace and Conflict Journal,* 1(1): 81–94.

Zimbabwe Human Rights Association. 1999. *Choosing the path to peace and development: coming to terms with human rights violations of the 1982–1987 conflict in Matabeleland and Midlands provinces.* Harare: ZimRights.

Zorbas, E. 2004. Reconciliation in post-genocide Rwanda. *African Journal of legal studies,* 1(1): 29–35.

Zupan, N. 2005. Development assistance and peace building projects in conflict areas: background, tools, lessons learned, and challenges ahead. *Internationale Politik und Gesellschaft* 4: 49–62.

## Website References

http://www.medterms.com
http://www.thefreedictionary.com

# On Durban University of Technology

With approximately 23,000 students, the Durban University of Technology (DUT) is the first choice for higher education in KwaZulu-Natal (KZN). It is located in the beautiful cities of Durban and Pietermaritzburg (PMB). As a University of Technology, it prioritises the quality of teaching and learning by ensuring its academic staff possess the highest possible qualification that they can get.

The Durban University of Technology is a result of the merger in April 2002 of two prestigious technikons, ML Sultan and Technikon Natal. It was named the Durban Institute of Technology and later became the Durban University of Technology in line with the rest of the universities of technology.

DUT, a member of the International Association of Universities, is a multi-campus university of technology at the cutting edge of higher education, technological training and research. The university aspires to be a "preferred university for developing leadership in technology and productive citizenship", and to "making knowledge useful".

As a butterfly develops from a pupa, so have the students at our institution. From the moment they register as green freshers, to their capping at the hallowed graduation ceremony, our students undergo an intellectual evolution.

*Website* http://www.dut.ac.za/



D. Ngwenya, *Healing the Wounds of Gukurahundi in Zimbabwe*,
The Anthropocene: Politik—Economics—Society—Science 19,
https://doi.org/10.1007/978-3-319-66818-5

# On Durban University of Technology

https://doi.org/10.1007/978-3-319-66818-5

# International Centre of Nonviolence (ICON)

ICON is one of DUT's ten focus areas. Its mission is to make strategic interventions in education that challenge structural violence and help develop a culture of nonviolence.

ICON seeks to make nonviolence real through analysis of the local and global context, through research and through reflective practice. These inform its actions and strengthen its capacity in the field of nonviolence.

Accordingly, ICON is active in the teaching nonviolence to undergraduates as part of in DUT's general education programme, using highly participatory learning methods. In addition, it has a large postgraduate programme in peacebuilding, with some 60 PhD and 15 master's students as at early 2017, drawn from many African countries. All postgraduate students follow an action research approach in their thesis work.

*Website* http://www.icon.org.za/current.html



D. Ngwenya, *Healing the Wounds of Gukurahundi in Zimbabwe*,
The Anthropocene: Politik—Economics—Society—Science 19,
https://doi.org/10.1007/978-3-319-66818-5

# Grace To Heal (Zimbabwe)

Since 2003, Grace To Heal (GTH) has been working with communities in Matebeleland, Zimbabwe to advance community healing, deepen community cohesion enhance democratic participatory decision making proccsses, at grassroots levels.

Violence, and organised and sustained political violence for that matter, tends to leave communities feeling disempowered and unable to function as a normal society should. That is, where people should be working together to development themselves, elements of mistrust, suspicion and general lack of self-worth and belief in one's abilities, all combine to militate against agency and resilience in the people. As a result, the community fabric is torn apart, community support systems dysfunctional and participation in activities that uplift a community's wellbeing greatly diminished. GTH works with these communities in order to rebuilt their belief in themselves and their capabilities, so that they can once again take charge of their destinitation, by being able to identify their problems, analyse and find sustainable solution to them. The nexus between trauma healing, peacebuilding and development informs the work of Grace To Heal. From community healing, to walking with communities through political and social conflicts, GTH has contributed to the betterment of communal wellbeing and an increased application of participatory decision making principles within the areas of operation.

Additionally, the organisation seeks to promote practitioner reflexivity through the Applied Conflict Transformation Studies course, which encourages the use of action research in the work plan as an effective way to bring about desired change. This Masters course is done out of Zimbabwe in conjuction with the Durban University of Technology, South Africa.

Key areas of GTH's work portfolio include:

- ***Trauma processing***—helping victims of violence, their families and communities, to deal with traumas;



D. Ngwenya, *Healing the Wounds of Gukurahundi in Zimbabwe*,
The Anthropocene: Politik—Economics—Society—Science 19,
https://doi.org/10.1007/978-3-319-66818-5

- ***Women empowerment***—unearthing female peacebuilding capacities, and promoting women participation in community affairs;
- ***Youth peacebuilding activities***
  Using sports, peace clubs and citizen journalism assist youth to find nonviolent and creative means to deal with their conflicts.
- ***Church and traditional leaders***—encouraging constructive involvement of church leaders within their communities, and bridging gaps to traditional leadership structures;
- ***Conflict resolution skills***—equipping local key actors with the skills to constructively resolve conflict in their communities, and assist others in doing so;
- **Research**—collecting insights from local peacebuilding processes and feeding them into symposia and debates to inform discussions on matters of peace and conflict.

*Grace to Heal* is a non-profit organization which empowers communities through conflict transformation, peace advocacy, justice, trauma healing, reconciliation & mediation.

***Website*** http://www.gracetoheal.org
***Address*** 7 Duncan Road, Suburbs, Bulawayo, Zimbabwe,
***Phone*** (263-9) 225 0267—**Contact email** gth@gracetoheal.org

# About the Author

Dr. Dumisani Ngwenya is the co-founder and executive director of Grace To Heal. He completed his doctoral studies at the Durban University of Technology's International Centre of Nonviolence in 2015. His research interest and work focus is around the issue of Gukurahundi and its after effects. He sees himself as a peace-practitioner first and an academic second. He has been involved in the field of peacebuilding since 2003. His work with Grace To Heal involves working with the communities of Matebeleland which were affected by the 1980s atrocities perpetrated by the Zimbabwean government which left an estimated 20,000 civilians dead and countless others tortured and maimed. This work includes identifying and mapping the mass shallow graves, documenting victims' stories and creating platforms for victims' families and survivors to confront their past. He has also been involved in peacebuilding efforts in communities torn by political violence. He also lectures part time at a local university and has been a visiting lecturer at the Centre for Peace and Conflict Studies in Cambodia. His current major project is the setting up of an Action Research based Masters programme-the Applied Conflict Transformation Studies (ACTS) course, in conjunction with the Durban University of Technology, in Bulawayo Zimbabwe.His major publications are:

"Our Branches have been broken": Using the Tree of Life methodology with victims of Gukurahundi in Matebeleland, Zimbabwe. *Peace and Conflict Studies* 23, 1 (2016),

The Consequences of not healing: Evidence from the Gukurahundi violence in Zimbabwe. *African Journal on Conflict Resolution*, 15, 2 (2015) (with Geoff Harris),

Healing from violence: an action research project among survivors of *Gukurahundi,* Zimbabwe, in *Peace and Conflict Review*, 8, 2 (2015) (with Geoff Harris)



D. Ngwenya, *Healing the Wounds of Gukurahundi in Zimbabwe*,
The Anthropocene: Politik—Economics—Society—Science 19,
https://doi.org/10.1007/978-3-319-66818-5

Healing the wounds of violence: a participatory action research project in Zimbabwe (2017), in Kaye, S. and Harris, G. (eds). *Building Peace via Action Research*: *African Case Studies,* Addis Ababa, Ethiopia: UPEACE.

*Address* Dr. **Dumisani Ngwenya,** 7 Duncan Road, Suburbs, Bulawayo, Zimbabwe.

*Email* dumiemngwenya@gmail.com

*Website* http://www.gracetoheal.org and on this book http://afes-press-books.de/html/APESS_19.htm

# About the Book

Between 1983 and 1987, an estimated 20,000 people from Matebeleland and parts of Midlands Province in Zimbabwe were killed in an operation code named *Gukurahundi* by state security agents; mostly the Central Intelligence Organisation and a battalion [5th Brigade] especially trained for this operation. Since that time no official apology or any form of healing process has been proffered by the ZANU PF government which was responsible for these atrocities. As a result, most communities in these areas have never been afforded opportunities to openly talk about their experiences and to seek relief for their painful memories of the past. If anything, the government has continued to cause enduring pain by periodically actively suppressing any such attempts. It has become an accepted norm that after violent conflicts that programmes aimed at reconciliation, healing and forgiveness should be undertaken as part of the peacebuilding efforts. Where such has not occurred, there is a fear that there might be a return to violence at some point in that country or community.

The question that this research seeks to answer is whether, in view of the absence of any apology or official healing programme, these communities can heal themselves? Using a participatory action research approach, this research sheds some light on what communities could possibly do on their own to deal with their hurts. It also identifies conditions that would make such healing sustainable and what currently prevents that from taking place. It finds that through a broadly-based array of actions such as creating safe and empathetic spaces for storytelling, both verbal and written, group-based healing workshops and other psychosocial approaches, as well as a critical analysis of participants' contexts in order to understand what needs transformation, it is possible for traumatised communities to attain a measure of relief from their emotional and psychological wounds. It also finds that this relief could be more sustainable if certain conditions were eliminated.



D. Ngwenya, *Healing the Wounds of Gukurahundi in Zimbabwe*,
The Anthropocene: Politik—Economics—Society—Science 19,
https://doi.org/10.1007/978-3-319-66818-5

# About the Book

# Index





D. Ngwenya, *Healing the Wounds of Gukurahundi in Zimbabwe*,
The Anthropocene: Politik—Economics—Society—Science 19,
https://doi.org/10.1007/978-3-319-66818-5

MIX
Papier aus verantwortungsvollen Quellen
Paper from responsible sources
FSC® C105338

If you have any concerns about our products, you can contact us on
**ProductSafety@springernature.com**

In case Publisher is established outside the EU, the EU authorized representative is:
**Springer Nature Customer Service Center GmbH**
**Europaplatz 3, 69115 Heidelberg, Germany**

Printed by Libri Plureos GmbH
in Hamburg, Germany

MIX
Papier aus verantwortungsvollen Quellen
Paper from responsible sources
FSC® C105338

If you have any concerns about our products,
you can contact us on
**ProductSafety@springernature.com**

In case Publisher is established outside the EU,
the EU authorized representative is:
**Springer Nature Customer Service Center GmbH**
**Europaplatz 3, 69115 Heidelberg, Germany**

Printed by Libri Plureos GmbH
in Hamburg, Germany